D0741866

Date Due

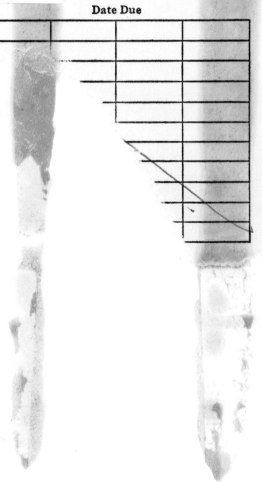

Columbia University Contributions
to Anthropology
Volume XXI

ZUNI MYTHOLOGY, 2 vols.

BY
RUTH BENEDICT

ZUNI MYTHOLOGY

Vol. I

BY

RUTH BENEDICT

AMS PRESS
NEW YORK

Reprinted with the permission of
Columbia University Press
From the edition of 1935, New York
First AMS EDITION published 1969
Manufactured in the United States of America

Library of Congress Catalogue Card Number: 75-82366

5-23-77

AMS PRESS, INC.
New York, N. Y.   10003

FOREWORD

The tales in these volumes were recorded during the summers of 1922 and 1923. The first summer was sponsored by the Southwest Society and the second by the Social Science Research Council of Columbia University.

Zuni accent falls regularly on the first syllable. Vowels have the continental values, and the following phonetic symbols have been used:

    ' glottal stop
    ł voiceless lateral
    · indicates lengthened vowel
    ḳ non-aspirated prepalatal stop (in early writers written ky or ki)
    c English sh

The informants are numbered as in Bunzel AES 15 : VIII. They are described in this volume, XXXVIII.

TABLE OF CONTENTS

Vol. I

Vol. II

INTRODUCTION TO ZUNI MYTHOLOGY[1]

Folkloristic studies, since the days of Cosquin and the students stimulated by the collections of the Grimm brothers, have been extensive rather than intensive. Whether the proposed problem was historical reconstruction, or a study of creative processes in mythology, the method that has been followed is that of far-flung comparative studies. This method has been used by Ehrenreich and the psychoanalytic students of myth, both of whom are interested in the role of symbolism in folklore, as well as by the modern school of Aarne, which is interested in reconstructing archetypal forms of folktales, and by students like Bolte and Polívka who are committed simply to documenting distribution.

The intensive study of one body of folklore has been scanted throughout the history of folkloristic studies, and little stress has been laid upon its possible rewards. The most valuable studies of this kind have tabled and analyzed the cultural behavior embodied in the tales, and these have been made only in American Indian material: Boas, F., Description of the Tsimshian based on their Mythology, RBAE 31 : 393—477; Boas, Kwakiutl Culture reflected in their Mythology, Memoir of the American Folk-Lore Society, in press; Ehrlich, Clara, Description of Tribal Culture in Crow Mythology, Journal of American Folk-Lore, 1935, in press. Such studies show the great amount of cultural material in myth, and stress the value of folklore for an understanding of the culture. This is not the only kind of intensive study of folklore. Boas has defined, and contrasted with other regions, the themes of Eskimo folklore, Folklore of the Eskimo, JAFL 17 : 1—13.[2] He has indicated the relation of

---

[1] References; F. H. Cushing, Zuñi Folk Tales, New York, 1929; listed *Cushing*. M. C. Stevenson, The Zuñi Indians, RBAE 23; listed *Stevenson*. Ruth Bunzel, RBAE 47; listed *Bunzel*. References to the two volumes of the present collection are listed I and II; the final section in each of these volumes contains abstracts of all Zuni versions of all tales, and comparative discussion of these versions. The abstracts, in these sections, of previously published tales referred to in this introduction, can be located by means of the Check List of previously published Zuni Tales, at the end of Vol. II. For abbreviations of journals in references, see I: 255. Italicized captions of incidents refer to the form in which these are listed in the Index of Incidents, Vol. II.

[2] See also Ralph S. Boggs, The Hero in the Folk Tales of Spain, Germany and Russia, JAFL 44 ; 27—42.

these themes to the cultural behavior and ideals among that people. In addition, there is also the possibility of the study of the native narrator, that is, the literary materials which he has at his disposal and his handling of them.[1]

These problems have seldom been attacked, and several circumstances have contributed to this neglect on the part of folklore students. In the first place, the most striking and obvious result of research in the early days of folkloristic study was always the fantastically wide distribution of episodes and plots, and everyone therefore joined in diffusion studies. In the second place, there are certain conditions which must be fulfilled before intensive study of one body of folklore can yield any considerable fruits, and these conditions have not often been met in the available collections. For the most profitable study of single bodies of mythology, folktales should hold an important place in the tribal life, not being relegated, for example, to children's amusement or used solely as word-perfect recitations of magical formulae; a large body of tales should have been recorded, and over as long a period as possible; the culture of the people who tell the tales should be well known; and folklore among that people should be a living and functioning culture trait.

These optimum conditions are fulfilled in the folklore of Zuni, the largest pueblo of the Southwest of the United States. Even compared with other North American tribes, mythology is a highly developed and serious art in Zuni, and the great number of tales that have been collected by many different persons extend over a period of fifty years. The culture of Zuni is well known, and in discussing the tales I have been able to use my own first-hand acquaintance with Zuni beliefs and behavior, as well as detailed accounts by other students. Finally, in contrast to that of almost all other tribes of the North American continent, folklore in Zuni is not moribund. The processes that can be studied in it are not reconstructed in a kind of folkloristic archaeology but are open to observation and experiment.

When these conditions can be fulfilled, intensive study of a single body of folklore is of first-rate theoretical importance, whether the problem at issue is historical reconstruction, the study of culture, or literary problems in the development of oral traditions. It seems obvious enough that studies in the two latter problems can be carried out best by careful intensive study, and that the students of symbolism, for example, have overlooked in favor of misleading comparative studies a method of work which can yield definite results. Even

---

[1] See, for a comparative study, D. Demetracopoulou, The Loon Woman, A Study in Synthesis, JAFL 46 ; 101—128.

in the matter of historical reconstruction, also, which is the chief end of comparative studies of folklore, intensive study has also much to contribute. The usual library-trained comparative student works with standard versions from each locality; in primitive cultures, usually one from a tribe. This version arbitrarily becomes "the" tribal tale, and is minutely compared with equally arbitrary standard tales from other tribes. But in such a body of mythology as that of Zuni, many different variants coexist, and the different forms these variants take cannot be ascribed to different historical levels, or even in large measure to particular tribal contacts, but are different literary combinations of incidents in different plot sequences. The comparative student may well learn from intensive studies not to point an argument that would be invalidated if half a dozen quite different versions from the same tribe were placed on record.

The two problems which I shall consider at the present time from the analysis of Zuni mythology are: I, the themes which their folklore elaborates and the relation of these to their culture; II. the literary problems of the Zuni narrator.

I

No folktale is generic. It is always the tale of one particular people with one particular livelihood and social organization and religion. The final form that a tale takes in that culture is influenced, often fundamentally, by attitudes and customs that cannot be discovered except with full knowledge of life and behavior among that people. It has always been obvious to students of every theoretical persuasion that folklore tallied with culture and yet did not tally with it, and the majority of students have agreed upon one convenient explanation of those instances where the two are at odds. Folklore, it is said, reflects not the customs and beliefs of the narrators of the tales, but those of many generations past; cultural survivals of earlier ages are perpetuated in folklore, and these, it is often felt, are the chief reason for the study of oral traditions. Even conditions of barbarism in which fathers are supposed to have eaten their children, and conditions of primal life when man first gained ascendancy over animals, have been said to be embalmed in folklore.

A conservatism that perpetuates long-discarded customs, however, is characteristic of a dead lore rather than a living one, and the great emphasis on the importance of survivals in the interpretation of folklore is evidently due to certain characteristics of oral tradition in Western civilization. European folklore was rescued from the memories of old men and women much as that of the Plains Indians is rescued today. It was recorded by collectors long after its heyday. Grimm's tales are found to reflect the manners and customs of the feudal age, not contemporary contacts with industrialism or with urban civilization, and the belief has become current that survivals of old customs are perpetuated in folklore through great lapses of time. This, however, is to generalize the senescence of folklore into a law by means of which mythology is elaborately interpreted. Folklore often remains current and can be adequately collected when it is no longer a living trait. North American Indians can almost always relate their folktales long after their aboriginal cultural life is in abeyance, and many valuable bodies of mythology have been collected in dead cultures from old men who learned the stories in their youth. The functioning of myth in culture and the processes of cultural adaptation, however, cannot be adequately studied in these cases. Comparison of variants under such conditions indicates mainly how much or how little different informants have forgotten of a dead culture trait, and such comparison is comparatively unrewarding. In Zuni tales are constantly told, and recounting folktales is an habitual occupation of a great number of the most important members of the community.

A living folklore, such as that of Zuni, reflects the contemporary interests and judgments of its tellers, and adapts incidents to its own cultural usages. Like any cultural trait, folklore tends, of course, to perpetuate traditional forms, and there is a certain lag in folklore as there is in contemporary statecraft or in morals. But the scope of this conservatism is limited in folklore as in other traits. It is never sufficient to give us license to reconstruct the items of a racial memory; and contemporary attitudes are always to be reckoned with, rather than those that have been superseded in that culture. In the present collection the cultural lag is apparent in many details of overt behavior. In the folktales, for example, except in those recognized by the tellers as Mexican, entrance to the house is by means of a ladder to the roof and down another ladder from the hatchway, yet doors have been common in Zuni since 1888 and are today universal except in the kivas. Old conditions, therefore, have been equally retained in the ceremonial house and in the folktale. The same may be said of the use of stone knives. Stone knives are still laid upon altars and used in ceremonies; and in folktales also heroes use stone knives instead of the omnipresent contemporary store knife. More elaborate modern innovations are also unrecognized in folklore. At present sheep herding occupies much of the life of Zuni men, and hunting is in abeyance. In the tales, however, all heroes are hunters, and there is no mention of sheep herding except in tales recognized as Mexican. In like manner men do not now come courting with a bundle of gifts for the girl, but in folklore this is a convention usually observed. Similarly, at the present time the activity of the medicine societies is centered in their great all-night ceremony at the winter solstice, the individual planting of prayer-sticks at full moon, and in not very exacting incidental activities. In the myths, on the other hand, every member goes every night to his medicine society and returns home when others are in bed.

The cultural lag that is represented by these differences between custom in contemporary life and in folktales covers, however, a short period, and by no means gives indication of an early cultural horizon such as can be reconstructed, for instance, from comparative studies of culture, still less from studies of comparative linguistics. The agreement between the conduct of contemporary life and the picture of life in the folktales is very close. The roles of men and women in Zuni life, the role of the priesthoods, the conduct of sex life, the concern with witchcraft, are all faithfully indicated.

Where there is a contrast between Zuni custom and literary convention, the divergence commonly rests upon other considerations than survival of older customs. Even in the divergences just mentioned, cultural lag is not a sufficient explanation. It may well be, as any native will assure you, that, in times not long past, men spent every night in their medicine society meetings. On the other hand, it is possible that in those times as in these, this was a conventional description of a golden age, and golden ages have often existed only in the imagination. The impulse to idealize must be reckoned with in folkloristic contrasts with contemporary life even when it is also possible to set the difference down to cultural lag. Similarly, courting with bundles may not be a survival of an older custom but a borrowed incident which is a folkloristic convention. Stone knives and entrance through the hatchway also have become conventional attributes of a less troubled and ideal age, and from this point of view should be considered along with the fabulous prowess of heroes as runners in the stick race.

This tendency to idealize in folklore has often been pointed out. There is another set of discrepancies in Zuni folklore that cannot so easily be disposed of. The most striking instance is that of the constant recurrence of polygamy in the tales. Zuni institutions are thoroughly monogamous. It is of course conceivable that the folkloristic pattern reproduces earlier conditions. Polygamy is allowed almost everywhere in North America outside the Southwest and even polyandry is accepted in certain nearby tribes. The absence of any taboo against multiple spouses is an old and general North

American Indian trait. To assign the Zuni folkloristic pattern, however, to such a reflection of an earlier background is difficult for two reasons. In the first place, all pueblo cultures have the Zuni taboo on polygamy and pueblo culture is exceedingly old and stable, as one may judge from archaeological evidence in material culture. It is doubtful whether any folklore can be cited from any part of the world that reflects cultural conditions as remote as those before pueblo culture took form, and there is, therefore, good reason for dissatisfaction with this explanation. In the second place, even if it were possible to interpret the Zuni folkloristic pattern of polygamy as a survival, we should still have to explain why the marriage with eight wives or with two husbands is prominent in Zuni mythology and not generally over North America. The simultaneous marriage with many wives was culturally allowed over most of the continent, but it does not figure in their tales as it does in pueblo folklore. The presumption that is indicated by a study of the distribution of this folkloristic pattern in North America is that in the pueblos polygamy is a grandiose folkloristic convention partaking on the one hand of usual mythological exaggeration and on the other of a compensatory daydream. Just as the hero of folktales kills a buck every day, or four in a single day, so he also is courted by eight maidens and marries them. When a hero is given supernatural power by his supernatural father, he signalizes it by accepting all eight of the priests' daughters who had flouted him, killing them, and resuscitating them to serve his triumph, I : 200. It is a grandiose demonstration of power, and of the same nature as the rain-blessing the eight wives bring back to the pueblo after their resuscitation, a blessing so great that the consequent flood fills the whole valley and the people have to escape to the top of the mesa. In the same way the hunter whose sister uses her supernatural power in his behalf marries wives from all the seven towns, and in his witch wife's reprisal she has him abducted by eight Crane girls who keep him as their husband for four years, II : 179. Marriage with many wives is a Zuni fantasy of the same order as raising the dead or travelling with seven-league boots in other bodies of folklore. It plays a fairy-tale role in Zuni mythology which is automatically rendered impossible in those areas of North America where tales of polygamy and polyandry have bases in fact. What compensatory elements the tale embodies it is hard to prove, but it seems likely that these are present.

Other contrasts between custom and folkloristic conventions must be explained as fundamentally compensatory. The abandonment of children at birth, see *Children are deserted at birth*, is a constantly recurring theme and is alien to Zuni custom. In real life it does not come up for consideration at all. Illegitimate children are cared for in their mothers' homes, and present-day gossips, though they specialize in outrageous libels, do not tell of any instance in which an infant has been done away with. All men and women, not only the parents, give children the fondest care. There is no cultural background for the abandonment of illegitimate children. It is harder to judge about the abandonment of young children in famine. The tales of migrations to pueblos where crops have not failed are based on fact and such incidents as *Children deserted in famine* may possibly have occurred, where children too large to carry and too young to make the journey were left behind, though actual reminiscences are always of tender protection of the child, see AES 15 : 59. The incidents, however, of the girl in childbed who overtakes her party, leaving the baby in the grinding stone, II : 27, are regarded as fabulous by contemporary Zunis, like all tales of women who are able to get up immediately after childbirth as if nothing had happened. The abandonment of the child and the impossible physical recovery are grouped in one category. When the story of babies abandoned at birth is used in explanation of Zuni custom, the narrator concludes from the incident: "That's why girls who become pregnant before marriage conceal their condition," II : 16, — which is true, — not "That's why they expose their babies."

The fact remains that abandonment of children is an extraordinarily popular theme in Zuni folklore. The clue lies in the fact that the hearers' identification is with the child, not with the mother. Even women, who would be expected to identify with the mother in telling these tales, comment on the reunion of the abandoned child with his mother from the point of view of the child. "He made her cry all right," a woman said with heat, and, "Oh, she (the mother) was *ashamed*." The plots are all concerned with the supernatural assistance and human success of the poor child, and often the whole plot is directed toward the triumph of the abandoned child over the mother or the parents. In Deer Boy B, II : 18, when the child claims his relationship to his mother, she weeps while all her family scorn her. In the popular tale of the *Deserted children protected by dragonfly* the parents return in poverty and miserably sue their children for favors. The daydream, from the point of view of the child, is completed by the final largess of the children and their appointment to priestly rank. In narrator 7's two versions of the Twin Children of the Sun, II : 46 and 52, the twins return, make a laughingstock of their mother, and force her to confess. These two versions, which tell of the children's abandonment at birth, contrast strongly with the other two versions, II : 43 and Cushing 429, in which the girl does not expose her children but is killed by a witch, II : 43, or by the priests, Cushing 441, as a punishment for her unconfessed pregnancy. Her sons therefore do not humiliate her, but vindicate their mother's memory. The point of the story is entirely different.

The popularity of the theme of abandoned children in Zuni has a psychological significance that parallels the familiar daydreams of children in our civilization which detail their parents' suffering at their imminent death. That is, it is the expression of a resentment directed by children against their parents and worked out into a daydream of the childrens' imagined vantage.

This resentment, and the narrator's identification with the child, is still clearer in the tales of boys whose gambling ruins them, I : 224, Bunzel ms I : 340, and of children who are scolded, see *Overworked Children*. At least the deserted children are pitiful innocents and the identification of the Zuni audience with them might be on the basis of their lack of any wrongdoing. But the same attitude is taken toward girls who will not do their share of the work, Parsons JAFL 31 : 234; Bunzel AES 15 : 185; and boys who gamble away all their mother's valuable possessions. Their triumph is not only recounted, but those who scolded them are held up to criticism and suffering is brought upon them. "Even though they saw them doing wrong, they should not have scolded them," AES 15 : 194.

Another popular theme in Zuni folklore which reflects culture somewhat obliquely is that of *Death sought by summoning the Apache*. These tales must be understood against the cultural fact that suicide is unknown and even inconceivable to the Zuni mind, and violence is culturally taboo.[1] There is no cultural channel for taking vengeance upon an unfaithful spouse,[2] and no idea of the possibility of ending one's own life. Folkloristic daydreams, however, provide for both. One of these is *Death sought by summoning the Apache*. The abandoned wife sends a message to the Apache to come to destroy the pueblo. She washes herself for ceremonial cleanness and dances in her finest costume. She goes out to meet the Apache and is the first to be killed. Her faithless husband and his mistress are said to be the next victims, II : 164. The daydream is particularly charac-

---

[1] Benedict, Psychological Types in Southwestern Cultures, 23rd International Congress of Americanists, New York 1928, p. 581.

[2] The one situation where physical violence is institutionalized in Zuni, as in other pueblos, is the conflict between the wife and the husband's mistress. The two women may meet in a fist fight, in contemporary custom as in folklore. The man does not take part. The only mention of this in Zuni folklore is II ; 107, Bunzel ms II: 299, and Cushing 16. For Cochiti, Benedict BBAE 96: 114.

teristic of Zuni in that it provides a means of achieving the imagined end without the necessity of any violent act save on the part of the Apache.

The same incident occurs at the behest of the priestly families, II : 170, when they regard themselves as wronged by their people; they, too, dress themselves in their best and go out to meet death at the hands of outsiders. The most aberrant use of the situation, I : 181, is that in the tale of the young husband who thought his wife protested her love too much — demonstrativeness is suspect in Zuni custom — and called the Apache so that her indifference to his death could be exposed. In each case the story is a daydream motivated by resentment, and maneuvers the daydreamer into the martyr's position.

The other compensations which serve the wronged spouse as folkloristic daydreaming are available only to persons who have access to supernatural power and these are told consequently only for priests and witches. They approach simple situations of revenge more nearly than the tales we have been considering. Revenge tales are not differentiated according to sex, since if women have witch power they attempt to kill, II : 123; 128; 141; 147; Bunzel ms II : 284, as men do also when they use the power of the priests, II : 78, 85, 89, Parsons JAFL 43 : 47; Bunzel ms II : 283. The witch stories are analogous to European witch stories, as Zuni ideas of witchcraft also are analogous to European witch beliefs. They mirror Zuni culture to the extent that the jilted woman kills or transforms the woman who has supplanted her more often than her lost husband or lover. Similarly the faithful wife kills her faithless co-spouse, II : 107.

The folktales of deserted husbands who have supernatural power at their command are tales of calamities brought about by priestly power. They are similar to the tale of the wronged wife, II : 164, *Death sought by summoning the Apaches*, in that the objective they have in view is not a simple vengeance against the spouse or the present lover but a general destruction of innocent and guilty alike. It is specifically stated that the wronged spouse is miserable and wants other people to be miserable too, II : 82. There is no singling out of the guilty such as constitutes the whole point of modern moral tales of infidelity, and which is retained to a limited extent in the more derivative witch tales. The characteristic daydreams of Zunis who are unhappy is that others should suffer likewise.

Another theme, which also reflects Zuni culture but with a difference, is that of violent action based upon secret enmity. Grudges are cherished in Zuni. They are usually the rather general-

II*

ized expression of slights and resentments in a small community. In actual life they give rise to malicious aspersions, but in folklore they are usually satisfied by nothing less than the death of the offender. People grudge others their prosperity, I : 134, II :161, and set about to destroy them; they grudge a man his success in hunting and attempt to do away with him, II : 110, 152; Cushing 145, Heye Museum 8 : 475; they are jealous of a supernatural who has brought a new dance to Zuni, and try to bewitch him, II : 155; a priest who has not been paid for instruction kills the delinquent, II : 85; the child who is scolded for shirking, Bunzel AES 15 : 185, satisfies her grudge by leaving so that her family fear she is dead and recover her only after search by the supernaturals; people are angry because a girl will not lend a dipper and they have to drink from their hands, therefore a feud starts and both girls are killed, I : 159. Men and women both resent any slight in courtship; the woman tries to kill the man who has refused her a piece of his game (a usual courtship gesture in the tales), II : 123, and men kill or bewitch girls who have laughed at them, I: 200, or refused them a drink (a courtship prelim- inary today as well), II : 158. The deserted husband ritualistically causes a drought, Bunzel ms II : 283, an earthquake, II : 85; 89; Parsons JAFL 43 : 47; or an epidemic, II : 78, which threatens to wipe out the whole pueblo. The deserted wife similarly summons the Navahos or Apaches to demolish the village, II : 164; 179; or attempts to kill her husband, II : 128; 147. Unlike those of the Plains, Zuni folkways have no place for an ideal of character which overlooks slights, however small, and their folktales provide exaggerated fantasies of reprisal. In a culture in which homicide occurs with such extraordinary rarity that instances are not even remembered, the compensatory violence of these reprisals is the more striking.

True to the peculiar ideology of Zuni these reprisals are easily phrased as "teaching people to love you," i. e. to act decently toward you. The despised children, whom the people spit at, throwing refuse and urine into their grandmother's house, get the help of Salt Mother who takes away all the clothing in the pueblo. They tell her: "The people at Itiwana hate us. We want them to learn to love us," II : 56. The people have to stay in bed all the time and in their shame are brought to the point of begging work from the poor children. The latter remove the curse when the people promise to "love them." The whole story is an excellent illustration of the strange way in which, according to Zuni notions, you teach people to love you.

Zuni folklore therefore in those cases where it does not mirror contemporary custom owes its distortions to various fanciful exaggerations and compensatory mechanisms. The role of day-dreams, of wish fulfillment, is not limited to these cases of distortion. It is equally clear in the tales that most minutely reflect the con-temporary scene. Zuni folklore differs from most North American Indian mythology in that the usual daydream is little concerned with prowess in warfare. Nor are there in Zuni accounts of super-natural encounters and the acquisition of power, such as fill the folk-tales of the Plains Indians. Zuni folktales are as faithful to Zuni fantasies in what they exclude as in what they include. Their most popular theme is the triumph of the despised and weak and pre-viously worsted. The poor orphan boy is victorious in hunting, in stick races, in gambling, and in courtship, see *Depised Boy;* those who do not have witch power are triumphant over those who have, see *Witch Contests;* the stunted ragamuffin Ahaiyute win first place in everything. The detailed story, I : 87, is a generic daydream of the Zuni male, and is interwoven with the woman's daydream, which is more specifically presented in the tale I : 145.

Zuni folktales give an extraordinary place to women. Except for one point which will be discussed presently, the sexes of the pro-tagonists are constantly reversed. Men, I : 85; 87; 91; 126; 184; 190; II : 121; 154; Cushing 1; 104; 185; 200; Parsons MAAA 4 : 302; 313; Bunzel AES 15 : 123; 139 ms I : 336; 339; or women, I : 121; 138; 179; 182; 211; Parsons MAAA 4 : 307; 322; JAFL 43: 19; Bunzel ms I : 339, may equally take the initiative in courtship. In these tales, when the man is the suitor, the women impose tests upon their suitors and refuse marriage, and when the woman is the suitor, the men do likewise. Men and women equally are taught marriage by supernaturals; see *Marriage is taught by Supernaturals to those who refuse it: youth: maiden;* and either men, I : 87; I : 133; 157; Cushing 19; Bunzel ms I : 288; or women, Bunzel ms II : 299, follow their spouses or sweethearts to the world of the dead. This evenhandedness in the role of the sexes, however, has one great exception. Women are thought to be more erotic than men are. Sex is not well understood nor its values rated high in Zuni, and they have not the cultural background which makes the "masculine protest" so common an element of male behavior in our civilization. Women are not thought to rate higher than men because they are more highly sexed; rather, it is felt that they make a dangerous de-mand upon men; and men fear this demand. This is strongly emphasized in the tales. The sexes are reversed in the rape tales. It is always the theme of the timid man that is developed, not of the frightened virgin. There is a group of tales in which the hunter flees from women who want sexual intercourse, see *Pursuit by dangerous women*. He takes refuge all along the way; the woman catches up with him and again pursues him. He is in a panic of terror. Even when he retraces his steps next day after the fabulous Goat Man has killed his pursuer, "he saw the footprints of Toothed Vagina Woman and his own footprints escaping from her. His heart beat to see them," II : 116. Even the powerful little Ahaiyute, the patrons of war, are saved from their terror only by the institution of the scalp dance; upon having intercourse with the Navaho girl they summarily kill her, and she pursues them as a corpse from refuge to refuge until they are taught the ceremonial of purification, see *Origin of scalp dance*.

The corresponding theme for women is differently developed. Except for Parsons JAFL 43 : 25, it is not sexual advances that are offered to women in such tales. The monsters offer to cut off their heads, II : 91; gore them, JAFL 31 : 235; wrap them in their snake's coil, II : 138; or to eat them, I : 76; 84; II : 105; Cushing 305; 365; Parsons JAFL 43 : 42, as they over and over again eat men and boys also, II : 22; 188; 196; Parsons JAFL 43 : 6.

One of the most popular stories in Zuni is that of the Rabbit Huntress, I : 76, of which four versions are recorded. Atocle, the scare kachina, swallows all the girl's clothing so that she is shamed in her nakedness, and tries to get at her to swallow her too, but Atocle is a female kachina and the girl is afraid because the ogress is going to eat her. Similarly in the tale of two girls trapped by an ogre with black and white scales over his body, the indignity he offers them is a stew of baby's bodies, and when he makes them louse him he is preparing in turn to louse them by biting them in the neck, Cushing 365, as in other tales where people are killed for food, see *Death in lousing*.

Even in such a story as that of the girl who bathes and is made pregnant by the Horned Serpent, I : 167, the tale has not the affect we might expect. All Zuni girls are taught that they will be entered by the mythical Serpent if they immerse their bodies in bathing — actually they never do so — but in folklore the stories that employ this taboo are not nightmare tales. The girl merely acquires a supernatural husband and is sent ceremonially to accompany him to his home as any girl may be who marries a supernatural.

When the subject is of proposed sexual intercourse, women are not pictured as frightened. The *Abduction* tales in Zuni, where the woman is enticed by a man who meets her casually and takes her to his house, contrast strongly with the stories of the frightened man. The man with supernatural powers, the abductor, uses his powers to bless her and to endow her children with power as often as he uses his powers to force her to do hard work. But the tales in neither case are stories of fear of sexual violence on the part of the woman; when the abductor uses her harshly the tale is a realistic reflection of the fact that men can require certain obedience from women when they have the power. Abduction stories in Zuni, in contrast to similar stories even in other pueblos, are handled as tales of the triumph of the husband (or of the supernaturals whose aid he secures) in recovering something that has been taken from him. From the point of view of the man, they become stories of the triumph of the weak and of the settling of a grudge, II : 91; 98; 100; 104; 134; 147. From the point of view of the woman, they are stories of handsome men they admire and desire, II : 100; 138; or if fear is suggested it is because of a threat to cut off their heads or eat them, see above. In the tale of Winter Man, Bunzel ms I : 340; who accosted a maiden at the spring, took her to his home in his kickstick and treated her cruelly, the girl herself is successful in all encounters and finally kills him. She is thoroughly adequate in the situation, and Winter Man's sexual demands are not mentioned. "Oh, a woman wouldn't be afraid," men have answered when I asked for a tale corresponding to the group, The Hunter is pursued by Women, I : 167, but with a woman as the victim.

Even when the story is of the violation of women, as in Bat Youth, I : 253, the women take matters into their own hands. The idea that men take advantage women in their sleep is not only folkloristic in the pueblos, it is current scandal, and I have been told of living Lotharios in Zuni and in Cochiti who have been successful in the practice. It is extraordinarily consistent with the man's clandestine subterfuges in sex expression. Bat Youth violates four girls in this way, but upon waking, their reaction is not one of fear. All they say is, "It is Bat Youth who has done this. Let us run after him and pay him back." They caught him before he reached the ladder of his house, and it was he who was so frightened he could not climb it. They tore off his clothing and shamed him in his nakedness. "That is why nobody thinks bats are pretty. Nobody says when he sees a bat, 'Oh, see that pretty bat flying!' And because of Bat Youth's shame bats still carry bedbugs."

Similarly erotic invitation is ascribed to women, not to men. Women doublecross their husbands and make assignations with lovers, and the lovers are reluctant, Handy JAFL 31 : 465; II : 78, and they take the initiative in sex play, I : 186; 190; 212; II : 49; Parsons MAAA 4 : 308; Handy JAFL 31 :458. A woman's ruse to secure sexual intercourse is the theme of The Thunder Knives. It is told of Badger Woman and of Horned-Toad Man, who was a doctor. She groaned terribly in pretended pain, begging him to massage her further and further down her body. When she got what she wanted, her pain was all gone. Since Horned Toad is the progenitor of the ancient stone knives called thunder knives in Zuni, she bore a pile of these knives, and the conclusion is, "That's why women don't want to conceive when they have intercourse," II : 224.

The timid man figures constantly, also, in tales of courtship evasions. Courtship evasions are of course not peculiar to men; both men and women exhibit their superiority by turning down suitors. It is an occasion for pride almost as common in the tales as prowess in hunting. It proves superiority, as well for the woman as for the man, see references on men's and women's courtship, I : XXI. In two versions of the same tale, the girl in one humiliates the suitors, I : 126, in the other, the youth, I : 121. These tales of tests imposed in marriage, now upon women, now upon men, are not reflections of Zuni culture. Women are scrupulously taught not to be dilatory in accepting an offer, and men are proverbially eager to get a wife. They are daydreams of power and they are almost equally available to either sex. Only the poor and despised may not exhibit this form of pride in folktales, I : 175.

Pride, however, must be curbed, and in all tales of reluctant suitors the role of the supernaturals is much in evidence. It is regarded as a specific function of supernaturals to teach the joys of intercourse, and without such teaching, virgins, both men and women, will be guilty of rejecting marriage. Even the Rabbit Huntress, who has had no suitors, and whose only irregular behavior was to assume the masculine prerogative of hunting to feed her aged parents, is punished by the encounter with Atocle, and her rescue by the Ahaiyute is in all versions the occasion of her instruction in marriage. In three versions, I : 76; 84; Parsons JAFL 43 : 42, one of the heroes marries her himself, and, when he has taught her, instructs her to marry the first human man who asks her, I : 86. In another group of tales, reluctant suitors, either men, I : 121, or women, I : 126; Cushing 104; Bunzel AES 15 : 165; ms I : 336, hide game so that men fail while seeking a deer as a marriage test; the supernaturals finally release the deer and win the bride or bridegroom, turning their temporary spouses over to human suitors when they have been instructed, I : 121; 126; Bunzel AES 4 : 165. This theme is illustrative of the role of supernaturals in Zuni. They are thought of as stepping in to keep people from making mistakes, and one of the most likely of these mistakes is that of reluctance in regard to cohabitation.

The girl, however, is never portrayed in these tales as fearing the wedding night and circumventing it, but this is a familiar incident for the man. In "The Mannikin Wife" the boy makes himself a figure of a woman out of grass and a blanket, and lies with it. "He was ashamed with all the nice-looking girls who wanted to marry him and so he had to make this mannikin for a wife," I : 222. The supernaturals step in as usual and teach him how to face the difficult situation of taking a human wife. In "The Man who married a Donkey" the son of the village priest is afraid of marriage and of the girls who court him and tries bestiality. "He thought how much better this was than taking a wife.... He thought all the time how sensible he had been not to take a wife and have all that trouble. He thought that this way he would never have any trouble," I : 237. He is disillusioned only when he finds that the animal's period of heat is short, and retribution descends upon him when his donkey offspring discloses the truth to his father. His father gets the help of the Ahaiyute and they kill the half-human offspring and the youth has the good fortune to win a human wife whom he now knows how to value. The supernaturals tell his father that he is to blame for not having given his son sex instruction and trained him to accept the proper responsibilities: "You are a priest and you have not done these things."

The theme of the man's fear of submitting to a woman is developed also by means of several fantasies. Two of these are obvious: the hide and seek game proposed to a wandering man by a woman who demands that they stake their lives on the game, and the fantasy that brides appear as hags or as corpses in the morning. In the *Hide and Seek Game* the man always loses and is killed by the woman, I :197; 199; Bunzel AES 15 : 251. "She seized him by the hair and cut off his head. She twisted his hair together, and she cut open his chest and took out his heart. She dug a hole in the earth and put his body in it and covered it with earth," I : 197. The dangerous maiden and her sister are of course punished.

The incident, *Brides appear old in the morning,* is a courtship test which men must surmount. In case they do so they are rewarded with a successful marriage, I : 219; Parsons JAFL 43 : 21; but the nightmare is transparent: "He was lying with an old, old woman. Her eyes were almost shut. She was skin and bones. She was too weak to sit up and she scratched herself all the time," I : 219.

The brides who appear as corpses in the morning, *Corpse Girls,* is used in a somewhat different connection. It appears in several tales, and points the moral that men who yield to feminine blandishments are really yielding to corpses, and will find skeleton arms wound about them in the morning. In three versions of Eagle Man, I : 134; 174; Cushing 48, the wife tells her husband that he is not to smile at the girls who come to dance for him. They look very pretty, however, and he disobeys his wife. Instantly he is in their power and they spirit him away to their village of the dead, which is alive only at night. He goes to bed with them, but they smell like rotten meat so that he does not have intercourse with them. "At sunrise he woke up and the roof of that house was all falling down around them and a dead girl lay on each side of him with their arms over his chest. He jumped up and threw aside their arms and ran as fast as he could," I : 134.

Witch tales also develop this masculine fear of women. They are fantasy, since actual witchcraft techniques are apparently not owned and taught in Zuni. Witchcraft is terribly feared, but it is a Zuni anxiety neurosis, and actual witch practices, in the Melanesian manner, are unrecorded. There are no stories of witch husbands, see however II : 158, but the fear is directed toward the wife, or the sweetheart whom the youth has passed over. She betrays him by leaving him upon the top of a rock from which he cannot descend, II : 143, or she calls the rest of the witches and attempts the life of the hunter, II : 123; 129; 148; Parsons MAAA 4 : 309; Handy JAFL 31 : 468; Bunzel ms II : 284.

The man's fear of sex which is constantly turned to the wedding night may be illustrated from still other stories. The Zuni noodle tales are especially told to describe the discomfiture of the suitor and the young husband, and some of these stories make use of a transparent symbolism. In one of them the girl he has just slept with sets meat before him and gives him the little salt pot. He cannot reach the salt at first and gets his whole fist stuck in the pot. He runs to his grandmother who tries to make him go back, work his hand out of the pot and give her property back to the girl. " 'No, I won't do it,' says the young man, and strikes the salt pot against the wall and breaks it, spilling salt all around," Handy JAFL 31 : 453. In another, a kitten scratches him between the legs while he is eating and he screams. When he sees it is only a kitten, he covers his shame by admiring the kitten and proposing that he take it to show to his grandmother. As soon as he gets around the corner, he swings the kitten against a wall and kills it. His grandmother tries to make him go back. " 'No, I'm out of it,' and he would not go back," ibid 452. The images of killing the kitten and breaking the salt pot are apt.

In all these tales it is evident that it is the Zuni boy, not the girl, who fears the wedding night and has to be fortified for marriage.

This theme is fully developed in "The Boy who had to learn to marry," I : 210. Zuni does not celebrate the innocence of the young girl but that of the young boy. It is he who is so naive that he runs home to his grandmother at the advances of a young girl. He tells his grandmother, "I like her in the daytime but nights I think I shall run away from her." His grandmother lets him sleep with her and fortified with his newly acquired knowledge he accepts the girl on the next occasion. "They always lived happily because the boy married before he knew anything about girls." It is a story of the ideal marriage, like the stories in our own romances of the sweet innocent girl who makes the most acceptable wife.

Another popular theme in Zuni is that of the reunion of families. This favorite Zuni conclusion had often been apparent in tales already discussed. The Deserted Children, II : 1, in contrast to the usual form of this tale in other parts of North America, ends with a happy reunited family; the story of the ruined gambler ends with the happy reunion when he is welcomed back, I : 214; tales of girls who are chastised and leave home end with the reconciliation when they are at last discovered after great search, II : 41; Bunzel AES 15 : 199; men who are taken in marriage in the sky land get homesick and return happily, I : 136. This is thoroughly in keeping with the strength of the matrilineal family bond in Zuni. In the conjugal relationship the theme takes a more unusual form. In these tales the favorite theme is that of the return of the husband to the first wife whom he has abandoned, see *Return in death to first wife*. This is strongly felt in Zuni, and the motivation may easily be missed by readers of another civilization to whom the theme is not familiar. It is a common interpretation of death, i. e. the husband returns in death to the wife to whom he had long since been false. In such a long tale as I : 171, the incidents may readily seem confused without an understanding of the force of the traditional conclusion. The man sleeps with a girl whose mother has entertained him when he is overtaken by night on the hunt; in the morning he finds skeleton arms wound about him and the mother pursues him as a rolling skull. Porcupine helps him to overcome Skull and he marries Porcupine Girl. After four years he meets Eagle Girl and goes with her as her husband to her home in the sky. He is faithless to her with Chicken Hawk Girl, but is reconciled to his Eagle Wife who warns him against Corpse Girls who try to play with him as they dance. He is snatched off by them, and he is stripped by his outraged Eagle Wife and falls, which brings about his return in death to his first wife, the ghost girl. All the erotic adventures merely give point to the favorite theme. The same story with other details is told, Bunzel AES 15 : 210.

The same theme is felt in the story of the deserted wife who calls the Apache to destroy the pueblo. The first to be killed are the wife who has summoned the enemy, her faithless husband, and his mistress, II : 169. After the story was ended, I asked, "What then ?" and the narrator said, "Oh, she got him back again. She was his first wife."

There is a singular mildness in Zuni tales, and this mildness is strangely at variance with the compensatory violence we have already discussed in the reprisal stories which have cherished grudges as their theme. In these latter the violence of the daydream is fabulous, and the very fact that it is not a reflection of Zuni behavior allows the vengeance to take the most extreme forms. In other tales the mildness of actual Zuni life and institutions are accurately reflected. The idea of trapping all the witches into an ambush from which they could kill Apaches and must therefore have to become bow priests is a curious one, II : 151. "So A·lucpa caught all the witches in the bow priesthood. They were forced to go into retreat and be purified. They were bow priests. Only one witch had not been able to go out. So one witch was left. That is why there is no witch society any more, because A·lupca made them all bow priests." This tale in no way calls in question the great prestige of the bow priesthood in Zuni, nor the fear and hatred of witches. Nevertheless the conclusion is felt as adequate. In a case of personal vengeance, the priest's son who has been distressed at his wife's demonstrativeness, calls the Apache to kill him in order to test his wife's faithfulness to his memory, I : 179. She is merely left to enjoy herself at the favorite yaya dance, by which he proves her affection was too shallow to allow for proper respect for her husband. "He turned into an eagle, and that is why we value eagle feathers."

Similarly, bestiality, I : 236, and sexual fetishism, I : 221, in the tales already discussed, are regarded as shameful, but the erring youths are aided by the supernaturals and protected by human beings and their misstep is corrected, not punished. In the former tale, it is the father of the boy who is rebuked because, though he was a priest, he had not given his boy the education which would have prevented the moral breach.

All the tales of abandoned children are similarly mild, and we have spoken before of the revision of the "Deserted Children" story in Zuni, II : 1, whereby instead of killing the parents, they are only humiliated for four days, even, in Parsons MAAA 4 : 316, for only one day. Pautiwa's rebuke to the proud maiden who has refused her lovers because she required them to bring her scalps is typical: 'Perhaps if you had been wise, you might have been beloved, but now you have wished for evil days," AES 15 : 145; as is also the comment on the girl who has scolded her lazy sister who did not do her share of the housework: "For even though these were children of a priest they did not love one another, and so they (the supernaturals) tried them for a while. They hid their sister from them. Even though they used to see her doing wrong, they should not have scolded her," AES 15 : 194. And narrators keep introducing into plots which demand revenge: "Let's not kill her. She's quite nice," I : 63; "Let's stop now. Don't let's kill so many people," II : 183.

II

The literary problems which confront a primitive narrator are easily misunderstood. The gap between the traditionalism of primitive mythology and the emphasis upon originality in our own literature is so great that the reader from our civilization confronted by a collection of folktales is often led to false conclusions. Many students have assumed that the fixity of tales is absolute or almost so, that the individual narrator has no literary problems, and that the tales originated in a mystical source called communal authorship. On the other hand, it would be as easy to interpret the tales as far more fortuitous than they really are, for from the point of view of the outsider the incidents out of which the tale is built might just as well be other incidents, the stylistic elements might as well be omitted or amplified in any imaginable direction. In fact, because of the diffuseness and ease of prose, it is far easier to mistake the problems of the artist in this field than, for instance, in the plastic arts.

There is no more communal authorship in folklore than there is a communal designer in ironwork or a communal priest in religious rites. The whole problem is unreal. There is no conceivable source of any cultural trait other than the behavior of some man, woman or child. What is communal about the process is the social acceptance by which the trait becomes a part of the teaching handed down to the next generation. The role of the narrator in such a body of folklore as that of Zuni remains as real as that of any story teller in any civilization though its scope is somewhat changed by the role of the audience.

On the other hand, even more serious misunderstanding of folklore is introduced by the outsider's inability to appreciate the fixed limits within which the narrator works. The artist works within definite traditional limits as truly in folklore as in music. The first requisite in understanding any folk literature is to recognize the boundaries within which he operates.

In Zuni, tales fall into no clearly distinguishable categories. The divisions I have used in this volume are for convenience of reference only, and have little to do with the literary problems of the narrator. Even the Emergence story, which is the Zuni scripture, is not reserved for the priests nor owned by them. It is freely repeated by any fireside by any layman, and all versions differ markedly, not so much in order of incidents as in the details introduced. Incidents of it, moreover, can be lifted and used as the basis of entertaining stories such as Cushing 398.

Tales of kachinas, also, form no special group. Kachinas are freely introduced even into European tales, and are heroes of romances who marry several wives, contest with witches, and win in stick races. Much of the stock saga of the Ahaiyute has evidently been ascribed to them since Cushing's day, see I : 285, and these little supernatural twins figure as supernatural helpers in tales of every kind. They make themselves a "kapitan" and buy a dog from a Mexican in a patently Mexican tale, II : 102. In other cases the Ahaiyute tales are direct transcriptions of Zuni daydreams, I : 87, and represent the wish fulfillments most desired by the people. A variety of stories are attributed to the Ahaiyute in one of several versions, and it seems probable that this tendency is still operative in Zuni. If that is true, still other stories that were not yet told of the twins ten years ago when these stories were collected may become Ahaiyute stories in the future.

It is in keeping with the fact that folklore is such a living and popular trait in Zuni at the present time that tales of European derivation are so little differentiated from others. The ones that are popular or have been told for some time or are retold by a good narrator often mirror the details of Zuni life to the last degree. Cushing fifty years ago published an excellent example of this in his day in the tale of "The Cock and the Mouse," which adapted an Italian accumulative tale he had himself repeated in Zuni, Cushing 411. In this volume "The Man who married the Donkey," I : 236, is an excellent example of such acculturation, as is also "Tail by Tail," see notes I : 273.

Animal trickster tales, which form so large a bulk of many North American mythologies, are little told. Children's tales, usually a few sentences that go with a nursery song, of the type of II : 223, Cushing 296, Bunzel AES 15 : 285 are little represented in this collection but they exist in greater numbers.

In all tales, therefore, since the short animal incident occurs so rarely, roughly the same objectives are present to the narrator. Of these stylistic aims, probably the one most relied upon is the endless incorporation of cultural details. In most mythologies the picture of cultural life than can be abstracted from the tales, as in the studies of the Tsimshian, Kwakiutl, and Crow, see I : XI, is a comparatively adequate description of most phases of social life, but in Zuni there is in addition a loving reiteration of detail that is over and above this faithful rendition. The most extreme examples are the long descriptions of ceremonies which are reserved for another volume of Zuni Ceremonial Tales. These have practically no plot but are strung together on some thread such as that of the Pekwin who grieved for his dead wife and was comforted by each of the three religious organizations of Zuni, which each brought out a dance in turn, and finally by the great ceremony of the Corn Dance. In one of these ceremonies more than forty participants in the dance are severally invited by the bow priests to take part. In each of the forty retellings the priests go to the individual's house, greet those who live there with the conventional greeting, "How have you lived these days, my fathers, my mothers, my children?" are answered, fed, thank them for the food, explain the part in the dance they wish them to assume and conduct them back to the priests' chamber or leave them to prepare for the occasion. In each case, also, the moment's occupation of the principal occupants of the room are described as the priests enter. Practice for the dancing and the great occasion itself are meticulously described in the same fashion.

The excess of cultural detail is similarly apparent in the present collection. The Corn Maidens I : 24, The Rabbit Huntress, I : 76, Ahaiyute marries the Bow Priest's Daughter, I : 87, Lazy Bones, I : 145, The Deserted Husband causes an Epidemic, II : 78, and The Navaho come against Zuni, II : 170, are all good examples. The tale does not merely assume the cultural background, as the tale of any people must; it itemizes each detailed observance and encounter.

The Zuni narrator, besides this general preoccupation, has a special obligation to relate certain details. The greeting formulas, with the offer of food to the visitor and his thanks, recur constantly. Localization is imperative, and certain places are the scenes of certain kinds of incidents, as Cunte'kaia is the scene of witch tales and Hecokta of ogre tales. Indication of points of the compass is marked, but is much less of a stylistic necessity than in the pueblo tales from Laguna, for instance, Boas AES VIII. The introduction of helpful animals is marked in all tales where such incidents are relevant. Such animals, according to their abilities, fly, gnaw, or kill, for the hero, see *Helpful Animals*. Stylistic obliviousness to incisiveness or condensation is obvious in all the tales and if anything is only the more marked in the text translations, Bunzel AES 15.

The Zuni narrator is almost always free to incorporate his special knowledge in a tale. If he has taken part in a Corn Dance, his incidents of the Corn Dance practice reproduce his own experience, which is then of couse retold by others. Men, as well as women, incorporate accounts of woman's childbirth ritual, I : 80, or of cooking techniques, II : 202. The Emergence tale is used as a basis for the incorporation of a variety of ritual with which a narrator is familiar, see notes I : 256.

Cushing's tale of "The Cock and the Mouse," Cushing 411, has already been mentioned. It is a striking example of the extent to which Zuni stylistic requirements operate to remodel a borrowed tale. He himself told a group of native friends a European accumulative tale and a year later recorded the same tale as he heard it told by one of his listeners. The European tale tells simply of the joint nut-gathering adventure of the cock and the mouse. When the cock had tried in vain to reach the nuts he asked the mouse to throw some down to him, and the nut cut the cock's head. He ran to an old woman to get it bandaged, and she asked two hairs for payment. He ran to the dog for these, who asked bread. He went to the baker who asked wood, to the forest which asked water. He went to the fountain, which gave him water, and so he retraced his steps and got his head bound up. The story is bare of all further details. In keeping with Zuni narrative standards, the adapted version begins with a description of the old woman and her turkey yard, "like an eagle cage against a wall." The cock of the original story has appropriately enough become a Zuni pet turkey, and the fact that the turkey has a beard while the cock has not, is capitalized in the resulting story. The old woman had only the one turkey and she was too poor to give it meat, so that the turkey was always meat-hungry. One day he caught sight of Mouse's tail disappearing in his hole and snapped it up for a worm. Now the mouse's tail was his "sign of manhood" and he vowed vengeance. So far the additions are by way of supplying the traditional literary motivation of the despised and put-upon who set out to overcome their enemies. The mouse, therefore, made friends with the cock, who allowed him to eat crumbs thrown him by the old woman, and finally brought the turkey a nut out of his own hoard. The turkey lamented that he was not free like the mouse to gather such nuts and the mouse offered to gnaw the fastening of his corral. This incident is the familiar *Helpful Animals:* rodent (mouse, gopher, etc.) gnaws (ropes, wall, tree roots, etc.). When the nut hit the turkey he was stunned, fell "dead" as the Zunis say, and the mouse avenged himself by gnawing off his neck bristles, his "signs of manhood," in exact compensation for what he had himself suffered. This is the familiar incident, II : 219 and is especially connected in Zuni with *Underground to the Monster*, where the rodent shaves the monster directly over his heart. When the turkey could get up he went to the old woman to have his head bound and she asked him for four neck bristles, i. e. his signs of manhood. But they had been gnawed off. He therefore went to the dog, etc., until at last he got to the spring to ask for water, and the spring asked for prayersticks which should pay the gods for rain. It came and he retraced his steps and was healed. The story is easily a better story than its original; it has been thoroughly adapted to its new cultural setting by the incorporation of all sorts of observations of Zuni life, motivation has been skillfully built up, and well known Zuni incidents have been appropriately introduced in a thoroughly workmanlike manner.

The second ideal of the Zuni stylist is in the building up plot sequences out of large numbers of incidents. A Zuni audience likes very long tales, and the majority of stories combine in different ways several well-marked incidents. These incidents are stock property, and their outlines are known to all the audience. It is impossible to understand Zuni stylistic problems without this realization of what is traditional material. The collections of Zuni folklore that are now available do not reproduce all the tales that are told or may be told, but they give at least the elements out of which these would be built up. The study of the different variants indicates the principles of composition, and the way in which these elements, and new ones when they are introduced, are handled by the native narrators.

The stock incidents available in the composition of Zuni tales are indicated in the Index of Incidents, and those which are used in any given story are listed in the footnote to each tale. The principle themes in the service of which these incidents are combined have been discussed above in this introduction. The narrator's skill is shown in his use of these stock incidents in elaborating these stock themes, and an examination of the tales shows clearly that this is no mean role. The way in which incidents are combined is certainly a main interest of the Zuni audience, and the skill with which this is done by the narrator can be illustrated over and over again.

Certain of these combinations of incidents are very stable, and such complex stories as the Box Boat II : 62, and the Sun's Twins II : 43; 46, follow the same sequence in Cushing's versions and in the present collection. Cushing's tales were recorded fifty years

III

ago, and from families with quite different ceremonial affiliations and clan relationships. The sequences of incidents in these cases had very likely become popular and fairly fixed long before Cushing's time, and they may well hold firm until folktales are no longer told in Zuni.

Even in such a tale as the Sun's Twins, however, the scope of the narrator in building plot is clearly marked. Version A in this collection, II : 43, reproduces the Cushing tale; it is the theme of the proud maiden magically impregnated by a supernatural, publicly killed because she was about to bear illegitimate children, and vindicated by her two sons at the direction of their supernatural father. The great contrast between these two versions is the cleverness with which the thoroughly non-Southwestern ceremony of the Cushing version (this part of Cushing's story has many Shoshonean analogues) has been transformed into the familiar ceremony of the Zuni scalp dance in the present tale, II : 45. This present version, moreover, has dropped the concluding incidents of the Cushing tale: the death of the two sons as a consequence of their disobedience to their supernatural father, the resurrection of one of them as the Skull Husband and the repetition of the original supernatural pregnancy of the priest's daughter with her death, also by a fall from the sky, in a public retribution. This omission of the concluding incidents consolidates the plot, just as the changes in the ceremony bring it into agreement with Zuni cultural behavior.

The difference between these two versions, however, and versions B and C in this collection is more drastic. The same incidents have been used in these latter versions to elaborate a different theme: that of the sons' humiliation of the mother who abandoned them at birth. By introducing into these versions this stock incident of abandonment in childbirth, the narrator is under obligation to develop his story differently. He uses the old Cushing situation of the yaya dance to which the twins come at the direction of their father to dance in the pueblo, but instead of vindicating their dead mother by honoring the eight "mothers" with whom they dance, they dazzle their proud mother who abandoned them, make her select them as her chosen husbands, and humiliate her by announcing their relationship and her act in abandoning them. Version C is concluded at this point, but Version B continues with the concluding incidents of the Cushing tale which were dropped in Version A.

This role of the Zuni narrator in adapting incidents to different themes is apparent in many tales. The narrator must follow out the implications of the new sequence he has chosen. The same infor-

mant tells in I : 130 and I : 171 a like series of incidents, the Eagle
Wife story with the broken taboo on laughing at the dance of the
corpse girls, but in I : 130 he has dropped the *Borrowed feathers*
incident which Cushing gives also in his version, according to which
Eagle Wife brings about her husband's death when he attempts to
return to earth and leave her, and has substituted a series of
miracles by means of which he overcomes all obstacles and is
ceremonially returned with gifts by the Eagles. The story has been
adapted therefore to the theme of the blessings acquired through
marriage with the supernaturals.

In his other version he retains the *Borrowed feathers* incident, but
he builds up to it by relating a series of faithless adventures with
other women to motivate his wife's retribution, introducing especially an initial incident of an affair with a ghost girl so that the
whole story is told to the favorite theme of the husband's reunion in
death with his first wife, i. e. the ghost girl.

Another version by informant 6, Bunzel AES 15 : 210, is a still
different treatment of these incidents. The initial incident is the
Bungler's Instruction in Hunting. The character of the hero is set in
this incident; he is a bungler, and throughout the story he is true to
this character. He ignores a supernatural's directions; he is an inept
lover; he is laughed at by his Eagle Wife for offering his rabbits to
the skeleton which was his Ghost Wife; when he leaves her, he
deceives Eagle Girl instead of asking for her help. In motivating
the husband's death in this way, the narrator has had to reverse the
order of the two marriages, but he has achieved as the others have in
different ways, an integrated story. The interpreter said at the end
of this tale, "He had all this trouble because of what he did to the
rabbits," AES 15 : 235, note 1, i. e., the rabbits whose killing he had
bungled at the beginning of the tale.

The incident of the *Butterfly pursuit* is another illustration of the
implications recognized by Zuni narrators in plot combinations.
Three versions, I : 199, A, B, and Bunzel, AES 15 : 248 combine this
incident with the *Hide and seek game with a dangerous maiden*. The
kachina identifications are quite different in Versions A and B, and
in the former since the hero assumes the form of the Ne'we·kwe, the
licentious clown, he summons Coyote and both of them punish the
girls with intercourse; in the latter since he is Paiyatamu, the
gracious impersonation associated with sun and flowers, flute music
and love, he transforms the sisters into butterflies, which are here
associated with eroticism, and sends them to the four directions to
call the rain, i. e. instruments of fertility magic. In the Bunzel version the narrator has carried out still further the associations with

III*

Ne'we·kwe, suppressing details which do not belong to this cult and emphasizing details that are in character.

These three versions contrast strongly with the Bunzel ms version, I : 337, The Origin of Ne'we·kwe. In this case the *Butterfly pursuit* has been used alone, without introducing the *Hide and seek game.* The story is of a proud maiden who had no time for suitors but occupied herself with her basket making. She wanted to catch the butterfly to copy its marking in her basket patterns, and she pursued it till it disappeared in the Ne'we·kwe spring. She followed and was taken in marriage by the Ne'we·kwe who had shown himself as a butterfly. When he had taught her the human role of marriage, she returned home and married, but eventually returned to her first husband, and her children were the Ne'we·kwe society. The incident, therefore, has been used to point two favorite Zuni themes, *Marriage taught by supernaturals to those who refuse it,* and the *Return in death to the first husband.*

Other examples of the recognition by Zuni narrators of the literary problems involved in various transpositions are discussed in the notes: the two versions of the Bridegroom is required to kill a Deer, in which the courtship test is imposed in one case by a girl and in the other by a youth; the three versions in which the test is possible of accomplishment and the two in which the unwilling youth or maiden supernaturally render it impossible, I : 303; the consequences of substituting a human husband for the Ahaiyute, Bunzel AES 15 : 123 in the version of the Girl who requires a Scalp of her Suitors, I : 87; the Tarantula steals the Youth's Clothing which is told in the present collection, I : 137 to the theme of the humiliation of a youth who refuses marriage and in the Cushing version, 345, without reference to this theme; the versions of Parrot Girl, I : 184; 190; of Deer Boy II : 12; 16; of the Deserted Child guided by Awl, II : 20; 25; of the incident *Transformation into Coyote* which in three out of four versions is the regular conclusion of Deer Boy in Zuni, II : 19; Cushing 146; Bunzel AES 15 : 115, and is used as conclusion also in a similar tale of a despised boy who gains a patron in Coyote, Cushing Heye Museum 8 : 395, but which is transferred in II : 111 to the initial incident of a plot which allows the development of the theme of the hunter's revenge upon his false friend.

The freedom with which plots may be built up is made clear also by a consideration of certain incidents which serve as stock introductions or conclusions to a variety of tales. Whenever the plot allows its use, the incident of *Supernaturals are sent to shrines* may be called in requisition. The *Orpheus* incident is popular in a similar capacity, as well as the *Contests to retain a wife*, and *Witch contests*. The *Apparation impersonated to punish evildoers or enemies* is used both as introduction and conclusion to several tales. The *Kachinas at Kachina Village provide food or clothing* is requisitioned in almost any tale in which it is appropriate. The *Marriage taught by supernaturals to those who refuse it*, the *Magical impregnations* by Sun or Horned Serpent, the *Famine is caused by misuse of corn in a game* are popular introductions in tales the plots of which differ completely.

These elements (incidents) are often cleverly adapted to serve the plot. This can be most clearly illustrated in tales from other peoples adopted in Zuni. The story of the *Mare Wife*, I : 236, becomes in Zuni a means of stating quite completely the native views of marriage and the necessary sex education of the boy. The story of *Tail by Tail* is completely and elaborately assimilated to the favorite theme of kachina origins, see discussion I : 273. The popular Shoshonean incident of *Odors as deadly* (usually identified with bullets) is adapted to a tale of famine caused by too much rainfall and a priest's device for overpowering and driving away the rain gods, Cushing 269. The noodle tales are adapted to the situation of the reluctant and self-conscious bridegroom, I : 341.

It is obvious that where such freedom in handling incidents is expected of a good story teller, it will often become impossible to trace with assurance a tale's genetic relationship with tales of other peoples. The likelihood that Cushing's satire on the scalp dance is a Zuni handling of the Turtle's War Party, and the Little Girl and the Turkeys of the Cinderella story is discussed in the notes, I : 294; II : 259, and in both cases the ease and freedom of the Zuni adaptation to its native themes and ceremonies is complete.

The Zuni narrator is also allowed freedom in the use of stock folkloristic devices. The loads made magically light, the runners who carry straws or gourds or feathers to run lightly, the inexhaustible meals provided by helpful animals, the magically surmounted precipices, are all legion. Good story tellers usually incorporate these devices at any appropriate point.

The greatest freedom allowed the Zuni narrator, however, is in the adaptation of the tale to explanations and origins. Such "that's why's" are a stylistic requirement in Zuni, and no American Indian folklore presents such a prodigality of explanatory elements. They are seldom standardized, so that the same explanatory elements occur in different versions even of the same tale, and good story tellers often give several to one tale. The explanatory elements attached to the story of the Deserted Children in four versions illustrates the freedom with which they are habitually inserted:

Cushing: Heye Museum 8. Hence to this day the dragonfly comes in early summer humming from one plant to another, yet never content with its resting place. 121.

For this reason the dragonfly is painted on the priests' ceremonial bowls. 121.

Hence we have today Guardians of the Corn, i. e. priesthoods. 124.

Hence to this day the priests or hosts of Zuni cast a morsel of food into the fire with a prayer to the ancestors. 115.

Parsons MAAA 4. That is why the yellow wolves who live on animals they kill are in hills in every direction. 321.

Benedict II. That is why we worship the dragonfly and why we are not allowed to kill it. 9.

That is why we always choose honest people for the priesthoods. 12.

Explanatory elements are added to European tales quite as readily as to old indigenous ones. The conclusion to an accumulative tale is: "And that is why medicine men never serve without pay," Cushing 421. The familiar *Tail by Tail* is concluded in all versions with different kachina origins, including always the coyote collars of the Saiyalia, I : 273. The *Substitute Race* gives the origin of ceremonial offerings to animals on the occasion of stick races, Cushing 283. Explanatory elements are in Zuni the recognized mark of a good story teller, and the Zuni audience delights in the ingenuity which the narrator displays in inventing them.

The scope allowed the individual narrator in Zuni folklore is evident also from the comparison of versions told by the different narrators. The tales were told in English by Informant 7 and those of the other informants were interpreted by a woman of the household. Both Informant 7 and the interpreter were asked to translate the stories literally. They were faithful in their rendition, as can be seen by comparing actual text translations in Bunzel AES 15, and I have not retained their inadequate English in the translation, any more than if I were translating from text. Informants 3 and 6 are brother and sister, resident of course in different households, but members of the same major priesthood and tied by all the bonds which hold the matrilineal group together in Zuni. Informant 4 is their mother, and Informant 8 their father, resident in the clan household for nearly forty years. This group had heard the same tales told constantly around the same fireside and contrasts between them are therefore due in large measure to individual preferences and to different individual experience. Informant 7 was of a rival faction, a man of more independent activities and psychologically more aberrant than the members of the other family. He was a medicine society headmen who in his young manhood was condemned by the priests as a witch and hung by the thumbs until he confessed. He turned informant against the priests and caused the elder brother bow priest to be imprisoned in a government penitentiary. The story is told Bunzel AES 15 : 44.[1] He was a person of great ability, of commanding presence, and with a great personal need for achieving eminence, which he had primarily sought in the medicine societies. He knew incredible masses of ritual and song as well as tales. Earlier in his life he had sought prominence in trading and making money, but, as he said, "That was no good." He had used this wealth to build one of the annually required new houses for entertaining the Ca'lako, and he was no longer active in trading. More lately he had gained position as the Zuni representative in transactions with the Whites, and at the time these stories were recorded was governor of Zuni, a secular office. It is clear that he likes elaborate plot better than the other informants, who prefer to indulge rather in cultural details. This is of course only relative, and Informant 7 gave long ceremonial accounts which will be published in "Zuni Ceremonial Tales." However, the wilder combinations of incidents are his, and the others stick closer to the beaten track in plot combinations.

There is also a contrast in ceremonial emphasis between Informant 7 and the other story tellers. The former was a headman of Little Fire Society, and had set himself to learn the tales and rituals of the medicine societies, those of which he was not a member as well as of Little Fire. His emphasis upon the medicine societies in his tales is very marked, II : 19; 35; 67; 158; 227; 228; though the emphasis is apparent also in tales of other informants, II : 37 (3); 150 (6); 188 (6). On the other hand, all the long tales of tenatsali divination, I : 35, II : 139 and all statements of its great power, I : 47, II : 141, "that is why people who have tenatsali always have the best of everything," are from the tales of the other family, which possesses tenatsali and plants prayersticks for it regularly.

It is characteristic of Informant 7 that he tells the only tales of skeptics and their conversion. The skeptic doubts whether the Sun receives the prayersticks planted for him and sets out on the journey to the Sun to assure himself, II : 62; the Ahaiyute doubt the power of the medicine societies and are humiliated until they are convinced,

---

[1] See also Benedict, Patterns of Culture, New York, 1934, p. 260.

II : 228. The point in another instance is that the skeptic is successful because he does not accept the oracle he is given: the gambler
takes offerings to an Ahaiyute shrine and is told he is too late. He
says, "I don't care for omens," and goes back to his patron, to whom
he says, "Somebody spoke to me, 'My boy, you are too late.' And
I said, 'What do I care for omens?' I said that." He challenged his
opponents and was successful, I : 164.

On the other hand it is characteristic of the family of the other
informants that they carry the general mildness of Zuni tales to
characteristic lengths. In her version of The Deserted Child guided
by Awl, II : 24, one of the women of this family (3) tells how Awl
spoke to the child and guided him to his parents. Informant 7, on
the other hand, tells how his foster mother, Coyote Woman, was
fattening him for a feast, chased him as he fled, and was only prevented from overtaking him by helpful animals who detained her with
offers of intercourse and finally humiliated her, II : 20. In two
versions of the Twin Children of the Sun, II : 46; 52, Informant 7
introduces the incident of the mother's abandonment of her children
at birth and makes the point of the tale the children's humiliation
of their mother; Informant 8 tells of no abandonment and makes
his conclusion the twins' vindication of their mother's memory. In
accounts of the origin of the scalp dance, Informant 7 tells of the
fight between the two brothers to possess the girl and "in the morning they took their bows and shot her," I : 54; Informant 8 gives
the story: "Elder Brother said, 'Let's not kill her. She is quite nice.
We will come back some day and enjoy her again.' Younger Brother
said, 'No, we will kill her as we planned. If we come back again to
play with her, she might like me best, and then you would be angry
again.' Elder Brother said, 'No, I shan't be angry,'" I : 63. Among
all the versions of the Ahaiyute's rain-making game in which their
grandmother is killed, Informant 8 is alone in saving the grandmother alive, and she says, "Please don't play those games any more,
my grandchildren. If you go on, you won't have any grandmother
any more," I : 14.

The most striking way in which the importance of personal bias
and experience is shown in Zuni tales is in the contrast between
tales told by men and by women. There is no taboo in Zuni which
restricts such choice. The differences that exist are the result of
unconscious preference on the part of the narrators. Men tell the
tales which feature extended accounts of the stick races, I : 97; 216;
II : 72; 186; Bunzel ms II : 274; of gambling, I : 15; 163; 224; and
of hunting, II : 110; 123; 130; 136; 148; 152. Women tell those

which detail cooking techniques, I : 29; II : 198.[1] The Cinderella
story, I : 32 is told by a woman, and the stories of women assisting
in childbirth who discover that the mother has initiated her baby as
a witch, II : 162; 163. Women also tell the only tales of poor little
girls who are overworked. "Every day the little girl worked all day
long. She ground flour and baked corncakes. One night she was
tired. Her mother said to her, 'There is no water. Go fetch a jar
of water.' The little girl cried, she was so tired she could not go for
water." A Moth takes pity on her and her mother grieves. Even
when the little girl is brought back she cannot restrain her tears
and so loses her again, II : 40. The little girl who becomes the foun-
der of the Crane Clan lives with her uncle and says, "My uncle is
always away in his fields, my aunt treats me badly, and I always
have to grind and carry water. My jar is heavy and I am almost
starved," II : 41. The kind of detail that distinguishes the women's
stories is characteristic; women give the only account of childbirth
observances, I : 80; women add to a description of a picnic, "The
mothers nursed their babies and laid them down comfortably," I : 12;
to an account of girls grinding for the priests, "Their sweethearts
waited to see in which house the girls were grinding. They drew their
shawls over their faces and went in to husk for them," II : 170. In
Informant 3's tale of the Deserted Wife, the mother, before she
sends her children away from the doomed pueblo, tells them, "My
dears, I shall wake you before sunrise. You alone I do not wish them
to kill. On no account turn back home when you see dust and smoke
rising. Don't think perhaps your mother is not dead, for I shall be
the first one to be killed. But I shall have ways to help you. I shall
go to Kachina Village and become a uwanami," II : 166, 167. There-
after the tale follows the fortunes of the children, not of the doomed
village. Two tales by women informants relate at great length the
good time people have staying at other pueblos during famine,
I : 29, II : 198. The one case of a mother's regret in abandoning
her child at birth and her care of it is in a tale told by a woman.
When the baby was born she picked it up. "She liked that baby,
but she was ashamed to take it home. She broke the soft leaves off
the weeds and made a nest to put it in. She broke the weeds and
branches and made a shelter over the baby. She nursed it," and
returned next day to renew the shelter and nurse the child again.
"The third day his mother went out in the evening to see if the baby

---

[1] See, however, in tales by men the bride's teaching cooking to the Ahaiyute
grandmother (8), I: 119, and the good corncakes Lazy Bones makes (6),
I: 149. These are less elaborate.

was still there. He was gone. She saw the deer tracks. She was sorry," II : 13, 14.

In two cases tales are told from the point of view of the men actors or of the woman according to the sex of the narrator. The version of The Deserted Husband told by a woman expatiates on the woman's grievance; her husband did not compliment her on her cooking, "he never said, 'How good!'" It details the wife's determination to cook at other people's feasts and arrange a meeting with a man; it tells how she made hersslf beautiful, and how she went home to look after her little daughter; "she was making dolls out of rags." It follows through her arrangements with her lover and her handling of her suspicious husband, II : 78. The men's versions (8 and 7) omit all this; they tell the story from the point of view of the man. They begin with the husband's proposal to bring calamity upon the pueblo because of his faithless wife, and relate the details of the kiva conversations, the ritual which causes the earthquake, the friend who informs on him, and the help of the Hopi priests, II : 85; 89.

In the Rabbit Huntress, I : 76, the woman's version (3) tells how the resourceful girl gets more than a man's good catch in her hunting and expends itself in an account of the making of the sand bed and presentation of the child and role of the father's mother in the birth of the child of her marriage with Ahaiyute. The man's version, I : 84, tells how the girl has no success in hunting and gets only two rabbits; instead of the women's details of the other version, it goes on to describe a second marriage to a human husband and how the latter followed her to the land of the dead.

The fear of sex on the part of men that is evident in Zuni folklore has been discussed as a dominant theme in their mythology. Nothing could make this point clearer than the distinctions between the tales told by men and women. All the witch tales in which this theme is embodied, all the Ahaiyute tales, all the *Hide and Seek Games*, all the stories of sexual fetishism and bestiality, are told by men. One out of the five *Pursuits by a dangerous woman* is told by a woman, but that is the single appearance of this theme in a woman's tale. There is no tale of a woman who fears intercourse. In addition a man (8) tells the tale of the husband's fear of demonstrativeness on the part of his wife and his arrangements to call the Apache, I : 181, and a man (7) tells of the six Corn Maidens who trap their husbands and kill them, I : 206.

One minor point remains for discussion in connection with the Zuni tales, and that is in regard to their accuracy as history. The historical reconstructions of early ethnological students in Zuni and in Hopi were based in large measure upon the statements in folk-lore. Thus Fewkes interpreted the history of the Hopi as a gathering of diverse groups, now represented by the clans, from the four points of the compass; he interpreted their social organization as a consequence of these originally distinct groups. Cushing similarly, though less insistently, interpreted Zuni migration legends. The comparison of the different versions, I : 258, note 4, makes it clear that the often-repeated migration incident, the *Choice of eggs*, is told with almost as many "that's whys" as any other Zuni tale and that these explanatory elements are strictly comparable to those in courtship or witch tales. They certainly give no basis for reconstruction of history. In other examples of "that's whys" that have historic reference. the same truth is obvious. Thus the tale of Tupe kills the Apaches, II : 203, is given as the origin of the scalp dance, an origin accounted for by half a dozen other tales, see *Origin of scalp dance*, and recounts a scalp dance said to have been held two generations before the tale was told to me. Obviously the scalp dance in Zuni has no such recent origin, and the narrator himself scouted the suggestion. His "origin" was a literary flourish. In the same way a true story of treachery against Navaho visitors which happened two generations ago is told by the grandson of the chief actor as an origin of albinos in Zuni, II : 207, yet immediately after telling the tale he named albinos who had been born considerably before the date of the incident. I did not point out to him the inconsistency and he saw none. The tale did not even represent history according to his own personal knowledge.

The lack of historicity in the tales is apparent in other ways than in the explanatory elements. In the albino story a comparison with the historical account of the incident recorded by Dr. Bunzel shows that even in so short a time the tale has been built up to a climax with repetitive incidents and otherwise modified, II : 207. The story of the battle which took place on Corn Mountain, at which time a friendship pact was made with the Lagunas, and the Big Shell cult vanquished the enemy, is told in two historical settings, once as the tale of a quarrel with the eastern pueblos, II : 204, and the other, the catastrophe of the Rebellion against the Spaniards in 1670, Boas JAFL 35 : 97. To the latter tale, as is indicated also by Cushing, RBAE 13 : 331, is added the story of the Spanish priest who saved the people and who elected to stay in Zuni rather than return to his own people. It is obvious that standard literary versions of battles may do service in different connections, and that it is impossible to trust their historical accuracy.

I. THE EMERGENCE AND OTHER KACHINA TALES.

THE EMERGENCE

Notes, 255

A (6)

They were living in the fourth world. It was dark. They could not see one another. They stepped upon one another, they urinated upon one another, they spat upon one another, they threw refuse upon one another. They could not breathe. They lived there four days (years). The Sun took pity upon them. He saw that the world was covered with hills and springs but there were no people to give him prayersticks. He thought, "My people shall come to the daylight world."

The earth was covered with mist. He threw his rays into the mist and there in the world his sons stood up. They were two (boys). Their hair was tangled, they had long noses, long cheeks. Next day they played together. The third day the younger brother said to the elder, "Let us go and look for beautiful places. I will go to Corn Mountain[1] and you shall go to the south Where the Cotton Hangs.[1] The third day they went. The younger looked over the world and he saw that nobody lived there. He said to himself, "Tomorrow we shall be old enough to work." When the next day came he called his brother. Elder Brother came and said, "What is it that you have to say that you have called me?" Younger Brother said, "We are four days old and we are old enough to work. This is a good world and nobody lives in it. Let us go to the southwest. There below the people are living in the fourth world. They are our fathers and mothers, our sons and daughters. There is no light there, no room to move about. They cannot see one another. They step on one another, they urinate upon one another, they spit on one another, they throw refuse upon one another. They should come to this world where they can see our father Sun." Elder Brother answered, "It is as you say. We will go and try."

The two went to the southwest and they came to the entrance to the fourth world. They went in and came to the first world. There

---

[1] These are Ahaiyute shrines. In the more esoteric versions the Ahaiyute are later representatives of the originally born Watsutsi and Yanaluha.

1

was just a little light there. They came to the second world. It was dark. They came to the third world. It was darker still. They came to the fourth world. It was black. The people could not see each other. They felt one another with their hands and recognized their faces. They said, "Some stranger has come. Where is it that you have come from? It is our fathers, the bow priests." They ran to feel them and they said, "Our fathers, you have come. Teach us how to get out of this place. We have heard of our father Sun and we wish to see him." The two answered, "We have come to bring you to the other world where you can see him. Will you come with us?" The people answered, "Yes, we wish to go. In this world we cannot see one another. We step upon one another, we urinate upon one another, we spit upon one another, we throw refuse upon one another. It is nasty here. We wish to see our father Sun. We have been waiting for someone to show us the way, but our brothers must come too. As the priest of the north says, so let it be." The two "needed" the priest of the north. He came and said, "I have come. What is it that you wish to ask?" "We want you to come into the daylight world." "Yes, we shall be glad to come. We want to see our father Sun, but my brothers must come too. As the priest of the east says, so let it be." (Repeat for east, south, west.)

They said to them, "Do you know how we can get to the daylight world?" Younger Brother went to the north. He took the seeds of the pine tree and planted them. He turned about and when he looked where he had planted the pine had already grown. He turned again and when he looked at the tree the branches were grown to full size. He tore off a branch and brought it back to the people. He went to the west and planted the seeds of the spruce. He turned about and when he looked where he had planted the spruce had already grown. He turned again and when he looked at the tree the branches were grown to full size. He tore off a branch and brought it back to the people. He went to the south and planted the seeds of the silver spruce (lokwima). He turned about and when he looked where he had planted the seeds the silver spruce had already grown. He turned again and when he looked at the tree the branches were grown to full size. He tore off a branch and brought it back to the people. He went to the east and planted the seeds of the aspen (łaniko). He turned about and when he looked where he had planted the seeds, the aspen had already grown. He turned again and when he looked the branches had grown to full size. He tore off a branch and brought it back to the people. He said, "This is all.[1]

---

[1] From the branches long prayersticks, telane, were made for the ascent, and prayerstick-making instituted.

We are ready to go up to the upper world. My people, make yourselves ready. Take those things that you live by (etowe)."

The bow priests took the long prayerstick (elbow length) they had made from the pine of the north. They set it in the earth. The people went up the prayerstick and came into the third world. There was rumbling like thunder. It was lighter in that world and the people were blinded. The bow priests said, "Have we all come out?" They answered, "Yes. Is it here that we are going to live?" They answered, "Not yet. This is not the upper world." They lived there four days (years). The bow priests took the crook of the west that they had made from the spruce. They set it in the earth. There was rumbling like thunder and the people came up into the second world. It was twilight there and the people were blinded. The bow priests said, "Have we all come out?" "Yes. Is it here that we shall live?" "Not yet." They remained there four days (years) and the two took the long prayerstick that they had made from the silver-spruce of the south and set it in the earth. There was rumbling like thunder and the people came up into the first world. It was light like red dawn. They were dazzled and they said, "Is it here that we shall live?" They answered, "Not yet." The people were sad. They could see each other quite plain. Their bodies were covered with dirt and with ashes. They were stained with spit and urine and they had green slime on their heads. Their hands and feet were webbed and they had tails and no mouths or exits. They remained there four days (years). The bow priests took the long prayerstick they had made from the aspen of the east and they set it in the earth. There was rumbling like thunder and the people came up into the daylight world. The two bow priests came first and after them those who carried the medicine bundles, the ķa'etone, tcu'etone, mu'etone and ɫe'etone. When they came into the sunlight the tears ran down their cheeks. Younger Brother said to them, "Turn to the sun and look full at our father Sun no matter how bright it is." They cried out for it hurt them and their tears ran to the ground. Everywhere they were standing the sun's flowers (sunflowers and buttercups) sprang up from the tears caused by the sun. The people said, "Is this the world where we shall live?" "Yes, this is the last world. Here you see our father Sun." They remained there four days (years) and they went on.

Followed by the blessings brought by the witches: corn, and life after death, as told Bunzel 592—3 and Parsons JAFL 36: 137—8. See abstracts below, I: 258, 260..

They came to Slime Spring (Awico). They lived there four days (years) and the bow priests said, "It is time our people learned to eat." They took the corn of the witch and they put it in the fields to itsumawe.[1] When it had grown they harvested it and the men took it home to their wives. They smelled it, but they had no way to eat. The bow priests were sad and Younger Brother said, "Elder Brother, the people have made itsumawe and I am sorry for them that they cannot eat. Let us cut them so that they can enjoy food." Elder Brother agreed and his brother said, "When everyone is asleep we shall go to each house and cut mouths in their faces." That night after the people were asleep the bow priests took their (ceremonial) stone knives and sharpened them with a red whetstone. They went to each house. They cut each face where the skin of the mouth was puffed up. The knife made the lips red from the red of the whetstone. They went home. When the sun rose the people found that they had mouths. They said, "What makes our faces so flat ?" They began to get hungry and the men brought in corn and water and they ate. That night they were uncomfortable because they had no exits. They could not defecate. Younger Brother thought, "We should cut the anus so that they can defecate." He went to his brother and he said, "These people should have the anus. Let us cut it tonight when they are asleep." Elder Brother agreed and they took the (smaller) stone knives and sharpened them on a soot whetstone. They cut the anus for all the people and the soot colored those parts black. Next morning the people were uncomfortable and they went outside. They thought they had broken open in their sleep.

They tried to break up the corn so that they could eat it better. They took whetstones in their webbed hands and rubbed the corn on the hearthstone.[2] They mixed porridge and made corncakes (hepoloka). After they had made it it was hard to clean their hands for they were webbed and Younger Brother said to Elder Brother, "I am sorry for my people that their hands are webbed. Let us cut their fingers apart." Elder Brother agreed and that night they took the (larger) stone knife and cut the webbed hands and feet of the people.[3] In the morning the people were frightened but when the sun had risen they did not notice any more. They worked better

---

[1] Increase by magic. Putting clay sheep on an altar and planting big clay peaches are acts of itsumawe. Planting a garden falls in the same category.

[2] The wide grinding stones found in the ruins are said by the people to prove that their ancestors once had webbed hands.

[3] There was no blood for the tissue was like cartilage. "They had not been eating long enough to have blood running through it."

with fingers and toes. The next day Younger Brother said to the older, "Our people have been cut. They still have tails, and horns. Let us cut them away." Elder Brother agreed and they took the (smaller) stone knife. They went to each house and cut the tails and horns from their people. In the morning the people were frightened but when the sun rose they did not mind any more. They were glad that they were finished. They stayed there four days. They came to Watercress Spring. They stayed there four days.

They came to Prayerstick Place. The bow priest said, "Our people are too many. It is better for us to separate. Who will go to the south side and who will go to the middle ?"

Followed by The People are given a *Choice of Eggs*, Bunzel 595; Parsons JAFL 36: 141. The conclusion in this version reads:

That is why we have crows and ravens who eat our corn and the people of the south have parrots with valuable feathers. Then the people separated. Those who had chosen the parrot egg went to the south.

Followed by the Birth of the Koyemci and Transformation of the Children into Kachinas exactly as Bunzel 595—6. At Hanłipinka they make a vain attempt to have the water spider find the middle of the earth but it is too far from center. They send the bow priests to visit Kachina Village as ibid 596—7, with the addition that Father Koyemci introduces himself as the priest's son who had intercourse with his sister and asks the bow priests to send the priesthoods to receive instruction in prayerstick making. The priests go and are received by Pautiwa (village priest), Saiyataca (Pekwin), and Calako (bow priest) and receive instructions.

The next day they started toward the east. The people of Łe'etone went to the north to Rope Hill and then to the east to the Nutria spring and turned back again toward the west. The people who were seeking the middle had come to Matsaka. They heard the Łe'etone coming at Eastern Road and went out to meet them. They brought the Łe'etone back with them into Matsaka and that is why salt weed always grows there. That is why Nutria is cold and the wind is from the east.[1]

At Matsaka, each family built a house for themselves. The bow priests said, "It is time to try again to find where the middle is." He called the Water Spider and he put his heart down at Matsaka. He touched the corners of the east and north, but he could not touch the corners of the west and the south. He said, "You are very near. I will go and find the place where my arms will touch the horizon in all four directions." The bow priests went with him.

---

[1] Łe'etone is a winter medicine bundle and brings cold.

Water Spider said, "I have to go back. Let us try Halona (ant place). My heart will be on an anthill.[1]" He stretched out his arms and legs and touched the horizon at the north, west, south and east. He was in the middle of the world. He said, "My people shall live here always. They will never be overthrown for their hearts will not be to one side (of the world)."

They returned to Matsaḳa and they said, "We have found the place. We shall go there. We have found the middle of the world." They left their houses standing in Matsaḳa and went to Halona[2] to the middle of the world.

Followed by the account of the first initiation of boys and the institution of the Łewekwe ceremony, to appear in volume of Zuni Ceremonial Tales.

B (7)

Notes, 259

The first section of this ritualistic emergence version is published with text, Bunzel 547—603, and the differences between the version recorded with text and without text are so slight that the latter is not given. The tale proceeds in the latter version, after the settlement of Zuni, with accounts of the first initiation of children, and the institution of the Łewekwe rites. Both of these are reserved for Zuni Ceremonial Tales. The conclusion of the version is the story of the departure of the Corn Maidens and the institution of molawia upon their return, I: 24—43.

A. THE ḲANA·KWE CONCEAL THE GAME (7)

Notes, 261

Long ago when the world was soft the people of Kachina Village went hunting. They hunted four days. The Ḳana·kwe were hunting also. On the fourth day the kachinas went southeast and the Ḳana·kwe went southwest and they made their surrounds for deer. The Ḳana·kwe circle overlapped the circle of the kachinas, and they began to fight. Ḳana·kwe Chief said to the Kachina Chief, "Deer belong to us. Mountain lions, mountain sheep, jack rabbits, cottontails, belong to you, but deer belong to us." Kachina Chief said, "Deer belong to us." They were angry. All that day they did not hunt any more. They fought all day. In every direction men fought, a kachina and a Ḳana·kwe.

---

[1] Associated with many magical rites.
[2] Really a district of Zuni. Across the creek from Itiwana.

When night came they separated. The Ḳanaˑkwe held council. They said, "We will shut up all the game. The kachinas will hunt and find nothing." They gathered together all the deer and the cottontails and all the game animals. They took a porcupine and pulled out his quills and made a corral for them. They called Spider and she made a web over the corral so that no one could see the game they had hidden.

Next day the kachinas went again to hunt. They found nothing. They looked and looked, but they could not find even the tracks of game. They looked all the time, every year, every year. They thought and thought. They said, "The Ḳanaˑkwe have rounded up the game and shut it away." Pautiwa went to Ḳamaḳa, and he said to the Ḳanaˑkwe chief, "My people hunt and hunt but they find no deer. We have thought much of this. We think your people have hidden the deer." Ḳanaˑkwe Chief said, "No, we do not know where the deer are. We have not hidden the deer." Pautiwa said, "We think you have hidden the deer. We will fight you." Ḳanaˑkwe Chief said, "Very well, we shall fight. Whoever wins shall have the deer. Whoever loses shall never have deer any more."

Pautiwa went back to Kachina Village. He said, "We shall fight with the Ḳanaˑkwe, and whoever wins shall have deer." For four days they made their bows and arrows. They went out and came against the Ḳanaˑkwe. They fought all day. It drizzled.[1] They were equal: nobody won, nobody lost. That night they separated. The next day they fought again. They fought all day. It drizzled. They were equal: nobody won, nobody lost. That night they separated. The next day they fought again. They fought all day. They were equal: nobody won, nobody lost. The fourth day the Ḳanaˑkwe took yucca and strung their bows. The kachinas strung theirs with deer sinew.[2] When it drizzled the sinew stretched so that it was useless. The yucca tightened. The Ḳanaˑkwe pressed back the kachinas and they ran. Those who lagged the Ḳanaˑkwe took prisoners. They took Koɬamana[3] and Itsepaca (a Ḳoyemci) and a Saiyaɬia. They won the fight.

After they had fought, Pautiwa said to the Ḳanaˑkwe, "Now the deer are yours. When you go to Itiwana you shall take deer to the people. We shall not take deer. When we go we shall take corn and seeds and many things, but you shall take deer. And you shall take

---

[1] The kachinas are identified with rain, which caused the sinew bowstrings of both contestants to loosen.
[2] As usual.
[3] Literally, kachina berdache.

with you Kołamana and Itsepaca, and the Saiyałia.[1] The people will be glad to see you coming to Itiwana.[2] We shall work together for our people. We shall never fight any more." That is why the Kana·kwe come to Itiwana bringing deer on their backs, and have with them Kołamana, Itsepaca and a Saiyałia.

B (3)
Notes, 262
Published only in abstract

THE KANA·KWE CHILDREN BRING THEIR MEDICINE BUNDLE (7)
Notes, 263

After this there was a famine at Kamaka. The Kana·kwe had nothing to eat, and they went to Acoma to find food. They left behind a little boy and his younger sister. One side of their faces was white, the other red (Indian flesh-color). They had nothing to eat. The little boy went out and caught woodrats. He cooked them, and he and his sister lived on them. After several years, he said to his sister, "We cannot live on woodrats alone. I must go and hunt deer so that we will have enough to eat." She said, "All right." He went out and travelled northwest till he came where Caliente is. He looked out over the valley and he saw two towns. He saw Ketcipawa and Hawiku. He said, "There are people. Perhaps they are my people's enemies; perhaps they would kill me."

He went back to his sister. He said to her, "I went hunting deer to the northwest and I saw two towns. There are people living there. Perhaps they are our people, perhaps long ago they fought our people. If we go to them and they take us in we shall have food. If they are our enemies and they kill us, it is well. We cannot live as we have lived. If they kill us we shall die together." His sister said, "All right."

They made ready to go. The boy put on his ceremonial blanket and he took his bow in one hand, and around his left wrist he fastened his medicine bundle. They started out. They went a long way. His sister said, "I am tired." He took her on his back and carried her in the blanket. He carried her a long way. He said, "I am tired." He put her down. She walked a little way, and they came to the spring near Ketcipawa. They could go no farther.

[1] These three kachinas always accompany the Kana·kwe.
[2] The Kana·kwe dance is one of the greatest of the give-away dances.

The daughter of the priest came to get water from the spring. She saw the Ḵanaᐧkwe children there. She ran back to her home. Her father said to her, "Why do you come running in?" She said, "I saw two children at the spring. One side of their faces is white, the other red. They have snout-like mouths. Under their eyes there are curlicues. They are dressed in beautiful white ceremonial blankets." The priest went to the bow priest. They were dancing the Lapaɫiakwe (obsolete dance). He said to the bow priest, "My daughter went to the spring. She saw there a boy and a girl. One side of their faces is white, the other red. They have snout-like mouths. Under their eyes there are curlicues. They are dressed in beautiful white ceremonial blankets. I have come to ask you to go and speak to them." The bow priest went to the spring. He said, "How have you lived these days, my fathers, my mothers, my children?" They said, "Happily." They said, "What do you wish to say?" He said, "I have come from our fathers to take you where they are." The boy said, "We shall go."

The bow priest led them to the plaza. He made a cross of meal for the boy, and beside it a cross of meal for the girl. The priest put his hands on the shoulders of the boy and moved him toward the six directions and made him sit down. He put his hands on the shoulders of the girl and moved her toward the six directions and made her sit down. He said, "We have sent for you to ask you who you are and where you have come from." The boy answered, "My name is Ḵaniɫana. I live at Ḵamaḵa and my people are the Ḵanaᐧ-kwe. They had no food, and they went to Acoma. They left me and my sister behind because we were young. I hunted wood rats and we have lived on them. We can live on them no longer, and I came hunting deer to the northwest and saw this town. Whether you are our people or the enemies of our people, I do not know. If you kill us, it is well. We shall die together. It is better that we die together than that one of us be left after the other has starved." The priest answered, "We are not the enemies of your people. Long ago your people fought the people of Kachina Village, but we are not the people of Kachina Village. We shall not kill you. Perhaps you have a medicine bundle?" The boy answered, "Yes, I have brought a medicine bundle. It is the Yellow Corn medicine bundle, — I mean, Black Corn medicine bundle, — and it is powerful." The priest answered, "You shall be our fathers and our mothers, our sons and our daughters. This medicine bundle shall be precious to our people and you shall live among us."

So the Ḵanaᐧkwe boy and girl were adopted among the people of Ketcipàwa, and they lived there. The Ḵanaᐧkwe girl married a boy of the Eagle clan and the Ḳana·kwe boy married a girl of the Turkey clan. The children of the girl learned the songs of the medicine bundle from their uncle, the Ḳana·kwe boy, and today this medicine bundle is in the house in Sunshine Place and belongs to the Black Corn clan.[1]

THE ANIMALS PLAY HIDDEN BALL (7)

Notes, 264

A version of Hidden Ball from the same informant as the tale incorporated in the Emergence Myth, Bunzel 598, with Ahaiyute bringing his ball for the play and giving the decision as to day and night animals. It concludes:

After four years the Ahaiyute returned (to Hanłipinḳa). They sent Mountain Lion to the north, Bear to the west to find black ants for his food, Wolf to the south to kill game animals, Wildcat to the east to eat meat, Coyote in front to play about, and Porcupine up into the trees. The birds the Ahaiyute sent to the big rocks to make their nests in holes and to kill rats and mice. They all went to the places assigned to them and the Ahaiyute returned to their home in Corn Mountain.

THE FLOOD

Notes, 265

A (8)

The people were living at Itiwana. The corn clan was the largest of all the clans. The young people of corn clan were very handsome, and they played with each other and lay together. Only one man could not overlook their wrongdoing and he was a priest's son and a member of corn clan. He thought to himself: "I will call my uncle, who was killed by the Navaho, and I will ask him for help." He made four prayersticks and took them to Hawiku. He sat down and dug a hole and sprinkled prayer meal in it. He held his prayersticks in his hand and prayed, "Help me, my uncle, you who were killed in the Navaho fight; come to me. My clan does wrong and I am calling on you for help." He put down the prayersticks and covered them. Presently he heard his uncle coming. He heard the moaning and rattling of a dead man in the distance. He was not frightened because it was his uncle. He saw his body rolling toward him. They went together toward Itiwana. It was dark, and when they reached

---

[1] The informant said that the non-esoteric versions of this story differed principally in that the children went to Hawiku instead to Ketcipawa.

Pinawa the uncle brushed against the boy and he became a dead man. He was sorry at this for he had an old grandmother, and he lived with her and with his sister who had a little boy and a little girl.

The dead man came down close to Itiwana. In all the kivas the corn clan was carrying on its shameful practices. The apparition went from kiva to kiva. People were terrified, and they cried out for they were afraid of the earthquake. Especially those who had been taking their pleasure in the kivas started to run toward Corn Mountain to save themselves. Everybody in the village began to run for refuge there.

All the others had left the village when at last the sister (of the priest's son) and her little children heard of what had happened. They went to their old grandmother, and told her they were going to Corn Mountain to take refuge from the earthquake. The grandmother climbed the ladder and they all set out as fast as they could toward Corn Mountain. The boy carried his little sister on his back. When they came to Matsaka, they felt the earth rumble, and the boy who was now the apparition turned into Kolowisi. They said to their grandmother, "Stay here, grandmother, and we will go on to Corn Mountain; it is too dangerous to wait for you." The grandmother said, "It is well. I have only a little while to live. Let the young ones go on quickly; I must die one of these days." They went on to Corn Mountain without her, and Kolowisi kept back the floods until they had reached the mountain. Then he let loose the waters and they filled all the valley.

One of the priests said to the people, "This flood has come upon us, because of the shameful practices of the corn clan. You were always taking your pleasure in the kivas. For this reason the apparition came to us and to all the kivas, and he has caused this flood. You who are of one clan should be as brothers and sisters, and never desire one another." All the people repeated what he had said, and they stopped these practices. They agreed that no one must have sexual relations within his own clan but always with those of others. That is why we have learned not to have intercourse with those of our own clan even if they do not live with us. And if one of them has a baby or dies in the farthest corner of the pueblo, we go there and help, and if they are providing a feast we grind for them.[1]

---

[1] Children are told that there will be an earthquake if members of one clan mate with one another; also if children begin sexual practices before they are of age.

B (3)

They were living in Itiwana. It was the lonesome days.[1] Two
men were out hunting and they saw that water had run into a
depression near Kwakina and frozen there. The ice was strong and
smooth. They came back to the village and went to Pekwin's
house. He said to them, "What have you come to ask?" "Our
father, we were hunting by Kwakina and we found a frozen pond.
We have come to ask you to make plans that all your people go
there to slide on the ice." "I shall be glad. My people are lonesome
these days. After I have finished my meal I shall go to the bow
priest." He went to the house of the bow priest and said, "I am
coming to ask you to call our people out to slide on the ice. They
shall make lunches on the third day and on the fourth we shall go
to Kwakina." The bow priest said, "All right. I shall call it out."
As soon as Pekwin had gone and the bow priest had finished his
meal he made proclamation. He stood right there at his door[2] and
he said, "My people, we shall slide on the ice at Kwakina. On the
third day the women shall prepare food, and on the fourth no one
shall stay at home. We shall all go to Kwakina to slide on the ice."
The girls were happy as they could be. They ground on the third
day for paper-bread and for corncakes and for tcukinawe. Next
morning they ate early. All those who had children put them on
their cradle boards to take along. The young men dressed in their
best clothes. The rich ones wore their bayeta shirts. The bow priest
walked first and Pekwin next, and in the rear came the old women
hobbling on their canes. They arrived at noon. The mothers nursed
their babies and laid them down comfortably and played with the
young men, pushing each other and sliding on the ice. They had
their midday meal and broiled jerked venison on the open fires.
The girls who had sweethearts slid with them and not with their
mothers. After the meal they skated again. Those who had babies
tended them first and then joined the rest. The bow priest and
Pekwin sat at one side smoking and the people skated for them.[3]
The people played harder and harder; the women pinched the men
and the men ran after the women and some of them got separated
from the others and lay together. Women who had children left
them with their people and went off with the men there were
playing with. Only a few people were left at the pond. Pekwin and

---

[1] See II: 25. After the winter dance series is over there is a period when
   there are no kachina dances.
[2] I. e. he did not go to the roofs.
[3] "It was like dancing for their two fathers."

the bow priest saw what was happening. The bow priest was angry. He called out, "My people, come back to this place. We don't want you to scatter by yourselves. Enjoy yourselves sliding on the pond." They heard him and they came back. They were ashamed.

The bow priest was angry because they had done this thing. The bow priest said, "You have done wrong. You should have stayed here together. Now there will be earthquakes. The people under the earth don't want you to behavè like this. They want you to do right." They heard the earth rumbling. Uhepono[1] was angry. The people cried. They were afraid that the earth would shake that night to tell them that they should not behave in that way. They got home and nobody had the evening meal. They got ready to go to Corn Mountain. The next morning they were ready. They sent a man to the place where the earthquake had been to see what had been destroyed. He came back. "No, it just shook the earth," he told them. They lived on Corn Mountain but there were no more earthquakes. At last they came down.

They had not planted. The poor people were starving that spring and the food was exhausted. They said, "We shall all die together. What shall we do? If we eat our children, some of us will be left alive." They were afraid to do it in the village. One man made a plan with his wife and they went out to camp. They had ten children, one every year. They went to the west side, and came to a place where there were lots of trees and made a shelter. The children were playing around. As soon as the shelter was made, the mother and father dug a hole. They gathered wood and made a fire in the hole. They told the other children to go away to play, and when they had gone they choked the baby and put it on a big stone in the coals. They supported another big stone on top of the child. They raked coals over the oven and roasted the baby. In the evening the children came home. The father had buried the head and they all gathered around and ate the meat. They asked, "Where did you get this?" "There are animals around here." "Where is sister?" "Something came up and caught her. She is lost." The next day they ate the next baby, and the next day they ate the third baby. They ate six of their children. Other families went off to other places and did the same thing.

At last the little children found out what was happening, and a little boy about eight years old ran off with his little brother three or four years younger. When the oven was ready for the younger

---

[1] A woolly-skinned underworld giant. He has eyes like saucers and human arms and legs.

brother, the parents looked everywhere, and couldn't find the two children. They had gone to the place Where the Cotton Hangs. They were starving. Spider Woman heard them crying and spoke to them. "What are you crying about?" The elder brother said, "We have nothing to eat. My mother and father ate my little brothers and sisters and I don't want my little brother eaten so I have brought him over here." Spider Woman said, "Come in. I shall give you something to eat." "How can I get in? It is so small." "Put your foot in and it will get big." They stepped into a big cave. Spider Woman invited them to sit down. She went into the other room of the cave and brought out cornmeal and poured a little water over it and mixed it with her hand. She gave it to them. They squeezed it a little drier and ate it. There was lots of it. The little brother was happy to have plenty to eat. He said, "Thanks, grandmother." The old woman said, "Eat lots." She got a handful of ground corncake meal from the other room and put it in a bag. She said, "Take this with you to your people. Give a little to all the families. Take the rest to your mother. Whenever they eat it it will be increased." They laughed and took it. The boys went around to all the camps and told each one, "We are bringing you sweet corncake meal, and whenever you put it in the bowl it will be increased." They came to their mother. She was glad to see them back. They told her the same thing and gave her the handful of flour. It increased all the time. All these camps had food to eat again. They ate and still there was plenty.

The people returned home to Itiwana. They grieved for their children and they buried all that was left of them on the west side at the Pit of Many Burials. They came to Itiwana. The people who still had corn let them have seeds to plant in the spring. Every day they went out to their fields. When the corn was just coming up the women went out to help hoe (as always). The fields were growing well and there was lots of corn. When the crops were gathered in, they were happy; for two years they had food.

The bow priests did not know that the people were still doing wrong. The men and women who had paired the day they went sliding on the ice still lay together. The third year the earth rumbled again. They did not think of an earthquake because they did not know the people were sinning. The earth shook again. A third time the earth shook. Each time the people who were doing wrong were frightened and did right for a while, but they sinned again. The fourth time the earth opened. Uhepono's great head appeared out of the hole and water poured out in a great flood. They ran toward Corn Mountain. The water almost overtook them.

Those who were slow were drowned and turned into snakes and frogs. The people lived on Corn Mountain. When the earth dried they went down. All those who had done wrong turned into stone. Only those who had not sinned had got to the top of Corn Mountain and been saved. The people gathered these stone frogs and put them on their altars. That is why we know how to do right and we do not do those things which cause earthquakes.

THE ORIGIN OF THE UWANAMI (7)[1]
Notes, 266

Long ago they were living at Pinawa. They gambled all the time. A young man lived with his grandmother. She made yarn for him and he took it to the kiva to stake in gambling. Late at night the young man made a cigarette and smoked. Spider Woman spoke to him: "Do you want to gamble?" "Yes." "Make me a cigarette too." He made a cigarette and lit it and gave it to Spider. She sat in the cuff of his mocassin and every time the young man puffed his cigarette, Spider puffed too. The people watched and they laughed. The side that was losing said to him, "Go and play. Perhaps you can win back the tally sticks." Spider said, "No, we can't play now." After a while the game was nearly over and Spider told the young man, "If someone asks you to play now, go." The bow priest came and told the young man, "Young man, you had better play. Perhaps you can win".

The young man went over. Spider said, "Wait, I will see where the ball is." She went down into the ground and looked; it was in the west cup and she came back and told him. He took up the two cups nearest to him. Then he took up the west cup and there was the ball. He covered with the blanket and hid the ball in his turn. Spider went underground and made a web around the ball. She pulled it under the first cup, and the player paid the boy ninety tally sticks. They played nine times and the young man won every time.

In four days the people wanted to gamble again. Pautiwa came and said: "In four days you shall go to Kachina Village to gamble with the kachinas." The bow priest made proclamation. The people took necklaces and bracelets and shells and feathers and blankets and belts to stake in gambling. They got to Kachina Village and Pautiwa greeted them. The kachinas bet deer and antelope against the things the people had brought. The young man bet his pile of yarn against a little yearling deer. They were ready to play. They spun an abalone shell, and the kachinas said to the

---

[1] Recorded by Ruth Bunzel.

people, "Choose." The young men said, "Green." The people said, "What are you talking about? Black!" It came down green, and therefore the kachinas hid the ball first. The two men who played for the people chose the wrong cup. They lost. When they started back to their places the floor opened and the two men dropped out of sight. The floor closed over them. The people were frightened. No one wanted to play the next game against the kachinas. They played four times. Every time they lost, and the floor opened. Six men were gone. Pekwin and the two bow priests were under the floor.

The people were angry. They said, "Let us send the young man to play. If he is lost it will not matter." They sent someone to ask him. "All right. I'll play." Spider helped him as she had before. He won every time, and every time one of the kachinas dropped under the floor. At last the kachinas stopped playing, and they paid the deer they had staked on the game. The people killed many deer. The kachinas said, "The six men you have lost shall remain here, and you shall pray to them always." They went into an inner room and mist came out of that room and there were the six men sitting, three and three. The people prayed to these six men and gave them prayer meal, and the six men said, "Now we are the Uwanami.[1] Whenever you need anything, come here and plant prayersticks and give us prayer meal, and we shall surely help you." The people went home. They had won lots of venison and they all ate.

That is the reason why the priests go to Kachina Village every four years at the beginning of the summer rain dances. They pray to the Uwanami and plant prayersticks. And that is why when a person dies he goes to Kachina Village. That is all.

THE THEFT OF THE SUN AND MOON (7)

Notes, 267

Long ago when the earth was soft Coyote was living at Omaꞏ-kwena. He was always hunting and he could not get anything. One day he was hunting rabbits and Eagle was killing lots of jack-rabbits. Coyote killed nothing but grasshoppers. Coyote said to Eagle, "My dear friend, we ought to hunt together." "All right." Coyote and Eagle went hunting together. Coyote never killed anything. One day Coyote said, "My friend, it is dark and I can't

---

[1] Rain Makers. There are six Uwanami representing the six directions.

see anything."[1] Eagle said, "That is true. Let's go west, perhaps we shall find light." They went towards the west looking for the sun and moon. They went a long way and they came to a broad river. Eagle flew right across it but Coyote could not fly. He stood on the bank of the wide river. Eagle flew back and Coyote said to him, "How shall I get across the river?" "You must fly across the way I do." Coyote could not swim. He sweated all over; his eyes were bulging and the current carried him way down stream. He got a foothold on a mud bank and waded out. He was shaking as if he had ague. The eagle said, "Why didn't you fly across? You've got hair." "But I can't fly with hair." Eagle said, "I can fly with mine. Let your hair grow like mine and you can fly." Coyote said, "I can't do that."

They still went on to the west and they got to Kachina Village. All the kachinas were dancing. Eagle and Coyote went in and Pautiwa made them sit down. They stayed and watched the dance. All the time they were looking for the sun. The kachinas had a square box and when they wanted light they opened it and it was daylight. When they wanted less light they opened another box and there was the moon. They danced and danced. They made a big fire and all the people danced around it and they had a good time. When the dance was over they went home. Coyote said to Eagle, "Now we can steal that box." Eagle said, "If we do that we shall be doing wrong. We had better just borrow it." They took up the box with the sun and Eagle carried it. They went up out of the lake and went back towards the east. He flew ten miles and Coyote ran along on the ground as fast as he could. Coyote said to Eagle, "Now my chief, let me carry that box." "No, you ought not to carry it. You would not carry it right." "I want to carry it." Eagle flew on. Again Coyote said, "Now my chief, let me carry the box. If anybody meets us and he sees my chief carrying the box and I not carrying anything, it will shame me." Again Eagle said, "No, you will not carry it right." Again Coyote said, "Now my chief, let me carry it. It is not right that you should carry everything." Eagle said, "No, I do not want to let you carry it." The fourth time Coyote said, "My chief, let me carry the box, it makes me ashamed that you carry it all the way, because you are the chief." Eagle said, "All right, if you will carry it right. Do not open it."

Eagle flew on four or five miles and Coyote came behind with the box. Eagle called, "Hurry up." Eagle was a mile and a half ahead and Coyote was on the other side of the hill. He got to a place where there were lots of weeds and flowers and he was hidden in

---

[1] The sun and moon had not as yet been placed in the sky.

2

the midst of them. He wanted to open the box and he sat down and lifted the lid. Eagle said, "You foolish man, I knew you were doing something wrong." Coyote took the moon out and it slipped away from him and went up to the sky. Immediately all the leaves of all the trees dropped off and it was winter. He took out the sun and it slipped away from him and it went up in the sky. All the peaches, pears, plums, watermelons, and muskelons were killed (by the cold). Eagle got there and found what Coyote had done. He scolded him and said, "What have you done? Now every year we shall suffer from cold weather." That is why the sun is so far away in winter that it does not warm us. Coyote sat ashamed. He said, "I guess we are not friends any longer." Pretty soon lots of snow began to fall. Coyote started back east. Eagle said, "Do not go home any more. You are bad. You have done wrong." Eagle flew up into the sky and Coyote could not get home any more. All the leaves had dropped down off the trees and snow was falling. If Coyote had not done this we should have had summer all the time.

CITSUKA (8)

Notes, 268

Citsuka and Kwelele were living with their grandmother at Cipapolima. They were great hunters and went every day to hunt deer. Citsuka never failed to come in with deer every night. He was a famous hunter and in Kachina Village they laid plans to get Citsuka as their son-in-law. They hid all the game to force him to come to Kachina Village.

At Cipapolima Citsuka and Kwelele could find nothing, no deer nor jack-rabbits nor antelopes nor cottontails. They had nothing to eat. They found one kernel of corn in their house, and they lived on that. Citsuka thought, "Next time I am hungry I will eat my ears."[1] He took one off, and gave it to Kwelele and his grandmother, and the other he ate himself. They were hairy. When they had chewed these, Citsuka and Kwelele went out again and searched until evening for deer, but they found nothing.

Down in the west there were little clouds around the sunset and Citsuka saw four lightnings playing in the clouds. He thought to himself, "There must be someone there who is making rain (i. e. dancing)." Next day he told his grandmother, "I think I shall go to the southwest, I saw four lightnings in the clouds. I believe someone is making rain." He said to Kwelele, "Stay with our grandmother. Stay happily." And he started for the west.

[1] The ears of his mask are indicated by two little white hairy tails.

He went on and on. He had nothing to eat. At last he came to Kokokci Mountain. He climbed it and looked down and saw the great lake below it. He was surprised for he had never seen a sheet of water like that, and he stood there a long time. He could see no one, for the kachinas were careful because they had hidden the deer. At last two kachina girls came out of the lake with a buckskin and began to wash it. He wondered if they were really women. He said to himself, "I know now that people live here, and I had better go down and talk to these women."

The kachina girls said to each other, "He will see us washing our buckskin. He will know then that we have hidden the deer." They started to run and hide, but as soon as they had straightened up he was standing beside them. He said, "What are you doing?" They said, "We are washing buckskin." They had food and they asked him if he would eat. Citsuḳa was almost starved and he said, "Yes, thank you." They spread out their sweet-corn paper-bread and they said, "Eat lots."[1] He ate almost all the food they had. When he had finished he said, "Thank you," and he asked, "Where are the rest of the people?" "In the house." "Will you take me in?" "Yes." The girls liked him because he was handsome. They took him into their house and all the kachinas stopped dancing. They asked him to sit down. They were wondering why he had come and one of them said, "What did you want to ask of us?" He answered, "I was living at Cipapolima, and there was no rain and no game. We were starving." Pautiwa answered, "Yes, there are no deer around the country but if you marry my daughter I shall give you deer. You can take them back to Cipapolima."

Therefore Citsuḳa married Pautiwa's daughter and he stayed there that spring with his wife. In the summer he took the deer Pautiwa gave him and went back to Cipapolima. He lived with his grandmother there until the time of the winter solstice ceremony in December. He came from the east to Itiwana and after the days of the fire taboo he came in to bring the new year. That same day Pautiwa came from his house in the west and met his son-in-law in the dance plaza of Itiwana and took him back with him to Kachina Village. Citsuḳa stayed with his wife all winter again and in the spring he went back to his grandmother in Cipapolima. That is why he is doing this still.

---

[1] It was formerly the custom for women to carry lunch to give to a man.

THE CORN MAIDENS
Notes, 269
A (7)[1]

....Then they danced the Corn Dance in Itiwana. They made the shelter of boughs and brought the Corn Maidens in. They were very beautiful. That night the bow priest guarded them in the kiva. He watched them, for they were beautiful. In the night Yellow Corn went out to defecate and the bow priest followed her. As she came back he laid hands on her. Yellow Corn resisted him. She said, "No, we do not know men. Our flesh is food for the people. If we were hot with desire the people's food would be spoiled." She escaped from him and went back into the kiva. She said to her sisters, "My sisters, I must tell you the trouble that has come upon us. We are beautiful, my sisters. When I went outside the bow priest followed me and laid hands on me. He desired me. I repulsed him but he persisted. He lifted my clothes. I told him, 'I am your mother. Shall I lie with my child? Your flesh is formed of my flesh.' What shall we do, my sisters?" Red Corn answered, "My sister, we must go away. If we stay here, someone else will desire us and our flesh will be spoiled. Already they have made us less valuable." Yellow Corn said also, "My sister White Corn, what have you to say?" She said, "There is only one thing for us to do. We must go." "Blue Corn, what have you to say?" "There is no choice. We must go." They talked together about how they should do this. They said, "We will go immediately. It is dark. We shall escape and no one will know."

They went out. The corn out of all the storerooms followed them. It was their flesh and they took it away when they went. Only a little bit was left in each house. They went toward the east, then far to the southeast, and a long journey to the south till they came to the ocean. It was night when they got there. Yellow Corn said to her sisters, "My sisters, how shall we hide ourselves?" They saw Duck. He greeted them. They said to him, "We are the Corn Maidens. We gave our flesh to our people but the bow priest looked upon us with desire. Therefore we left our people and escaped. We have come to the ocean. How shall we hide ourselves?" Duck answered, "I shall hide you, my children." He spread his wings. Yellow Corn, Red Corn, White Corn, took shelter under his right wing, Blue Corn, Speckled Corn and Black Corn took shelter under

---

[1] This version was told as the concluding incident of the version of the emergence story B, I: 6.

his left wing. Duck rose and dived under the waters of the ocean with the Corn Maidens.

That spring people planted their corn fields and all the plants were killed by the frost. The people were poor. Next year they planted their fields again but there was no rain. No corn grew. The third the people were hungry and the fourth year they had nothing. They lived on cactus and venison and wild seeds. For six years no corn grew. The seventh year people were dying. The priests of the council met every night because their people were starving. They said, "Our corn mothers have disappeared all these years. Their trails went to the east and there are no footprints returning." They planned how they could recover them. Every night and every day they prayed their corn mothers to return. The priests said, "We will ask the birds of prey to look for our mothers." The village priest took shell and coral and turquoise and sent for Eagle. Eagle came. He went to the ceremonial room of the village priest. The priests were sitting there all skin and bones. Eagle said, "What is it you have to say to me that you have sent for me?" The village priest said, "Our father, our son, we want to ask you to find our corn mothers. They gave us our flesh and the bow priest laid hands on Yellow Corn when she went to defecate. They left and we have no corn. I have precious beads with which to pay you." Eagle answered, "Very well, I will try." Early next morning Eagle flew up into the sky. He could not find the corn mothers. At sunset he came back to Itiwana. "Did you find them?" "No. There were no traces of them." He sat down in the corner of the ceremonial room of the village priest. (Repeat for cokapiso, and Chicken Hawk). They sent for Crow. He went all the way to the ocean. He went under the waters of the ocean. Underneath there was lots of corn, yellow corn, blue corn, red corn, white corn, speckled corn, black corn. He ate and ate. White Corn said to him, "What do you eat my flesh for?" "I like it." Red Corn said, "Eat all you want." He ate lots. He came home. The village priest said, "Did you find the corn mothers?" "No." The people did not know what to do. They sent for Hummingbird. That night Crow was sick. He vomited. Everybody saw the corn kernels he had eaten. They said, "Where did you find those?" "I didn't know it was corn. Perhaps I found it to the east, perhaps to the south or the west or the north. I don't know." Next morning Hummingbird came. The priest told him, "Crow found our corn mothers but he did not know it was corn." Hummingbird answered, "All right, I will try." Next morning he went up and down, up and down by the ocean, four times he went the length of the

ocean. He saw nothing. He came back. "Did you find them?"
"No, I saw nothing." The priests did not know what to do. They
sent the birds home.

They said, "We will ask Ne'we·kwe Youth (Ne'paiyatamu)."
They sent the bow priest to Ashes Spring to ask him to help them.
He greeted him and he said, "Sit down. What is it you have come
to ask?" "Our Corn Mothers have disappeared. We are starving.
I have come to ask you to search the world for them. We need you."
Ne'we·kwe Youth answered, "Very well, I will try." He came back
with the bow priest to Itiwana. He went into the ceremonial room
of the village priest. He saw them sitting there all skin and bones.
He greeted them. They said, "Sit down." He said, "What is it that
you have to ask me that you have sent for me?" "Nine years ago
our mothers, the Corn Maidens, disappeared. The bow priest
desired them and they left us. We are starving. We have sent Eagle,
cokapiso, Chickenhawk, Crow and Hummingbird, but they could
not find them. We want you to try. Look all over the world for us."

Ne'we·kwe Youth went up to the Milky Way. Before sunrise he
saw Duck dive under the waters of the ocean with the Corn Maidens
under his wings. He returned to the ceremonial room of the village
priest. He said, "I have seen them, I know where they are. But I
cannot bring them back alone. I need your help. Go into retreat.
Do not stir, do not urinate, do not drink water, do not eat, do not
smoke, do not sleep, do not speak to each other. Sit with your arms
crossed on your breasts. We shall try to recover them. Make six
prayersticks that I may plant for our Corn Maidens." Next morning
Ne'we·kwe Youth took the yellow prayerstick the priests of the
council had made and went a little to the southeast and planted it.
He came back and sat down in the ceremonial room with the priests.
They were still in contemplation. They did not move, they did not
speak. He stayed with them a little while. He took the blue prayerstick and went out four or five miles to the southeast and planted it.
(Repeat for the red prayerstick which he plants fifteen miles to the
southeast after remaining three hours in the ceremonial room; for
the white prayerstick which he plants still further to the southeast
after a still longer stay, for the black prayerstick which he plants
still further in the same direction; and the spotted prayerstick
which he plants on the shores of the ocean.) Ne'we·kwe Youth came
back to the ceremonial room of the village priest. Still the priests
had not moved, they had not smoked, they had drunk no water,
they had not spoken. He said in his heart, "Poor people,[1] this is

---

[1] Because they were so uncomfortable.

the last time I shall stay with you. Next time I shall surely find the Corn Maidens."

He came up out of the ceremonial room and went to the edge of the ocean. Red Corn and Speckled Corn were standing by the edge of the water. They saw Ne'we·kwe Youth planting his black prayer-stick in the water. They disappeared under the ocean. Ne'we·kwe Youth watched them go. They came where their sisters were and said, "A man has come. He will find us here soon." Yellow Corn answered, "We cannot help it. He is Ne'we·kwe Youth. He has been in retreat with the priests. They have not stirred, they have not smoked, they have not drunk water, they have not spoken, they have made themselves poor." Ne'we·kwe Youth went down under the waters of the ocean. He came where Yellow Corn was. "How have you lived all these days, my mothers, my children?" "Happily, thank you. Sit down." He asked Yellow Corn, "Where are your sisters?" "In the other room." "I want to see them." Yellow Corn brought them. Ne'we·kwe Youth greeted them. Yellow Corn said to him, "What is it you wish to say that you have come this long distance and found us here?" "I want you to come back to Itiwana." "No, we cannot come." "Yes, you must come." Four times Yellow Corn refused and the fourth time she said, "Yes, we will go with you. When we come to Itiwana, if nobody is worried, if everybody is happy all the time, if they always pray as they should, if they always think good thoughts, we shall stay and give our flesh again to the people." "Thank you, it is well." He went out. A little way from the edge of the ocean he found a rabbit. He took it back to Yellow Corn. He said, "This is an animal that is happy all the time. It is good to make the people glad." She said, "Yes, kill it." He hit it a blow behind the ears. He took a sharp stone and slit the skin and drew it off. He took a bone from its foreleg and a bone from its ear and made an incision in them. He bound it with sinew that he took from the rabbit's back. He made the whistle[1] and put it in his mouth. He said, "Now, I shall play for you and you will follow me." He went out and they followed him. They came to the pueblos of the east, San Juan, San Felipe, Laguna. They came on toward Itiwana. They came past Corn Mountain, Matsaka, Red Bank. He came in blowing his whistle. In their ceremonial room the village priest heard. He made four crosses with cornmeal on the roof in the four directions. He came down and made a road for Ne'we·kwe Youth to bring in Yellow Corn. Yellow Corn sprinkled pollen as she followed Ne'we·kwe Youth into Itiwana. The village

---

[1] The whistle, bitsitsi, is blown when he brings in the Corn Maidens. Ne'-we·kwe Youth is commonly known by this term.

priest led her to the cross of meal that he had made to the north. He made her stand upon it. He touched her with his eagle feathers and turned her to to the four directions. (Repeat for the meal cross to the west, south, east. Repeat for all the corn sisters, each one in turn having a more elaborate ceremony. Yellow Corn's presentation should take "only about half an hour and Sweet Corn's about four hours.") All the corn sisters sat down in a row. Ne'we·kwe Youth prayed and made the sign of blessing with his arms and everybody inhaled from their hands. He said, "The Corn Maidens left us because one man desired them and wished to lay hands on them. We are their flesh and they give us themselves to eat. If they give it to us again and we plant in the spring for the rain to water we shall be fed again with their flesh. They will be our mothers and we shall be their children. If at any time we think evil thoughts or are unhappy they will go away from us again and we shall have nothing. When we dance the Corn Dance we shall carry their flesh in our hands. We shall not see them but they will be there in spirit. They will be among us and when we speak to them they will hear us." The people answered, "It shall be as you have said." Yellow Corn said to the priests, "At the end of the year[1] send for us and we will come to Itiwana. Ne'we·kwe Youth will always lead us. Pekwin will go first (make the road) and Pautiwa will follow Ne'we·kwe, and after him Father Koyemci. My flesh is your flesh. When you put my flesh in the ground it sprouts and does not die. It is like your bodies. When they are buried in the ground they do not die. Our flesh is like your flesh." It is so. The people went home. That night, late, when everyone was asleep, Yellow Corn said to her sisters, "Let us go to give our people corn." They came up out of the kiva and went to each house. Yellow Corn took one grain of yellow corn. She bit it and dropped it in the first house. She went on to the next. Blue Corn took a kernel of blue corn. She bit it and dropped it into the first house and went on to the next. (Repeat for Red Corn, White Corn, Speckled Corn, Black Corn and Sweet Corn.) They went to each house and left the village. Next morning each corn room was bursting with the flesh of the corn mothers. Everyone had plenty to eat but after this corn ears never filled out to the tip. Because the bow priest tried to lay hands on Yellow Corn, Zuni corn is never perfectly kernelled.

B (8)

The people were living in Itiwana. They did wrong. They played the stuffed bag game and they filled the bags with the meal of

---

[1] On the last day of Ca'lako the ceremony of molawia reenacts the recovery of the Corn Sisters by Ne'we·kwe Youth known in the cermony as Bitsitsi.

paper-bread and tcukinawe and sweet corncake and popcorn meal. The women ground armsful of corn and baked all their best food and ground it. All that year they wasted their corn. At harvest the men brought in their first new corn and the mothers of the houses brought out the last year's mother corns out of the storerooms to meet the fresh corn. They laid the old corn mothers in the basket in the center of the floor and upon them they put the first ears of the new year. The old corn waited for the new corn. When all the corn was harvested, the women took the ears into the storerooms and prayed, "We are glad that you have come to our house. Increase always. Do not fail us." The fresh corn said to the old corn, "How have you lived these days ? Give us now the room you have occupied." The old corn answered, "Yes, you are treated well at first because you are new."

Every village harvested. They brought in the long, perfectly kernelled ears and they laid them in dirty places and fed them to the burros. They did not honor them. They did not pile up neatly the ordinary ears. Elder Sister Corn said to her younger sisters, "My sisters, I think we must go away and hide from these people. They step on us and crush us. Every day we give our flesh to them in vain. Let us go far away so that they will learn how much they need us." Youngest Corn Sister answered, "Yes, I shall go to every house and tell the corn. We shall go quietly all together so that no one will hear us." She went and waked the corn. She went to every storeroom. She said, "Our flesh is not counted valuable and we shall go away. We shall come back again sometime when they have learned to be careful of our flesh. Let nobody know we are going. Be ready in four days. We shall leave our bodies here but they shall be used up quickly for there will be no life in them."

On the fourth night they said, "Now, my sisters, we shall go to the ocean. White Corn Sister will go first because she always 'makes the road'. After her Yellow Corn, Blue Corn, Red Corn, Speckled Corn. Black Corn shall come behind so that nobody can find where we have gone." The corn came together from every storeroom and went to the east. Then they went south until they came to the ocean. On the water they saw Mother Duck swimming. The corn came to a marshy place and said, "I think this is far enough. They cannot find us here." Mother Duck said, "Strangers have come. I will go and talk to them." They saw the Duck coming toward them. They waited till she came closer. When she was near they said, "How have you lived these days, my mother, my child ?" They were persons but when the Duck turned her head they all turned to ears of corn except the youngest sister. She said to

Mother Duck, "We have come from Itiwana. We gave them our flesh but they did not hold it valuable. Can you help us to hide ourselves from them ?" Mother Duck thought to herself. She said, "I will go and ask the others. Wait for me." She went to Father Duck. "People have come from Itiwana. The people treated them carelessly and they have come here to hide that the people may learn how valuable they are. They asked us to help them find a hiding place." Father Duck said, "There is only one way to hide them. Are you strong enough to cover them for four years ?" Mother Duck answered, "You are right. I thought I should ask you to hide them but you have shamed me. I found them and I am the one to hide them." She said to Father Duck, "How shall I conceal them ?" "Let them lie down on a little island in the marsh and, no matter how stiff you get, you shall cover them with your wings for four years. If nobody is looking for them, I shall take your place once in a while, while you clean yourself and drink." "Yes, it shall be as you say. We must tell them to go over to the island." They returned to the Corn Maidens. They were all corn ears. Father Duck took Yellow Corn and Mother Corn took White Corn and they laid them with their heads to the east. Father Duck gathered cattails and reeds to make a nest for them. Mother Duck went to the water and filled herself with insects. She drank and drank. She ate enough for a year's supply. She came back. Father Duck was making the nest and they finished it together. When it was done, Mother Duck settled on the nest facing west. She brooded them.[1]

In Itiwana they did not know that the corn was gone. It was light and tasteless but they did not know it was dead. In the mornings they did not go into the storerooms and greet the corn, "How have you lived till morning, my mothers, my children ?" When they needed an ear of corn they grabbed whatever they wanted with the right hand.[2] That winter when they danced the winter dance series they made sweet corncakes and flavored them with squash blossoms. They baked lots and took them to those who were dancing. Kanatcu threw away lots of food.[3] The women said, "Our corn is going fast. Mine is only so high in the storeroom" (a couple of feet from the floor). The others said, "Mine is so high," "So high." They kept on having throw-away dances. Finally it was time for planting. The men dug the field and put in the corn. The

---

[1] Itsumawe, to reproduce magically.

[2] It is proper to take the corn with left hand because it is not used so much and therefore by sympathetic magic the corn is not so quickly used up.

[3] In the popular throw-away dances.

women said, "How much have you planted?" "Not much." "I
think you planted too much. Our corn is nearly used up." All over
the village the people talked among themselves. In most of the
houses the storerooms were empty. Some had a little left because
they had been more careful. In the houses where the corn was gone
the women went to other houses to embroider white blankets. They
got eight or ten ears of corn in payment, and their families lived on
it for four days. Then the women went back to work again.

They harvested hardly any corn. Families had just one donkey
load for the whole summer's crop. The people said, "My corn is
owinahaiya."[1] Winter came. People gave away a whole cornfield or
a peach orchard for one griddle cake. They were starving. Some
people went to the east and some to the west. The people of Acoma
and the people of Hopi received them and they worked for them and
were fed. Only the priests and kachina priests and the valuable
families stayed in Itiwana. They had nothing to eat. They went
about to the empty houses and looked for kernels of corn in the
cracks and in the spider webs and in the dirt piles. They found bits
of old leather and boiled them. They roasted cactus stalks. They
said among themselves, "There is nothing to do. We must go to the
east or the west as the others have done. Our fathers who have the
care of our roads (of life) have failed us. We shall die."

The village priest considered the hunger of his people. He called
the bow priest. The bow priest came and greeted him. He made him
sit down and the bow priest said, "What is it that you have to ask,
my father?" "Our people are starving. They have gone to the east
and the west. It must be that our mothers (corn) are offended for
our fields do not grow any more. There is only one thing to do. My
people must return again to their rooted place. We must find where
our mothers went for it must be they have taken their lives (hearts)
from us." "Yes, we shall send our best runner and call the people to
return." The bow priest chose a young, good runner and went to
his house. He greeted him. The young man said, "What is that you
have come to ask, my father, that you have come to my house?"
"Yes, I have come to ask you to help us. Our fathers (priests) wish
to find our mothers (corn) again that we may have crops. The
village priest wishes to see you." "All right, I shall go and find out
what he wants me to do." He went to the ceremonial room of the
village priest. The priest greeted him and made him sit down.
"What is it that you have to say that you needed me, my father?"
"Yes, my son, our people have suffered since our mothers left our

---

[1] I. e., a fraction of the whole. Owinahaiya is the great scalp dance series,
so long that only a portion is sung at a time.

houses empty. Some of our people have gone to the east to find food. I want them to return to Itiwana." "All right, my father, I will do as you say. I will go to Acoma. I have one thing to ask. Will you make the downy feather for me so that I shall run easily?" "Yes indeed, I will have it ready for you when you start early in the morning. Go back to your house and tell your father I am sending you." The village priest took a straw and tied to it a downy feather. In the feather he tied a little snail shell.[1] He went into an inner room and found a tiny water gourd. He made a sling for it of yucca fiber and laid it with the feather in the basket. He prayed, "Now I have made you into persons that you will give swiftness to my son whom I have asked to go on this errand. Help him to go quickly so that our mothers will return to us." He presented the basket to the six directions and set it down.

At the boy's house his mother washed his hair, and dressed it. His father said to his mother, "You have a few dried peaches left. Let us eat them together now. Our son is going far away. It is dangerous to go to unknown places and our son might never return." His mother cooked the peaches and they ate. At sunset they said to their son, "Now, my son, sleep so that you will wake before sunrise. Everything is ready." They all went to bed at sunset. Next morning before sunrise they awoke. His mother said, "When will you be back?" "Perhaps in four days." They went to the river to wash their faces. The boy said, "I am going. I am ready now." His mother gave him sweet corncakes flavored with pumpkin flowers and he tied them in his blanket around his belt. His father took his hand and prayed, "May you have a clean heart. May you have a strong heart." He said good-bye to his sisters and brothers and went to the ceremonial room of the priest. The priest was already up and praying for the boy. He greeted him. He tied the gourd around his waist and said, "If anyone asks you what the gourd is for, say 'I carry it to drink at the spring,'[2] but do not drink at all the first day." He gave him the downy feather. He took it in his left hand. The priest said, "In the east tell one of the priests that all the people are to return here together." "All right, my father, I am going. Stay happily and pray for me as I go." "I will. Go happily." The boy went out. He did not have to run. The feather and the gourd carried him lightly without effort.

He came to Blue Paint Mine at sunset. He was not tired. "I will

---

[1] Snail shells are maze symbols, and magically insure that a runner can find his way in any maze. The exaggerated concern for this journey is ceremonial. In practice the trip to Acoma is made with little thought.

[2] The gourd, like the feathers, magically insure lightness of foot.

go right on." Before sunrise he saw the smoke of Acoma.[1] "I wonder if this is where I am going." He came to the river. The women were coming with their jars for water. He was shy. He saw his own people among them and they recognized him. They said, "You have come, haven't you? Are there crops in Itiwana?" "Wait, I shall tell you afterwards. I want to see the Itiwana priest." He laid his gourd under a tree and stuck his downy feather under his belt. The Itiwana priest was eating his morning meal. The men who came with the runner greeted him. They said, "A runner has come from Itiwana to see you." The priest made him sit down. All the people of Acoma thought he was an important priest because his clothes were beautiful.[2] The priest's wife brought food and said, "Eat." He took a little. His lunch was in his blanket. He laid it in the basket for the people. The men of Itiwana reached for it and ate it greedily. They were glad to have home cooking. The runner ate the food the priest's family had set before him. "Thank you." "Eat lots." The priest said to him, "What is it that you have come to say, that you have come this long distance?" "The village priest sent me to tell you to call his people back to their rooted place. Let them all make the journey together at one time so that no one will be left behind." "All right. We have no Itiwana bow priest here. I shall ask an Acoma bow priest to make proclamation." He sent a messenger for an Acoma bow priest. The bow priest came in. He took off his right moccasin, and he said, "What is it that you have to say?" "I will tell you. My son has come from our father, the village priest of Itiwana, to tell our people to return. He wants nobody to stay behind. For three days we shall make preparations to return. Will you make proclamation now while my son is here, so that he will tell our father priest and he will know that we are coming?" "All right. I will go immediately." He went out into the street. "For a long time the people of Itiwana have been here in our village. Now the village priest of Itiwana has sent a messenger for you to return. Make no excuses but prepare for the trip. My people, let them be well provided with food for the journey. We shall all see each other again some day." The Acoma people were sorry that their helpers were going to leave and the Itiwana people wept that they were going back to their home where there was no corn.

The Itiwana priest said to the runner, "Return and tell our father that we shall come. We shall start in four days." "All right, I shall go." The people of that house gave him paper-bread and he

---

[1] The interpreter said, "How pretty the places were!"

[2] People of other pueblos are described as marvelling at the fine costumes, fine cooking, and remarkable abilities of their Zuni visitors.

wrapped it in his blanket. After the morning meal he started again for his home. The Acoma people said, "There he goes, the messenger from Itiwana." They followed him with their eyes as long as they could see him. He took his gourd from under the tree where he had laid it and tied it in his belt again. He took the downy feather from his belt and carried it in his left hand. He did not have to run, he was carried along lightly. A little after noon he came to Blue Paint Mine. He came to the Uprooted Trees. Before daylight he came to Summit (the top of the Zuni Mountains).

Just as the people were rising in the morning he came into Itiwana. He went to the house of the village priest. Already he was awake and praying for him. The runner greeted him, "How have you lived till this day, my father?" "Happily, since you have reached here." The priest rose and breathed from the boy's hands. His wife also breathed from his hands. They made him sit down and the priest said to his wife, "Now let your son eat first before he speaks." His wife set out paper-bread and corn mush flavored with datila (tsupiawe). He ate. "Thank you." "Eat lots." They moved back. The village priest said, "My son, let me hear of your journey." "Yes. I got there in one day and one night. Everybody was glad to see me. Our people are happy there but they were glad to come when they heard that you needed them. I went to the Itiwana priest and gave your message. He called the Acoma bow priest and he made proclamation to the people that they should start in four days. They will make the trip in two days." "Thank you, my son. Nobody makes the journey as quickly as you do. As soon as you have rested, I shall call you to go west to summon our people who have taken refuge there." "Yes, indeed. I shall go home and tell my father and mother that I have returned." He went out. Everybody on the street ran to him and breathed from his hands. At his house his father and mother greeted them and they also breathed from his hands. They ate their morning meal together.

For three days the kind people in Acoma gave the Itiwana women corn to grind for the journey. They made tcukinawe and on the third day they sewed buckskin into bags to hold the flour. Everything was ready. The men who had burros put them in the corrals. On the morning of that day the Acoma bow priest made proclamation. "Our people, this is the last night that we shall all be here together. You ancients (aliconawe, those who lived in that place, i. e. Acoma people), go to your houses and give hospitably to the people of Itiwana when they come to say goodbye." The Itiwana people had their evening meal and went to the houses of their Acoma friends. In every house they gave them paper-bread or a bowl of flour. They visited all night.

Early before daybreak the priests started ahead with the women and children without eating.[1] They travelled while it was still cool. The men stayed behind and packed. They filled their canteens. Some had burros and some carried their possessions with pack-straps. By noon the women had reached Blue Paint Mine. The priest said to them, "Rest a while till the men overtake us, and then we shall eat." They sat and rested. The mothers nursed their babies and what was left in their breasts they let the older children have. They saw the dust of the men's party in the distance. When they came up they soaked paper-bread in water from their canteens and ate together. The priest started ahead with the women and children and the men followed behind. They were singing the Salimobiya songs and therefore they were happy. By evening they came to the Uprooted Trees. The priest said, "We will sleep here." They built fires under the trees and ate. The priest said, "Let us dance as our ancients (aḷiconawe, i. e. Acoma people) do." They built a large fire and danced heme·cikwe. They had a good time. Before it was late the priest said, "Let us remember we are travelling (i. e., remember to sleep early)." He appointed a good speaker to wake the people in the morning. They slept. In the morning they all got up and the priest went ahead with the women without eating. Before noon they came to Summit. The priest said to the women, "Let us rest here till the men overtake us." They ate and went on again. At sunset they came to Nutria. "We are almost home. We will eat supper here tonight and travel on in the moonlight." After they had eaten they travelled as far as Black Rock. They slept there and early in the morning they came to Wild Animal Place. They were singing heme·cikwe songs. They stopped east of the village and changed their clothes. By the time they got to Rock Horn all the people of Itiwana were watching for them on their roofs.

The priest who had brought them from Acoma went directly to the ceremonial room of the village priest. "How have you lived all these days, my fathers, my mothers, my children?" "Happily, thank you. Sit down." "You have sent for us, my fathers, and we are here. I have brought my people this journey to their homes. None are missing. None of your flesh is dropped (no one has died). We are your rear people and we hope that you are glad to see us." He breathed from his hands and the village priest said, "Yes, my people, your hearts were satisfied with the good food of Acoma and it made me sad. We are one people and our mothers with the quiet hearts (corn) have left us all. I have called you that we may seek for our mothers and discover why we have no crops." Again he

---

[1] On all such journeys, people eat the morning meal as they go.

breathed from his hands. They all prayed for blessing from their ancients, the Ahaiyute, and whoever had been wise enough to hold their roads (give them life). The village priest said, "I am glad you have had a good journey." "Yes, my father, we sang as we travelled so our women are not tired. Now I shall go to my home. Stay happily." He went. All the people who had come from Acoma went to their own houses. That evening the village priest called the bow priest to his ceremonial room. He greeted him. "Now I have called you to make proclamation that whatever food our people have brought with them shall be used sparingly." "I shall make proclamation." He went to the housetops and called, "My people, whatever food you have brought with you, use carefully that we may come to the end of our roads." Everybody went outside their doors and listened to his message and they obeyed it. They put water in all their food and made it go far.

The runner rested at his house. He went to the ceremonial room of the village priest. He greeted him. "My father, I have come to tell you I am rested. What shall I do now ?" "Some of our people have gone to the east and I want to send you to them also with the message. I will prepare you for your journey and make the downy feather. Our bow priest is in Hopi. Take him the message and have him lead the people back." "My father, if you have the downy feather ready now, may I take it to my house so that I may start very early in the morning without coming to get it ?" "Yes, I shall bring you the feathers as soon as I have made them into persons." "Thank you, my father, I will go home. Stay happily." The village priest made the downy feather. He prayed incessantly. When he had finished it, he laid it in the basket. He made himself ready and took the downy feather that evening to the house of the runner. The boy heard him coming. He said, "That is my father." They set a seat for him. He came down the ladder. "My fathers, my mothers, my children, how have you lived these days ?" "Happily, thank you." They set out a basket. He laid the downy feather in it. He said, "You must put this feather in an empty room." The boy's mother took it into a room that had nothing in it. "That is all I came for. Stay happily." He went back to his own home.

Early in the morning the boy started for Hopi. He travelled fast. He came to A'mosa. He came to the Sunflower Stalks. He came to Red Spring. He got almost to the Hopi mesa and lay down to rest. Before sunrise the men from Hopi came out to race before dawn. He passed them and overtook the women carrying water up the mesa trail. He came into the village. He went to the Itiwana bow priest. In that house they were eating the morning meal. They

heard him coming and the bow priest said, "That is my son." He
went to meet him and they set out a seat for him and brought food.
He ate a little. "Thank you." They moved back. The bow priest
said, "What is it that you have come to say that you have come this
long distance ?" "In Itiwana our people are starving. Our father the
village priest wants you to return to our rooted place that you may
help him to discover our mothers and who has hidden them from us."
"Yes, we shall be glad to help him. We are treated well here but we
are glad to go if he needs us. I shall make proclamation immediately
so that you can tell our father that we are coming." The bow priest
put on his blanket and went out. "My Itiwana people, our father
the village priest has sent to ask us to return. Let everyone go.
If anyone wishes to return here after we have done our part he can
come back again. In four days we shall all go together." The Hopi
people wondered what he had said. "What is wrong in Itiwana ?"
they said to each other and they went to their Itiwana relatives
to ask. The bow priest told the runner, "Tell our father we will
start on the fourth day." "That is all. I will go now. Stay happily."
"Return happily." The Hopi people watched him till he was out of
sight. He ran easily because the downy feather made him light-
footed. He passed Red Spring. Almost immediately he was at the
Sunflower Stalks. That evening he came to the spring at A'mosa.
By midnight he was in Itiwana.

In Hopi all the Hopi women and girls ground toasted sweet corn
to make paper-bread for the Itiwana people. The Hopi village
priest sent for the Hopi bow priest. He said to him, "I have called
you to make proclamation to our people. The Itiwana people are
returning in four nights. I want everybody to be happy. On the
fourth night we shall have waha."[1] "I shall be glad. This will please
them all." The bow priest went to the top of the houses. "Our
brothers will be here only four nights longer and our father wants
us all to be happy with them. On the fourth night we shall have
waha." All the Hopi girls ground meal for the Itiwana people.
At night those families where there were girls cleaned out one of
their rooms. Related girls came there for that night and they
leaned out of the low open windows and played with the boys.
The boys tried to pull them out of the windows and the girls tried to
snatch the boy's blankets. If a girl got a blanket the boy had to go
home and get food to redeem it. The Hopi boys and girls taught the
Itiwana young people for three nights how to play. The third day
everybody made paper-bread and ground sweet corn. They made

[1] The festivities of the fourth night are called waha, onomatopoetic for
laughter. It is a night when Zuni and Hopi sweethearts sleep together.

3

the food ready for the journey. That evening they had waha. Boys and girls of Hopi and Itiwana slept with their sweethearts. They left the seed of Itiwana in Hopi and took the seed of Hopi to Itiwana. Before it was time for people to go to sleep the boys and girls went to their own houses. Everybody was happy.

Next morning the bow priest rose before daylight and called the people. "We want to reach home. Let the women and children start without eating and the men shall pack and come later." The people rose and the bow priest started with the women and children. They travelled singing the owinahaiya songs.[1] At Red Spring the women rested till the men came up. They ate and started again on their journey. The men carried the babies to let the women rest. By evening they came to the Sunflower Stalks and they slept there. Next day they rested at the spring at A'mosa and at evening they came to Itiwana.[2]

Early in the morning the priests of the council met in the ceremonial room of the village priest. The bow priest who had brought the people from Hopi went in and greeted them. "How have you lived all these days, my fathers, my mothers, my children?" They made him sit down. The village priest said to him, "I have sent for you because we are starving in Itiwana. Perhaps our mothers (corn) have left us. Perhaps someone has hidden them. We must be all together so that we can discover where they are. Shall we ask tenatsali or jimson-weed to find them for us?" The priests of the council thought and they said, "It is best to call our fathers the tenatsali. Let us make prayersticks for they do not come unless we work for them (make the prayersticks)." The priests made prayersticks for the tenatsali. They cut the wood in short thumb lengths and painted them. Their wives washed their (husbands') hair and their bodies and they went again to the ceremonial room of the village priest. Each of them took a tenatsali prayerstick and they went out to all the directions and planted them. They met again in the evening after they had eaten. They said, "The room has to be empty." They took everything out and put it in the other room and set a basket of feathers in the middle of the floor.[3] The priests sat around the room. The village priest said, "No matter how sleepy we are we must not let our minds wander. We must do our part that our fathers, our sons (tenatsali) may help us." They made a

---

[1] "Hopi harvest songs; only one is sung in Zuni in the scalp dance."

[2] "It is downhill from Hopi so it takes less time to make the journey than from Acoma."

[3] If anyone interrupts the ceremony the tenatsali youths are supposed to become the feathers in the basket and remain invisible.

small fire (for light) and they prayed. The Tenatsali Youths came into the back of the room. They were like shadows. They said, "How have you lived all these days, our fathers, our children ? We have received the feathers that you sent us and we have come to find what you need of us." "My fathers, my children, for many years my people have been starving. Some of them went to the east and some to the west to find food. My heart beat slowly (I was unhappy) and at last I sent for all of my people to come together in Itiwana. Now we have called you to help us. Perhaps our mothers have left us. Perhaps somebody has hidden them that all these years we have had no flesh." "We will try to find them for you, our fathers, our children. Put anxiety out of your hearts so that we may be able to do our best. No matter how tired and sleepy you are, stay awake till we have returned." All the priests got up and came into the middle of the room and sat upright in a circle.[1] The Tenatsali Youths went out. Elder Brother went to the north corner of the world and returned. Younger Brother went to the south corner and returned. They met and said to each other, "Did you dream (lit., see anything in the night) ?" "No, I heard no sound. There was no breathing, no talking." Elder Brother went to the east corner of the world and returned, Younger Brother went to the west corner and returned. They met and said again, "Did you dream ?" But they had heard nothing. It was still before daylight. They went into the ceremonial room of the village priest. The priests had not shut their eyes all night. The village priest had a cigarette ready. He took an ember from the fire and lit it. He smoked to the north and asked Elder Brother what he had found and he answered, "I have sought to the north corner of the world and heard nothing. There is no breathing, no talking. Everything is quiet." (Repeat for south, east, west; Younger Brother answers for south and west.) The Tenatsali said, "We will try for four nights. Think of nothing else. If we do not succeed we shall have to call someone who is wiser than we are."

Repeat for four nights and add: On the second night the wife of the village priest cleaned out the room and removed all the furniture. On the second night the Tenatsali went to the waters of the world in the four directions. On the third night they searched the sky. In preparation for the third night they asked the priests to make them downy feathers so that they would be able to ascend. "Pekwin and the village priest made a downy feather for each of the Tenatsali. They tied them with cotton string, and the village priest

---

[1] So that they would not be tempted to lean against anything.

3*

gave them to the Tenatsali youths." They ascended to the sky on the downy feathers and reversed the feathers in order to descend.

On the fourth night they searched the underground world. They asked for a right-armed[1] prayerstick, a short thumb-length stick, and tied owl tail[2] feathers to it. When they had finished, Pekwin said to the village priest, "We should not send our fathers away without gifts. Shall we not make them prayersticks to give them on this last night ?" The village priest answered, "Thank you for suggesting this. I will call the bow priest." The bow priest came. He went to the others and told them to make prayersticks to please the Tenatsali, who had helped them to try to find the Corn Mothers.

The Tenatsali returned to the ceremonial room of the village priest. "Our fathers, our children, we have been everywhere. We could hear nothing. We are sad but we have done our part. We wish to help but we have failed." The priests bundled together the prayersticks they had made for the Tenatsali and the village priest said, "Our fathers, our children, we are happy that you have tried to help us. Whenever we need you, we hope you will come to us." He gave them the bundle of prayersticks. "We shall always help you and some day we shall succeed. Call our brother Jimson Weed. He may be able to find our mothers."

The priests went to their own homes and slept for two nights. They told their people that they had tried to find their corn mothers but they had failed. When they were rested, the bow priest called the council again to their ceremonial room. The village priest said, "Now we shall call our father Jimson Weed." They worked together on the prayersticks. They cut two sticks of thumb length and tied maiya feathers and bluebird feathers to them and painted the sticks blue.[3] They laid the sticks in the basket. That evening they all came to the ceremonial room and sat in a circle in the middle of the floor. Jimson Weed came and sat in the corner of the room in the shadow. He said, "Now, my fathers, my children, you have called me. What have you to ask of me ?" "Yes, we needed you. Our mothers have left us. Perhaps somebody has hidden them. We want you to look for them." "Yes, I shall help you. I never search more than one night." "Yes, whatever your rules are, we shall follow them." "Sit straight. Do not sleep. Do not let your minds wander. Do not speak." He took the prayersticks that they had made and returned to his home.[4] He planted his prayersticks. He

---

[1] "Because you can dig up anything with your right arm."

[2] "Owls can see in the dark so the feather gives light in the underworld."

[3] The variety of jimson weed which the Zuni use has a blue flower.

[4] His home is south of Tenatsali Place.

went south looking everywhere for the Corn Mothers. He went to the east. He passed close to the lake where Duck was covering the corn ears but he could not find them because they were made invisible by the black corn that was laid in the nest last. He went north but he could not find them. He went west and returned to the ceremonial room of the village priest. The priest took a cigarette and lit it with an ember and smoked him from the six directions. He said, "What is it that you have found?" "Yes, my fathers, my sons, I have been to every part of the world but I could find nothing. Perhaps no one is wise enough to find them. But if you are strong enough, let me have a little boy with a perfect body,[1] one of your own children." The priests sat with bowed heads. The bow priest said, "We do not want to starve. If I had a son like this, I would give him. Let us do this quickly, that we may receive what we have asked for." The village priest said, "I am the one to bring my son." He rose and went into the other room. His wife was asleep. He woke her. "Is our son asleep?" "Yes." "Our fathers need him in our ceremonial room to tend the fire." His mother washed him. Poor child, his father said to him, "My son, do not be frightened. When you eat what we will give you, you will have supernatural power. When you sleep you will dream and when you wake tell us all that you have seen." "Yes, my father." His father said to him, "When you go into the room say, 'How have you lived these days, my fathers, my mothers, my children?' " They went into the ceremonial room. The little boy greeted them and they let him sit next to his father. Jimson Weed said, "Now let us be alone while I let him eat." The priests went into another room and Jimson Weed said to them, "I will tell you when we are ready." He said to the boy, "Sit down facing the east." Jimson Weed went close to him, to one side, and turned into the jimson plant. He gave him his right leaf and his left leaf, his top leaf and his bottom leaf. The boy sat straight and ate them. When he had finished, Jimson Weed became a person again. The boy stiffened and moaned. In half an hour he was quiet and Jimson Weed called the priests to return. The boy was journeying and he talked in his sleep. Jimson Weed took him everywhere. When he was about to wake he was restless again. Jimson Weed said to the priests, "Go into the other room again. He will not be comfortable if you stay here." Jimson Weed went to the boy and touched the boy's chest to take his (jimson weed's) flesh from him. The boy awoke. He was weak. The priests came back and sat down. The village priest took a cigarette and smoked his son from the six directions and said to him, "What is that

---

[1] One with no sores or scabs, bites or wounds.

you have seen?" "Yes, I have been to the plains, the lakes, the tall trees and the high mountains. Jimson Weed went with me. Sometimes we travelled high up and sometimes low down. I looked into the eagles' nests on the cliffs but there was nothing there but their eggs. I looked into the hawks' nests in the high trees but there was nothing there but their young. I looked into the springs to the north but there was nothing there but water weeds. (Repeat for east, south, west.) This is all that I have to say." The priests were troubled. Jimson Weed said, "My fathers, I have done what I could. This is the first time I have failed. Call the Ahaiyute; they are very wise. They will find our mothers for you." "All right. We will do this." "Go to your houses and sleep well before you try again. You will need strength. Put aside all anxiety so that our fathers (the Ahaiyute) may be successful." The village priest took his son into his own house. His mother never knew what he had done.

The next day the priests came to their ceremonial room and brought their boxes of valuable feathers. They said, "Now we shall make crooks for the Ahaiyute." They finished them and the bow priest planted them. That evening the priests all came together again in their ceremonial room. The Ahaiyute came. "How have you lived these days, my fathers, my children?" "Happily, thank you. Sit down." "What is it that you have to ask of us?" "Yes, our people have nothing to eat. Everybody is starving. Our hearts are heavy. We want you to find our mothers and make our people happy." "We shall try. Wait for us till we return. Sit straight, do not sleep, do not let your minds wander, do not speak. Let us have ashes so that we may see."[1] The village priest went into the other room. He dipped up a gourdful of ashes and gave them to the Ahaiyute. They each took a handful and went out. Elder Brother threw his ashes into the sky. It made a thin line across the sky. Younger Brother threw his handful and it made a wide road. They went up along the Milky Way that they had made. It turned about slowly to take them in all directions, west, south, east and north. It hung low down over the low place where Duck was hiding the corn but they could not see on account of the black corn. The Milky Way brought them again to the roof of the ceremonial room of the chief priest and went up into the sky again. The Ahaiyute made the Milky Way when they were looking for the Corn Maidens.

They sat down and greeted the priests. The village priest took a fagot and lit a cigarette. He smoked them in the six directions and said to them, "What have you to say, my fathers, my children?"

[1] Ashes are white and give light in the darkness.

"Yes, we have been in every direction. We heard no sound, there was no breathing, no talking, in the west, in the south, in the east or in the north. Someone who has great power must be hiding the Corn Maidens. Perhaps someone you have never seen, someone who has never been into Itiwana, can help you to find them. He may have power." "Who is this?" "He is Duck. You do not have to make prayersticks for him. Go to the headman of Ne'we·kwe. Tell him to call his society." "Thank you, my fathers. We will do as you say." The priests went home to sleep. Next day the village priest called the bow priest. He said, "Go to the headman of Ne'we·-kwe and ask him to come." The bow priest went. "Our father has called you to come to his ceremonial room." Ne'we·kwe headman got up immediately and went with the bow priest. He came into the ceremonial room. "How have you lived these days, my fathers, my children? What is it that you have to ask of me? I am a poor man but you have called me." "Yes, we have been looking for the Corn Maidens. We are not happy and our people are starving. We have asked the Tenatsali but they could not help us, we have asked Jimson Weed but he could not help us, we have asked the Ahaiyute but they have failed. We hope you may succeed and bring our Corn Mothers back to us again." "My fathers, I shall try. I am poorer than you but I shall see what I can do. I shall go back to my house and make prayersticks. When I have planted them I shall meet with you here tonight." "Thank you for your help. We shall be ready for you tonight." Ne'we·kwe headman went to his own home. He took his box of feathers and laid out the valuable ones. He took pure white turkey feathers and downy feathers from any bird and he made beautiful prayersticks. His wife said to him, "What are you making? Why did the bow priest call you?" "They asked me to help them. I am not a rain priest but they have asked me for my aid. Have pollen ready." She brought out pollen and put it beside the prayersticks. He thought he was a rain priest. He dressed himself and took his prayersticks and went to the west. He dug a hole and sat down beside it. He faced east. "Now whoever are my fathers, my children, anyone who can help me,[1] my fathers in the ceremonial room of the village priest have asked me for my help. Help me to find the Corn Maidens. Especially you who live in Ashes Spring, whom I have never seen, of whom I have heard so much, I have made prayersticks for you. Help me." He planted the prayersticks. That evening his wife set out the evening meal early and immediately

---

[1] Instead of the usual, "Those who were headmen of Ne'we·kwe before me in their lifetimes," he uses this indefinite form because in this origin tale "no headmen of Ne'we·kwe had died yet."

he went to the ceremonial room of the village priest. No one was there yet.[1] The village priest was still eating. "How have you lived till this time, my fathers, my mothers, my children?" "Happily, thank you. Sit down." The priest's wife set food before him and the priest said, "Eat with us before we go into our ceremonial room to speak together." "I have already eaten. I will go in and wait for you." He went out and went into the ceremonial room. The village priest finished his evening meal and joined him. All the priests of the council came. They smoked together. They sat and prayed that Duck might come from Ashes Spring. He came down the ladder. He had short legs, fat stomach, small pointed head. He was covered with gray down. He wore a green necklace of frog spittle and a headband around his head. He greeted them. "How have you lived till this time, my fathers, my mothers, my children?" The priests were amazed. They had never seen him before. He sat down facing the east. "My people, you have sent for me. I thought I was the least of the raw people but you have asked for my help. How can I be of assistance?" "Yes, indeed, we are in great trouble. My people are starving. I am unhappy. I need your help. I am glad you have come." "Yes, my fathers. If you can wait for four years (days) without sleeping or going to your wives, I will try to do what you want. I will try to find the Corn Maidens. If not, I can do nothing." They sat with their heads bowed. The village priest answered, "Yes, we must do what you have asked. We think we are able. I want my people to know that I am willing to undertake this." Ne'we·kwe Youth[2] said, "However tired, however sleepy you are, sit straight. Do not lie at your ease. Drink before I start and do not drink or eat again till I return." They went into the other room. The village priest asked his wife for food. She set paper-bread before them and they ate. They said to Ne'we·kwe Youth, "Eat also," and he answered, "Put food in the fire for me and it will nourish me." When they had all finished their meal they went out of the house to urinate. They came back and sat in the center of the room. Poor men, they could not eat, they could not drink, they could not speak, they could not sleep. Ne'we·kwe Youth said, "I shall be gone for four years (nights). Stay happily." He went out. He went to the south and returned again to Ashes Spring. He looked everywhere. All day he stayed at his home at Ashes Spring. The second night he went out. He went to the west. He looked every-

---

[1] The whole description emphasizes the self-importance of the society head-man when he is called upon to help the priesthoods.

[2] This term is used during the rest of the tale, Duck being a Ne'we·kwe supernatural.

where. He came back and stayed for the day at his home. The third night he went to the north and returned again to his home in Ashes Spring. The fourth night he went to the east. He looked everywhere. He went four times back and forth across the east, he went around in a circle, he saw Duck sitting in a low place. He said, "That must be the one who hides the Corn Maidens." He turned himself into a duck also. He went down and faced the east and greeted Mother Duck. "How have you lived till this time, my mother, my child? I have been looking for you for four years (nights)." Immediately the corn ears became persons and Ne'we·kwe said to them, "My mothers, my children, I have been sent to bring you to Itiwana. My fathers the priests have been looking everywhere for you." Yellow Corn answered him, "My father, we came here because our flesh was not honored. They scattered it everywhere. They stepped in it, they dropped it in the dirt. It was wasted. We are persons. We feel and smell and we are hurt when we are dropped in the dust and stepped on. We came away to hide from our people till they knew how to value us. Mother Duck has taken care of us all these years. This is our home. I do not know whether my sisters will want to return or not. What do you think, my sisters? Our fathers have sent for us. Are you willing to go?" They answered, "We have been here for four years but we have not been happy. If our people in Itiwana welcome us and honor us we shall be happy to go back. They will dance us.[1] If we stay here, we shall never dance." They were happy because their people had sent for them and they could dance with them. They called Mother and Father Duck. Ne'we·kwe Youth said to them, "The Corn Maidens are going home again. We are happy. The people in Itiwana will value them and treat their flesh with honor. We shall wait for evening." That evening they dressed themselves. They took cattails and green things growing in the marsh and stuck them in their belts. Ne'we·kwe Youth said to them, "Now you shall walk in this order; Yellow Corn, Blue Corn, White Corn, Red Corn, Black Corn, Speckled Corn. You will no longer be hidden.[2] I will walk behind." They came quickly to Itiwana. The priests of the council were all in the ceremonial room of the village priest. Poor men, they had not eaten, they had not drunk water, they had not slept, they had not spoken. When the Corn Maidens had almost reached the village,

---

[1] The great Corn Dance is a dance to allow the corn to participate in dancing. The ears are held and "danced".

[2] During the time that they were in hiding, Black Corn had been placed in the rear of the sisters so that they were covered with darkness, i. e. invisible. By rearranging them in this normal order, their invisibility comes to an end.

Ne'we·kwe Youth said to them, "My mothers, my daughters, I am now taking you to the ceremonial room of the village priest. If they weep, if their faces are covered with tears, do not mind, because they love you. They are ready to welcome you and will do anything to please you." He went to the roof of the ceremonial room. He was a person. He went in. He led the Corn Maidens. They stood in the shadows but the priests heard the noise of their coming. Ne'we·kwe Youth said, "How have you lived these days, my fathers, my mothers, my children? Rest now, my fathers, I have brought our mothers back to our home." Immediately the priests wept and rose. They took gourds and drank water. They greeted the Corn Maidens and made them sit down. The village priest took a fagot and lit a cigarette and smoked them from the six directions. He said to Ne'we·kwe Youth, "What have you to say?" "My fathers, I went four times to the south, to the west, to the north, and to the east. Far in the east I found my mothers, my daughters. I asked them to return to their homes. They had been sad while they had been away because they had not danced. If we will dance them and honor their flesh they are willing to come back and live with us." The village priest answered, "We are glad, our mothers, our daughters. Our stomachs have been empty for four years. We have been unhappy. Our people have died. We will dance you. We will honor your flesh. Stay with us and make us happy." He said to Ne'we·kwe Youth, "You shall be the father of the Corn Priests (towaciwani). Every year on the last day of Cala'ko, the people shall entertain you. You shall bring in the Corn Maidens (at molawia). We shall all stay here together tonight, my daughters." They set out six baskets and the Corn Maidens became ears of corn of the six colors and Ne'we·kwe laid them in the baskets with their heads facing to the east. The priests, poor men, dropped asleep where they sat and Ne'we·kwe went to Ashes Spring, leaving his shadow in the ceremonial room. At sunrise the village priest woke. He remembered what had happened. He said to himself, "Perhaps it was a dream. Perhaps our father has taken our mothers back again." Then he saw the corn lying in the six baskets. He waked the others. They said, "Here are our mothers. How did our father (Duck) look?" They remembered the green necklace of frog spittle that he wore, his little pointed head, his headband tied around his hair, his gray covering and his nakedness. They said, "I think this is the way our father looked."[1] They said to Ne'we·kwe headman, "Now you shall impersonate our father and bring in the Corn Maidens every year to our daylight people. The people shall entertain you on the last day

[1] I.e. they made like this the duck whistle Bitsitsi carries.

of Cala'ko and our father (the Duck superatural) will be glad."
That is why on the last day of Cala'ko we dance the molawia, and
we call our father Bitsitsi[1] because he whistles like our father Duck.

SALT WOMAN MIGRATES (8)

Notes, 272

The people were living at Itiwana, and Salt Woman lived at
Black Rock Lake. The priest made proclamation that all the
people should go for salt. "My boys and my girls, tomorrow we
will go out to the salt lake and bring salt." They liked to go, for
they had a good time. They baked sweet corncakes and paper
bread (folded) and early in the morning they were ready. The men
took fawn-skin bags to fill with salt. The girls dressed up in their
good clothes and took the food. They put black blankets around
their shoulders and went to the houses of their chums. The girls
went two by two and the boys went two by two. Everybody
looked for their sweethearts; two boys would ask two girls to eat
with them, and the girls would spread the food.

Salt Woman was standing there waiting. She was afraid they
would soil her. She said, "This is the first time you have come.
I shall see how you treat me." She sat and watched them. They
were careful; only one or two urinated. The young men and girls
had a good time and behaved well. They filled the fawn-skin bags,
and the girls took off their moccasins and waded into the lake too.
At last the priest asked, "Are you all ready?" They started home,
and the young men carried the salt. They came home singing the
dance songs and the girls danced. Just before sunset they came into
Itiwana. They spread buckskins on the floor and emptied out the
bags in a heap upon them. They laid with it a perfect ear of corn and
spread a black blanket over it and put many beads on it. They lifted
prayer meal to their lips and inhaled and sprinkled it over the salt,
and they prayed, "Salt Mother, we are glad you have come to this
house. We are glad of your flesh. Increase and come many times
again."

They used the salt freely. It was easy to go and get it, for it was
only a little way off. When the people's supply was gone, again the
priest made proclamation, "On the fourth day we shall go to the
salt lake and get salt. The women shall grind for the lunches and we
shall bring the salt." The women ground and they baked sweet
corncakes and made paper bread. On the fourth day they dressed

---

[1] Onomatopoetic for the sound of his whistle. The common name for the
unmasked impersonation who figures in this ceremony.

themselves and went with their chums to the salt lake. The men filled their fawn-skin bags and the women waded with them into the salt lake. They did not ease themselves nearby. They came home and emptied the salt and put the perfect ear of corn and the valuable beads with it and prayed that it would come again.

Again the third time the priest made proclamation that they should go to the salt lake and bring salt. They were careless. They spat and eased themselves nearby, and when they brought the salt home they wasted it so that they might go again the sooner and enjoy themselves. The Salt Mother was very sad.

Turquoise Man lived east of the south side of the salt lake. The bow priest made proclamation that the men go to gather turquoise. Their wives made lunches. The men took their kick-sticks and raced to Turquoise Place. They found pretty turquoise there, and they treated it as if it were a common thing. They had so much they wasted it. Turquoise Man said to himself, "My flesh is valuable but they waste it." Salt Woman said to herself, "It is not good to be here. The people waste my flesh. I am not feeling comfortable in this place. I shall go to Turquoise Man and tell him, for they are wasting his flesh also. The people will have to go a long way for our flesh." Salt Woman went to Turquoise Man. He lived in a cave in Turquoise Mine. When Salt Woman came, he said, "Sit down." She sat down and he asked her, "What is it that you have come to say?" "I have come to ask you what you think. These people come and waste our flesh. If we go far away, they will value us. Shall we go far away so they must come a long way to get us?" "All right. Where shall we go?" "Some other place. Eight days ago they were here, and in four days they will come again. I shall wait till they have taken a little supply of my flesh and we will go the same day. Then I shall come here and we shall find out which way to go."

That same day at Itiwana they made proclamation to go to get salt again. "On the fourth day we shall go to the salt lake and get salt. The women shall grind for the lunches and we shall bring the salt." The women ground and they baked sweet corncakes and made paper bread, and on the fourth day they dressed themselves and went with their chums to the salt lake. They went there. They saw very little salt. Salt Mother did not sit there as she had before. She stayed inside her house. They said, "There is very little salt." Another said, "I think that it is the hot weather. It has melted." So they worked hard to get a few handsful of salt. The bags were only partly full. They got sores on their hands from digging for the salt. They said, "I think this is enough. We shall come again. There will be more next time." They came back with their half-filled bags of salt. They came in singing. They emptied the salt and put the perfect ear of corn and the valuable beads with it and prayed that it would come again.

When it was dark, Salt Woman put on her white feather. She came up through the water of salt lake to Turquoise Man and asked, "Are you ready?" "Yes, wait a few minutes." He brought out prayer meal to carry in his hand. Salt Woman led Turquoise Man. They walked a few yards and nothing ever grew there again. They went to Eagle Rocks, and there Salt Woman said, "Wait here. I will leave my white feather." So she took the white feather tied in her front hair and stuck it in the ground and Turquoise Man sprinkled prayer meal upon it. He said, "This is what I brought this for." They walked on, and the feather turned into a rock cropping out of the earth.

They went farther to the south, and turned and came to the west and came to the home of the Tenatsali Youths. They went in, and they asked them, "What have you come to ask?" "We were living at Black Rock and the people did not value our flesh. We are going farther away, then the people will have a hard time to get us." The Tenatsali said, "What do you want before you go?" "Will you give me some meal and some tenatsali sticks? I will take it where I am going and leave it there." So they went into the other room and brought out a bunch of tenatsali. Salt Mother said, "I shall take this to my house, and it will be valuable." She thanked them and went on. They went on to the south till they came to Salt Lake. She said to Turquoise Man, "This is where I wanted to be. I shall stop here and go in. Go to the East and make your home there." So Turquoise Man went to the East, and he came to the country beyond Santo Domingo. He stayed there two nights and left his outer clothes there. He went on, but we do not know where he went. He settled in the white people's country, and that is why the white people have better turquoise than we can get.

After a few days the people had no more salt. Again the priest made proclamation for them to get salt. "On the fourth day we shall go to the salt lake to get salt. The women shall grind for the lunches, and we shall bring the salt." The women ground and made sweet corncakes and paper bread for the lunches. On the fourth day they dressed themselves and went with their chums to the place where they were accustomed to go. When they came in sight of the place where the lake had been, there was no lake there. They went up to it. It was only a damp place. They could see the way she had gone, for the weeds along her path were brushed by salt. They were sad. They had no good time. They were worried about how to get salt. Some dipped their hands into the mud and licked the salty taste from their fingers. They did not want to come back with empty sacks. Salt Woman had left her dress there, and they took that up. The priest said, "We shall go home." His heart was sad because he had brought the girls and boys out and there was no salt. They got to Itiwana. The people were waiting, because they liked to hear their songs. But there were no songs. "Maybe they are tired," the people said. The village priest met them and they said, "We have not had a good time. Salt Woman has gone and the weeds are brushed with salt along the way she has taken." They went into their houses. The village priest said to the priests of the council, "We shall meet in our ceremonial room. We can send to find out where she went. After supper we shall meet." They went to their houses. After the evening meal the priests of the council went to the ceremonial room of the village priest. They talked of this. "Why did Salt Woman do this?" they asked. "We were careless with her flesh. The people played near by when they went after her flesh, and we wasted it as if it were common. She didn't like it and has gone away." "Shall we send one of our young men to look for her?" They chose their best runners. Two of the priests went also to carry the bundle of prayersticks.

So they made the feathers. They made prayersticks. They did not tie on duck feathers.[1] The runners carried the food for the journey and the priests carried the prayersticks, and they went to the east to Black Rock Lake. There they followed her tracks. They came to the rock feather. They knew that it was new, and they knew that she had made it. They followed her trail all the way to Tenatsali Place. Just before they got there, at K̦amak̦a, they were tired and stopped to eat. They sat down and ate the ground-up sweet corncakes and drank tcukinawe. They drank at the spring. They were ready to go. The runners went ahead, and the two priests behind. They had never been to Tenatsali Place. It was Salt Woman who showed them the way to the tenatsali. She blessed our people. Where the spring was, they saw a rock like a house and they saw her tracks leading into it. They said, "Father, go in first." The priest went in first, and there were two little boys in that room. They were kind. They asked, "How have you lived these days? We are glad to see you here. It is hard to come all the way from Itiwana. What are you coming to ask for?" "Our Salt Mother used

---

[1] "Turn around feathers" added to many prayersticks to show that the maker is an initiate in the kachina society. The feather faces in the opposite direction from all other feathers on the stick.

to live at Black Rock and our people were careless with her flesh. Now she has gone away. We are looking for her. We have followed her tracks to this place." "Yes, this is our home. She came here and went on south. It is not far away. You will get there today." The priest said, "My sons, I am going to ask you a question. I should like to know if you know anything valuable?" "We shall be glad to tell you. We shall be glad to tell you. That is why Salt Woman stopped here at this house, so that you should follow her and learn what we know. We are the ones who make the clouds and the rain and bring the kachinas from Kachina Village to Itiwana. We make your thoughts. If you take our flesh and put it in a covered jar in an empty room and keep it away from common people, it will help you. No one must touch us unless he is sick or in need." So they told the two priests, "Go back home and make prayersticks for us. Do not use turkey feathers. Use eagle feathers or bluejay feathers for our sticks. We have been wishing every day to have you come here that we might tell you. Salt Woman showed you the way, and now it has happened as we wished. Plant prayersticks for us in every direction (from Zuni) and we shall be glad to help you. We shall be way over here, but we shall do everything for you." The village priest was happy. He only said, "Thank you, my boys." "Before you go we shall go out and get the tenatsali sticks for you." They came in and gave them to the priests. They said, "It was we who made Salt Woman come this way to lead you here. It was we who made you know in your ceremonial room that two of your priests should come here with the runners. You thought you would send outside people (i. e. the runners) and we put it into your minds that you must come too." The priests said, "When we need your flesh, we shall come here again." "Other priests shall come with you also. But when you come, do not come as you came this time. Follow the road straight from Zuni." "We shall do what you say. We are going now. Live happily a long time."

They went on toward Salt Lake (south and then east). They saw a great lake before them. They were afraid to approach because they had been unkind to her. They were wondering what she would say to them. When they got close, the runners hung back because they were outside people. They let the priests go first. The priests took their moccasins off and waded into the lake. The salt cut their feet. They were close to her house, coming down the steps, but they could not bear the pain. They ran out and sat down where they had started from. Again they waded into the lake, but the salt cut their feet. They were almost in her house, but they ran back for the pain was too much. They came just to the door. Their feet were bleeding.

The third time they waded into the lake, but the salt cut them so badly that they had to run back. They rubbed their feet with clay. "Ouch, ouch!" they cried. They waded out the fourth time and went into her house. She was dressed in a white embroidered blanket and she had a white feather in her hair.[1] She was glad to see them. She asked, "What is it that you have come to ask? Why have you come this long way?" "My dear daughter, we are looking for you. We have had a hard time finding you." "Yes, it was too easy for you to get my flesh. You were careless and spat and eased yourself on me. I do not want these boys and girls to play and step on me. You know better. Did you think young people knew better than you? After this I want the older people to come for my flesh. Make proclamation for the men to come. It is not the women's part to come for salt. When I was at Black Rock Lake and the winds blew from the west, I could smell the smell of people. Therefore I came here, and now the men shall come for my flesh and bring prayersticks." "Here are your prayersticks. We have brought them." She took them, but there was no reversed duck feather. She said, "I am pleased with these, but not entirely. There is no reversed duck feather. You are initiated men (in the kachina society). You should have put the reversed feather on the prayersticks you made. When you go home, tell the others that when they come for salt, all those who are initiated should always put the reversed feather on their prayersticks. These feathers look as if you were giving them to a dead person.[2] I am not dead, I am living always. If young children come without the reversed feather in their prayersticks, I will know it is because they are not yet initiated." She told them this, "You shall take a little salt with you. When you get near Zuni, call out for your fathers' sisters to come to wash your bodies. They shall give you a present, and you shall give them a little salt in return. If other men wish to come, they may come also for my flesh. Their fathers' sisters shall wash them the first time, but when they come a second time, their aunts shall not wash them. I shall be valuable now that I am far away." "All right. We shall do as you say." They came out with their fawnskin bags full of salt. Just before they started, Salt Woman said, "Do not go around by the way you came. You can go straight to Zuni. There is a road there." They set out, but they could not find the road.[3] They went over mountains and

---

[1] When it is not cloudy this feather stands up straight. When it is about to rain, it is heavy, and makes the clouds come.

[2] Prayersticks to the dead have no reversed duck feather.

[3] This, like the cutting of their feet, was punishment for the people's carelessness at Black Rock salt lake.

precipices. It took them four days. Their food was gone, and they killed butterflies to eat. On the fourth day they climbed a mountain and they saw Itiwana. They burned a pile of wood as a signal to show they were coming. The people in the village saw it and thought it was a signal that the Navahos were coming. They were frightened. Those who had gone to find Salt Woman had already been gone eight days. About noon they came in past Sand Hill and called, "We are coming in. When we get to Halona our fathers' sisters shall come to wash our bodies before we have anything to eat. They shall bring us a present." Their aunts ran to their nephews' houses to be ready. They came in. Everybody was watching. Their moccasins were worn out and their hands and faces were covered with clay (from Salt Lake). They came into their houses and spread the buckskins and poured out the salt. They put the perfect ear of corn with it and covered it with a blanket and put beads with it and scattered prayer meal. They prayed, "Salt Mother, we are glad that you have come to this house, we are glad of your flesh. Increase and come many times again."

Their fathers' sisters broke up soap-weed root and made suds to wash their hair. They said, "You are our child. We are washing your hair who have been coming from Salt Lake so many days." They brought in bowls of grain to give to their nephews and they washed their whole bodies. The head aunts filled up the bowls with salt and all of the fathers' sisters took them home. That is why we still bring in the salt in this fashion.[1]

TAIL BY TAIL (8)

Notes, 273

The Ḵanaʻkwe lived on Corn Mountain.[2] Every day they danced and after they had danced they had a throw-away of corn boiled in the husk. All the animals gathered around and caught them.

Coyote heard about this and he said to his people, "Let us go up to the top of Corn Mountain where these generous dancers[3] give away their corn." He went all around the country and gathered together the coyotes. They could not tell how to get up there and at last one said, "We will take corn cobs and break them in two and

---

[1] When a young man goes for the first time to Salt Lake, his father's sisters tell of it and say, "We should wait for our child." So they make bowls for him, or grind, or bring a present from the store, and when he comes back, they wash him and he gives them salt.

[2] The Ḵanaʻkwe do not live on Corn Mountain. See discussion, 273.

[3] The Ḵanaʻkwe are the proverbially generous givers.

stick them into our anuses. We will puff up with wind and we shall be light enough to get to the top of Corn Mountain easily." So the coyotes had a big corn husking and they broke the corn cobs in two and stuck them in their anuses. Coyote said, "Nobody must take them out for if they do we shall all fall down and be killed."

They all went up easily, one after the other, up Corn Mountain and they got almost to the top. The could hear the Ḳana·kwe singing their songs, for they were almost there. They liked to hear the dancing going on close by. They were so happy one of them pulled out his corn cob. He broke wind and they all fell down to the bottom and were killed. They all lay dead at the bottom of the cliff that they had wanted to climb to the very top so that they could get something good to eat. Just then Saiyali'a came that way and he saw the coyotes all lying there dead. In the beginning when he first came from Kachina Village Saiyali'a had no fur collar, and now he said, "This is just what I want for a collar. I will skin the coyotes." He went back and got the rest of the Saiyali'as[1]. They came and skinned the coyotes and made fur collars so that they never got hoarse any more. That is why the Saiyali'as always wear collars of coyote fur.[2]

THE BOY WHO BROKE HIS VOWS (3)

Notes, 274

Published only in abstract.

_____

[1] There are four permanent Saiyali'a masks.
[2] Bunzel 919.

II. AHAIYUTE ADVENTURES

THE AHAIYUTE DESTROY MONSTERS (7)

Notes, 287

Long ago the people were living in Itiwana. Cloud Swallower
stood in the east. He swallowed each cloud as it came up and there
was a great drought. He was like a giant elk; his neck was half a
mile long. The Ahaiyute lived with their grandmother on Corn
Mountain. One morning she said to them, "In the east there is a
monster who eats the clouds, therefore there is no rain. You must
not go there, he is dangerous." "All right." Next day the Ahaiyute
went to the east. They heard someone speaking to them. It was
Gopher coming out of his hole. Gopher said, "Wait a little." They
stood still. "Where are you going?" "Oh, we are going to kill Cloud
Swallower." "Come into this hole." The Ahaiyute went in. Gopher dug
a hole deep down into the ground for those two boys. Gopher said,
"Over there Cloud Swallower is asleep, I will make a way for you."
He tunnelled till his hole was directly under Cloud Swallower's
heart. He began to gnaw his hair. Cloud Swallower started up. "No,
wait, grandfather. I want your hair for my nest." Gopher shaved a
circle over his heart and went back. He said to the Ahaiyute, "I
have shaved the hair over his heart; go through my hole and shoot
him quickly where I have shaved. He will fall dead." They went.
They drew their bow and shot him. Cloud Swallower started up and
put his antlers down. The Ahaiyute ran back, Younger Brother
ahead and Elder Brother behind. The antlers grazed his back, but
just as it touched him the monster fell dead. His great head is there
yet where he died.

They came back to Gopher and said to him, "Come and see if he is
dead." Gopher went up and touched him. He called to them, "He
is dead." The Ahaiyute came up. They said, "Now there will be
rain. He will not eat the clouds any more." They said, "We will cut
open his breast." They took his heart and threw it to the east and
it became the morning star. They took his liver and threw it and it
became the evening star. They took his lungs and threw them and
they became the Seven Stars. They took his entrails and threw
them and they became the Milky Way. They went home to Corn
Mountain.

4*

Next day their grandmother said to them, "Do not go to the south, there are owls there. They are dangerous." "All right." Next morning the Ahaiyute went to the south. In their house there were great owls sitting in rows and rows. They never winked. They sat staring straight ahead. Back in the corner there was one girl owl and one boy owl. The Ahaiyute came in. The owls said, "Sit down by the fire." Younger Brother had brought salt (from the Salt Lake) in his hand. When he sat down he threw it into the fire. The owls were staring with their eyes fixed and open. When the salt began to pop it popped into their eyes. It killed them all. The Ahaiyute cut them up and plucked their feathers. Over in the corner little girl owl and little boy owl were still alive. They said, "If you kill us there will be no more owls." The Ahaiyute said, "If we let you go, do not live as human beings (in houses). Do not kill men. If you do, we will come and kill you. Kill jack rabbits, cotton-tail rabbits. Live in trees and caves." "All right." They flew off. The Ahaiyute took their big bundle of owl feathers and went home to Corn Mountain.

Next morning their grandmother said to them, "In the southwest there lives an old giant who has a horn in the middle of his forehead. He always kills people. You must not go to Noponikwi." "All right." Next morning the Ahaiyute went to the southwest. They took the trail along the cliff of Noponikwi. The giant's children lived in a cave at the foot of the cliff. They were all girls. When people went by on the trail Hakisuto (forehead horn) raised his leg and kicked. He knocked them over the cliff and his children ate them. The Ahaiyute got there. They greeted him and said, "We are passing by." "All right, you can go past without any danger." They started. Just as they were opposite he said, "Ouch, I have a cramp in my leg." His leg kicked. Younger Brother said, "I suppose you want to push me off." "No, I have a cramp." They started again. Just as they got there the giant said, "Ouch, I have a cramp in my leg." He kicked, but they jumped back. Again they started and the giant said, "Ouch, I have a cramp in my leg." He kicked, they jumped back. The fourth time Younger Brother said to Elder Brother, "Next time he does that I will catch him and throw him over." They came up. The giant said, "Ouch, I have a cramp in my leg." Younger Brother got him by the leg and threw him over the cliff. He dropped down where his children lived. They ran up and began to eat. They ate his foot and his thighs and his body and his arms. They came to his head and they saw the horn on his forehead. They cried, "Our father, we have eaten our father." The

Ahaiyute came down and killed the children. They went home to Corn Mountain.

Next morning their grandmother said to them, "Away up in the north a woman and her granddaughter live. They kill people. Don't go there." "All right." Next morning the Ahaiyute went to the north. They got there. They saw nice girls. They went in. The girls said, "Which is the elder?" Younger Brother said, "This is my elder brother. Why did you want to know?" "I am the younger sister and this is my elder sister. I shall marry the elder brother and she will marry the younger brother." They went into the house to sleep. The girls tied on red head bands. The Ahaiyute said, "What do you do that for?" "We always do that when we get married." "All right." When the girls were sound asleep Younger Brother spoke to them. They did not answer. He knew they were asleep. He got up and took the girls' head bands off. He took the white head bands from around his own head and his brother's and put them on the girls' heads. He tied the red headbands on his own head and his brother's. The girls' father came with a sharp stone knife. He saw the white headbands in the dark. He said, "These are the husbands." He cut the girls' heads off and threw them outside and put their bodies in the cellar. The Ahaiyute said, "Let's go home." They went home to Corn Mountain. Next morning they told their grandmother, "We killed those girls." She said, "Thank you. Those girls have killed lots of people."

Their grandmother said, "Nearby in the west there are eight girls living with their grandmother. Don't go there. They have teeth in their vaginas. They will cut you and you will die." "All right." In Tsukipa (Big Belly) the Lehaci lived. They were six young men and they lived with their grandfather. The Ahaiyute went there. They told the six boys to get oak wood and make themselves each a false penis. Then they told them to get hickory wood and each make themselves a second. When they had finished Younger Brother went down west where those women lived. He said, "Do you girls want us to come and dance tonight." "Yes, how many are there of you?" "There are eight of us and our grandfather." "That is just right. There are eight of us and our grandmother." "We shall come tonight." Younger Brother went back. He told them, "They want us to go to dance late tonight." They went down. Their grandfather carried the drum. The girls said, "Come in." They went in and danced and sang their songs:

> "The Lehaci don't know girls.
> The Lehaci don't know girls.
> They just sleep here."

The eldest sister said, "Which is the smallest boy ?" "Ma·sewi[1] said, "I am." Elder Brother said, "I am." They quarrelled. All the boys paired with the girls. The youngest took the youngest. The grandmother said to the girls. "These Łehaci are going to die soon." The girls said, "Poor boys, pretty soon we shall kill them." They lay with the girls. The grandmother took the grandfather. All the men took out their false members. They used them cohabiting. They broke the teeth from the women's vaginas. The blood ran. When the oak members were worn out, they put them aside and took the hickory ones. By daylight the teeth of these women were all worn out. They were broken in pieces. The grandfather told the boys, "We shall beat the drum all the way home." No one of them was killed. They went back home to Tsukipa, and Ahaiyute went back to Corn Mountain.

They left the eight girls and their grandmother sleeping. When they had gone Coyote came. He had intercourse with each of the girls. He pulled a hair out of his moustache and planted it between the legs of the first girl and breathed on it. He pulled another hair out of his moustache and planted it on the second girl and breathed on it, and he did the same to the third girl and the fourth. When he had given a hair to each of the girls he went back home. The girls woke. They scratched themselves. They said, "What is the matter ?" They each had pubic hair. They said, "Why does it smell ?" It was Coyote's odor. These women never killed men any more.

Ahaiyute grandmother said to them, "A girl lives down by Snake Place. She is dangerous. Do not go there." "All right." Next morning the Ahaiyute went to Snake Place. The girl said, "I wonder what is the matter with those boys. Which one of you would like me ?" Younger Brother said, "I would." Elder Brother said, "No, I." Again she asked them. They fought. The girl said, "Which one ?" The younger slept with her and then the elder. In the morning they took their bows and shot her. She died and they went out. Next day they came to Badger Place. They found a nice girl there and again the younger slept with her and then the elder. Next morning they took their bows and arrows and shot her. She died and they went to the Hopi country. They found a nice girl there and the elder slept with her and then the younger. Next morning they took their bows and arrows and killed her and they went to the Navaho country and they found a nice girl there. The younger slept with her and then the elder and in the morning they took their bows and arrows and killed her. They went on. They had not gone far when

---

[1] The little-used personal name of Elder Brother. It is the name always used in Keresan tales.

the girl[1] they had killed came following them. The boys ran. When the sun came out there were lots of dead persons' heads rolling after them. The boys got to the Hopi country and there they were having the yaya dance. "Save us, save us. There is a dead person following us." "All right, come into the kiva." They put Hopi trousers and blankets and headdresses on them and gave them necklaces. They stood with the girls to dance. The dead person came following them. She came down into the kiva. The boys ran. They went way up to the Navaho country. The Navahos were having a ceremony ("praying with rings"). "Save us, there is a dead person following us." They put Navaho clothes on them and fixed their hair Navaho fashion and put quivers over their shoulders and they prayed with rings. The dead person came following them. She touched them. They ran. They went far to the east to Big Spring. There were great fields of sunflowers there. They said to the sunflowers, "Save us. There is a dead person following us." The biggest sunflower said, "Sit on my hair." They sat down. The dead person came. She said, "Where are my husbands?" She found them. She shook the sunflowers and those two boys jumped out and ran away to the east. There were bluebirds there. "Save us, there is a dead person following us." The biggest bluebird said, "Come up under my wing." Elder Brother sat under one wing and Younger Brother under the other wing. The dead person came. The birds made a great noise but the dead person said, "Where are my husbands?" She struck the biggest bird and Elder Brother jumped out from under one wing and Younger Brother jumped out from under the other wing and they ran way east to Cipapolima. They came to the Knife Society room. "Save us, save us, there is a dead person following us." "All right." They dressed them. They tied buckskin round their waists and gave them bandoleers and buckskin warhoods and quivers and a war club and bows and arrows.[2] The White Bear of the Knife Society gave them a flint knife. He said, "You must take her scalp. When she comes in, take hold of her. No matter if she is already dead, kill her and put her by the altar." The dead person came. She called, "Have you seen my two husbands?" White Bear said, "Yes." The dead person said, "Send them out." "Come in and get them." "Send them out to me." "Come in and get them." "Send them out." The fourth time she went into the house. She was a fine looking girl in a nice woman's dress. She said, "Where are my husbands?" "There." She said to

---

[1] These four girls are the same individual, who returns to life each night because she has not been ceremonially killed.

[2] That is, they dressed them in the costume of bow priests.

them, "Let's go home." "All right." They got up. Elder Brother walked ahead and the girl in the middle and Younger Brother behind. They went up to the roof and down the ladder. When they had gone fifty yards Younger Brother hit her with his war club and Elder Brother shot her with his bow and arrow. They killed her and mashed her body all up. They took the scalp and threw it up four times and put it in their belt. They took the corpse by the foot and dragged it a long distance and laid it on its back. They said to it, "Count the stars till you have numbered every one." They went back with her scalp to the room of the Knife Society.

Followed by the account of the institution of the scalp dance, reserved for Żuni Ceremonial Tales.

Variant: THE AHAIYUTE DESTROY MONSTERS AND OBTAIN

CEREMONIAL OBJECTS (7)[1]

This version opens with Cliff Ogre thrown as food to his Children; Underground to the Monster; Death in the Eyes (owls) as in version A.

Next morning their grandmother told them, "Well, my grandsons, don't go to the southeast because a bad man and a bad woman live there." "No, we won't go there." After breakfast they went out and the elder said to his brother, "Let us go to where these two bad people are and let us kill them." They went a little way and caught a jackrabbit and took out the guts. They filled them with blood and put blood on their necks. Then they went down to the mesa to the southeast and they looked inside a hole. Soon an eagle came down. He took the two Ahaiyute and carried them up to his cave. He had two little eagles. As soon as they came there he told the little eagles, "Here is something for you children to eat," and he put them down in there and went off. The little eagles jumped down and went over to eat the young men. The young men said, "Ouch!" and the eagles did not touch them. Then the eagle's little sister said, "Why don't you eat them?" He said, "They talk. I can't eat them." The sister said, "No, they are not dead." Then he went over again and when he wanted to touch them, they cried, "Ouch!" and he was scared. Soon Eagle Woman said, "Why don't you eat them?" He said, "Those boys talk." She said, "No, they are dead." She took them up and they had jackrabbit blood on their necks and their guts were hanging out. So she fed them to the children and said, "Now eat. These people are dead." Then she

[1] Recorded by Ruth Bunzel.

went out. The Ahaiyute got up and asked, "What time will your father come home?" The little eagle said, "As soon as there is a light sprinkle of rain he will come home." Then they asked, "When will your mother come home?" They said, "With the fourth sprinkle of rain our mother will come home." They sat down and waited. Then there was a little shower of rain and the eagle came and they saw him and killed him and hid him away. Pretty soon there was another shower and then another came. Then they saw her and killed her. Finally they said, "We are going to kill the little eagles." The little eagles said, "You must not kill us because if you kill us there will be no more eagles." The Ahaiyute said, "If we let you live you must not kill any more people. You may kill cottontails and jackrabbits. That will be all right for you." The eagles said, "All right," and they turned them loose. Then they stripped the feathers off the eagles.

They came out of the cave and wanted to go down but they could not get down. They saw an old woman down below looking for cactus fruit. They took a stone and threw it down at the old woman. She looked up and saw the Ahaiyute there and asked, "How did you get there? Didn't the eagles eat you?" They said, "No. They will not eat people any more. Now you had better come up and get us. We don't know how to get down." Bat Woman went up after them and asked them, "Where are the two eagles?" They took her there and showed them to her. Bat Woman filled her basket full of little soft feathers to line her nest and she put the two Ahaiyute in the basket. The boys said, "Your basket is not strong enough. It is only spider-web." Then Spider Woman filled her basket with stones but it did not break and the two Ahaiyute got in. Bat Woman said, "Shut your eyes and do not open them until I let you." She flew away singing a song. Then she came down.

> "Ha'actiana ha'actiana
> Tcepana łen ła tcepanałen ła łe
> Ha'actiana ha'actiana
> Tcepanałen tcepanałen
> Łen łen."

They came right down. When they were halfway down, Elder Brother said, "I think I will open my eyes." Younger Brother said, "No, don't." They went a little farther and one of them said, "I guess we can open our eyes now. I am tired." The other said, "No, don't." After they had gone a little farther he said, "I guess I'll open my eyes," and the other said, "No." They went a little farther and he said, "Now I am going to open my eyes anyway."

He opened his eyes, and they all dropped down on their grandmother, the two boys and Bat Woman and the basket, and they mashed her down and made her back hurt. Then the two little Ahaiyute laughed at their grandmother because she was so mean-looking. She gave the boys some wild grapes to eat and after a while the boys said, "Grandmother, we are going to tell you something. If you do this it will be all right but if you don't do it it will be bad luck. You have lots of feathers in your basket. Put your basket on your back and shut your eyes and go up to that rock. Shut your eyes and don't open them until you get there." She started to go and soon she came to some sunflowers and she could not get through. She went first to one side and then to the other and could not climb up and the Ahaiyute laughed. Soon their grandmother became tired and opened her eyes and all the eagle feathers turned into summer birds, all kinds of summer birds, black birds and white birds, and they all flew away. The old woman tried to catch them but could not and then all her feathers were gone. She came back to them and they said, "Now, grandmother, we must go home and you must go home too." Then they went home.

They went home and told their grandmother, "We have killed the two eagles," and they showed her the tail feathers and wing feathers. Then their grandmother said, "All right. The two eagles killed many people, and it was dangerous to go there because the eagles carried off the people and ate them."

Next morning as they were eating breakfast their grandmother said, "Don't go near Twin Buttes because an old woman lives there who is mean and kills many people." The two Ahaiyute said, "All right, we won't go there." They went out and after they had gone a little way to hunt rabbits, Younger Brother said to Elder Brother, "Let us go where that old woman is. Let us see what kind of woman she is." So the two Ahaiyute went to Hecoktakwi, this side of Twin Buttes. They went up to the top of the mesa and hid, and after a little while one of them looked down and saw the old woman. The old woman was working, fixing her dress. Then one of them took up a piece of rock and threw it at the old woman. The little stone dropped down and the old woman just turned and looked around. The two boys hid, and she did not see anyone. About an hour later they picked up another stone and threw it at the woman again. The old woman turned and looked up, but the two boys had hidden behind the rocks. After a while one of them looked over the edge and the woman was working again, fixing her dress. He picked up a stone and hit her again for the third time. The rock dropped down and the old woman turned and looked up, and the two boys hid again. Then the woman said, "I want to know who hit me." The younger boy said, "Well, next time when we hit that old woman, don't hide." The old woman went back to her work, and a little later the boy picked up a stone and threw it down. The stone fell and the woman turned and looked up, and the two boys were standing there on the top of the mesa. Then the woman said, "Well, my boys, come down. What is the matter? Why did you hit me?" The two Ahaiyute said, "Let's go down and see her."

The two Ahaiyute went down and the woman spoke to them. "Well, my grandsons, I am glad to see you. Sit down here." She made the elder sit on her right side and the younger on her left side, and she held their heads in her lap and combed their hair. She told the two boys, "Now, grandsons, go and get some wood and we shall make a fire and cook some dinner." The two Ahaiyute knew that they would die in a little while, and one of them picked up a stick of wood and said, "This wood will cook my body." Then the other picked up a stick and said, "This wood will cook my body," and they joked about it.

A little later the two boys came back, each with an armful of wood, and the old woman made a fire and put lots of stones in the fire to make them hot. She put a big cooking pot on the fire and filled it with water. The two boys piled wood on the fire to make it burn hard, and the stones got red hot and the water boiled. Then she said to Elder Brother, "Sit here on my right side, and, Younger Brother, sit here on my left side." She combed their hair again, and after a while she bit the neck of the elder brother, and he died, and then she bit the neck of the younger one and killed him too. Then the old woman said, "You foolish boys, now you are going to die." Then the soul of the elder one came out of his body and went into the water jar, and the soul of the younger one came out and went into the cooking pot. She took the elder and put him into the cooking pot and boiled him, and then she took a red hot stone from the fire and laid the body of the younger on it and put another red hot stone on top of his body. She went out.

After a while the old woman said, "I guess I will get something to eat now. I shall eat the younger one as my first course." She went in and put the boiled meat in a dish, and took the younger one from between the red hot stones and put him in a basket. She ate some of the meat, and while she was eating, the elder Ahaiyute, who was in the water jar, said, "Too bad! I made the meat dirty with my excrement." Then the old woman was angry and she said to the water jar, "Why do you talk like that?" and she took a stone and threw it at the water jar and broke it to pieces. Then the elder

Ahaiyute came out and went into the mixing bowl. After a while she sat down to eat the boiled meat. Then the younger one, who was in the cooking pot, said, "Too bad, I urinated in the stew!" Then the old woman was angry and she took a piece of wood and broke the cooking pot, and the younger Ahaiyute went out of the cooking pot into a small bowl. After a while she ate again, and the elder one said something. She took up a stick and broke the mixing bowl. Then, later, while she was eating, the younger one said the same thing, and the old woman was angry and took a piece of wood and broke the small bowl. The elder brother went into her right nostril and the younger brother went into her left nostril. The old woman ate some more and the two boys began to scratch the inside of her nose and she began to sneeze and cough, and after about an hour she died.

After she was dead the two Ahaiyute came out of her nose. The old woman lay there dead. Then they took an arrow point and skinned her from her feet up, and left the body in the house. They went out and got grass and weeds and brought them back to the house and stuffed them into the old woman's skin. They stuffed it full and sewed up the feet. Then they put her dress on it, and it was just like the old woman. They put a stick in each leg and tied a belt around the waist. They went back into the house and they saw lots of food there, corn and wheat and pumpkins, They went into the second room and it was full of wheat. They went into the third room and it was full of melons and pumpkins. They went into the fourth room and it was full of beans. After they passed through the fourth room they were in the other world. They went out and saw a trail. They followed it. They walked about three miles to the other side of a mountain, and there they saw a village where people were living.

After sunset they came into the village and stood looking at the houses. After a while people came out of their houses and went into the kivas. After they had been in there a little while lightning came out of the door, and they heard a sound like thunder. After a couple of hours the two Ahaiyute looked into the window of the kiva and they saw two men. One of them had a smooth round stone which he rolled and which made a noise like thunder, and the other man had an instrument for making lightning. It was something like a board, and it made lightning. The two Ahaiyute watched them, and late at night the people put away their things on a shelf in the corner of the kiva. After a while the men who stayed in the kiva went to sleep. Then the two Ahaiyute went into the house quickly, and the younger took the lightning under his arm, and the elder took the thunder. As he took it up it made a little noise, and all the people woke up. The boys ran away, and all the people ran after them. They went to the east and the people almost caught them. They found the house where they had killed the old woman and went in. The people could not catch them, but they said, "Never mind, we will get you some day."

They went through the house and came out to where the old woman's body was standing. The elder put the old woman's belt around his waist and ran as if the old woman were chasing him. They came over the hill and called to their grandmother. Then Younger Brother tied the woman to his belt. Elder Brother called out, "Oh, someone is chasing my younger brother! Grandmother, someone is chasing my brother! He has almost caught him!" The old woman heard them and went into the house and picked up a big stick, and a grinding stone in the other hand. She put ashes on one side of her face, and soot on the other side, and ran out as fast as she could. She crossed the Zuni river. The two boys were coming down the hill. Elder Brother was about ten yards away and the younger one a little way behind, with the old woman coming after him. Their grandmother stood there, and Elder Brother came up and said, "Grandmother, someone is trying to catch my brother; you had better hurry!" The old woman ran as fast as she could. She picked up some pebbles and spat on them and waved them around the head of her grandson.[1] She took the stick and hit the old woman as hard as she could, and the old woman fell down. Then she took her grinding stone and mashed her head with it, and the two Ahaiyute laughed and laughed at their grandmother. Their old grandmother was angry and wanted to kill the old woman. The elder one said, "Well, grandmother, you had better stop. That old woman is dead, she is not alive." Then their grandmother saw that the old woman had died the day before. The Ahaiyute just laughed and said, "That old woman was mean, so we killed her. We kill everyone who kills people and now the people do not need to be afraid any more, because we have killed all the monsters in this country." Then their grandmother said, "Thank you. You have killed all the mean people. Now there are no more dangerous people here any more."

Then they went home and their grandmother gave them something to eat, and she ground flour while the the two boys played in the house. The elder brother used the lightning sticks and shot lightning from the door, and the younger brother rolled the thunder stone and made a noise. Soon their grandmother said, "Where did you get those things? You had better throw them away or give

[1] To remove misfortune.

them away. You have no right to them. They belong to the Uwanami." "No, they don't," they said and they began to argue with their grandmother. Soon they said, "Let's go out." They went out. Clouds were coming up all over, from the east and the north and the west and the south. The clouds were all over. Soon it began to rain. It rained hard. The two boys used their lightning sticks and their thunder stone. Soon their grandmother began to cry out. The whole house was flooded. There were about two feet of water in the house, and their grandmother cried. The younger one said, "You had better put grandmother some place where she will keep quiet." The elder one went into the house and the water came up to his knees. In the corner was a big open cooking pot. He took his grandmother and threw her into the pot. Then he went out and played again. He laughed all the time. Soon the water came high up in the house, and soon the house would be full of water. Then their grandmother cried out again. Soon the water came up to where their grandmother was, and their grandmother was drowned. Soon the water came up over the roof and their grandmother was washed out. Then the younger one saw her and said, "Look, our grandmother is dead." Then the elder one stopped playing with the lightning, and the younger one with his thunder. They got a stick and sharpened one end and made a hole in the wall of the house. The rain had stopped and the water ran out of the house. Then the Ahaiyute dug a hole and buried their grandmother, and the Ahaiyute were alone for about four days. After the four days Elder Brother said, "Now we had better go away. We cannot stay here in this house." They went to Corn Mountain. He put his younger brother in Corn Mountain, and the elder brother went to Twin Buttes. They threw away their thunder and lightning, and the Uwanami came to get them back.

The Ahaiyute killed all the monsters. That is all.

Variant: THE GHOST PURSUIT (8)

The people were living in Itiwana. The Ahaiyute lived on Corn Mountain. Every day the Ahaiyute went hunting deer. One day they told their grandmother they were going to the west. They said to her, "Give us lunch. For three nights we are going hunting." She stirred up cornmeal balls, and Younger Brother bundled twelve of them in his blanket.

Next morning they started. They went beyond Hecokta and they came to a Navaho hogan. There was a pretty girl there all alone. Her father and mother were herding. The Ahaiyute said to her,

"Where's your father? Where's your mother?" She said, "They're out herding." The Ahaiyute said, "Will you eat our lunch with us?" She liked Younger Brother because he had the lunch. They talked. They went off together and played a long time. Younger Brother had intercourse with her and gave her the lunch.

Elder Brother was impatient waiting for his brother. He called, "Come on. I'm in a hurry." His brother came. Elder Brother said, "Where is our lunch?" His brother said, "The Navaho girl took it." Elder Brother was very angry. He talked to his brother. Younger Brother said, "It's no use getting angry. Go ahead and have intercourse with her yourself so you won't be angry with me. Then we'll kill her." "All right."

Elder Brother went up to the hogan to play with the girl. He said, "Where did you get that lunch you have?" She didn't say anything. He said, "My brother took that lunch. It was mine. Let me have my lunch." The girl did not want to give up the lunch. When he reached for it, she held on to it and pulled him into the hogan. They played together, and Elder Brother had intercourse with her. All the time Younger Brother peeped at them through the cracks of the hogan.

Elder Brother came out of the hogan. Younger Brother said, "We are going to kill her now." Elder Brother said, "Let's not kill her. She is quite nice. We will come back someday and enjoy her again." Younger Brother said, "No. We will kill her as we planned. If we came back again to play with her, she might like me best, and then you would be angry again." Elder Brother said, "No. I shan't be angry." Younger Brother insisted, "We will kill her."

They went together to the girl. They were pleasant with her. She was shy. Younger Brother drew his bow and shot her. They both shot her full of arrows. They ran away.

They got as far as Hecokta, and they heard the dead person coming. They ran as fast as they could. They thought they would not be safe from her at their grandmother's so they ran on past Corn Mountain. They ran to Cipapolima. They thought that the medicine societies were at Cipapolima,[1] and that they would be safe with them. They went into the first room, and it was empty. She was at their heels. They ran out again, and just as they got out she was coming in. They ran back toward Corn Mountain, but she was close behind them. They thought there would be no one to protect them from her at their grandmother's so they went on to find the medicine societies at Itiwana.

At the east edge of the village they stopped. They could hear all

---

[1] For the story see The Origin of the Medicine Societies, reserved for Zuni Ceremonial Tales.

the societies singing. They[1] had just come from Cipapolima, and they were all meeting in their society rooms. The Ahaiyute ran toward the house of Little Fire. The members were thinking of nothing but their ceremony. They paid no attention to the Ahaiyute. They slid down the ladder (without stopping to step rung by rung). They said, "My fathers, my mothers, is there any way to save us from the person who is following us?" "No, we don't know of any way to save you. Sit down here." They sat down in the middle of the floor. The dead person came to the hatchway. She called down, "Where are my husbands?" Four times she called. Then she came down. All the people were terrified when they saw her. The Ahaiyute ran out of the room as fast as they could.

They came to the room of Uhuhukwe. They slid down the ladder. They said, "My fathers, my mothers, how have you lived these days? Is there any way to save us from the person who is following us?" They answered, "Sit down here." They pointed behind the altar where the headmen sit, and the Ahaiyute went back of the altar and sat there. The dead person came to the hatchway, and she said, "Where are my husbands?" She called four times. Then she came down. The people were frightened. The Ahaiyute ran out.

They came to the room of Big Fire. They felt they would be safe there. They did not slide down the ladder. They said, "My people,[2] is there any way to save us from the person that is following us?" They said, "Go behind the altar. The White Bear will save you."[3] The Ahaiyute took seats behind the altar. They nudged each other and said, "My, I guess we're safe now." The dead person came to the hatchway. She called in, "Where are my husbands?" They answered, "There are no husbands of yours here." She said, "Yes, I saw them come in. They are in there." They answered, "Come in and get them." She called again, "Where are my husbands? Send them out to me." They answered, "Come in and get them." Four times she called, and then she came down the ladder. When the people saw the dead person they were terrified. The Ahaiyute ran out and came to the room of the Hunter's society.

They thought that in the Hunters's society they would be safe, for there were only men in that society. They said, "My people, how have you lived these days? Do you know any way to save us from the person who is following us?" They answered, "Sit behind the

---

[1] The beast gods, loc. cit.

[2] The narrator explained that the fuller form of address used before had not helped them so they abandoned it.

[3] The headmen of the medicine society who sit behind the altar are the representatives of White Bear, Wildcat, and Mountain Lion respectively.

altar. Wildcat will protect you." They went behind the altar and sat down. They nudged each other, and said, "Now we'll be safe." The dead person came to the hatchway. She called down, "Whoever is in there, send out my husbands." They answered, "We do not see your husbands here." "Yes, they are in your room." "Come in and get them." "Send them out to me." Four times she called for them, and then she came down the ladder. When they saw a Navaho dead person coming into the room, all the people were terrified. The Ahaiyute ran out as fast as they could. They ran to the Bedbug society. It was midnight, and the men and women were dancing. The Ahaiyute said, "My people, how have you lived these days? Do you know any way to save us from the person who is following us?" They answered, "Sit behind the altar. Mountain Lion will protect you." They went behind the altar and sat down. They nudged each other and said, "Now we'll be safe. Mountain Lion will save us. There is dancing here and they are using rattles."[1] The dead person came to the hatchway, and she called down, "Whoever is in there, send out my husbands." They answered, "We do not see your husbands here." "Yes, they are in your room." "Come down and get them." "Send them out to me." Four times she called for them. She came down the ladder. When the dancers saw a dead Navaho woman coming into the room, they were terrified, and stopped dancing. The Ahaiyute ran out as fast as they could.

They came to the Ciwanakwe society. Their dance was still going on in Ciwanakwe. The Ahaiyute came into the room, and all the women stopped their dancing to look at them, they were so ugly. The Ahaiyute said, "How have you lived these days, my people? Do you know any way to save us from the person who is following us?" The men of Ciwanakwe answered, "Go and sit with the women." They went over to sit by the women, and all the women drew away from them. Someone said, "They are the little Ahaiyute." The Ahaiyute heard them. They nudged each other, and they said, "We're safe now, sitting with the women." The dead person came to the hatchway. She called down, "Whoever is in there, send out my husbands." They answered, "We do not see your husbands in here." "Yes, they are in your room." "Come in and get them." "Send them to me." Four times she called. She came down the ladder. When they saw a dead Navaho woman they were terrified. She went directly to the place where the Ahaiyute were sitting among the women. They ran out as fast as they could.

They came to Ne'we·kwe. The members were all dancing drawing

---

[1] "The ghost would be overcome by the dance."

5

sickness from the people.[1] They were growling like bears, and they danced drawing out in their hands the sickness of all the people who had come for curing. The Ahaiyute were interested. They said, "My people, how have you lived these days? Do you know any way to save us from the person who is following us?" They answered, "Go and sit with the drummers." The Ahaiyute went over to the place where the choir was. They pretended they knew the songs and they made a show of singing with the choir and keeping time.[2] They nudged each other and said, "We are safe now. The singing will protect us." The dead person came to the hatchway. She called down, "Whoever is in there, send out my husbands." "We do not see your husbands here." "Yes. They are there." "Come in and get them." "Send them to me." Four times she called. She came down the ladder. When the people who were curing saw the Navaho dead person come into the room, they were terrified and stopped doctoring, and the choir stooped singing. The Ahaiyute ran out as fast as they could.

They came to Cuma·kwe. The women were dancing their dance[3]. The Ahaiyute came in and said, "How have you lived these days, my people? Do you know any way to save us from the person who is following us?" They answered, "Go into the middle of the line of dancers." They put them in the middle line of dancers, with two girls on one side and two on the other. The Ahaiyute danced.[4] They said, "Now we are safe for we are dancing." The dead person came to the hatchway, and she called down, "Where are my husbands?" They answered, "We do not see your husbands here." "Yes, they are in that room." They answered, "Come and get them." Four times she called, "Send out my husbands." She came down the ladder. When the people saw the dead Navaho woman come into the room, they were terrified and all the women who were dancing scattered. The Ahaiyute ran out as fast as they could.

They came to the room of the Snake Society. They were dancing the curing dance and the bow priest of the Snake Society was

---

[1] The differences in the performances in the Medicine Society rooms indicates the passing of the night. At any given hour all societies are supposed to be similarly engaged.

[2] The pantomine of their failure here is very humorous to the audience of the tale.

[3] Cuma·kwe's special dance with the women four abreast, and rhythmic movements of the hands which are clasped over an object held about breast high, and lowered in four successive rhythmic movements.

[4] Laughter at a pantomime of their awkwardness.

curing.[1] He drew out the cactus spines from the body of the sick person and vomited them upon the corn husk. The Ahaiyute watched him; they were interested. They said, "How have you lived these days, my people? Do you know how to save us from the person who is following us?" They answered, "Go and sit by the headman by the altar." They went and sat by the headman by the altar. They nudged each other and they said, "Now we are safe for the Bow Priest of the Snake society is curing." The dead person came to the hatchway, and she called down, "Where are my husbands?" They answered, "We do not see your husbands here." "Yes, they are in that room." "Come and get them." Four times she called, "Send out my husbands." She came down the ladder. When the people saw the dead Navaho woman come into the room, they were afraid and they scattered, and the Ahaiyute ran out as fast as they could.

They came to the room of the Knife society. In this room they were sitting quietly, resting after the curing dance. The Ahaiyute came in. They said, "How have you lived these days, my people? Do you know of any way to save us from this person who is following us?" The headman of the Knife society had supernatural power. He said to them, "Is it true that she is your wife?" No one else had talked in this way to the Ahaiyute, but the headman of the Knife society said, "It was not right, after she had become your flesh, to kill her." The Ahaiyute were ashamed. The headman said, "You two boys must think in your minds that you are brave men."[2] He sent men to bring the leather war bonnets[3] and they put them on the Ahaiyute. They brought also the war clubs (loaded at one end). The headman said, "It was wrong to kill this woman with whom you had had intercourse. Therefore carry out our directions. Take this stone knife. When she comes into the room, hit her with the war club. Hit her only once and kill her with the blow. Take the body to the west, and take her scalp with the stone knife, and call the rain.[4] Then lay her on her back. Do not lay her on her face. Say to her, 'Lie there and count the stars.' If she lies on her back, she will count the stars and never finish."[5]

The Ahaiyute stood in the center of the room, Younger Brother on the south side, and Elder Brother on the north side. The dead

---

[1] In ceremonies the bow priest of this society is their chief medicine man; this preeminence does not hold on other occasions.

[2] I. e. put on a show of bravery.

[3] Distinguishing regalia of the bow priests.

[4] Taking a scalp of itself calls the rains.

[5] Therefore never be free to trouble them again.

5*

person came to the top of the ladder. She called down, "Where are my husbands?" The headmen answered, "Come down and get them." She called four times, "Send them out to me." She came down the ladder. As she came down, the Ahaiyute hit her with the war club, and she fell down. They took her up and went out to the west. They took the stone knife and scalped her. They laid her down on her back, and they said, "Lie there and count the stars." She could not trouble them any more. They took up the scalp, and they returned to the room of the Knife Society. They laid the scalp on the roof.

The headman had made a broad meal road from the ladder to the altar. When the Ahaiyute came down the ladder, he said to them, "Look hard at this road of cornmeal. Perhaps something has happened to it." They looked and there were the tracks of Chaparral Cock. Younger Brother said, "It was coming in." Elder Brother said, "It was going out." So they quarreled. The headman said to them, "Look behind the altar." They looked, and there was the chaparral cock. Younger Brother took it in his arms, and he said, "My, it's pretty." Elder Brother stroked its feathers. He said, "It is pretty." He stretched out the wing feathers separately and then the tail feathers. Nobody could tell how the chaparral cock came to be behind the altar. The headman said, "Count the feathers." They counted and Younger Brother said, "There are twelve." The headman said, "So many days will there be of taboo (in the scalp dance)." The Ahaiyute did not know what he was saying. He said, "It is your wife. She has become the chaparral cock. Hang her scalp up from the roof."

Followed by the account of the institution of the scalp dance. reserved for Zuni Ceremonial Tales.

THE AHAIYUTE OBTAIN CEREMONIAL OBJECTS (8)
Notes, 290

The Ahaiyute lived with their grandmother at Eastern Road. The eagles had a nest at Pierced Rock, and the Ahaiyute went to this place to hunt. They were looking for feathers for their arrows. They did not like their arrows unfeathered; they wanted to make them pretty. They went to Pierced Rock and they saw the eagle flying from his nest. They said, "How shall we get feathers?" They could not get them. The eagle's cliff was too high for them to climb down to the nest from above. They sat on the ground and watched for the mother eagle to come home. After a long time they saw her coming with a dead fawn. They saw her carrying it in her claws.

They had a good idea: "We will kill a young deer, and the eagle will carry us to the nest like dead fawns." They went home. When they had had their supper they told their grandmother what they had seen. Their grandmother said, "Do not go there. There is no way to get down." They said, "Of course we always do what you say."

The next morning they told their grandmother that they were going to hunt and asked her to make them a lunch. She browned lumps of cornmeal in the ashes. Elder Brother carried the lunch. They started out to look for fawns. They went to Pierced Rock. One of them gave a call like the mother deer. A fawn thought it was his mother and ran toward them. They killed two fawns and skinned them whole. They hid the flesh of the deer and crawled into the skins. They lay down like two fawns in the shade of a tree near where the eagle was accustomed to sit.

Finally mother eagle saw them. They watched her flying nearer and nearer. "There she comes," they said. "Lie still, brother." She pounced on Younger Brother and carried him up to her nest. She laid him down by the nest. She dropped down again and took Elder Brother. She took him up also and dropped him down by the nest for her young ones. She sat back in the cave and watched the two dead fawns and her children, craning her neck, and thinking to herself, "What a nice dinner my young ones will have." She flew off, and the Ahaiyute lay very still as if they were dead. The young eagles came over to the fawns to pick out their eyes. Younger Brother said, "What are you going to do to me?" The eaglet jumped back. When she saw the fawn was as quiet as ever, she tried again, and again the fawn said loudly, "Ouch!" The little eaglet drew back, and Younger Brother said, "Let's get up and ask when their eagle mother will be back." They both got up and pulled off their fawn skins. The Ahaiyute said to the eaglets, "Where did your mother go?" "To hunt." "How long will she be gone?" "When the storm clouds come with the fine rain." "Where did your father go?" "To hunt." "How long will he be gone?" "When the storm clouds come with the big rain." They thought, "We had better take the feathers before the father and mother come." They killed the eaglets and took the feathers, and filled the fawn-skin bags with eagle feathers. They laid the eaglets out with their heads to the east.

They were ready to get down, but they couldn't find any way. They were frightened because they had already killed the eaglets and there was no way to escape from the eagles. Elder Brother said, "What shall we say to the mother eagle?" "We shall say that she had no right to bring us up here. We were sleeping in the shade and she brought us up."

Soon the mother eagle came and lit where she had been sitting before, and she saw that her eaglets were dead. "Who killed my children ?" The Ahaiyute sat on their fawn-skin bags full of feathers. They tried to hide them. She asked, "Who killed my children ?" Right away the Ahaiyute said, "We did. We thought you would never come back. They were starving so we thought that we might better kill them." "They had lots to eat when I left. I brought two young fawns." "No, we were the two fawns. You had no right to bring us up. We were sleeping in the shade." "I never brought up little ugly-looking things like you." She talked crossly to them. Younger Brother nudged Elder Brother to kill her on the spot, and he seized his bow and shot her with his arrow. Again they pulled the feathers out and put them in their fawn-skin bags. They hid the mother eagle and laid her out like a person.

They thought to themselves that they would wait for the father eagle. At last the father eagle came and sat at the entrance of the cave. He wondered where his young ones were or he thought his wife was still out hunting. He asked the boys, "Where are my eaglets ?" "We haven't seen them." "You must know. You are the only ones who have been here." They were angry and raised their bows and knocked him down too. Again they pulled out the feathers and pushed them into their bags. They were happy because they had so many feathers.

They were very hungry, and they kept looking to see how they could get down. They cried because they could not see any way. Squirrel climbed up to see what was the matter. They pretended they hadn't been crying. They said, "We didn't cry. We just looked down and were talking about how we could get food." "I heard you crying, don't deny it. I have a way to feed you." He went down to his house again, and looked for something to eat. He took pumpkin seeds that had been ground in the metate and mixed them in water. He took some up in a little bit of gourd which he held in his mouth. The Ahaiyute looked down and saw him coming, and they thought to themselves, "Such a little bit!. One will have a little drink and one won't have a bit." Squirrel brought it up and said, "Here, boys, eat it." They ate and ate and ate, and they had all they could hold. They thanked him. Squirrel said, "I will get pine-tree seeds from Kachina Village and plant them below the cliff so they will grow up." He went to Kachina Village.

They were dancing there. All the kachinas stopped dancing and said, "Our grandfather is coming." They asked him to sit down. "What is it that you have come to ask ?" "These Ahaiyute went up to kill the eagles. They pretended they were young fawns and mother eagle took them up to her nest. They cannot get down and they are starving. They have a grandmother. I have come to ask for pine-tree seeds to plant under the eagle cliff." They brought the seeds and gave them to Squirrel. He said, "Thank you, be happy."

He started back in the evening. He brought the pine seeds back and planted them way down at the foot of the cliff. He went into his own house. The next morning the boys were sleeping in the eagle's house and their grandmother was wondering where they were. When they woke at sunrise a tall pine was growing up to their very ledge, with great branches strong enough to bear a man. Squirrel was singing and making it grow. He came up and told them to climb down. The Ahaiyute put their fawn-skin bags on their shoulders and climbed down. They were happy and thanked Squirrel. They said, "Now we will feather our arrows when we get home." Squirrel said, "Be careful, don't go where any kind of flowers are growing, sunflowers, or any summer flowers, or your feathers will all become birds and fly away." "All right. What any one tells us to do, we always do it."

They came to the first patch of flowers and they went around it; they came to the second patch of flowers, and they went around it again. At the third they were pretty good too, but when they came to the fourth, Younger Brother said, "Our sacks are tied tight; I don't believe what Squirrel said." "All right." They went right through the flowers. As soon as they came to the middle, both of the fawn bags burst and summer birds of all sorts flew out. They tried to catch them, but the bags were empty. They thought that there were still some feathers left in their sacks, but when they reached into them the bags were empty.

When they got home their grandmother said, "Where have you been all night?" They were ashamed to come from hunting without anything, so they said, "Oh, we just slept somewhere." Again the next day they went to hunt. They said, "If we find more eagle feathers, let's not go into the flower patch." They looked for eagles, but they couldn't find any because they had not kept their promise the first time. At night they went home. That evening after the evening meal they said to their grandmother, "You always tell us about the Saiyałia who lives at Hecoktakwi." "You boys must not go to any of those places," said their grandmother. "I don't want either of you boys killed. It is dangerous." "We always mind whatever you say." But they said, "Just as soon as you get up in the morning, you must put up a lunch for us." "All right." Their grandmother browned cornmeal balls in the ashes. After the morning meal they took the lunch and went out. Elder Brother asked,

"Which way shall we go?" "To Hecoktakwi. We asked grandmother about those kachinas last night. Don't mind what our grandmother says." "All right, let's go there."

They went. It took them a long time and it was dark when they got there. They heard the Saiyaɫia in the kiva initiating three or four little (Saiyaɫia) boys.[1] "Let's go in," the Ahaiyute said. "If they push us out, it's all right." They peeped in and saw them whipping the boys. Elder Brother said, "They might whip us." "It won't hurt." They went in. The Saiyaɫia looked up. The Ahaiyute looked different from their little boys, but they let them stand there. Nobody asked them to sit down. One of the Saiyaɫia came up to them and took Younger Brother by the arm and led him over to be whipped. They whipped and whipped him until he was dead. Then the Saiyaɫia went to Elder Brother and said, "Your brother went to sleep." They took him to be whipped, and they whipped and whipped till he was dead too. Then the Saiyaɫia brought out the stone knife to cut off their arms and legs to put into the pot for their little newly-initiated Saiyaɫia to eat. They keep turning the pot while they finished whipping the little Saiyaɫia boys, and after they were done they served the flesh to the little Saiyaɫia boys. They ate their flesh, but their voices were still alive. The Saiyaɫia ate with their children. When they had finished, the little boys went home and the Saiyaɫia stayed in the kiva. The Saiyaɫia heard a voice: "What you have been eating was dung. What you have been eating was dung." They could not see anybody. The voice was coming from one of the yucca blades they had whipped with. They broke it, and then they heard again, "What you have been eating was dung. What you have been eating was dung." It was another yucca blade. They broke that. All over the room voices were calling, "What you have eaten was dung. What you have eaten was dung." They ran to every corner trying to stop the voices but they could not. The Saiyaɫia were sneezing and their noses were running, and finally out jumped the Ahaiyute from their noses. The Saiyaɫia sneezed them out. The Ahaiyute caught up their bows and arrows and shot the Saiyaɫia, and they turned into deer.[2]

The Ahaiyute took off the deer's skin whole and they stuffed the big buck with twigs and leaves and set him on his feet. They dressed themselves and tied on strips of shredded yucca which they tore from the (Saiyaɫia) whips, passing the strips over their shoulders and crossing them on their chests. When they had finished, Younger Brother said to Elder Brother, "Let's go through their houses. They

[1] "There are only a few Saiyaɫia so they initiate very few boys at a time."
[2] It is a fundamental Zuni belief that kachinas when killed become deer.

might have something we want." So they went way down into their
cellar and there they kept their rain-making things, the lightning
frame and the arrows and the thunder stones. They took those all
out and laid them across their left arms. Elder Brother said, "You
lead; I will drag the stuffed deer, and you call out to grandmother
that something big is chasing us." His brother said, "All right." Just
as he was getting near the house he called, "Help! Somebody is
running after us!" Their grandmother was parching corn in the pot.
She set it down and wiped ashes over one side of her face and soot
over the other,[1] and she picked up a big stick from the fireplace and
ran out. Ahaiyute said, "There she comes, funny looking!" She
cried, "Where is the fight?" "Here it is!" She hit that deer, and she
hit and hit till she was exhausted. The Ahaiyute laughed and
laughed. Their grandmother cried, "You bad boys! You are always
up to something!" She was angry.

After they had eaten the Ahaiyute asked their grandmother to
clear out one room so that they could play their rain-making game.
"Don't do that," she said. "Those are what the Saiyalia use to
make rain, and the Uwanami will come and take them away from
you." They said, "No, we will play the rain-making game." Their
grandmother cleaned the room and took everything out. They shot
the lightning frame, and rolled the thunder stone and shot the
arrows. The lightning came and the big clouds rolled up. It began to
rain. It rained harder and harder. At last the water poured in
through the hatchway. Their grandmother stood up to her knees in
water. She called out, "Please stop, my grandchildren." They went
on playing the rain-making game and they shot the lightning frame
and rolled the thunder stone and shot the arrows. Their grandmother called out, "Grandchildren, grandchildren, stop, stop!"
She was standing to her thighs in water. She called out, "Please stop,
my grandchildren." They went on playing the rain-making game;
they shot the lightning frame and rolled the thunder stone and shot
the arrows. Their grandmother called out, "Grandchildren, grandchildren, stop, stop!" She was standing to her middle in water, and
she called, "Please stop, my grandchildren!" They went on playing
the rain-making game; they shot the lightning frame and rolled the
thunder stone and shot the arrows. Then she called out, "Grandchildren, grandchildren, please stop!" She was standing up to her
neck in water. She called once more, "Please stop, my grandchildren!" They went right on playing the rain-making game; they
shot the lightning frame and rolled the thunder stone and shot

---

[1] A face painting associated with impersonations of the dead.

the arrows. They did not hear her call any more. They looked in and only her little knob of hair was bobbing up and down on the water.

The younger said, "We had better stop. Grandmother isn't there." They climbed down and broke a hole through the house wall to let the water out. Their grandmother turned her head on her shoulder and talked (in baby talk), "I'm afraid of you, grandchildren." They said, "Look at her! She is coming out all right." "Please don't play those games any more, my grandchildren. I was drowned. If you go on, you won't have any grandmother any more."

The water went down, and they ate the midday meal. After they had finished they went to Corn Mountain and looked again for an eagle to feather their arrows. They climbed the mountain and they saw a nest they thought they could get to. Younger Brother said, "Will you hand me down?" "How could you get up again?" "Some way. If you won't go, I'll go." Elder Brother took hold of his brother's hand and climbed down to the eagle's nest. When he was half way down, his brother could not hold on any longer. He called out, "Oh, I'm tired." They lost hold, and Elder Brother lost his balance and fell the rest of the way to the eagle's ledge. He fainted. Younger Brother called, "I didn't mean to, brother." His brother was angry, and he did not answer. Then Younger Brother called, "Are you still there?" Again he did not answer.

He said to himself, "I'm going to kill these two eaglets." He asked them, "When does your mother come home?" They answered, "She comes with the fine rain." "When does your father come home?" "He comes with the big rain." He took his arrows and killed the eaglets and put the feathers in the fawn-skin bag. His brother on top called, "Pull them all out, don't leave one." His brother was sitting with his hands clasped over his knees and his head in his arms. Elder Brother called, "I'm ready. Pull me up." "How can I pull you up? How can you carry the bag?" "I can do it this way." He tied it with yucca fibre crossed on his chest and he tried to jump up and catch his brother's hand, but he could not jump high enough. He cried. Another squirrel heard him, and he came and saw Younger Brother at the top of the cliff, who said, "My brother is way down there; he wanted to get eagle feathers and now he can't get up." "I have a way." He went down and said, "Get on my back and I will carry you up." Ahaiyute said, "I'm too heavy." "That's all right. Don't talk back to me, or I won't carry you up." "All right, I will get on your back." He got on Squirrel's back and he carried him up. Squirrel said, "You have everything you wanted, but if you go through the flowers you will lose all your feathers." "We know that. The other Squirrel Man told us that."

"All right. I have told you again." They went towards home, and they were as careful as they could be. As soon as they saw flowers they went far around to avoid them, no matter how long the road was. It took them all the evening to get home. They got home after sunset. They were happy because they were home and had eagle feathers to feather their arrows. That's why one likes to feather his arrows with valuable eagle feathers just as the Ahaiyute did. That's why there are eagles still in the cliffs where the Ahaiyute found them, and pine trees growing in this country now.

VARIANT (3)
Published only in abstract
Notes, 292

This version begins with the tale of Atocle Woman's lousing the Ahaiyute and biting their necks to kill them. She roasted and ate them. They left their voices in her pots and baskets and called out that she had eaten dung. They caused her to eject them by sneezing, upon which she fell dead.

Upon being killed, like all kachinas, she became a deer. They stole all her rain-making ceremonial objects and stuffed her as a huge deer to fool their grandmother. They played with her rain-making objects and caused a flood. Their grandmother drowned:

"There was their grandmother floating on top of the water. Her knob of hair was bobbing up and down. This is why when anybody has two boys they mind just like the Ahaiyute."

III. TALES OF COURTSHIP

THE RABBIT HUNTRESS

Notes, 295

A(3)

The Ahaiyute lived on Twin Mountain and Atocle Woman at Hecokta. The people were living in Itiwana. A priest had an only daughter who helped him in his work. She did all the work of a man. Her father was not able to go hunting, so she said, "My father, I will go and bring in rabbits." That night her father made the high fur moccasins for her. He sprinkled water on the skin, and spread sand over it (to give an even moisture). He cut them and sewed them.

Next morning the girl started toward Hecokta. She did not tell her father that she was going in that direction. She found a great many rabbits. She killed twelve, and she killed one deer. She killed more than a man's good catch. She had planned to go home that night, but when she killed so much, she thought she would go up into the mountains and stay all night. She thought to herself, "I will find a cave and spend the night." She climbed the mountain and found a cave just big enough for her to get into. She went in. She thought, "This is a good place. I shall skin a rabbit and stay here tonight." She built a fire inside close to the mouth of the cave, and she roasted one of her rabbits and ate it. She was still eating when she heard Atocle calling in the distance. Atocle was calling, "I smell rabbits cooking. I smell a human being." The girl's heart beat violently. She put wood on the fire to make it blaze up and keep Atocle out. Atocle Woman came close to the mouth of the cave, and she said, "Ha! I am coming in and eat you up. Give me a rabbit." Atocle was afraid to come in past the fire; she was afraid she would burn her hair. Atocle called, "Throw out the rabbit." The girl threw out the rabbit, and Atocle stuffed it whole into her mouth. Again she called, "Throw out a rabbit." The girl threw out another rabbit and Atocle Woman ate it whole. She called out again, "Throw me a rabbit." Again the girl threw out a rabbit and she ate it whole. She called for her rabbits till they were all gone. Then she said, "Give me more." The girl answered, "I have no more." "Throw out your clothing." She took off her woman's belt;

she thought Atocle wanted it to wear, but instead she swallowed it
as she had swallowed the rabbits. Atocle called, "My, isn't this good!
Throw out more clothing." She took off her moccasins and Atocle
swallowed them. Atocle called out, "This is very good. Throw out
more!" She took off her black knit leggins and she threw them out.
Atocle ate them. She said, "Now this is good. Throw out more."
Poor girl, she took off her black woman's dress and she threw that
out. Atocle ate it in one mouthful. Poor girl, she was holding herself
naked in the corner of the cave. Atocle took her crooked stick, and
she thrust it in to the mouth of the cave and tried to hook the girl's
head with her stick. She thrust it in again and tried to hook her
arm. She thrust it in again and tried to hook her leg. The girl was
crying in the far corner and the stick would not reach to where
she was.

On Twin Mountain the Ahaiyute's grandmother said to her
grandchildren, "Your grandmother[1] is going to eat somebody. Go
and save the girl." They took their bows and arrows and they
started. When they came near to the cave at Hecokta they hid
close by. Atocle called out to the girl, "Now I shall come in and
get you." She stuck her head into the mouth of the cave, but it
was too small and she could not enter. Younger Brother said, "Now
let's shoot her." They let fly their arrows, and she fell, a deer.[2]

The Ahaiyute went to the mouth of the cave. When the girl saw the
youths she covered her genitals with her two hands. The Ahaiyute
said to her, "Where are your clothes?" She said, "Atocle Woman
has eaten my clothes. She ate all my rabbits, and when she had
finished she asked for my clothes and ate those. Every time she
called for more, I threw out another garment. She ate even my fur
moccasins." The Ahaiyute said, "We will get your clothes for you.
They are inside her stomach. We'll get them." They skinned the
deer and opened its stomach. There were the rabbits. They took
them out, eleven of them. The girl was happy. She thought to
herself, "Now I shall be able to take home the rabbits I killed."
But the Ahaiyute said, "Don't take home these rabbits. They are
no good any more. We will kill other rabbits for you." They threw
them into the fire and burned them. They took out the girl's
clothes; they took out the woman's belt and the fur moccasins and
the black knit leggins and the woman's dress. They gave them to
the girl and she put them on.

The Ahaiyute said, "Sit down and rest, and we will hunt rabbits

---

[1] The Ahaiyute were in the habit of calling their grandmother "Atocle"
in jest.

[2] It is a fundamental belief in Zuni that the kachinas if killed become deer.

for you." The girl sat down and rested, and the Ahaiyute went out and each killed twelve rabbits. When they had twenty-four rabbits they brought them to her and they said, "We will take them home for you to your father and mother."

The girl's father and mother had been worried all night. They had been praying that she had gone to the mesas to the south. They heard someone coming. It was their daughter, and she came in with lots of rabbits and the two youths following her. Her father and mother were overjoyed. They said, "Why didn't you come last night ?" She said, "I went toward Hecokta and I killed twelve rabbits and I thought that next morning I would kill some more. So I went up the mountain till I found a cave. I went in and roasted a rabbit to eat. Just as I was eating I heard Atocle coming. She came to the mouth of the cave and called for my rabbits. I gave her all I had and she ate them. Then she called for my clothing, and when I gave them to her, she swallowed every one. She poked her crook into the cave and tried to drag me out, but she could not. She tried to force her way in, but the mouth of the cave was too small. Just then these youths came up and shot her and she turned into a deer. They skinned her and opened the stomach and took out the rabbits and the clothes she had swallowed. They threw the rabbits into the fire and they went out and hunted for me. They killed all these rabbits. These are the youths who saved me."

Her mother and father greeted the Ahaiyute who had saved the life of their daughter. The mother set out the paper-bread and the food and they ate together. The father kept thinking to himself, "If one of these youths marries our daughter I shall have help. They are good hunters." When they had finished their meal, he said, "I have something to say. Perhaps one of you will marry my daughter." Before the words were out of his mouth, Elder Brother answered, "I will." Younger Brother was angry. He gave Elder Brother a black look, and he said, "Very well. I shall go home to my grandmother. She will be waiting for us to come." He got up and went home. As he went along he thought, "All boys get married, and the girls take the flour to the boy's mother's house. When my brother brings his wife to my grandmother's with the flour, I shall tell my grandmother not to speak to them. As for me, I won't speak to either of you, for I am jealous." He got home. His grandmother said, "Where's brother ?" "He's over in Itiwana. He's married the priest's daughter that we saved last night. Atocle ate her eleven rabbits and her clothes and tried to hook her with her crook and to force her way into the cave. We shot Atocle, and we cut open her stomach and took out the rabbits and the clothes. The girl was going to take home the rabbits, but we told her 'No', and we threw them on the fire and hunted twice as many for her. We took her home and her mother and father were glad. Her father said, 'Will one of you marry my daughter ?' I didn't have a chance to speak. My brother said right off, 'I will', and my brother married the girl. When the girl comes to bring the flour, do not say a word to either of them." His grandmother said, "Very well."

Next day about sunset they came. The girl had the basket of flour. Younger Brother had heard that it is always the second day that the girls bring the flour to their mother-in-laws so he was watching for them. He saw them in the distance and he ran in and told his grandmother, "Grandmother, they're coming. Now don't say a word to them." Again he went out. He saw them nearer. He ran back again, "Grandmother, they're coming. They're coming now. Don't speak to them." He waited a little while and he ran up the ladder again. He poked his head out. They were right there on the roof. He went back down the ladder. His grandmother was roasting corn. He said to her, "Don't speak to them."

They came to the top of the ladder and they said, "Ca. lift me down[1]." Before the grandmother had a chance to get to the ladder Younger Brother called out "Yes," and he scrambled up the ladder and handed down the flour himself. His grandmother said, "Well, indeed! you didn't even want me to speak to them!"

They both waited on the girl. The grandmother had a pot of venison cooking on the fire. She brought out her paper-bread and set out the stew. They ate, and when they had finished, they said, "Thank you." The grandmother took the basket the girl had brought and emptied the flour in the inner room and filled it again with dried venison. She piled it carefully on the basket. She went to a cavity in the wall and took out the stone that closed it. She took out a red-and-black-bordered white blanket and a black woman's dress. She put them down on a dancer's kilt and folded it over them and put them on top of the meat on the basket.

Elder Brother and the girl went home to Itiwana. When the girl was tired carrying her basket Elder Brother carried it for her. They reached Itiwana. Her mother was very pleased with the dried venison because they had had no son to hunt deer for them.

Elder Brother lived in Itiwana with his wife. His wife became pregnant. In a few days she had twin boys. They were very happy. Elder Brother ran to his grandmother on Twin Mountain to tell her

---

[1] That is, "Take what I am carrying." This is the usual greeting when anyone is bringing something.

to come to make the sand-bed for the babies[1]. He got there. He was so happy he skipped all the steps on the ladder. His grandmother was roasting corn. He called out, "I have twin babies in Itiwana. Come and make the sand-bed for them." His grandmother was so excited and happy, she forgot her back-shawl, and she hobbled along on her cane as fast as she could to Itiwana. Younger Brother, too, was pleased that his brother had twin boys.

Elder Brother ran on ahead of his grandmother. He got home. His wife was waiting for the grandmother to come to make the sand-bed. His grandmother was still a long way behind. He was impatient. He went to his wife's room and he got a straw. He inhaled through the straw and his grandmother was there beside him. She had been just bobbing up and down, too tired to make any progress.

He went down the ladder and his grandmother followed him. The girl's mother had the hot water ready. The grandmother came in and she rubbed up against the people[2] in the room and she said, "Oh, I am so glad to hear about my grandchildren!" She went over to the babies and she rubbed up against them and she said, "You look like your father." She was so happy she could hardly talk.

She took soap-weed root and she made the froth. She washed the babies. She prayed, "Father Sun, make these boys grow up strong and healthy all their lives." She washed their hair and rinsed it. She washed their bodies, and while they were still wet, she took ashes and rubbed them with it.[3] Ahaiyute ran out to bring in sand for the sand-bed. She dried the children on a woman's ragged dress and wrapped them in it. She took a hot flat stone from the fire and drew it through the sand-beds to make them hot. She mixed the sand up with her arms to give it an even heat. When it was hot, she put the stone back in the fireplace to heat for another warming. She put down corn-ears for the babies at the outside of their sand-bed. She took the babies and put them in their sand-bed. Over them she put the blanket. When the babies were in their bed, she made the bed for the mother. When it was ready the mother came and lay down upon it on her chest.[4] The mother and the babies stayed in their sand-beds for four days. The girl's mother helped the grandmother to warm the sand-beds when they got cool. Every evening the grandmother went to her home.

---

[1] The duty of the father's mother.
[2] An affectionate form of greeting.
[3] This is still invariable Zuni custom, to insure hairlessness. Of course it produces sores on the babies' skin.
[4] So that the milk will flow readily.

The third day Ahaiyute went out to hunt so that his wife would have fresh meat when she came out from the sand-bed. He went down to the mesas to the south of Zuni. He killed a big deer. He brought it in the night before to have it all ready. They were overjoyed to have the babies and the deer.

The fourth night the grandmother did not go to her house. The girl's mother set the pot in the fireplace and cut up the venison. She put it in the pot. She soaked white corn and skinned it in the mealing stone, and put the shelled corn in the pot. They let it boil all night. Early in the morning before earliest dawn the grandmother woke up and built the fire so the others would wake. The mother of the babies woke, and then her mother. The grandmother put water on the fire to heat and she threw cedar twigs into it.[1] The grandmother took one of the twin babies with the ear of corn that had lain beside it, and the girl's mother took the other baby with the ear of corn that had lain beside it. Before sunrise they went out and stood facing the east. The grandmother prayed and said, "Father Sun, we are bringing these babies to show you. They were born in our house four days ago. We are bringing these babies to show you to ask that you will give them health and good fortune all their lives." They took prayer meal and scattered it toward the sun.

They came back to the house. The grandmother washed the heads of the babies, and she rinsed them and prayed, "Father Sun, make these boys grow up strong and healthy all their lives." She washed their bodies and she rubbed ashes over them while they were still wet. She dried them on an old woman's-dress and wrapped them in it. She laid them on the floor and heated the water to wash their mother. She took a brew of cedar-water to the mother to drink. She brushed the sand from the sand-bed into a ring and put a stump-seat in the middle. The mother of the babies came and sat upon it. The grandmother took the pot of cedar water and set it beside her. She took a gourd and poured the water over her and washed her body with her hand. The mother of the babies stood, and she washed her legs. When she had finished she went to the antlers on the wall and took down the girl's dress, and her belt, and her shawl, and her black knit leggins. She brought them to her and she put them on. The grandmother gathered up the sand and carried it up the ladder to the roof.[2] She took it all out. The mother of the babies helped her mother to set out the

---

[1] To give it a sweet smell, and to stimulate milk.

[2] Her grandson could not help her with this, for to touch it would make him womanish.

feast. They sat down and ate. They were all very happy. They finished, and the grandmother was anxious to start for home. She said, "Thank you." They gave her a great pile of paper-bread in a blanket, and sweet Indian corncakes (hepaloḵa). She had no way to carry a bowl of meat-stew, so the mother of the girl wrapped a fore-leg of the deer and put it with the paper-bread in the blanket. She started home.

Younger Brother was watching for her. He saw her coming a long way off. He ran out to meet her so that she would not be tired. He ran up to her, and he panted, "You here, grandmother? You tired?" "Of course I'm tired. I'm bringing you fine corn cakes, my child." "Let me carry home the bundle. Alas, don't hurry." He took the paper-bread and the sweet corncakes and the deer's leg wrapped in the blanket and he ran home. His grandmother came on as fast as she could. She wanted to get home for she knew what good presents were waiting for her there. Her grandchild reached home and built a fire and made a deep bed of coals. He cut a slice from the fore-leg and spread it on the coals and cooked it. His grandmother came in and they ate. She had two breakfasts that morning. They were pleased with the presents, especially with the sweet corn cakes.

In Itiwana the twins grew up in one day big enough to play with the other children. On the fourth day they were old enough to go across the river to play. They used to pull off a child's arm, or his ear, and stick it back on again. Every day they did this, and the children went home and told their parents. Their parents saw that the boys had done no harm to their children, but they thought that someday they would get the children's arms and ears mixed up and they would look ridiculous. They said to their children, "Do not play with those boys." The children continued to play with them.

The Sun was angry that they continued to do this. One day when they pulled off a boy's arm and tried to put it back, the Sun interfered so that it was impossible to put it back. The children all ran back to their parents and they said, "A boy has been all pulled to pieces." The people ran out where the boys had been playing, and the twins ran home. They found the boy that the twins had pulled to pieces. They said, "We must make proclamation that these twins shall be killed on the fourth day." When they had gone home, the Sun came down and put the little boy together again. The people were glad, but they thought, "Perhaps next time the children will be pulled in pieces and will not come together again." The bow priest made proclamation and he said, "My people, on the fourth day these twins shall be killed. They have done evil things."

When the fourth day came Ahaiyute had bows and arrows ready for them. He dressed them as he himself was dressed, with dancer's sash and leather hood.[1] He told them to go out and wait for the people who were coming to kill them. He said, "Do not be afraid. You shall not really die." They went out. They walked down toward the river and people shot at them and they died. The people left them where they fell[2] and returned to their houses.

As soon as the people had gone toward their homes, the priest, the grandfather of the twins, went to Pekwin. He entered. He greeted him. Pekwin said, "What is it that you have come to say?" "I have come to tell your people that they have sent away my grandchildren, and now they must make the games for them: lapotciwe, and hidden ball, coliwe, and kick-sticks.[3] They must make also little bows and arrows, and fasten to them bits of petrified wood. They must make these for my grandchildren, and for their father and for their uncle. Their father will take them to live at the place which he has appointed."

Therefore he had proclamation made: "My people, you will make the games for the twins: lapotciwe, and hidden ball, and coliwe, and kick-sticks. Every year we shall think of these youths, and make them fresh hearts." The bow priest went down from the roofs, and the people worked on the games for the twins. Pekwin went to every house to see that everything was in readiness. He went the rounds the second time, and he saw that there was nothing missing. He went to the house of the mother of the twins. Their father was there, and Pekwin told him, "Everything is ready." He answered, "Tell them to bring everything to this house." Pekwin went around the village and gathered everything and brought them to the house of the mother of the twins. Ahaiyute said to his wife, "When evening comes, you too shall go with us. We are not allowed to live in this place. You shall come and make the road for us (with prayer-meal). Walk ahead and lead us, so that this evening we may go to the places that are appointed."

That evening the twins were alive again. They walked to their house. The people saw them, and they said, "Those twins had supernatural power. They are alive. They will live here again, and they will continue to kill our children." In their own house, the twins had evening meal with their father and mother just before sunset. When they had finished their mother dressed herself and put on an embroidered ceremonial blanket. She took a pottery

---

[1] The bonnet of the bow priests.

[2] "Because they knew they had supernatural power."

[3] For the games of the Ahaiyute, see Stevenson 317 sq.

6*

basket of prayer-meal in her hand and she led the way. The twins and their father took their games on their left arms, and just as they left the house their uncle came from his home. They gave him his games and he stepped into line and went with them. They started. The mother made the road to the outskirts of the village, and she threw the meal outward, and went back to her home. She was very sad.[1]

The Ahaiyute and the twin children went out from the village toward the south. They came to Wool Mountain and their father said to the younger of the twins, "This is where you shall live (go in.)" They came to Panitanima, (also to the south of Zuni) and he said to the elder of the twins, "This is where you shall live." They went on toward the east, and they came to Corn Mountain, and the father said, "This is where I shall live." They went on toward the east, and they came to Eastern Road. The younger brother of their father said, "This is where I shall live." The grandmother went on alone toward the west,[2] and she came to Twin Mountain. She said, "This is where I shall live." That is how they each found their homes. And that is why every year the people make the games for the Ahaiyute. One year they renew the hearts of the elder pair of Twins, and the next year the hearts of the younger pair of Twins.[3] If the people had not fought them and expelled them from the village, they would still have remained nearby, and played their dangerous games.

B(7)

The people were living at Matsaka. An old man and an old woman lived with their granddaughter. It was the middle of winter. The old man was too old to hunt and they never had any rabbits to eat. The girl talked to her grandfather and she said, "I would like to have a rabbit to eat. If I were a boy I could go hunting." "It can't be helped. You are a girl. We can't have any rabbits." The snow was waist deep on the ground and the girl said, "It is just the time to go hunting. There is lots of snow." At last her grandfather said, "All right." She put up a lunch and started out to the northwest. She came to Hecokta. By sunset she had killed only two rabbits and the snow was falling thicker than ever. She lost her way in the snow storm. She got into a canyon and there she found a cave. She

---

[1] None of them are sprinkled with meal because they wear no masks.

[2] Though it is not stated, each one is supposed to remain at his shrine, and the others go on without him.

[3] That is, make new images of these supernaturals.

squeezed her way in. She put her rabbits down on her blanket and she went out to get wood. She brought it in and made a fire in the cave. She sat down and took off her clothes and dried them. She had only stockings on. Long after dark she heard someone calling. She went out and called back, "Here I am." She heard the cry again. "Come up here," she cried. She heard the cry again. It was Atocle. She was frightened. Pretty soon Atocle got to the mouth of the cave. Her gray hair was streaming over her face. She had a big basket on her back. Her eyes were bulging and she carried a crook. She said, "Give me something to eat." The girl threw her a rabbit. She ate that whole. The girl threw out another rabbit. She ate that whole too. She said, "Give me something more to eat," and the girl threw out her overshoes. She ate those whole and she said, "Give me something more to eat." So the girl threw out her stockings and her dress and her belt and her back scarf and her blanket. At last she was naked. Atocle said, "I am going to eat you now." She tried and tried to get in but the entrance to the cave was too small and she could not. She tried to hook the girl with her crook. She said, "Wait a minute, I will get you yet."

Up on Twin Mountain, the Ahaiyute were living with their grandmother. She heard Atocle banging at the cave. She told her grandchildren, "You boys go up and kill Atocle. She is trying to get a girl in a cave. Take your bows and arrows." The Ahaiyute went off as fast as they could. They knocked Atocle down with a club and they went to the cave and looked in. There was the girl all naked. She covered her genitals with her hands. They said, "Where are your clothes?" "Atocle ate them." They went to Atocle and cut open her stomach and took the clothes out. They were wet. They scraped them clean with a stick and gave them to the girl. They picked out the two rabbits and scraped them clean also and they said, "No, we won't give these to the girl. We will leave them for Coyote." The girl said, "All right."

Next morning they started back home. The Ahaiyute killed lots of rabbits for her and she carried them on the end of her stick. There were lots of rabbits, thirty or forty. Just after sunset they got home. The old man and the old woman threw their arms around the girl. They had thought she was dead. She was happy to be home and she skinned a rabbit and cooked it for their supper. The Ahaiyute stayed and ate with them and after they had eaten, the grandfather said, "You were almost killed." Elder Brother said, "It was I that saved your grandchild's life. Let her be my wife." So he stayed and married the girl and every day he went out to hunt for rabbits.

The girl had twin boys. In four days they were grown and she wanted their father to make bows and arrows for them. He said, "If I do that it would be dangerous." He would not make them for them. After four or five days, the two boys were out playing and they went to Eastern Road where the two (other Ahaiyute) had their home. They were glad to see the two boys. Their grandmother brought out broiled wood rats and mush balls and gave them something to eat. Afterwards the four boys played together, running the stick race. After that they played games.[1] Then the Ahaiyute gave each one a bow and arrow and a kick-stick, a stone knife and a turquoise rabbit stick and they went home again.

After their evening meal they showed their father what they had received. He said, "Where did you get these ?" "At Eastern Road." The father knew that it was dangerous. One of the boys sat down. He cut his brother in two with the stone knife which the Ahaiyute had given him. His mother cried. Right away he stood up again. He was alive again. The other one took the stone knife and he cut his brother in half. All night they played, doing this to each other. Their father said, "Never do this to an Indian boy." The elder brother said, "No, we will not." Next morning they went out playing. There were lots of children and they followed them. The twin boys cut each other in two and they stood up again whole. The children said, "Do it to me. Do it to me!" "No. My father said, 'No, you must never do it to an Indian boy.' " They said, "Do it just the same." "Perhaps it would kill you. You would not come to life again. We are different from you. Perhaps when we cut you in two you would stay dead." "Do it anyway." "But if one of you dies we shall get into trouble." At last the elder twin said, "All right. I will cut you in two." He took the stone knife and cut one of the boys in two. He took the stone knife again and cut another boy in two. He cut another and another. They all lay there dead. There was only one child left. An old man was coming by, bringing food in from the east. Just as he got there, the last boy ran away and the man went on to the town and called out that the twin boys had killed all the children. All the people went out and got the bodies and put them together and brought them into their own houses. The people were angry. They wanted to kill the twin boys because of what they had done to their children.

In his own house Ahaiyute said to his wife, "We (I and my children) must go away from here. If any man, rich or poor, wants to marry you, marry him and be happy. I cannot have children by you. I am a raw person and my children are dangerous." His wife

[1] The narrator abbreviated the account at this point.

said, "I will go with you." "No, you can't. We must go now. The people will come and try to find us. I will go to Corn Mountain and the boys will go to Turquoise Mine near Santa Fe."

The people came to their house to try to kill them but they had gone and the people did not know where they went. The girl stayed in her own house and that winter she married again. Her new husband killed deer and rabbits. One night the Navahos came and the woman and her husband killed the Navahos and took their scalps and made the war dance, (because she had been the wife of Ahaiyute).

Her husband hunted deer every day. One day while he was gone, his wife died. When he came home they had buried her in the graveyard. The man went to the graveyard and stayed there with his head in his arms. He could not eat. For three days he watched by her grave.[1]

THE GIRL WHO REQUIRES A SCALP OF HER SUITORS (7)

Notes, 298

Published only in abstract

AHAIYUTE MARRIES THE BOW PRIEST'S DAUGHTER (8)

Notes, 299

The people were living at Matsaḳa. The bow priest had a daughter who never went out. She wove black women's-dresses and white blankets and did the grinding. She never went out even to see the dances. She was old enough to marry.

It was ko'uptconawe (the time of the winter kachina dance series). Every four days they danced their prettiest dances: first tcakwena, then the mixed dance (wotemła). Every day they were dancing. The bow priest said to his daughter, "My daughter, go out to the plaza during this ko'uptconawe. Be like the other girls." She said nothing; she did not refuse. Every day she stayed indoors weaving black women's-dresses and white blankets, making baskets and grinding. Her father thought he would not speak to her about it again. She stayed in always, she only went out to ease herself. Her father thought, "If my daughter married like other girls, I should have help in the fields. I am tired of working alone." But she did not change; for a whole year she did not marry.

[1] Followed by Orpheus tale. Not recorded. See Index, Vol. II, *Orpheus* for the tale.

Her father thought, "I shall make proclamation for a rabbit hunt with the women.[1] My daughter will be given a jack-rabbit[2] and in this way she will get a sweetheart." He went to the housetops and called, "My people, now it is time for us to have a rabbit hunt with the women. In three days the women shall have the lunches ready and whatever rabbits we catch we shall give to the women." On the third day they were grinding for paper-bread and for sweet Indian corncake. Her mother said to the bow priest's daughter, "My dear, grind for the corncake, like the other girls." She said nothing. On the third evening the bow priest made proclamation again. He said, "My people, we shall meet for the rabbit hunt on the west side of A'mosi." He came down.

That evening everybody set sweet Indian corncake (hepaloķa) to bake, but the bow priest's daughter did not make one. Her father said to her, "I will dress you for the hunt in a new black woman's-dress and new belt and you shall wear a new red and black bordered white blanket, and new white buckskin puttees and necklaces of beads. You will be able to hold up your head." His daughter said nothing at all.

They thought that next day she would go when she saw others going. Her mother got up early and took out an Indian corncake for her daughter. She brought it in and said, "Now we are ready for the morning meal. I hope you will go with the others today. All the girls are going on this rabbit hunt. You have everything you need. No one will be better dressed than you." The daughter made no sign of going. Her father grew tired of waiting; he got ready and rode around the village calling them to the hunt. The girls were all dressed with their best white buckskin puttees and red and black bordered white blankets. They went towards the west. The young men took the girls they liked on their horses, but the daughter of the bow priest did not go. Her mother was sad because she would not dress up like all the other good-looking girls and find a sweetheart on the rabbit hunt.

They hunted rabbits, and in the evening all the girls came in, and all of them were carrying rabbits, enough to last their families eight days. Her mother said, "I wish you had gone and brought rabbits."

Again her father thought of what he could do. "It would be good for her," he thought, "if she went out among the people. I can't

---

[1] The elder bow priest is the hunting society's executive or bow priest. This society is responsible for the ceremonial rabbit hunt.

[2] The men give their rabbits to the women to bring home and they pay afterwards with baskets of flour.

make her do anything I want her to do." He thought. "I will call the yaya dance. I will go to the village priest and he will call the Cuma·kwe society to call the yaya dance. Then my daughter will go out." When evening came he went to the village priest's house. He greeted him. He sat down. The village priest said, "You have come for something?" "Yes, I came to ask if you will go to Cuma·kwe and ask for the yaya dance. I want my daughter to come out among the people. She never goes out, even to get water. She weaves black blankets and white blankets and makes baskets and grinds, and she does not even look out to see what dances we are dancing." So the village priest said, "I will go and ask them to dance for your daughter to come out among the people. What days shall we ask them to dance?" "Whenever it is convenient." "I will go to the headman of Cuma·kwe as soon as I have had my morning meal tomorrow." "That is well. I am glad you will help me. I am going home. Be happy these days." He went out.

The village priest made the long cigarette to take to the headman of Cuma·kwe to ask for the yaya dance. Next morning after he had eaten, he went to the house of the headman of Cuma·kwe. He went in and sat down. Cuma·kwe chief said to him, "You have something to ask?" "Yes, I have come to ask for the yaya dance. The elder brother priest came last night to ask me if I would come to you. His daughter will not go out among the people. Her mother and father have tried to persuade her, but she never goes out. She will hear the dancing and the drums, and she will wish to dance the yaya." Cuma·kwe headman said, "Which form of the yaya dance do you want, the eight day's yaya, or the short four day's yaya?" "The short yaya; the eight day's yaya is much more trouble. He wants the dance right away, as soon as it is convenient." The headman of Cuma·kwe said, "That is well. I shall be glad to call my society together tonight. Then we shall make plans for the short yaya, and in four days we shall have the yaya dance in the plaza for the bow priest's daughter." "It is well. I am going. Be happy all afternoon." He went to his own house.

That evening the headman of Cuma·kwe called his society together. He returned home and waited for them. They came in, one after another. When they were assembled, they said, "Is there anything you wish, our father?" The headman answered, "Today the village priest came to ask us to bring the yaya dance on the fourth day for the bow priest's daughter. She never comes out among the people. We hope that she will come out when we bring the yaya dance. This is what I called you together to say to you. We shall work four days on the feathers and have the yaya dance.

for the bow priest's daughter." "All right, tomorrow we shall come after the morning meal and make the prayersticks." The headman said, "It is late now, we shall go home to sleep." So they all went home.

Next day after the morning meal they all came again to their society house and brought their willow sticks and boxes of valuable feathers. They sat in a circle and each cut four sticks, three short, and one long for the crook. They tied on the valuable feathers: eagle-tail feathers and blue-jay feathers. They put also onoḷiḳa feathers for a prayer that the bow priest's daughter would come out among the people. Everybody talked about this girl who never came out; they wondered if she would come tomorrow. They went in (to retreat) and for three nights they slept in their society house.

They chose the yaya leaders and gave them their pendant hair feathers. When they were ready that night, the yaya leaders gathered the girls together to practice in Heiwa kiva. The bow priest and his wife talked to their daughter about the yaya. Her father said, "I shall have a good new buckskin for your puttees; I shall scrape and dress it and cut it in two for you to wear the days of the yaya. It is a wonderful dance. Go and dance, my daughter, and be like the other girls. I know that you are prettier than any others in Itiwana and have better clothes." She did not say a word in answer.

The third night it was time for Cumaikoli[1] to come in from the east. Everybody in Itiwana went out to see them coming. Her mother said, "Daughter, let us go out to see Cumaikoli come in. You don't even know how he looks." The daughter said, "I am busy, I cannot go." "You can always weave and grind and make baskets, but this is the only time you can see Cumaikoli." But she would not go. They thought she would change her mind when she heard the drums next day. Everybody was busy making Indian corncake. Poor mother, again she made it for her daughter. In the morning when everybody was going out early to take the corncakes from the oven her mother brought in the baking. They tasted it. The father and mother talked to their daughter, "Now everybody is ready. All the women have laid their best dresses out in the sun to be ready to put on." The daughter said not a word. Everybody washed and dressed their hair, and put on their best dresses and moccasins. The bow priest brought his valuable buckskin and cut it in two. "Please, my daughter, go out! They are having this dance for you. I have cut this valuable buckskin for you." She was weaving and she did not say a word.

---

[1] This is the single masked dancer who comes for yaya. He is a favorite in Zuni.

The yaya dancers came out to the plaza. She did not stir. The mother and father were tired. The mother said, "I am going to dress and go out to dance. The buckskin that your father cut for you I shall wear it myself." She dressed herself, but the girl went on weaving. The mother went out and danced. When the yaya was over, everybody said, "We could not make her come out." After this her father paid no attention to her. He thought maybe they were too good to her, and that she was spoiled. At last one day her father planned to ask for the Corn Dance (la·hewe). He thought she must come out to dance. He thought, "This is the most valuable of all the dances." He asked the village priest to call the Corn Dance. But she did not come out.

Her father thought one day, "Now there is nothing I can do to change my daughter. Our people say it is good to have a daughter because she will marry. But mine does not marry." He thought he would offer her to the best hunter and make proclamation that whoever brought in game should have her. So he made proclamation and said, "My people, especially my young men, whoever goes out and brings in an elk or deer, so that he could make my daughter happy, shall marry her." The young men thought that surely they would marry the bow priest's daughter.

Next morning their mothers waked them, "Get up, go and hunt. Perhaps you will marry the bow priest's daughter." The young men went off in every direction looking for deer. The handsomest man was a priest's son. He went with his friends to the mountains to the south. At Eagle's Nest they sighted a great deer and killed it. There were four young men hunting together, and they quarrelled as to which of them saw the deer first. At last they agreed that it should belong to the one whose arrow had made him fall. They came up to the deer, and the arrows of the others were in his legs, but that of the priest's son was in his heart. The others were jealous because the priest's son had won the bow priest's daughter. The priest's son skinned the deer and gave the others pieces of flesh to take home. They were discontented that they had nothing with which to court the bow priest's daughter. The priest's son got the deer ready to pack home. He cut a straw of red-top grass and put it on top of his burden so that it was light to carry. At dark he came into Matsaka and behind him were the three men carrying their pieces of meat and some rabbits. He went straight to the bow priest's house.

The bow priest and his wife and daughter were in their house. The father said to this daughter, "My dear, I have made proclamation that whoever brings game and is the best hunter shall marry you. Please, when they come, choose the one you like best, and the deer that he has killed will be ours. The rest will go home." She never said a word. Her mother thought, "When they come in she will change her mind." They heard someone coming. It was sunset. The priest's son called, "Ca! Come and pull me in." The mother and father ran over to the ladder and brought him in. The girl sat in the corner and never said a word. They came in bringing the deer and the boy came last. The mother ran to get the embroidered white blanket and prayer meal. She spread out the blanket in the middle of the floor. They laid the deer with its head to the east and the mother asked if they should clothe it (i. e., sprinkle it with meal and put turquoise upon it). The father said to the priest's son, "My son, sit down with me and let us talk. I do not wish to clothe the deer if my daughter does not wish to marry you." The mother set out the stump for the priest's son, and he sat down. The bow priest asked, "My daughter, what is in your mind? Do you wish to marry this boy? If you do, we shall clothe the deer and pray over it and you will live together." The girl did not answer. Then the father said, "My daughter, answer and do not waste time. This boy is hungry. If you decide, we shall clothe the deer and he can have something to eat. If you don't want to marry him, he will take it to his own house to clothe and eat." She said, "No, I do not want to marry." The bow priest said, "It is well. You must take your deer. I am sorry my daughter does not wish to marry you."

"That is all right. I do not have to marry your daughter." Poor mother, she hated to see the deer go away. She helped the priest's son put it on his back. He said, "Be happy all night," and went out.

As soon as he was gone they heard someone else coming. The father said, "My daughter, please marry one of these men. I need help in my work." The young man called, "Ca! Pull me in." The father went and brought him in. They laid his deer on the blanket. The father said, "Sit down, my son, until we have decided. I do not wish to clothe the deer if my daughter does not wish to marry you." So the bow priest asked his daughter, "My daughter, what is in your mind? Do you wish to marry this boy? If you do, we shall clothe the deer and pray over it and you will live together." The girl did not say a word. The father said, "Hurry and do not waste time. This boy is hungry. If you decide, we shall clothe the deer and he can have something to eat. If you do not want to marry him he will take it to his own house to clothe and eat." The girl said, "I do not want to marry." The boy said, "That is all I came for. I will go." The mother helped him put the deer on his back and he said, "Be happy all night." He went out.

Soon they could hear someone approaching again. "Ca! Pull me in." The father brought him in. The girl sat in the corner and did not say a word. Again they asked her if she wished to marry this man, but she said, "No, I do not wish to marry." Every day the young men brought deer, but the bow priest's daughter would not marry.

The Ahaiyute heard that the bow priest had proclaimed that anyone who killed a deer should marry his daughter. It was evening and they could not get any deer that night. They told their grandmother that they were going to marry the bow priest's daughter who lived in Matsaka. Their grandmother said, "I know there are many handsome men in Matsaka and they have failed. She'll never marry one of you." The next morning, however, they said to their grandmother, "We are going to hunt. If we don't come tonight you will know that we have married the bow priest's daughter." "All right, I will think that" (irony).

The rest of the young men saw them hunting. They laughed and said, "They will never marry the bow priest's daughter, but we will." The Ahaiyute went along close to Corn Mountain, and at Rib Place they found a big deer asleep in the shade. They quarrelled. The eldest claimed, "I saw it first!" "You didn't say so!" "I saw it, if I didn't say so!" "Well, there's no use quarrelling; the one who makes it fall down shall claim it." So they sat down and drew their arrows. The younger shot and the deer fell. He was happy, but he didn't want his brother to be angry, so he said, "I shall go to marry the bow priest's daughter and I will bring her to our house and we will both have her." "All right, but I don't trust you." "This time you can trust me. We shall both marry her." "It isn't nice to marry the same girl[1]. You killed the deer and you may take the girl." So he helped his brother skin the deer. They slit up the legs and laid the skin back and took out the intestines. The younger said, "I am going to give you a present." He pulled out the heart and the wind pipe and gave them to his brother. Then he got a straw of red top to put on top of his deer pack and soap weed to make a head pad to carry it upon (the front legs on one side and the hind legs on the other). The elder twin started off for home and then came back to where his brother was. "How funny you look!" he said, "You'll have to walk back to Corn Mountain afterwards, and have your long trip for nothing. She'll never marry you!"

For four days the young men had come bringing deer to the daughter of the bow priest and she had refused them all. As the

---

[1] This is strictly upheld in Zuni custom, but in folklore it is not the case.

dirty little Ahaiyute came with his frizzled hair, the people saw him carrying his deer on his shoulders. They laughed and laughed. "That poor little Ahaiyute is coming to marry the bow priest's daughter. All our handsome boys have gone courting her and now here is this dirty little boy." They said, "She'll turn him out." Ahaiyute climbed up the ladder. The deer dropped on the ground. He was sweating under his load. The mother and father of the girl were in the house; they sat without raising their heads. They said, "There's another one coming." Ahaiyute called, "Ca! Pull me down." The father said, "Somebody is all choked up!" He rose and went up the ladder. There was this dirty little boy. The bow priest thought, "My daughter will cry when she sees this funny little thing." The mother went into the inner room for the embroidered blanket and prayer meal and they laid the deer with its head to the east. The father said, "Wait a minute. Do not clothe the deer till we have talked a little." The Ahaiyute said, "My people, how have you lived these days?"[1] in his choked voice. "Happily, thank you," the bow priest's daughter answered. The mother was surprised for she saw that her daughter liked him. Ahaiyute sat down and clasped his hands around his knee.[2] "I'm so tired," he said. The father said, "Of course you are." Then he turned to his daughter, "My daughter, will you marry Ahaiyute? If not, he will take back his deer." The girl said, "I will marry him." They were surprised. They were pleased with the deer, but not with the man. The mother got up and set out food for him. Then the mother and father clothed the deer. They put beads on his neck and spread a black blanket and a white embroidered blanket over him and they sprinkled prayer meal and prayed, "We are glad you have reached this house. We hope that you will come many times." They brought food. Ahaiyute ate. He was very hungry and ate lots. The mother and father took the blanket off the deer and cut a piece of its flesh and cooked it on the coals. That very night they ate part of it. Afterwards Ahaiyute and the bow priest hung the meat in the room. The family were all happy. Late in the night, the father said, "Now, my daughter, make the bed in the inner room." She got up and went into the inner room and made the bed, and Ahaiyute followed her. They slept together. So the Ahaiyute married the bow priest's daughter after all the handsomest boys had failed.

The bow priest and his wife were still up. All the people in Matsaḵa had seen Ahaiyute go in, and they wanted to find out if he had been accepted. They selected a boy to go and look. "I will go and

---

[1] He should have said this when he first came in.
[2] An undignified position.

look," he said, "but how shall I find it out?" They said to him, "The
boy and the girl will be in the inner room and you can't see them,
but if you see the venison hanging on the walls you will know he is
married to the girl." He went up on the roof. He smelled the
roasted meat. He thought, "It looks as if they were married! But
maybe he left a little piece of meat." He came in. He greeted them,
"My father, my mother, how have you lived this evening?" "Happily, thank you. Sit down." So the boy sat down. "The deer has
come," he said. "Yes, it came." What they had roasted they laid
out for him to eat. "Where did this deer come from?" he asked.
"My child has brought it in to me." "It is late now, I am going
home." "Wait a minute." They cut off a piece of meat and gave
it to him. He said, "Thank you. Good luck with the deer, and may
the deer come again." He took the flesh home. Everybody was
waiting to find out what news he had. "Yes, the Ahaiyute has
married the girl," he told them. They exclaimed, "What is it that
girl wants! All our nicest young men tried to marry her, and now
she has taken the little Ahaiyute." The people went all around the
village telling that the bow priest's daughter had married the
Ahaiyute. They told all the men that they shouldn't go out to hunt
in the morning. But they were not sure yet; they wanted to see with
their own eyes. Sure enough, the next morning at sunrise Ahaiyute
came out of the bow priest's house to go back to his grandmother's.

After his brother took the deer to the bow priest's house Elder
Brother Ahaiyute went back to his grandmother. She said to him,
"What is that, my child?" "This is my brother's heart. I killed him
and I took this out to bring to you." The grandmother snatched the
heart away from him and cried. Ahaiyute laughed and said, "My
brother went off looking so funny carrying a big deer to the bow
priest's daughter. If he doesn't come home to-night we'll know he
is married to the bow priest's daughter." "I'm sure he won't
marry that pretty girl!" When night came they waited and waited,
but he didn't come. Every little while Elder Brother Ahaiyute
sighed and said, "I wish I could marry just like that!"

In the morning the grandmother said, "Poor child, he did not
come. Maybe he slept in the mountain somewhere." "No, he's
married. If he comes in, don't speak to him. I shan't notice him.
I am very angry." "All right."

Younger Brother Ahaiyute climbed up Corn Mountain. He was
lonesome for his brother and his grandmother, and he came as fast
as he could; he couldn't get there fast enough to tell them that he
was married. His grandmother was toasting corn and his brother
was sitting in the corner. As soon as he came to the top of the ladder,

Elder Brother cried, "Oh, there's my brother!" "I thought you said that we were not to speak to him!" Younger Brother said, "Why?" "Your brother is jealous because you're married." "I'm going to bring her someday soon. She told me that she would come in a few days." They sat down and ate their meal. They were all happy because Younger Brother had married the nicest girl in Matsaka. Younger Brother said, "I came just to tell you I was married, so that you wouldn't be looking for me. I am going back. Grandmother, what have you to send my wife?" "Oh yes, I have something to send her." She got an embroidered black woman's-dress and buckskin. He put them upon his shoulder. He didn't fold them into a bundle; he wanted them to show.[1] He came down Corn Mountain.

He got down near the village. The people said, "My, there's Ahaiyute coming. I guess he went to get a black dress and buckskin for the girl." The young men hated him. He came down into the bow priest's house. His wife was grinding. He had the black dress and buckskin on his shoulder. The mother called the girl to come, and she came and took them off his back and hung them on the wall. He sat down, and the mother set out venison and paper-bread. When he had eaten he went out to hunt rabbits. In the evening he brought in eight. Every day he brought in game: sometimes deer, sometimes many rabbits.

The young men were more and more jealous. They talked of what they would do. They went to the priest's son to ask him if he would ask his father to call a race with Ahaiyute. The priest's son went to his father and said, "Father, I have something to say." "What is it? I shall be glad to know." "Will you call a kick-stick race with Ahaiyute? He is living with us." "If you want it, I shall go to the bow priest and see if he wants his son-in-law to run a race with you."

When the next evening came the priest went to the bow priest. He came in. He greeted him, "My fathers, my mothers, how have you lived these days?" "Happily, thank you. Sit down." The bow priest put out a stump and made him sit down. His wife set out roasted venison and paper-bread. He ate. The wife took away what was left. The bow priest said, "What is it that you have come to say?" Ahaiyute and the girl sat in a corner. The priest said, "My son suggested to me that we run a stick race with your son-in-law. He suggested that I ask you to let your son-in-law run. We shall have a good time." "How do you feel about this, my son?" Ahaiyute answered, "As long as they want me to run with them, I shall not

[1] This is extremely bad form.

say no." The priest asked, "When will it be convenient?" The bow priest said, "In four days we shall run the race." Ahaiyute said, "All right, I shall be ready in four days." The priest said, "This is what I came for. We shall have the race on the fourth day." He walked out. "Be happy all day," he said.

He went home. His son was waiting. As soon as he came in his son said to him, "What have you to say?" "Ahaiyute is ready to run the race with you." "I shall go to the rest and tell them that we must practice for the race." He went out. He didn't go into their houses. The boys were outside in the yards. He said, "My father has been to the bow priest and asked if Ahaiyute will race with us. He will be ready on the fourth day." "All right; we shall practice and the best runner will race against Ahaiyute. We will practice every morning." The next morning they got up early. Ahaiyute never practiced. Some of them went in one direction and others in other directions to practice for the race. At sunset they came in. All day each day they practiced. They were sure they would win. For three mornings they practiced.

On the third day, Ahaiyute went to hunt. He came home to his midday meal and after he had eaten he went home to his grandmother. His brother was outside. He saw his younger brother coming, so he ran in to tell his grandmother. "You haven't been home for a long time." They had a good time. Then he said, "My grandmother, my brother, the Matsaḳa people are going to run a stick race. I have come to tell you I am not sure I can win. I have come for things to bet." The grandmother answered, "We are not poor. We have relatives to ask for help in the race. Go to the Owl at Owl Spring and ask your grandfather there to help you. You can take this along to pay him." She took prayer meal and put it in a buckskin bag. "All right. Give me the things I shall bet." The grandmother got two buckskins and two black womens'-dresses. "This is all I came to tell you. I will come again," he said, "I am going home." He walked out with the two buckskins and the two black blankets. He went to his wife's house. As he got close, people said, "There is that Ahaiyute bringing things to bet." He came to his wife's house.

The priest made proclamation: "My people, nobody shall go to work in the fields today. We will run a stick race with Ahaiyute." The racers in the stick race thought that they should hold their (preliminary) ceremony in the ceremonial room of the village priest (because he had asked for the race) but his son refused. They looked for a ceremonial room to meet in. They chose that of a stick-race man[1] ("one wise in stick races"). They went in. They took with them an embroidered white blanket, and paper-bread, and turquoise ground with white meal and folded in cornhusk. They sat in a circle. The stick-race man came from the inner room. He asked, "Are you all here now ?" "Yes." "Which of you is the best runner ?" They chose the ones who had run the fastest in the practice race. They chose three, and said, "We shall chose the others after we have practiced again tomorrow." The stick-race man said to these three, "Have you food for our forefathers ?" They took out their corn husks with the paper-bread and turquoise, and he said, "Now, my boys, those who are to run tomorrow come with me and we will take food to our forefathers." They went out. Those who were left took food and fed it into the fire and they said, "Our fore-fathers, whoever ran in the stick races in your lifetimes, choose our side and help us to win."

The four went out to the east. They stood in a row facing east, and the leader said, "My people, my forefathers who were stick-race men, and you who ran in the stick-races in your lives, choose our side and help us to win. We are giving you valuable things." The stick-race man scattered the offering in a line. Then he said, "Now my boys, listen carefully. If we hear the owl or hummingbird, or water making a noise in the stream, or its bank falling in, it will be a good sign for us." They walked back. He said to them, "Do not look around whatever sound you hear. If you do, we shall lose our race. No matter if you hear an owl, walk straight ahead." They listened and heard a crow. They didn't know whether that was good luck or bad. "We have never heard whether a crow is good luck or bad," they said. They walked into their ceremonial room. The others were smoking. They sat down. The others said, "What did you hear ?" "We only heard a crow." "What is the meaning of the crow ?" Nobody knew. They said, "I hope it is good luck. I think the crow was telling that we will win." The stick-race man said, "We will sleep a little, and our dreams will tell us."

In the morning early Ahaiyute got up and went out to Owl Spring. Owl was just going to sleep for the day. Ahaiyute said, "How have you lived these many days, my grandfather ?" "Happily. What is it that you have come to say, my grandchild ?" "They are going to run a stick race with me today and my grandmother told me to come to you to find what to do. I'm bringing this to pay you." And he gave him the prayer meal. "Thank you, I shall be glad to help you," his grandfather said. "Pull a feather from my left wing and carry it when you run. When you carry this close

_____

[1] It is obligatory to sleep in the ceremonial room before a race.

to them in the race my sleeping will overcome them and they will
be too tired to race.[1] Choose the position on the right for the race;
let them run on the left."[2] "I will." Owl lifted his wing and Ahaiyute
pulled a feather. Owl said, "I know you will win."

Ahaiyute walked away with the owl feather. Just about sunrise
he reached home. In their ceremonial room the boys who were to
race took the emetic. They drank quantities of warm water and
vomited to take away bad luck. Afterwards the wife of the stick-
race man brought in (paper-bread and a bowl of water). He dipped
the paper-bread in the cold water and gave it to the three who
were to run. When they had eaten they lay down in that room and
rested. The stick-race man made the kick-stick. He took cottonwood and shaped it. When he finished he stood and prayed, "My
forefathers, you who used to be stick-race men, be with us and put
into my mind what I should ask of you. Help us so that we shall
win this race." He held the stick to his mouth and breathed from it.

That morning, before the midday meal, Ahaiyute and the bow
priest went into the inner room alone and the bow priest made the
kick-stick for his son-in-law. Ahaiyute lay with his hands clasped
behind his head and his legs kicked up.[3] The bow priest finished
the stick.[4]

After midday meal all the women dressed in their best to go out
to see the race. Ahaiyute's wife, who never went out at all, put on
her buckskin puttees and dressed herself. About the middle of the
afternoon they came out to bet. Ahaiyute's grandmother had
given him two buckskins and two black women's-dresses, and
his mother-in-law gave also three buckskins and three black
women's dresses and three women's belts. The bow priest made
them up into a bundle and brought them out to the plaza. The
stick-race man brought out a buckskin and a black women's-dress
and the three others who were to race brought their bundles
also. All the relatives of Ahaiyute's wife bet on his side against the
rest of the village. They paired off these things that had been bet
on the race; Ahaiyute's buckskin they tied against that of the
stick-race man, and those from his mother-in-law against those
of the three runners. The women of the pueblo were all dressed as
if for a dance with beads and black blanket-dresses, and they

---

[1] An owl's feather is put beside a child who will not sleep in the day. They
take it out of the box of valuable feathers.
[2] This side has ever since been the lucky one.
[3] A very unceremonious position.
[4] He did not pray over it because Ahaiyute was a raw person.

7*

climbed up to the house tops with the young men.[1] The people of the village brought out their possessions to bet on the race. The women brought red and black bordered white blankets and black women's-dresses and women's belts, and they wagered them. Ahaiyute's wife too came to the plaza carrying a red and black bordered white blanket to wager. Nobody had ever seen her before. She was pretty. Her cheeks were as red as if they had been painted. The people were surprised that she looked just like the others and was not shy and talked as easily as anybody. Her mother was glad that at last her daughter was out among the people.

When all had bet, the stick-race man tied the bangs of the three racers together (sticking out in front) and took off their clothes except the G-string. Ahaiyute didn't have any hair to tie up! He had just a wildcat G-string tied with buckskin thongs. The stick-race man said, "Go and tell Ahaiyute to meet us a mile south of the village. We are ready. Do not turn your heads as we go." He went first and the three behind followed with folded arms. Out came the bow priest and Ahaiyute. They walked with folded arms too, but Ahaiyute was pert. People nudged and giggled when they saw him, but his wife paid not the least attention to this. Under the wildcat skin Ahaiyute had tied the owl feather, and the bow priest carried the kick-stick. They came to the starting point. The stick-race man marked the starting line with his toe. He said to Ahaiyute, "Which side will you have?" "I will take the right. There is only one on my side, not three as there are on yours."[2] "What mark will you choose for your kick-stick?" "I will choose the middle." So his father drew out the red ochre paint and Ahaiyute moistened his finger and rubbed it on the paint and drew it around the middle of the stick. Then the leader of the other side took his stick and marked two lines around the ends.

They started. Ahaiyute ran ahead and the other runners fell behind because of the owl feather. Ahaiyute thought, "I better let them get ahead of me," so he fell behind. Everybody was riding along the course on horseback and shouting to them to come along. They sent a messenger back to tell the people that Ahaiyute was behind. The people were all out on the roofs watching the race in the distance.

The course went around by Badger Place and turned at Hawk Hill and ran close to Eastern Road. At Piled Rocks, and Where the Willows Grow, and Where the Red Stones Stay Ahaiyute was still

---

[1] Not customary now. "They must have been crazy."

[2] That is, it is fair for him to choose the luckier side because he is under a handicap in running alone.

way behind, but at Hecokta he caught up and shot ahead like a hummingbird. After he passed the runners they hardly ran at all! All those on Ahaiyute's side cheered him. Two of the runners they took back to Matsaḳa on horseback and only one still tried to finish out the race. Ahaiyute came into the plaza. He drew his hands four times up the pile of things which had been wagered and each time he breathed from them. "Just in this way I shall win next time," he said. Then he went to his house. When the runner who had raced with him came in he was exhausted, but little Ahaiyute was not a bit tired. The bow priest and his relatives took up the pile of winnings. All the rest were angry because they had lost. The people who had bet on Ahaiyute came into his house, and the mother had venison and paper-bread ready for them. The bow priest spread out a bordered white blanket and piled the buckskins, black women's-dresses and belts upon it and put over it another bordered white blanket. The bow priest's wife took prayer meal and breathed from it and said, "Now we are glad our clothing has reached us here. We are glad you have come to live in this house. We ask you to tell other (garments) to come also." So they sprinkled prayer meal on the pile of clothing. Afterwards they set out the paper-bread and venison. "Let us eat lots because we have won," they said. The girl sat down by Ahaiyute; she was happy that he could do this (win races).

In the houses of the other runners they also set out a feast, and they talked about how they would run another race with Ahaiyute. The stick-race man said, "My boys, practice every morning. We know now how fast he can run." The runner said, "Yes, to-day I did not know how fast he could run but next time we can overtake him. We shall have a good race next time." They had a big dinner. They said, "We shall send the messenger to him so that he will know that we want to run again. When shall we run?" So they said that in four days they would run again, and they sent a messenger to him to tell him that in four days they wished to run. The leader said, "I will go."

In Ahaiyute's house they had finished their feast and were sitting on the wall benches. They heard someone coming. The bow priest said, "The other side is coming to ask for another race." The stick-race man came in and greeted them, "My fathers, my mothers, how have you come to evening?" "Happily, thank you. Sit down." He sat down and the wife of the bow priest put down paper-bread. "No, thank you, I have eaten," he said. The bow priest said, "What is it that you have come to ask?" "My runners want to have another race in four days. They wanted me to find out if your side will race with them on the fourth day." The bow priest said to his son-in-law, "How about it, my son-in-law? The runners want to run a race in four days." "Just as they say; I never refuse." "This is all that I came for," said the stick-race man, "I am going. Be happy all night." He walked out. The bow priest said, "Those boys want to beat you. I know you'll never be beaten." All that evening they were happy over the garments hanging on the pole. The little Ahaiyute was not tired at all. Finally the bow priest said, "I think it is time for you to go to bed. We are tired." Ahaiyute and his wife went into the inner room.

The stick-race man went back to the others who were waiting for him. He sat down. The oldest asked immediately, "What did he say?" "He accepted; he would not refuse. My sons, you must go everywhere barefoot. Perhaps you were afraid of the cactus."[1] "All right, we will go barefoot." "All the others who didn't run in the race today shall practice too, for some of you may run better than the ones who were running today."

Next morning, before people were up, the young men who ran races went out in every direction to practice. They went out to climb the big hills. They tried to calculate how long it would take them to run the whole course.

Ahaiyute never practiced. On the third day he took four buckskins and four black women's-dresses and went to his grandmother's. Everybody was watching and they said, "There's Ahaiyute going to his grandmother's and he is taking her her winnings." He climbed up Corn Mountain. Elder Brother saw him just as his head came over the top. He ran in and told the grandmother. She wouldn't believe it. "He hasn't been here for so long," she said, "I think he is dead." Elder Brother said again, "He's coming in." He came in. The buckskins and the black women's dresses were all hanging down around him. His grandmother took him in her arms, "What is it that you have brought?" she said. "I won them, my grandmother." She lifted them and spread them out. She laid one buckskin on the ground and piled the other things on it. She took a pinch of meal and held it to her mouth and prayed, "My clothing, I am glad you have reached us here, and may many of you come to stay with us." She sprinkled the corn meal on the garments. Afterwards they talked, and she set out the little corn-mush balls (pupanowe). No matter how good the paper-bread he was eating[2] was, Ahaiyute had missed his grandmother's corn-mush balls. He said, "I need to ask a question again. I am having to run another race; what shall I

---

[1] The races are run barefoot.
[2] In his wife's house.

do?" "You shall go to your grandfather, Tecamiḵa,[1] and he will help you. But you must take him his batons (yamune). Ask your father to make them for you. These will make him glad and he will help you." "All right, thank you. Do you want me to wager again the clothing I won for you?"[2] "Of course I do." She gave him again the clothing that he had just won. He put it on his shoulder and went back to his wife again.

The third day he came into the village bringing his grandmother's winnings to wager again. After dinner he sat back with his father-in-law and asked, "My father, I have something to ask." "What do you wish to say? I shall be glad to hear." "Will you make Tecamiḵa's sticks for me? I have to go to ask him for his help. I could make them myself if I knew how." "I will surely make them for you." He went into the inner room. He took cottonwood sticks and brought his box of feathers and set them out in the inner room. He put the sticks in a basket and made a cigarette. He lit it with a brand, and smoked it. "Now you will be the batons of Tecamiḵa. I hope he will be pleased with you. Whoever is our grandfather on the south side[3], I am giving you this smoke to please you." Afterwards he scraped off the bark with a stone knife till the sticks were white. He painted one with blue paint (akwile) and the other with black prayer-stick paint. He wrapped four turkey feathers with cotton thread and hung them from the stick. When he finished he bundled the yamune with corn-husk. He called his son-in-law in and said, "Now I have made the sticks. Take them to Tecamiḵa, and I hope that he will be pleased with them."

Ahaiyute put the sticks under the string of animal fur tied around his waist and went out to the south where Tecamiḵa is. He got out to Tecamiḵa's place. As he got near he unwrapped the corn husk. Tecamiḵa was lying down by his house. He got up,[4] and said, "How do you do, my grandson?" "How do you do, my grandfather?" "Are you coming in?" So he went in. "What is it that you have come to ask?" Ahaiyute answered, "The boys in Matsaḵa want me to race tomorrow and I have come to ask you to help. I am bringing you these yamune to pay you." "I am very glad of the yamune. My old ones are all worn out." He showed him his old ones in his hands. The feathers were all worn off. Ahaiyute gave him the new ones. "I shall be glad to help you," his grandfather said. He rubbed himself and rolled up a big ball of cuticle and patted it

---

[1] Echo, a masked impersonation. See Bunzel 1036.
[2] The regular practice. Each time one wagers one's last winnings.
[3] Tecamika lives to the south of Zuni.
[4] Always expressionless, "staring". His voice is without intonation.

until it was about an inch thick. It was black with red particles.[1]
"When they ask you to paint the sticks," he said, "use this on their
sticks and they will be stiff and slow just as I am." "All right,
thank you. I will come again to see you. Be happy all your days."[2]
He walked out and got home late in the afternoon. His father-in-law
said, "Have you come? Lay down in the basket what you are
bringing." He went into an inner room and laid the cuticle ball in
a basket. He came out again. He sat down by his wife and played
with her.

That night after dark the runners went to their ceremonial
room. The men of that house had paper-bread ready for them. They
said, "My fathers, how have you lived these days?" After all were
in the house, the stick-race man said, "I wish to know who came
out first in the trials." "There were two who ran fastest." "I don't
think it is good to have three on one side and one on the other. We
had better try one more this time," he said. The boys did not want
this. They wished two. The stick-race man let them have their way.
He said, "Those who are to race, take food for our forefathers. The
others will remain here and make their offerings." They went out
with the stick-race man and the others fed their offerings to the
fire and prayed, "Our forefathers, whoever ran in the stick races
in your life-times, choose our side and help us to win." The others
went out to the east, farther than before. They stood in a row facing
east and the stick-race man said, "My people, my forefathers who
were stick-race men, and you who ran in stick-races in your lives,
choose our side and help us to win. We are giving you valuable
things." The stick-race man scattered the offerings in a line, then
he said, "Now my boys, listen carefully. If we hear the owl, or
humming bird, or water making a noise in the stream, or bank
falling in, it will be a good sign for us." They walked back. He said
to them, "Do not look around whatever sound you hear. If you do,
we shall lose our race. No matter if you hear an owl, walk straight
ahead." They listened and they heard a coyote. The stick-race
man was not sure if it was a good sign. "There is a coyote, I hear
it," said one. "I think it is a good sign," the stick-race man said.
When they got back the rest asked, "What did you hear?" "Coyote."
"The other day it was a crow, so now we know that a crow is not a
good sign. This time it is a coyote and we shall find out if this is
a good sign. We will sleep, and in our dreams we will find out if we
are going to win."

---

[1] Tecamiḳa's body paint is black with red spots.
[2] Only a raw person would say this to a kachina.

Ahaiyute didn't practice at all and that night he went as usual into the inner room and played with his wife.

The next morning, in the runners' ceremonial room, the mother of the house brought in a big pot of water and set it in the fire until it was warm. The two runners drank and ran long feathers down their throats and vomited. Afterwards they lay down and rested before they ate. The mother of the house brought in paper-bread and soaked it in cold water and they got up and ate. Then they lay on the floor again and rested. In the middle of the afternoon the stick-race man told the men to go out and get the clothing they had planned to wager on the race. Each brought a buckskin, or a black woman's-dress, or a red-and-black bordered white blanket, or a belt. The stick-race man and those who were to race, brought their things (to bet) to their ceremonial room.

In Ahaiyute's house his wife gave him the garments he had won on the last race and the bow priest took them to the plaza. The stick-race man brought a bundle (to wager) from his side; he went back and got another until all were in the plaza. The bow priest went back and got another and they paired the wagers and tied them together. All the people came out for the race. Ahaiyute's wife dressed herself again in her best. The stick-race man went back and tied the runners' hair. They walked in file out of the pueblo to the starting point. The bow priest carried the kick-stick that Ahaiyute had raced with in the last race, and the stick-race man had the one his side had used. They lined up at the starting point and the stick-race man said to Ahaiyute, "Which mark do you choose?" "We will not use the same marks as before. I shall paint your stick for 'middle', and next time, if you want me to race again, you shall paint my stick." He took out the paint Tecamiḳa had given him. He asked his father for the red paint, and substituted for it the cuticle ball, and he marked their stick in the middle with it. Then he used the red paint to mark his on the ends. "Now we are ready," the stick-race man said.

Ahaiyute started off ahead; the other runners were stiff. Their stick was heavy. Then they ran neck to neck. Both sides were happy, and those on horseback cheered the runners. Through Badger Place they ran abreast, and at Hawk Hill, and Eastern Road. They went on to Piled Rocks, and Where the Willows Grow, and Where Red Stones Stay; but at Hecokta Ahaiyute gained on them. At A'mosa they almost overtook him. But at White Rocks he was far ahead of them and they could not catch up. Their legs were like wooden stumps. The horsemen put them on their horses and brought them back to Matsaḳa. Little Ahaiyute was near the

Burnt Wood Place. He came into the plaza, drew his hands four times up the pile and breathed from them and said, "So I shall win the race another time." He ran home to his wife. Everybody was surprised that those little short legs could run so fast.

He stepped into the house. His father came to meet him. "You are bringing in good luck, my son," he said, and he breathed from his own hands. He went out to bring the bundles of garments they had won. His wife and the women of her family went to the other houses to get those things they had won on the race. Again they spread out the white blanket and piled the buckskins, and black women's-dresses, and women's belts upon it and put another white blanket over the pile. The bow priest and his wife took prayer meal and held it to their lips and said, "Now we are glad you have come to live in this house. We ask you to tell others to come also." They breathed from the meal and sprinkled it on the pile of clothing. Afterwards they set out the feast. The relatives all came and ate with them.

In their house the stick-race man and the runners also feasted. They said, "Let us eat lots, so that we shall forget all that we have lost to-day." They comforted the stick-race man: "When we race again we shall get back what we have lost. We will run our best." He said, "My sons, I'm afraid not. Ahaiyute is a great runner." Again they said, "We will ask him to race on the fourth day." After the meal they sent the stick-race man to the bow priest. Those at the bow priest's house had finished supper when he came in. He greeted them. The bow priest asked, "I know you have something to say?" "Yes. Again my boys are planning another race on the fourth day." He turned to his son-in-law and said, "How about it, my son-in-law? The runners want to run another race in four days. Do you wish to run?" "I have nothing to say, I will not refuse." The bow priest said, "We shall be ready on the fourth day." The stick-race man went out. "Be happy all night," he said. He came to their ceremonial room. As soon as he sat down, the others asked, "What have you to say?" "He never refuses. You boys will not give over racing. I hope this time you will win the race." "I think that we had better go home, we are tired. We shall practice tomorrow." So they went home.

The next morning they went in every direction and practiced. When the third day came, after the meal, little Ahaiyute went to his grandmother. He didn't take anything back this time, for he knew she wanted to stake it on the next race. His brother was in the house with his grandmother. He was lonely, and just sat in the corner holding his knee. He jumped up, and the grandmother dropped her sticks, and they embraced him. They were anxious because he had brought no buckskins. He said, "I lost all my wife's things and your buckskin." She said, "My poor grandchild! did they win all your garments that you staked on the race!" "Yes, they took them all. I came to tell you that I had lost everything." The grandmother was sad. Then he said, "I didn't lose at all, I won everything. Now they want to race again. Where shall I go for help this time?" The grandmother said, "Go to your grandfather Hawk at Hawk Hill. I know he will help you." "What shall I take to please him?" "Nothing, just use polite words. That will be enough." "That is what I came for. I will come again."

He went out and went straight to Hawk Hill. On a little pile of rocks Grandfather Hawk sat. "Have you come? What is it that you have to say?" "I have come to ask you to help me. In return I may do something for you." "Surely, what do you want?" "At Matsaḳa the runners have run two stick-races with me. They wish to run a third time. If there is anything that you can do, I should like you to help me." "Yes, pull a feather from both of my wings, and carry them on your hips, then I know that you will run faster than they." Ahaiyute pulled out a feather from the right wing and from the left wing, and said, "Thank you, my grandfather. Now I am going home, and I shall come to see you again." He walked home and reached there in time for the evening meal. He did not tell them about the help he had received from the Hawk.

Again that evening, after the evening meal, the runners prepared prayer meal and ground turquoise. They went to their ceremonial room. They said, "How have you lived these days, my fathers?" They all came in. The stick-race man asked, "Are you all here?" "Yes," they answered. "Which is the fastest runner?" They chose three. Then he said, "We will go out with the offerings, and the others will feed our forefathers in the fire." So they went out farther than before. The stick-race man said, "My children, when we have asked them to help us and have left our offering, do not turn around no matter what you hear." "All right." Again they stood in a line, and the stick-race man said, "Our forefathers who were stick-race men and ran in the races in your life times, we are giving you paper bread, and prayer meal, and valuable turquoise to please you." They scattered their offering and then listened. The stick-race man said, "If you hear an owl, or a hummingbird, or water running, or a bank falling, that will be a good sign." But there was no sound. As they came back they heard somebody following making sounds like a dead person.[1] They were warned by the

---

[1] The rattle of a skeleton.

stick-race man, "No one may turn around, for if he does he will be pulled back."[1] Somebody stepped on their heels. They were frightened, but did not turn. They got to the village. They went quickly, for they were scared. They walked into their ceremonial room and they asked them, "Did you hear anything?" The last man said, "Somebody followed me and stepped on my heels. I wanted to turn but our father would not let me." The father said, "That is a good sign. As he caught up with us, so will we catch up with Ahaiyute." They smoked awhile. Then the stick-race man said, "Now we will sleep for a time and our dreams will tell us if we are going to win." They lay down on the floor.

At Ahaiyute's house he slept with his wife.[2]

When morning came their mother (of that ceremonial room) heated water and waked the runners to make themselves clean. They drank lots and stuck the longest turkey or eagle feather completely down their throats and vomited. They were exhausted and lay down to rest. Then their mother handed them the paperbread and they dipped a piece in water and soaked it, and ate it, and drank cold water. After this they lay down again on the floor till the middle of the afternoon.

Ahaiyute also lay down in his house. In the middle of the afternoon the stick-race man and the runners went out to their homes to get the things which they were going to wager. Each brought a buckskin and a black woman's-dress, or a black woman's-dress and a woman's belt. They brought them to their ceremonial room and the stick-race headman took them to the plaza. Ahaiyute laid out the things that he had won at the second race, and the bow priest took them to the plaza. There were many things left. The two sides paired the garments they had staked and tied the pairs together.

The people dressed themselves in their best. The bow priest's daughter said, "My father, leave the belts for me to match against the women," for she staked the belts that she had made. People went to the tops of the houses and bet on their sweethearts, and Ahaiyute's wife bet on him. When they had all bet, the stick-race man tied the hair of the runners with string. Ahaiyute fastened the hawk feathers in his G-string of wildcat fur. They were ready to go out to the starting place. The stick-race man and the bow priest were carrying the kick-sticks. They came to the place. The stick-race man said, "We shall paint your stick for you this time." So it was given to him. He marked the stick with red paint.

---

[1] By the dead. That is, he will die.
[2] That is, again he did not observe the customary taboos before a race.

At Ahaiyute's first kick his stick went only a little way. The people all bet even more heavily against him. This time they knew that he would lose. He ran heavily, and the men on horseback called out, "You dirty, ugly fellow! You will lose this time and the bow priest will kill you. You'll stop running and the bow priest's daughter will have to bring water to you."[1] The runners[2] were ahead at Badger Place, and at Hawk Hill, and at Eastern Road, and at Piled Rocks. At Where the Willows Grow Ahaiyute overtook them. The men on horseback hooted like owls (to frighten him with a bad omen) and cried out, "He's gaining; he's coming up, Short-legs-like-a-frog!" A little past where the Willows Grow they passed him again. At Where the Red Stones Stay Ahaiyute overtook them once more, but before they came to Hecokta they passed him again. They were together through A'mosa, and at the White Rocks. The runners were running well this time, because Ahaiyute had not put any magic upon them. The people sent messenger after messenger to the pueblo, one with one message, another with another. At the Place of Burnt Wood they were neck to neck, but at Snake Place Ahaiyute spurted ahead and came in first to the plaza. The people were all sick. They cried, "You woolly hair, you long chin!"

All the time of the race the bow priest had been in his house facing east, sitting with crossed ankles held tight together.[3] He prayed, "Now my forefathers who were stick-racers in your lifetimes, make me to tie the legs of the other side so that we will win this race." All through the race he sat rigid and motionless. Ahaiyute came in and said, "My fathers, my mothers, my children, how have you lived these days?" His father looked up and Ahaiyute said to him, "You may rest now. We have won." "Thank you that we have won again." He breathed three times from his own hands and went out to the plaza to bring in the winnings. His relatives helped him to bring in all the things, and the people hated Ahaiyute.

At Ahaiyute's house, and at the stick-man's house the pots were ready for the feast. In Ahaiyute's house they brought in the pile of goods and prayed and sprinkled it with prayer meal and prayed, "Now we are glad that you have come to live in this house. We ask you to tell others to come also." At the stick-race man's house the runners gathered as soon as they put on their clothes, and the feast was set out. They said, "Let us eat lots to forget the things we have lost." One runner said, "I'm glad to lose so that when I go to

---

[1] To revive him.
[2] Of the opposite side.
[3] A magic practice to lock the legs of those who ran against Ahaiyute.

Kachina Village my grandmother won't lie with me[1]." The women said to the men, "Do not race again because all our garments are gone already." "Do not be afraid. We shall win one of these days! We will try just once more." The priest's son said, "Now my brothers and my uncles, whoever you are in this race, I wish my father (the stick-race man) to go to Ahaiyute and ask him to race with me on the fourth day. We shall stake our garments on this race, but he shall stake his wife." Nobody laughed. They were thinking that they could all sleep with her in succession if they won. They said, "I wonder if he will bet his wife?" "Yes, he is not like us, he is a raw person; he will bet his wife." After they had finished eating, the stick-race man said, "I will go to ask him if he will run on the fourth day and stake his wife." He walked out.

In Ahaiyute's house they were still eating. He said, "How have you lived these days, my fathers, my mothers, my children?" "Happily, thank you. Sit down. Eat." He sat down and ate. After a little they finished and moved back. The bow priest said, "What is it that you have come to say?" "The priest's son wants to race with your son-in-law. He says, 'Let the Ahaiyute stake his wife on the race. We will put up our most valuable possessions against her.'" The bow priest turned to Ahaiyute and said, "What do you think, my child; will you wager your wife?" "Just as they say. I always take them up. I know that they are jealous of me because my wife would not have them. That is why they race with me." The, bow priest said, "That is true." Then he turned to the stick-race man, "Tell your boys to bet their most valuable possessions, especially many beads. My daughter is most valuable." "All right. Be happy all night." He went back to the ceremonial room. The young men were anxious to know. Right away they asked, "What did he say?" "He always answers yes. He wants you to wager valuable beads against his wife." Some said, "We should not ask him to put up his wife against our beads; we are poor." Then the priest's son said, "But we may win, and one of us will live with the bow priest's daughter and Ahaiyute will lose her." The stick-race man told them that it was time to sleep. "Then we shall practice and we shall try to win Ahaiyute's wife," he said. They all went home.

Their women were getting tired,[2] but still they helped them with their wagers for the fourth race. Ahaiyute was troubled on account of the fourth race. Last time he had barely won. On the third day

---

[1] A woman will say also, "I am glad I have lost, so that my grandfather will not lie with me in Kachina Village." If she wins, she will say, "I won't let my grandfather lie with me in Kachina Village, the old man!"

[2] Of staking their possessions on a losing side.

he thought, "I will not go to my grandmother this time; I will go straight to the Hummingbird. I have always heard that he is the swiftest." He went out to Badger Place where the sunflowers grow. He carried corn pollen with him. He got to the sunflowers and he saw a hummingbird hovering over them. Hummingbird waited for him. Ahaiyute said, "My friend, will you stop while I ask you something?" Hummingbird sat quietly in the flower and said, "What is it that you have come out in this direction to ask?" "My friend, I came here because I have always heard so much about your swiftness. They want me to run a fourth race with them and stake my wife against their most valuable possessions. I have come to ask help so that I shall not lose my wife." "Pull a feather out from the under side of each of my wings. Put it in your G-string and you will win. Maybe you have brought something with you to pay me?" "If I haven't anything with me now I will bring it next time." "I want only corn pollen. I come here to hover over these sunflowers to get their pollen to make me yellow again. The corn pollen spewed over me will make me yellow." Ahaiyute took out his little bag of corn pollen and put a pinch on his tongue and spewed it over him. "Thank you, I will help you whenever you have need," said Hummingbird. Ahaiyute answered, "I hope I shall be able to do something for you someday. I will come again to see you." He walked home to his wife. He didn't tell his father-in-law where he had gone for help.

The stick-race man and the runners met again. The priest's son went with his father into his father's ceremonial room. His father gave him a little from-the-beginning black paint.[1] He mixed it with red paint and wrapped it in a corn husk and tied it in his shirt. His father told him, "The stick-race man will take you out, and before you leave your ceremonial room you will untie the paint and carry it in your fingers so it will be hidden. When they ask you to mark your stick, wet your fingers and mark it with this sacred paint." His son said, "Wait for me until evening. Be happy. Leave the door open for me." He went to his ceremonial room (i. e., stick racer's). He greeted them, "How have you lived these days, my fathers?" The stick-race man said, "We are all here, we are waiting for you. But I knew you were coming, for this is your turn. We two will go out with the food for our forefathers; the rest will feed theirs into the fire." They went out. The stick-race man said, "Before, we have been to the east; we had better go to the west this time.[2] They got a little

---

[1] Only the priesthoods have this paint.

[2] "Because a priest's son is running, it will bring the rain, therefore they go west."

way and the stick-race man told him, "We will feed them and listen. When we go back, do not turn around no matter what you may hear. If you do you will lose, and if it is a voice of a dead person, they will pull you back." They stood in a line and held their food, and the stick-race man prayed, "Our forefathers, who were stick-race men, and you who ran in the races in your lifetimes, we are giving you paper-bread and prayer meal and valuable turquoise to please you." The priest's son prayed, "I am a child of a priest. Uwanami priests, please come and bring rain, we need you." They scattered their offerings and listened. The stick-race man said, "If you hear an owl or a hummingbird, or water running, or a bank falling, that will be a good sign." They heard blue doves quarrelling. The priest's son said, "Do you hear that? What is it?" "It is blue doves quarrelling." Both listened. "Maybe it means that if Ahaiyute lost his wife he might quarrel with us," they said. They walked back, and as they got near the village they heard the crow, but they said, "Maybe it won't be bad luck this time." They came in and sat down and smoked. One of the men said, "What did you hear?" "We heard blue doves quarreling, and, close to the village, we heard a crow." Some said that it was bad, and some said that perhaps it wouldn't be bad luck this time. They smoked awhile and talked. They hoped they would win the girl. "We will go to bed to find out in our dreams," they said, "Our dreams always tell us truly." So they slept.

In his house Ahaiyute's wife made herself ready. Her mother said, "If the others win, you will have to go to the priest's son. There will be no way out. Even if you are married to Ahaiyute and not to them, they will take you." The girl put water on the fire and put cedar twigs in it to make a sweet smell. Ahaiyute sat and watched her. When the water was warm she made her mother bring the sand in to make a ring. She set a stool out and she dropped her black woman's-dress and held her hands over her genitals and her mother helped her wash herself. Ahaiyute was watching her sharply. He said, "What will I do if I lose you? I shall never get another wife like you." She bathed in the cedar water and stepped out of the sand ring, and her mother carried it out. The girl put on her dress. The mother said, "That is all; tomorrow I shall wash your hair."[1]

His wife went into the other room with Ahaiyute. He had seen how beautiful his wife was in the bath and he could not wait to

---

[1] The morning is the proper time for hair washing. If you wash your hair in the late afternoon you will be a big liar; if in the evening, the people of Kachina Village will "pull you back", except at the winter solstice ceremony when the medicine societies meet.

embrace her. "Make the bed right away," he said. So she made the bed and lay down. He embraced her and said, "Do you love me?" "Yes, I love you!" "I am afraid I shall lose you!" They were awake all night. "Tell me truly, will you be glad to go to the priest's son to sleep with him tomorrow night?" "No, I love you best." "Tell me truly, do you love me better than you would love him?" "Yes, I do!" And they embraced again.[1] Every time the bow priest and his wife waked they heard them talking. "Poor children! They are talking all night. I know how they hate to lose each other!" Just before daylight they went to sleep. Next morning when the mother got up, they did not stir. She said, "How my son-in-law is snoring!" About seven o'clock they got up. All the other runners were up and the priest's son had taken the water and vomited. Afterwards he rested awhile and the stick-race man's wife handed in the paper-bread again. Once more the stick-race man soaked it and the runner ate it. They all came and ate with him. Afterwards they lay down until the afternoon.

In their house the bow priest's wife had breakfast ready and the girl came out and helped her set out the meal. They ate. They felt sad. When they finished, the mother warmed water and pounded yucca root and made a suds. She told her daughter to come and kneel down before her.[2] She washed her hair carefully, and rinsed it. While it was drying the girl's father's sisters came to help her mother with the feast. In the priest's son's house his father's sisters also came and helped. They parched the corn and loosened its husks in the grinding-stone and got it ready to put in the stew, so that they would be ready for the feast when he brought the bow priest's daughter to his house.

There was great excitement. Nobody had ever staked his wife on a race before, and besides a priest's son was running. The girl rested in the morning, and her father doubled together chains of turquoise and coral and white shells and tied them around her neck in a heavy collar of beads with heavy loops of beads hanging in front. He fitted them to her throat. Then he cut a buckskin in two for puttees. Her mother was fixing a new black blanket into a woman's dress. She laid out all new clothing and took out a new red-and-black-bordered white blanket and new moccasins. Everything was ready before dinner. Her father's sisters set out the food. The girl ate before she dressed for the race. Everybody said, "I hope our house wins so that you will not go to the ceremonial room of the priest." Her father said, "My daughter, if we lose and the

---

[1] That is, again he did not observe the traditional taboos.
[2] "Very old fashioned, but some still do it."

priest's son comes for you, go with him directly, so that you will receive long life when you go into the priest's ceremonial room." "I will." They finished dinner. The girl asked her mother, "Please tie my hair." "Yes, I think that we had better start. It takes so much time to dress a woman!" She sat down and brushed her hair. Her mother tied it up and fastened it with the narrow woven hair belt. Next she put her moccasins on and they spread out a blanket so as not to soil the new buckskin puttees. Her mother wrapped them. She put them on smooth and tied them tight. When they were done her foot was tinier than ever. She put on her new woman's dress and spread her legs till the skirt was tight and then adjusted it evenly and tied the belt. Then her father tied all the beads on her neck. She put on the red-and-black-bordered white blanket and sewed it together at the neck with cotton thread threaded in a deer-bone bodkin. She was ready and she sat down. The Ahaiyute was putting on his G-string. Now they were all ready.

The stick-race man told the young men to bring their valuable wagers. They went home to fetch them, especially the priest's son. He brought one chain of coral (the most valuable beads), and one chain of turquoise, and one of shell, and ten black women's-dresses, and ten buckskins, and four belts to wager against the girl. The other runners brought garments to match against those the Ahaiyute put up. They each brought a white blanket, or a black woman's-dress, or a belt. The stick-race man said, "I will not carry them all myself to the plaza. You shall go also and carry what you have brought." They walked to the big plaza. The stick-race man walked ahead, and when they came to the plaza he took out his prayer meal and sprinkled some on the ground. After this he laid a piece of buckskin down and piled carefully on it all the things the priest's son had staked against the wife of Ahaiyute, and what the others had bet.

Then he went to the bow priest's house to get the girl. Everybody said, "He has gone for the bow priest's girl!" He walked in. "How have you lived this while, my fathers?" he said. "Happily, thank you." "My daughter, are you ready? I have come for you." "Yes, wait a minute until I get my things." He sat down. The bow priest took out four buckskins and four black women's-dresses and eight belts. He put them in a blanket and put them on his back. The stick-race man went out ahead, then the girl, and then the bow priest. The girl said to her mother, "I hope that I shall be back this evening." The people said, "There she is coming out." She was very, very beautiful. They thought that they might win her.

They came to the big plaza. The stick-race man said to the girl, "Wait a moment." They tied together what the bow priest had brought and the garments the runners had wagered. Then a woman who lived at the big plaza brought out a stump, and said, "This will be better." The stick-race man said, "Thank you," and he put it against the pile of clothing and spread a buckskin over it. He put his hands on the girl's shoulders and moved her to the six directions and made her sit against the pile of clothes. He said, "Now, my daughter, you will remain here this afternoon, and whoever comes first to get you, whether it is the Ahaiyute or the priest's son, he shall be your husband." The stick-race man and the bow priest went to get their runners ready. The stick-race man said, "Now my son, be strong, I have brought the bow priest's daughter out. Be strong!" He tied the boy's hair. The bow priest said to his son-in-law, "Are you ready?" They walked out to the starting place and made the line. The Ahaiyute was to have the right, the priest's son the left. They pulled their red paint out, and the bow priest asked the priest's son which mark he chose, and he answered, "The middle." So the Ahaiyute had the ends. The priest's son marked his with the priest's from-the-beginning paint. They laid the sticks on their toes. The stick-race man called, "Ready!" Off went the sticks. They ran neck to neck. The people were mad with excitement. At Hawk Hill the priest's son was ahead. Ahaiyute caught up with him, and at Eastern Road the two were together. At the crossing of the river they were still together. At Piled Rocks and at Where the Willows Stay the priest's son was ahead. But Ahaiyute caught up and they ran neck to neck all the way around the course until they passed White Rocks. They sent messengers back on horseback, saying, "We don't know which one is coming out ahead; they are coming together." They came to Burnt Wood Place. They got to Badger Place and Ahaiyute ran with all his might. People called to the priest's boy, "He's ahead! Run! Run!" But he could not. In the plaza they were saying, "They will both come in together." Just then in came Ahaiyute and seized his wife in his arms. He cupped his hands and breathed from them, "This is the way I shall win lots of wives!" The people pulled him to pieces with words. He went home with his wife behind him. Just then the poor priest's son came running in. He went to his house and there was the pot boiling and the aunts waiting for him to bring the girl to the priest's ceremonial room.

Ahaiyute came into his house and behind him the girl's moccasin was just showing up at the top of the ladder. Her mother was overjoyed. "You have come," she cried. She ran up to her son-in-law and stroked his shoulder, saying over and over, "Good runner! Good runner!"

8*

The bow priest went out to the plaza and the relatives helped him bring in all the clothing and the beads. The garment pole was loaded full. All the relatives came in to eat, and the sisters of the bow priest set out the feast. They were happy in that house, but in all the rest of the village they were angry. However, they had feasts just the same. The stick-race man said, "There is nothing that we can do against Ahaiyute," and they did not challenge him again. But other men said, "We will play a game with him and win our clothes back." "No," said the stick-race man, "he has power, we can do nothing against him."

At the bow priest's house, when four of his sisters were ready to go home, the girl gave each of them a belt. The aunts went home. The bow priest arranged the clothes.[1] Those who had come to the feast were still smoking at the bow priest's house. They asked Ahaiyute if he had been tired. He answered, "I was tired, but I didn't want to lose my wife." At last they thought that it was time for them to go to bed. "Be happy all night," they said, and went home. Ahaiyute and his wife went into the inner room.

The stick-races were finished. For four days Ahaiyute lived in the pueblo and went hunting. He brought in venison every evening. After four days he said, "I will go to my grandmother's. I will come back again." His wife said, "I don't want you to go until I grind for your grandmother. Then you shall take me to your house." "All right. I will wait until you have the flour ready." She told her mother that she wanted to visit Ahaiyute's grandmother. Her mother said, "All right. That is the way to do. You must grind lots before you go and take the basket of flour to her." So the mother went into the other room and brought out corn and the girl shelled it. The mother parched it. The daughter spread it out afterwards to cool. There was so much it covered the whole room. People said, "The bow priest's pretty girl is grinding for the Ahaiyute." So she ground for him, and her arms showed bare as she knelt by the grinding stone. They were beautiful. She ground two great basketsful in two days. The second evening she finished and her mother said, "I will pile it so that it will be ready for you to take in the morning." She spread out a blanket and put the basket in the center and piled the flour in the basket and packed it in tight, and what fell on the blanket she gathered up and put back.

The girl was excited because she was going to visit Ahaiyute's grandmother. Her mother said, "I shall put the pot on the fire so that we may have an early breakfast." The mother washed the jar

---

[1] "They did not sprinkle prayer meal this time because they had won so much."

and put the meat in. She soaked the corn and skinned it on the grinding-stone, and put it in the pot. She brought it to a boil, and all night, when the fire burned down, she got up and put more wood on it. The next morning the stew was ready. Her daughter was up early, earlier than ever before, and she dressed in the clothes that she had won at the stick-races. She put on a new black woman's-dress, and a belt, a red-and-black-bordered white blanket, and new buckskin puttees and new moccasins. They set out the meal and all sat down to eat. The mother said, "When will you come back?" Ahaiyute answered, "We are going for four days. We shall be back on the fourth day. I have been away from there for nearly a month. I know that they miss me. I want to go back for four days." The mother and father both said, "Of course they do, and we shall miss you too." They finished and the daughter said, "I am ready now." Ahaiyute picked out the grandmother's garments, those which he had wagered and those she had won, and put them on his shoulder. They walked out. "Be happy four days. We shall be back on the fourth day." The mother and father said, "Be happy going." The father carried the basket of flour out for his daughter and put it on her head.

They walked off; his wife followed Ahaiyute, the little Ahaiyute and his big wife. The young men said, "There's that Ahaiyute and his pretty wife. Let's go and hide around and scare him and he will run away, and we shall get his wife." The boys ran around ahead. Ahaiyute and his wife got to Ololowicka.[1] He said, "Let's rest; this is where we always rest." So she set her basket off onto a high rock, so that she might slide it back onto her head. Ahaiyute put a stone under his foot and put the little stone on the groove and be-gan pushing it around the groove. He said,

"Ololowiwicka, wiwicka,
This is the way we make baskets!"

His wife put a stone under her foot and pushed it around behind, but she did not sing. She giggled. He said, "You must sing too, we won't be rid of our tiredness if you don't." So she sang too,

"Ololowiwicka, wiwicka,
This is the way we make baskets!"

Then they went to the heap of stones and took one and spit upon it, and twisted it four times around and threw it on the pile. After-

---

[1] The place, not the impersonation of the same name. The place is along the lower part of the Corn Mountain trail. The grooves are plainly marked in the rock, and the pile of rocks is near by.

wards they sat down and played together. Then Ahaiyute said, "I think that we had better go now." The girl went to her basket and pulled it onto her head. It was almost too heavy for her to lift. They walked along the trail to Corn Mountain. He reached out his hand and pulled her up the hard places of the trail.

They came up. Ahaiyute's brother was in the house. He was lonely. He heard footsteps, tum-tum, tum-tum. "Somebody is coming," he said. Ahaiyute called, "Ca." "What do you want?" "Come out and pull us in." The brother ran up, but he couldn't lift the basket himself. So both Ahaiyute and the girl took hold of it on three sides in order to lift it down the ladder, and the grandmother ran for a blanket. They emptied it. "Sit down, sit down!" they said. The girl sat down. They talked lots (i. e., they were kind and happy). The grandmother got the mush balls out of the ashes. She said, "I was going to make some new cakes, but I didn't." She had lots of red coals and she spread dried venison over them. She set out the meal, "Let us eat." They talked; they were happy. The grandmother kept jerking her head up to admire the clothes which she had won in the stick-races. Ahaiyute told them how the people had treated him at Matsaḵa. "They ran four races with me," he said, "They wanted to win my wife from me — but I won!" "Isn't that nice that you didn't lose your wife."

For four days they lived there. That evening the grandmother asked, "Are you going back home?" "We are going in four days." Ahaiyute's wife helped his grandmother with the grinding all day. In the morning she got up early and boiled the water, and when it was boiled she took some of the corn meal she had brought, and put a little water in and stirred it thick. She rolled it between her hands till she made a little roll hang down. She pinched this off into a basket and she shook the basket until it all rounded into little balls. Then she poured it in the pot and boiled it awhile. Just then the grandmother got up. She kept a corncob under the edge of her blankets and when she waked up she pulled it out and scratched herself all over with it. She put on her dress and tied her belt so that the fringes hung in front.[1] She came to the fire. The girl was sitting by the fireplace waiting for the pot to be ready. The grandmother didn't see the girl at all. She went to start the fire, and she burned her fingers! She fell back and sat down right on the girl's lap. The girl was laughing. "What's the matter, grandmother?" She started and jumped up; then she saw her granddaughter. She came close and stroked her arm and said, "My granddaughter, my granddaughter! I had forgotten that you were here. I came out to

---

[1] There is much laughter at this ineptitude.

start my fire." "I have made boiled dumplings." "How nice that is," and she went to get venison. The girl soaked the meat and set it out. She took the hollowed stone and put water in it and set it in the middle, and she put salt and hampasa in it. She cut the meat up into four pieces and laid it around the stone, and she set the corn dumplings out in the baskets on either side of the stone. They took wooden spoons with which to eat the dumplings. The grandmother said, "Please show me how you make these when you do it next time. Teach me all you can." They sat down to breakfast.

Afterwards the Ahaiyute planned to go out to hunt. They worked on their bows and arrows. The girl heated the cooking stone and put some water on to boil. When the stone was hot, she greased it with fat, and she poured water in her meal and spread out the batter on the stone with her fingers. When the cake was done on one side she turned it. She made two. She rolled them up in her blanket and gave them to her husband. The grandmother watched everything she did, so that she could do it after the girl left. The Ahaiyute said, "We shall be back before evening," and they went hunting. The girl made another cake. The grandmother said, "May I taste it?" "Yes, eat lots." And every time the girl made a cake the grandmother ate it all up.

The Ahaiyute went a little way (still on top of Corn Mountain) and they found a big doe with two young. They shot it and it fell. They skinned and cleaned it. It was late in the afternoon when they brought it home. The girl and the grandmother were ready. The girl had made paper bread and the grandmother was in a hurry to have them come home to eat the fine evening meal. The elder brother was happy because he had his brother, and his brother was happy to be with him again. The girl was watching for them. "They are coming now," she said. The grandmother got the prayer meal to bring in the deer. She thought the girl had never seen that done before. She spread the embroidered blanket and the Ahaiyute laid the deer with its head to the east and put beads on it and the black blanket over it. The grandmother prayed, "Now we are glad you have reached here. Be many, and come many times again." They were happy all night.

For four days Ahaiyute and his wife stayed at his grandmother's house, and the girl taught the grandmother every kind of cooking. When the fourth day came, Ahaiyute said to his grandmother, "Now we are going back, but we will come again." "That will be nice. Come as often as you can." The next morning they got up early. The girl said, "I do not think that we will stop for breakfast; then we can get home before it is hot." The grandmother filled up the basket with dried venison. Ahaiyute and his wife said, "We shall be back in a few days." The grandmother and his elder brother were still in bed. They said, "All right, we shall be glad to see you again." They walked out with the basket of meat.

They came home to the girl's house. The girl's mother expected them to come back in the evening, but they came before they had finished breakfast. They heard them on top of the roof and said, "Somebody is coming." They came in. The mother got up and she said, "You are coming? Why did you come so early?" "We liked to come before it was so hot." The girl had the basket on her head and the mother took it and went into the inner room to hang up the meat. She came out and said to the others, "Eat." They ate.

Ahaiyute lived with his wife a few days more. He could see that the people did not like him because he had won so much. He said to his father, "Now I shall go home again. I am not like you; I am a raw person. I cannot stay here. If you wish to give me something, I would like you to make for me two crooks, one for myself and one for my brother." The bow priest said, "I will not make these crooks myself. I must go to my village priest to ask the council to make these crooks for you. They will make them."

He went to the village priest and greeted him, "How have you lived these days, my fathers, my mothers?" "Happily, thank you. Sit down." He sat down. "What is it that you have come to say?" "Please make two crooks for my son-in law, one for him and one for his brother. He wants us to make these for him before he leaves us again." "Of course we will make whatever they ask. They help us a great deal." Then he said, "I will call the others, and we will make them tomorrow." "All right, this is what I came for. Be happy all night." He went out and returned to his home. He told his son-in-law that they would make the crooks in the morning.

That evening the village priest went to the homes of the members of his priesthood and told them to come to the ceremonial room and bring their boxes of valuable feathers. The next morning, after the morning meal, they went. They went in and greeted the village priest, "How have you lived these days, my fathers, my mothers, my children?" "Happily, thank you. Sit down." They sat down, and took their moccasins off. The village priest said, "I have called you because our son is ready to go home, and he wants crooks for himself and for his brother. His father-in-law was here last night and put this request before me." "All right." So they worked with their feathers. They put out these of the eagle, chaparral cock and bluejay, and hummingbird. They put the feathers in the basket and blew smoke upon them and asked to have good luck with the rain. They prayed, "Now that we are making the crooks into persons to give to Ahaiyute when he goes to his home, make rain for us." They made the crooks and put them in the basket. They said, "He will come and get them. He will give us a blessing for them."

While Ahaiyute's wife was washing his hair, his father, the bow priest, put on his buckskin war-hood. Ahaiyute put his on too. The bow priest took prayer meal in a basket and they went to the ceremonial room of the village priest. They greeted them, "How have you lived these days, my fathers, my mothers, my children?" "Happily, thank you." The village priest rose and lifted the two crooks and put them in Ahaiyute's hands. He held them in his own and moved them toward the six directions, and said, "We have made these two crooks for you. Please ask the people of Kachina Village to bring us rain." "I will do what you ask." "We are glad to do anything you need. Live in the daylight a long time." They walked out together and the father (bow priest) "made the road" for him up Corn Mountain, and he went back to his home. So that is why the bow priest always "makes the road" home for the Ahaiyute after the winter solstice ceremony.[1]

THE BRIDEGROOM IS REQUIRED TO KILL A DEER
A. YELLOW CACTUS GIRL (7)[2]
Notes, 303

Long ago the people were living in Hecoktałupstina[3]. The village priest had one son who had no wife. He killed many deer and brought them home, and he had many buckskins in his house. About seven miles away at Ḳakwena lived a girl who wanted to marry him. One afternoon the girl carried a basket of corn meal to Hecoktałupstina. She reached there about six o'clock in the evening. The boy's mother asked her what she wanted, and she said, "I want to marry your son." His mother said, "If my boy wants you, all right," and his father said the same, "If my boy wants to marry you, all right." The girl said, "All right," and she stayed in the house. After supper she made a bed in the other room, and the mother came and spoke to her son, and said, "Son, you had better go into the other room, your bed is ready there." He went in and he said to the girl, "We can't sleep in one bed." The girl said, "Why?" He said, "Well, maybe you are not a good girl. Tomorrow grind some corn, and I will go out to look for deer and antelope. If I kill deer or antelope or any large game, I will bring it home before sunset. Then you will

[1] The principal Ahaiyute ceremony. See Bunzel 526.
[2] Recorded by Ruth Bunzel.   [3] Yellow House.

be finished grinding. Then I will know that you are a good girl. But if I do not kill anything I shall know that you are a bad girl." The girl said, "All right." She made a bed for herself in the corner with the girls, and he slept in the other bed.

Next morning the girl got up and made breakfast. She set it out on the floor and told everyone to come to breakfast. Then the girl shelled corn and the boy took his bow and arrow and his prayer meal bag and went out towards the south. After he had gone a little way he came to a spring, "Our fathers, I give you prayer meal. Do not show me any deer or antelope. Hide all the game from me. I don't want to get married. I don't know if I shall be happy with a wife." He went on looking for deer and could not find any, because they had all been hidden away. In the evening before sunset he came home, and the girl asked him, "Did you kill deer?" He said, "No, I suppose you are a bad girl, and that it is best for you to go back home." The girl said "All right," and went into the house and took her basket and went back to Ḵakwena.

Next morning a girl from Pinawa wanted to go and see that boy. She took a basket of cornmeal and went there. About sunset she got there and the boy's mother and father said, "A girl is coming. What is the matter, son? Why don't you marry one of these girls? Why do you make them all go back home? You must not do that." The boy said, "The girl doesn't like me." After a while the girl came and asked him questions, and wanted to marry the boy. His father asked him, "Do you want to marry this girl?" and the boy said, "Yes, I guess I'll marry this girl." After supper they went into the other room and he asked the girl the same questions as he had asked the other girl, and said to her just the same things.

Next morning he went out to hunt deer, and he prayed at the spring just the way he had the other time. After he came home he spoke to the girl just the same way as he had done before, and the girl went back home.

Next day a Pinawa girl came and spoke to him the same way. The following morning he went out to hunt deer the same way, and he did not kill anything, because he had prayed to have all the deer hidden, and he could not see anything. This was the third time.

The fourth one was a girl living on a mesa six miles from here, at Meactekwe (Cactus Cave). She was Yellow Cactus Girl. She had seven sisters, and she told her sisters that she was going out for willow to make baskets. Soon she brought the willow and made a basket. It was January and there was a lot of snow on the ground. Then the girl took cactus fruit and put it in the basket between corn husks. She put in the large brown cactus fruit, and took it to the man's house. She knew that the boy did not want to marry her, but she went there anyway. She was a nice looking girl, but no one knew where she came from. She belonged to different people. The boy's father asked her what she wanted, and she said she wanted to marry his son. He said that if his boy wanted her he was willing. Late at night his mother made a bed in the other room. Then she came out and told the boy to go into the other room. They went in, and he said to the girl, "We can't sleep in one bed." "Why?" He said to her, "Tomorrow you will grind flour, and I shall go out to hunt deer, and if I bring home deer, then I shall know that you are a good girl." She said "All right," and made a bed for herself in the other corner.

Next morning she got up and made breakfast, and he took his prayer meal and went out. When he came to the spring he sprinkled meal and prayed, "My fathers, I give you prayer meal. Do not show me any deer. Please hide all the game from me, because I do not want a wife." Then he blew the meal and went on, and all day he did not see anything. Meanwhile the girl stayed home and ground flour. Towards sunset he came home, and the girl asked him, "Have you come?" He said, "Yes, I have come." "Have you killed any game?" He said, "No, I guess you are not a good girl. You are not the kind of a girl I want." Then the girl answered him and said, "You prayed to have all the deer hidden. You could kill deer if you wanted to. But you prayed to have the deer hidden, and of course you couldn't see any. You can't fool me like that. I am not a bad girl, but you are a bad man. Now I am going home." He said, "Yes, that is good." Then the girl took his heart out and put it in her dress, and he acted like a crazy man after that. She went out. His mother stopped her and said, "Here, take your basket." She said, "No, maybe you will need the basket," and she went out over the snow.

That night after the girl went away the boy could not sleep. Next morning he felt sick and could not go out for deer.

When the girl came home her seven sisters asked her, "Where is your husband? Why didn't you bring your husband with you?" She did not answer them but went into the other room and went to sleep. She slept all night and all the next day. When she came in she took prayer meal and prayed and said, "My sister, my mother, my aunt, my cousin, punish that Yellow House boy. He does not want girls." Then she went in and slept. She did not eat but slept all day and all night for four days.

All the time the boy could not sleep. He wanted to sleep, but he could not. He was sick. He could not talk right, and he became very weak. For four days he could not eat anything, and he was all skin and bones. Then his father said, "Who was that girl who was here last ? She was no Zuni girl. Maybe she was one of the raw people and made my boy sick. I want to know who she is." He asked everyone but no one knew who that girl was. He took prayer meal in a basket and went out to the south. The little sister stayed with the boy, and when they were alone, the cactus basket started to talk, and said, "Call your father back. He is not going the right way." The girl went out and called her father back. He came back and she said, "Someone just talked to me and said you were not going the right way. She went to the northwest. You will see her tracks in the snow." He went out again and saw the tracks going to Cactus Cave.

When he got there he saw seven girls in one room. They all looked alike, and all were pretty. The man greeted them and they asked him to sit down. One of the girls asked him what he wished. He asked them, "Which one of you girls came to my house ?" "We never went to your house." "Oh yes, one of you went to my house some time ago." "Our sister went to your house some time ago." "Where is she ?" "She is in the back room. As soon as she came home she went to sleep and she has not waked up." "Well, you had better go in and wake her up. I want to talk to her." One of the sisters went in and told Yellow Cactus Girl to wake up and come out, because someone wanted to see her. She asked, "What does he want to see me for ? I don't want to go out." The sister went out and said she did not want to come out. The man said, "My boy is sick. That is the reason I want to see her." The girl went back and told her sister, "You had better come out. He told me his son is sick. He is dying, and that is why he wants to see you." The girl said, "Let him die. A bad man like that should die." The girl went back and told him that her sister did not want to come out, and she told him what she had said. He said, "Tell her my boy is almost dead. She had better come out." She went in again and said to the girl, "You had better come out. He says his boy is nearly dead, and that is the reason he wants to see you." She said, "I don't want to talk to him, because his son treated me badly." The girl went back and told the man what she had said. "Tell her she must come out. I won't go away until I have seen her." Then for the fourth time she went in and said, "Now, my sister, you had better come out and talk to that old man and tell him what you want. He won't go away without seeing you. Go out and see him, and then he will go away." Then the girl said, "All right. I will come out in a little while." She was angry now. Then the girl went out and said, "My sister will be out in a little while." Pretty soon the girl came and talked to the old man and asked him what he wanted. He told her, "My son is very sick. That is the reason I came to see you. You must go back with me and see my boy." She said, "No, I won't go." "My daughter, I want you to go with me." "No, I won't go. You have a bad son. He did not treat me right. He treated me badly, and that is the reason why I won't go and see him now." "Yes, I want you to go with me. It doesn't make any difference. My boy is bad, but I want you to go with me anyway because I don't want my boy to die." "All right, I will go with you. If you give my seven sisters what they want, I will go with you." The man said, "All right," and he went home and got eight large buckskins. He gave each girl a large buckskin. Then the girl took a basket of cactus fruit and went to Yellow House.

The boy lay in a corner. He was all skin and bones because he was not able to eat or sleep. The girl sprinkled water on the floor and began to sweep. Soon she came to sweep near the boy's bed, and he spoke to her, but she would not speak to him. After she finished sweeping she put some food on the floor and put down her basket of cactus fruit and told the people to come and get supper. The people all sat down and ate. Then she went over to where the boy was and told him to get up. She put her hands behind his neck and he put his arms around her shoulders, and she pulled him up. He could not get up alone, because he was so weak. He had not slept for ten nights. After he got up she told him to eat supper, and he sat down. Then she chewed some salt and gave it to the boy and told him to wash out his mouth with salt. He washed his mouth two or three times and then he ate supper. After supper she said, "Don't sleep tonight. Watch everyone. Some girls have no husbands, and some boys have no wives. Watch tonight." The boy said, "All right."

Then the girl took corn pollen and went out and prayed. She said, "My mother, my sister, my aunt, my cousin, come to my husband now. Don't leave me alone." She sprinkled corn pollen and went into the house. Everyone went to bed and slept, and the girl lay down on the right hand side of the boy. About midnight they heard someone walking on the roof. The girl asked the boy, "Are you asleep?" and he said, "No." She said, "Well, watch now. Someone is coming." Then a girl in a fine white dress and white moccasins came down the ladder and lay down on the left of the boy.[1] Four times during the night the cactus women came and lay down with the boy. When it was near daylight and just getting light no more girls came, and the Cactus Girl said to her husband, "Now let us go to sleep. No one will come now."

[1] When a man takes a wife, the girl always lies down on the left of the man.

Next night the same thing happened, and it happened for four nights. On the fifth day she went out and sprinkled corn pollen and prayed, "My mother, my sister, my aunt, my cousin, leave me alone now. Do not come. Leave my husband alone." Then she went in and lay down beside her husband and said to him, "Now, my husband, listen to what I am going to tell you. You say you don't want a wife, but I know that you need a wife. You won't be happy until you have a wife. You will lie awake at night and worry, and you won't be able to sleep. Last night you saw four girls. It didn't matter that you had no wife, you slept with a girl at night anyway."

The four girls did not come back again, and Cactus Girl stayed there. After a while the boy was satisfied with his wife. She was a good wife and never quarrelled. Then one day the girl told him, "I must go back home. I cannot stay any longer. Now you see that you will be happy when you marry. If any girl comes and wants to marry you, marry her. Not two, but just one girl."

After a month he got lonesome for his wife and went to look for her, but he could not find her house, only a cave filled with cactus, so he went home.

That is the reason why a Zuni never has two wives. It is not good to have two wives, but one is all right.

B. THE FROG HUSBAND[1]

The people were living at Halonawa. Many boys wanted to marry the village priest's daughter. The boys met in the kiva. One boy said, "I am going to the village priest's house. I want to marry his daughter." He went there before sunset and he took along presents of clothing for the girl. The girl brought food and sat down with the boy to eat. After a while, when they had finished, her father took tobacco and corn husks and asked the boy to smoke. Then he questioned him and asked him, "What do you want?" He said, "I want to marry your daughter." The old man said, "Well, maybe my daughter doesn't want to. What do you say, daughter?" "Well, I think I'll marry this boy." The boy stayed a little while and about nine o'clock at night the girl made a bed in the other room and came out and told the young man, "Let us go to bed." The young man got up and the girl said to him, "You had better bring these things with you." He took the blankets and buckskins and moccasins and brought them into the back room. Then the girl said to him, "We cannot sleep in one bed." "Why?" "You did not bring what I want." "What is it that you want?"

[1] Recorded by Ruth Bunzel.

"Well, tomorrow morning you must go out and hunt deer and bring me fresh meat." The boy said, "All right, I will try." So the young man slept in one corner and the girl slept in her own bed.

After daybreak next morning the boy got up to go. The girl gave him something to eat and the young man said, "Your father has a bow and arrow?" The girl said, "Yes," and went in and got the bow and arrow and gave them to the young man. He went out and hunted deer all day but could not find any. In the evening, he came home and the girl asked him, "Did you kill deer?" The young man said, "No." She said, "Well, if you cannot kill deer you are not my husband." "All right," said the young man, "I will go." She said, "Yes, take your things and go."

He went up to the kiva and the boys said, "Here comes the village priest's son-in-law," and they made fun of him. One asked him, "Did you marry that girl?" He said, "No." "Why not?" He said, "She wants someone to hunt deer and I could not kill any deer." "Well, I guess you are too lazy. I think I will marry her." He went to her house and she said the same thing to him, and the next morning he went out to hunt but he could not find any deer. The girl told him, "You cannot stay with me if you cannot kill anything." The boy went back to the kiva and the boys said, "Here comes the village priest's son-in-law." "No, I did not marry that girl, because I could not kill deer." Then another boy said he would try. He went out next day to hunt deer. He went to the east and there he saw a bear. "I will ask the girl if she wants bear meat and if she says yes I will go and get it tomorrow." He went home and the girl asked him, "Did you kill any deer?" He said, "No, I did not see any deer, but I saw a bear. Do you want bear meat? If you do I will go and get it for you tomorrow because I can kill bears." "No, I don't want bear meat. I want deer," she said. "Well, then, I must go back home." And the young man went home.

At Itiwana there was a Frog. He said, "I guess I will go and see that girl. I see lots of young men coming away, so I guess I will marry that girl." Frog went up to the house and jumped up the ladder. The girl's father said, "Now, my daughter, someone is coming in. What is the matter with you? Now don't send this one away. Someone is coming now." Frog jumped down and came right over where the people were eating supper. He sat down by the fireplace and the children were all frightened. The girl said, "Come and eat," but he said, "No, I am not hungry." Then her father asked him, "What do you want?" "I want to marry your daughter." The father asked the girl and she said, "All right, but

I guess you are too slow. You must kill deer for me." She was not scared and did not say no to him. Then they went into the other room and the girl said, "We cannot sleep in one bed." Frog said, "Why?" She said, "You must go out and hunt and if you bring me meat I will marry you." The Frog said, "Why, I can't kill deer. I am too slow." The girl said, "Well, if you want to marry me you must kill deer." Next morning, before daybreak, Frog wanted to go. The girl gave him something to eat and he asked for a bow and arrow and the girl brought them to him and put them on his back and tied them with buckskin thongs. Frog jumped up the ladder and went out.

He went about two miles to the south of Zuni and there he cut a hole in his head and stepped out of his frog skin and stood up a man. He hid his frog shirt in the ground. He had on a fine shirt and fine buckskin leggins and fine turquoise necklace and turquoise in his ears. He went on and went up into the hills. About sunrise he met a mountain lion. He talked to him and Mountain Lion asked him, "My grandson, where are you going?" "I am going to hunt deer, because the village priest's daughter wants venison and I want to marry her." Mountain Lion said to him, "I will help you find deer. Just follow me." They went a little way and he saw many deer and killed one. He skinned it. He took a stick and tied the meat and the head to the stick and carried it back to Zuni. He came to the place where he had left his shirt and he put the meat down on the ground and put on his frog shirt. He took up his load and came jumping along carrying the meat. It was still early morning and many boys were standing on the roof of the kiva. The village priest's little girl was playing on the roof, and she saw Frog coming with the meat and ran into the house and told her mother. The girl was grinding corn and her mother said, "You had better go out and meet this man because he is bringing meat." The girl was frightened. Frog came jumping along. He hopped right into the house and dropped his meat.

Frog stayed all day in the house and the children were all frightened. They did not like to see the Frog in the house. Towards evening they prepared supper and the girl said, "Eat," but Frog said, "No, I am not hungry." After supper, the girl and her father and mother sat down. They did not talk. They were all frightened. About midnight the girl's father told her, "Well, my daughter, you had better make a bed and go to sleep. It is late now." The girl went into the back room and made a bed and came out and told Frog, "Let us go in." Frog went in behind the girl. He said to her, "Please give me a cup of water. I am thirsty and I want to drink." The girl said, "All right," and went out. As soon as she had gone, he pulled off his shirt and he was a fine looking man. He sat down. The girl's father asked her, "What did you come out for?" The girl said, "I came to get a cup of water for that man." She got the water and went back and when she saw the man sitting there she was frightened. "Where is the man I brought in?" she said. "I am the one. Why don't you give me my water?" The girl was too frightened to say anything and just stood in the door. Three or four times the young man asked for his water. Then he took up his frog shirt and held it up and asked the girl, "Which do you like better, the frog or me?" She said, "Well, I like the young man better." Then he said, "Well, then, you had better bring me my water." She gave him the water and he said, "Now tell your father to put my frog shirt away." The girl went out and said to her father, "You had better come in. The young man wants to see you." The father went in and said, "Well, my son, what is it?" He said, "I want you to put my frog shirt away. I do not need it now." He took the shirt into the other room, where he had his sacred things, and he put it with his sacred things and the young man stayed there with the girl.

Next morning, at daylight, he told his father to bring out his frog shirt. He put it on and went after deer. He brought meat in again early in the morning at about eight o'clock. Then he took off his shirt and sat down and all the people knew that Frog was a young man. After four or five days the people began to talk about it. "I suppose that man runs fast in order to be able to kill deer. Maybe we could run against him in the stick-race. You had better see about it. Let us have four men on each side, four men on our side, and on the other side the village priest's son-in-law and the village priest's three sons. We shall be running against one family." Then the bow priest went down to the village priest's house and told him that the people wanted to run a foot race against his sons in four days' time because the men had seen the frog that had come to his house. Frog said, "I do not run very fast but I will do as you say. I know that you all want my wife." He told his three brothers, "We shall run against them and bet all we have."

Three days after that he went out at night and put on his frog shirt. He went into the river and went by way of the river to Kachina Village. When he got there the people were all dancing. Pautiwa said, "We had better stop. Our grandfather is coming and maybe he wants to tell us something." Then they all stopped and questioned him and he told them, "Up at Halonawa the people want to run a race against me tomorrow. Will you help me?"

9

They said, "Yes, we will help you." They made four cigarettes and gave them to him and told him, "When you are running, go about two miles and then take off your shirt and give it to your father and let him bring it back to his house and put it in a basket. After you have run about four miles, light the cigarette and we will come." He went. He went right back to his house.

Next morning his wife bathed him all over and washed his hair. In the afternoon his father took out a big pile of buckskins and blankets and beads and dresses and bet against everyone in the town. Some people in the town still had some things left. Then his father came back and he led out his daughter and staked her against the things the people had wagered. The runners began to run. The course was along the south road. The other side was about a mile ahead. Frog Man went two miles to where his father was waiting for him and he took off his shirt and gave it to his father to bring home. His father took it into the house and put it in the basket. Frog kept on racing.

He had gone four miles. He lit a cigarette and when he had gone another mile he saw clouds coming up over the whole sky. He went up along Western Road and now it began to rain. Frog was still behind and soon it was raining heavily. The man ahead of him lost his kick-stick in the water and he could not find it at all. He was looking for his stick when Frog Man came along and passed him about half a mile outside of Zuni. Frog won the race. The whole town lost all they had and the young people brought the things into his house.

After a while he told his wife, "Now I must go back home. If any poor man comes and wants to stay with you, he will be your husband. Treat him well. I cannot stay with you for life because I belong to the other people (supernaturals)." The girl wanted to go with him. "No, I cannot take you with me. When your time comes you will die and when you go to Kachina Village you will stay with me." The young man went back to his home in Kachina Village. The girl married another man and her husband killed deer for her and they lived together. After a while the girl became sick and died. After four days she went to Kachina Village and met her husband. That is why when a woman dies and goes to Kachina Village she always lives with her first husband.

EAGLE MAN (7)
Notes, 305

The people were living at Ḳakima. The village priest had four daughters and one son. His son's name was Itiwana, and he had a young eagle that he had taken from the nest. He hunted game for it every day. He did not till his fields, he would not do anything for his sisters. All day until late afternoon he was hunting for his eagle. His sisters said, "My brother does not till the fields. He hunts every day for his eagle. Let us kill the bird. If we kill it he will work in his fields." The eagle heard what they said to one another and that afternoon when the boy came back with a jack-rabbit the eagle did not eat. He turned his head away. He had always caught at the food before and swallowed it quickly. The boy said, "What is the matter? Are you troubled about anything?" The four sisters were out in the fields hoeing and the eagle said, "Let me go. I will go home." "Why?" "Your sisters are angry and they want to kill me. I will not stay here any longer. I have a home and I want to go back to it." "No, I won't let you leave me." "I have to go. Let me out." "If you have to go I shall go with you." The eagle said, "Go and get food for us to carry on our way and find a bell to take so that your sisters can hear us as I fly." The young man went back to the house and got some food for their lunch. He found six bells and took them with him to the roof. He replaced the door over the hatchway and the eagle said, "Are you ready to go?" "Yes." "Let me out." He opened the cage and the eagle said, "Now get on my back." "How can you carry me? I am too heavy." "Take hold of my wings and sit upon my shoulder." He did as the eagle told him. "Put your weight on my shoulder. Fasten the bells on both legs and shut your eyes until we get to my home. If you look we shall drop down and die." He tied the bells on and got on the eagle's shoulder. The eagle said, "Are you ready?" "Yes." The eagle flew up and up toward the southwest. Down there his sisters were working in the cornfield and the eagle flew low so that they could see him and he said to the young man, "Shake your legs so that they will hear the bells ring." The girls looked up when they heard the sound of the bells and they said, "It is our brother. Our brother has gone with his eagle." Those girls cried and cried.

The eagle circled up into the sky and went through the sky-hole into the next sky. The crows were living there and the eagle flew up through that sky and went through the hole into the next sky. The Chicken Hawks were living there and he flew up through that sky and went through the hole into the next sky. The Night Hawks were living there and he flew up through that sky and went through the hole into the next sky. He flew into the fourth world and that was the home of the eagles. He lit on the rock at the entrance, and he told the young man to open his eyes. He did not know where he was. They climbed up on top of the houses and went down the

9*

ladder, but nobody was there. The house was empty. Eagle came
into the house and took a flint knife. He dropped down upon it
and slit off his eagle shirt and stood up a fine girl. The young man
looked at her and said, "My dear." Just then the eagles began to
come home.

The first eagle laid down his deer and took off his shirt and hung
it on the wall, and he stood up a man. The next eagle laid down his
deer and took off his shirt and hung it on the wall and stood up
a young girl. Pretty soon another came in and when he took off his
shirt he was a man. Pretty soon another came in and when he took
off his shirt he was a girl. Finally there were about twenty-five
women and twenty-five men. The house was full. All the eagles'
shirts were white as snow. They had black combs and yellow bills.

The chief Eagle said to the young man, "My son, we are glad
you have come. Stay and live with us in this house." The young
man lived there and he took his eagle for his wife. The chief said,
"This is my daughter. You have married her and you will always
stay here."

Every day the eagles went out to hunt jack-rabbits and deer.
For ten days that young man stayed in the house all the time. After
that time the chief asked his children to make an eagle shirt for the
young man so that he could go out hunting with them. They took
a deerskin and sewed it up like an eagle shirt and one eagle pulled a
feather out of his right wing, another eagle pulled a feather out of
his left wing and the next eagle pulled a feather out of his right
breast and the next eagle pulled a feather out of his left breast until
they had feathers enough to make a shirt, even down to the little
downy feathers. They made an eagle shirt for the young man just
like theirs.

Next morning after all the eagles had gone out hunting, only
that one eagle girl stayed with her husband and she said, "Put on
your eagle shirt and we will go out." He put on his shirt and fastened
it tight and they climbed to the top of some stones and the girl said,
"Stand on the top and fly off." He fell down to the bottom; he
couldn't fly. Again he tried and again he fell down. He couldn't
do it. The girl carried her husband to the west corner of the house
and she said, "Fly from here. Shake your wings. When you fall I
will fly under you and make a wind to support you." He jumped
off and fell and when he was half way down the girl flew underneath
and made a breeze so that it lifted him up and he learned how to fly.
He went way to the southeast. She said, "Look for rabbits." Down
in the sage brush he saw a tiny steam rising. The girl said, "Maybe
that is a rabbit. Go and catch it." He dropped down upon it but he

ran his beak into the earth and the girl got the rabbit. She laughed at him. Then they took off their eagle shirts and sat down in the shade to rest awhile. When they had played together they put their shirts on and flew up over the other side of the mesa and she caught a small deer. The girl said, "Now we are going home," and they flew up through the skies to the eagles' home. After a while the other eagles came bringing their deer.

Next day that young man did not eat any of the morning meal. He did not know how to eat meat raw and that was the way the eagles ate their food. He got weaker and weaker. He said to his wife, "I shall have to go." "Why?" "I cannot eat raw meat, it makes me sick." The eagle chief said, "What are you talking about?" The girl answered, "My husband cannot eat raw meat." The chief said, "Go out and gather some bundles of wood and cedar bark and we will make a fire and cook food for your husband." When all the eagles got home that young man went to the top of the house and put wood and cedar bark in a pile with lots of chips underneath. The eagle chief flew up and circled around high in the air and dropped down like an eagle, "Hm, hm!" He breathed on the pile of wood and the fire started up and burned that pile. The smoke came out of it and made all the eagles black and spotted as they are today. The young man brought the carcass of a deer and roasted venison and ate it. The chief said to him, "We had white shirts and in winter no one could see us, but now we are all speckled. It is not good for us to have fire here. In the morning fly to the northwest three miles and a half. There an old man and an old woman live who cook food just as you do. They will feed you. Do not go farther for bad people live in that direction."

Next day the young man put on his eagle shirt and he flew to the northwest and saw a gray house. An old man was sitting on the ladder. The young man said to him, "My fathers, how have you lived these days?" "Happily, thank you. We have waited for you and you did not come." Koloka called his wife and said, "Come and talk to your grandson and give him some food." She got a bowl and put some peas and beans in it and brought some paper bread. The old man said, "Make yourself at home." The old woman said, "Eat lots." After he had eaten they sat and smoked. The old man knew he came from the eagle's country. He said, "If you stay here, you must be careful. There are bad people in this country. Do not go farther to the west. They are dangerous." "All right." He stayed a little while and he said, "I must go back home."

He flew a little way toward the west and he saw great ruins near by and no people moved about. He went down nearer and sat on the corner of some of the houses and all around he saw skeletons lying. Everywhere there were dead people. It was a pueblo as big as Zuni. For the evening meal he went home again to his wife. She knew where he had been and she was angry. She said, "Where did you go?" "I went to the house of the old man and the old woman." She said, "I know where you have been. I know you are bad. I told you not to go there. After sunset they will come for you from that dead man's pueblo and you will have to go."

They ate their evening meal and when they were through, somebody came to the hatchway and called, "Where is our husband? We are coming to dance for our husband." The chief said, "We are waiting for you." The girl said to her husband, "Do not laugh if those girls smile at you. Do not smile at them." Pretty soon those people came. A girl dropped in down through the hatchway and fell on the floor like a dead body. Blood ran out of her mouth. Another girl fell in through the hatchway and hit the floor like a dead body. They stood up two fine girls with smooth plump arms and big black eyes. They were very pretty. The young man sat next his wife and she said to him, "Be careful. Do not laugh." He thought to himself, "My wife is just like a woman, for these are nice girls." When they laughed, he laughed back and those two girls came over and caught him by the arms and carried him up out of the hatchway and back to their own country.

As soon as he got to their country they set out something for him to eat. Their house was a nice house, like the houses in Zuni. They boiled venison and gave him muskmelons and watermelons and pumpkins, but he did not touch them. It got late and those two girls said, "Let's go to bed." They lay down and the boy lay in the middle and they put their arms over him. They were fine looking girls but he said to himself, "These two girls smell like rotten meat." He liked them but he did not have intercourse with them. Towards morning he fell sound asleep. At sunrise he woke up and the roof of that house was all falling down around them and a dead girl lay on each side of him with their arms over his chest. He jumped up and threw aside their arms and ran as fast as he could.

He got back to the eagle country and his wife said to him, "What did you laugh for? I do not want you here any more." "Those were two nice girls." "Go back to your nice girls. Let them teach you." He said to himself, "I must get some hot water and wash my stomach." He went out and went to the house of the old man and woman and the old woman heated some luke-warm water. When he had vomited he was clean and she gave him some breakfast. He said to the old man, "What am I going to do? Those two girls are

coming for me again today." "Why did you go down there in the
first place ?" "I was foolish." The old man told him to get an ear of
perfect white corn and shell it and take turquoise and coral and
white shell and grind two handsful of prayer meal. He said, "Take
your bow and arrow and take your wife. Put her half a mile outside
of the southeast corner of that pueblo. Make a circle of prayer meal
all around the town. Begin at the east and close it at the southeast.
Shoot your arrow into the circle and you will overcome these bad
people."

The young man did as the old man told him and late in the afternoon he flew down to the dead people's pueblo and waited for the
sun to set. Just at sunset all the dead people woke and the father
and mother of those two girls said, "Their arms are broken and
their two legs."[1] They came out into the streets and they saw that
where the young man had made the circle of prayer meal the whole
pueblo had been lifted up into a great mesa. They tried to get down
the cliff but they couldn't. The young man set his lightning arrow
to his bow and shot through the circle of sacred meal and the whole
pueblo shot up into the sky on the other side of the ocean. The
young man said to his wife, "Now we shall go home." He took her
back to the eagle country.

The eagle people began to talk about how they would send the
young man back to his home. The medicine men were looking for
him all the time. They had set up the altars of the medicine society
and they prayed that they might find the son of the village priest.
The chief Eagle said to him, "Your brothers are looking for you,
we must send you home." The young man said, "All right." Next
morning all the eagles went out hunting deer. They brought them
back and packed the venison to give to the young man to take to his
home. First they brought him his eagle shirt and twenty-five eagle
men and twenty-five eagle women carried the meat down through
the four skies. They landed eight or nine miles southeast of Ḳakima.
They made a camp and all the eagles went back home except the
young man and his wife and the chief Eagle. The chief called the
Chicken Hawk and as soon as Chicken Hawk had come he said,
"We are sending back the young man to his pueblo. We have lots of
venison but we need bowls." Chicken Hawk said, "I know a Navaho
camp to the northeast and I will go and get these things." The
Navaho were going down to the water with their sheep and Chicken
Hawk sailed down and got those things and brought them back.
Eagle said, "We need a bow for our son." Chicken Hawk said, "I

---

[1] Where the young man had thrown them off when he jumped up from the
bed.

will get it." He went back to the Navaho camp and got a bow, a quiver of arrows, baskets, and a cap.

In Itiwana there was an old man who was despised by everybody. He was poor and old. He asked for help to find the son of the village priest. They[1] told him to go to the medicine men to ask for a a fetish[2] from their altars. They said, "Perhaps our fathers will help you." The old man went to the medicine men. He started for Zuni. He stopped once and he stopped a second time and he stopped a third time and the fourth time he came to Zuni to the medicine men.[3]

The people were all looking for that young man. The old man said, "You must look for him in the north and in the west and in the south and in the east and up and down and then he will be waiting for you here." His father was sick in bed and his mother and sisters were grieving for their son. The old man said, "If I have good fortune I will bring your son home again. For forty days you have been looking for him. I will try and our fathers will help me." "All right." He asked for the young man's clothing, his shirt and his sash. He asked the medicine men for a fetish. The head medicine man offered him his fetish but he asked the next medicine man for his fetish. He asked the medicine man third in rank for his fetish and the medicine man fourth in rank. He said, "I do not want these." A medicine man who was not an officer at all gave him his fetish and he said, "This is the right one." He went out and he prayed, and he waved his fetish to the north, to the west, to the south, to the east, and there the young man stood before him. He went into this house and his sisters cried, "Our brother has come." They embraced him and they said, "Why did you go and leave us ?" His mother would not believe that he had returned but they said, "Yes, our brother has come." He came in and the old woman got up and they brought in all the venison which the eagles had sent. They ate their evening meal and they honored the old man whom everybody had despised. He had more power than the medicine men. Eagle Man said, "This man is my real father.[4] He brought me home. You must never despise him." His mother and his sister called him by relationship terms. They honored him and gave him venison. That is why we always honor old men.

---

[1] The supernatural beings. The story is obviously abbreviated at this point.
[2] The stone image of an animal, etc., set out by priests on their altars.
[3] The four ceremonial stops. The old man evidently is supposed to have been to Kachina Village or Cipapolima to interview the supernaturals.
[4] I. e., ceremonial father.

THE TARANTULA STEALS THE YOUTH'S CLOTHING (8)

Notes, 307

Long ago the people were living at Matsaḳa. The Ahaiyute lived at Eastern Road, and the Tarantula lived over at Badger Place. Pekwin had one son and one daughter. The son was handsome. His mother was proud of him. All the girls wanted to marry him. Every other day he went to his field to work, and on the other days he went hunting. He was a great hunter. He always brought in deer. One day he thought to himself, "I am not dressed well. I will put on a nice shirt and moccasins and fringed leggins and leather bow-guards." When he had dressed, he looked at himself in the selinite mirror. He said, "I have no red powder on my face." He pulverized red ochre and rubbed it on his cheeks. When he had finished, he thought he was handsome. He went out to Badger Place to hoe. There the Tarantula saw him coming, and he said to himself, "That boy has beautiful clothes." He thought, "I think you are going somewhere. Some day I will talk to you and get your clothes."

The next night the boy came back from hunting, carrying a deer. The Tarantula was watching the priest's son; he thought he was a handsome boy with the deer on his back. The Tarantula said, "My boy, you are coming, aren't you?" The boy looked but he could not see anybody. The Tarantula said, "Here I am." The boy took out his stone knife and cut a piece of meat and gave it to the Tarantula. The Tarantula said, "Thank you, my son." The boy went on to the village. Everybody was watching for him. All the girls had been grinding that day to take meal out to that boy as he came in. Every day they did this. They met him with their meal that he might give them a piece of his meat and want to marry them.

His mother saw him coming. She went to meet him with her prayer meal, and prayed, "Oh my children,[1] we ask you to come in again to our house that we may never lack venison." She sprinkled the road to bring them (boy and deer) home. They entered the house and she prayed again: "Always when my son goes out to hunt, our children, be plentiful. Come again many times to our house." When they had come down the ladder, she set her basket of cornmeal on the floor and brought out an embroidered ceremonial blanket and spread it on the floor. On this the boy laid the deer with his head to the east, and his mother brought out beads and put them on the neck and ears of the deer. When they had dressed the deer, they covered him with another ceremonial blanket.

[1] Refering, as in the prayers following, to the deer.

Then everyone in the house took cornmeal in his hand and prayed, "We are happy, our children, that you have come here again. Return always to our house." They breathed from their hands and sprinkled the cornmeal, and breathed again from their empty hands. His mother was always glad to have her son come from the hunt, because he never came empty-handed.

Next day, when the morning meal was over, the boy went to his field again at Snake Place. The Tarantula was watching for him. He thought, "I shall talk to him, and some day he will be my friend, and I shall take his clothes away." So when the boy came, he spoke to him. "You are going, aren't you?" "Yes." "Where are you going?" "I am going to my field." "Where is your field?" "It is over in Snake Place." "May I come with you? What are you going to do?" "I am going to hoe." "I can help you cut the weeds and you will finish in a few days." "I shall be glad to have you come." So they went together to Snake Place. When they got there, the Tarantula exerted himself to be polite. He said to the boy, "Go and sit in the shade, and I will cut the weeds for you." The boy did as he was directed. But the Tarantula said to himself, "Some day I will get your clothes." When he had finished his day's work, he said, "It is late now. We shall go home, and come again tomorrow." The boy answered, "Tomorrow you can rest, for tomorrow I am going to hunt." They went back home. When they came to the Tarantula's house, the priest's son said, "Come with me to my house, and eat with us there." But the Tarantula said, "No, I am ashamed." The boy answered, "All right. Thank you for your help. I will do something for you someday." They parted, and the boy went on home.

As he was on his way home, a woman came to his house in Matsaḳa, carrying a basket of cornmeal. She brought with her her five sisters, each carrying their baskets of meal. The boy's mother heard them. She told her daughter, "Somebody's coming." The women were walking heavily. The mother did not feel happy at the visit of these women. "You're coming, aren't you?" she said to them. She took their baskets of flour, and went into the inner room and emptied them into the grinding stones. She came back bringing paper-bread, and said to them, "Eat." They ate, and they said, "Thank you." Then the boy's mother said to them, "What is it that you have come for?" The eldest of the six sisters answered her, "We have come to marry your son." His mother said, "He is not here, I do not know when he will be back. Perhaps he will marry you. It is for him to say." The mother filled two of their baskets with dried peaches, and two with fresh meat, and two with dried meat, and on the basket of the eldest sister she laid a woman's belt. They said, "We will go now. We will come back when he is here." They went out.

As they were returning to their house, the priest's son came from his field. The evening meal was waiting for him, and they sat down. While they were eating, his mother said, "My son, those six girls of the Sand Hill Crane clan who live in Paɬtowa[1] came with corn-meal this afternoon. The eldest sister had the largest basket. If they come after the evening meal, if you go into the other room, excuse yourself until you find out if she is a clever woman."

As they finished their meal, the eldest sister came into their house. The boy's mother said, "There she comes." The boy looked up. She came down the ladder. They said, "Sit down." She sat down with the boy, and ate with him.[2] After they had finished, she went to the wall-bench, and the boy got up and sat beside her. Then his mother told her son to go into another room, and the girl went too. The boy forgot what his mother had told him. He liked this woman. He told his mother to make the bed. His mother was angry. She took in the bear skin and the sleeping blanket. The boy lay down and the girl also.

The boy said, "I shall sleep in the same bed with you, but we shall not marry. Tomorrow we shall see if you can grind the corn between morning and noon. I will go out and hoe my field; if you finish before noon, we shall marry." So the next morning when the girl got up, she asked the boy's mother for some corn. His mother said, "No, wait until after the morning meal; then I will bring it." They had their morning meal. Again, after it was over, the girl asked her mother-in-law for corn and the mother went into an inner room and picked out the hardest popcorn. It was hard and shiny. When the girl saw it, she cried. Then she thought to herself, "It is always the nicest looking boys who are most valuable. It is their mothers who give the girls the hardest corn." She comforted herself and sat down and began to shell it. The mother did not even parch the corn for her. The girl had to put the pot in the fireplace for herself, and parch the kernels. She stirred it over the coals, and the boy went to the field again. She finished the parching, and spread it out to cool, and winnowed it in the basket. When it was ready she put it into the grinding stone. It was so hard it flew out under her stone. She could not break it.

Over in the field, the priest's son finished his hoeing before noon, and came back to his home. Poor girl, she was still grinding. She

---

[1] One of the named sections of Zuni.
[2] "A queer thing for her to do."

was almost exhausted. Every few minutes she went outside to urinate to rest herself. She saw the boy coming, and she said to herself, "He is coming, and I have not finished." She went back to her work. When he came in, he stopped where she was, and he said to her, "We shall not marry now, because I find you are not good at grinding." The woman cried. She rose and got her blanket, put it upon her head and went home. She sat and cried. Her sisters said, "It is no use for us to try. We have worked hard. Anyway, we can marry other boys even if they are not priest's sons." But the priest's son thought some of the other sisters would come. He said to himself, "Perhaps I shall marry them."

The boy asked his mother to bring him food. His mother said, "Yes, my dear." She set out the meal and the boy sat down and ate. When he was through, he said, "I am going back to my field again." He still had the biggest patch to do. As he passed through Badger Place, the Tarantula was watching. He said, "I shall speak to you again so I will get your clothes." When the boy came along, he said, "You are coming, aren't you?" "Yes." "Come over here. Sit down and you can get rested before you go to your field." So the boy sat down a little way back from the hole. The Tarantula took out a cigarette and they smoked. He said, "I see you have many girls wanting to marry you. Let me put on your clothes and you can see how you look. You really cannot see yourself in that glass. If I wear your clothes, you can see yourself as the girls see you." The boy said, "I shall be glad to see how I look." He took off his shirt and trousers and his fringed moccasins and the wrist-guard and his beads. The Tarantula put them on, one after the other. The boy was naked. He was ashamed and tried to cover himself with his hands. "What shall I do?" he said. The Tarantula said, "Just cover yourself with your hands; we are the only ones around here. See how fine you look." The Tarantula backed off a little, "Now can you see better how you look?" The boy answered, "Yes, that is just the way I look." The Tarantula backed farther toward his hole, and said, "Now you can see better." The boy said, "Yes, that is fine." At last the Tarantula got to his hole, and he sang out, "You look just like me. People hate you." He jumped into his hole, and made off with all the boy's clothes. When the boy saw that his clothes were gone, he cried, "What shall I do?" He ran to the hole and tried to dig an entrance, but he worked and worked, and he had no success.

Pekwin came from Hecokta that evening, and his wife said to him, "Our son has not come home yet." He answered, "He must be coming soon." It grew very late, but still he did not come. His father went out to look for him late at night. He came to Owl Place. As he went he sang:

> Kanaite[1] tell me where you are, Ķanaite.
> Ķanaite Ķanaite.

Owl Mother heard the Pekwin's voice. She said, "What are you doing here, father?" He said to her, "Have you seen my son? He came out to his field today; I am looking for him, but I cannot find him." Owl said, "Do not cry. You will find him at Snake Place. He is crying over there." His father said, "Why is he crying?" Owl said, "His is crying because the Tarantula offered to show him how he looked by putting on his clothes, and disappeared with them into his hole. Your son is naked. He tried to dig the Tarantula out of his hole, but he could not succeed. He is crying over there." The old man asked the owl, "Do you know how to get my boy's clothes back?" Owl answered, "I do not know unless the Ahaiyute will help you. Go now to your son. He is still there; go and say to him, 'Let your clothes go, you have lots of clothes at home.' He will not wish to give up his clothes. Therefore you can go to the priests tomorrow and work on prayersticks for the Ahaiyute and ask them to help you."

Pekwin thanked her and went on to his boy at Badger Place. The boy saw his father. He cried again. He said, "Father, I have lost my clothes. The Tarantula took my clothes and went into his hole. I have dug and dug, and I cannot get them. What shall I do?" His father said, "Let them go." The boy said, "No. I cannot give them up."

His father went home and told his mother and sisters that the boy had lost his clothes and did not wish to come home without them, that he wished to wait at Badger Place until he had recovered them. His mother made lunch and took it out to him. As she came near, the boy covered himself with his hands and cried again. She said, "Poor child, how did you come to let the Tarantula have your clothes?" "He told me he would let me see how I looked, then he ran into his hole." The boy cried again. His mother said, "Well, your father has gone to the other priests and they are making prayersticks for the Ahaiyute. They will help you get the clothes." So when the boy finished his meal, she comforted him again, and said to him, "You will be back tonight."

The father of the boy went with the other priests of the council to their ceremonial room. They all greeted one another and asked what he had to say. He said, "Yesterday my son went to the fields.

---

[1] Name of his son.

For two days the Tarantula had helped him in his hoeing, and on the third day he asked to exchange clothes with him. He was going to show him how he looked. Then he backed into his hole with the stolen clothes. My son could not get them back. I went out to look for him last night, and I lost my way. At Owl Spring Owl told me how to get his clothes. She directed me to come to you; together we should make prayersticks for the Ahaiyute and ask them to help us."

The priests answered him, "We will do as you have said," and they worked on the prayersticks. They made three for Elder Brother, and three for Younger Brother. After they had finished they placed the sticks in the basket, and they prayed, "We are giving you these to pay you to help our son who has lost his clothes. If there is any way, we ask you to help our son." They sprinkled prayermeal and the father of the boy took the prayersticks out to the shrine of the Ahaiyute at Eastern Road.

The Ahaiyute were living there with their grandmother. They said, "Somebody is coming." The priest came in with his bundle of feathersticks. Their grandmother said, "How do you do, my son?" He answered, "Well." She said, "Sit down," and placed a stump for him to sit on. He presented his prayersticks to the six directions and laid them down. The grandmother went to the fireplace and took out mush balls from the ashes and brought dried venison. He ate. When he had finished, he said, "Thank you," and the grandmother removed the food. She said, "What have you come for?" He answered, "My sons, I need your help. My fathers, the priests, have made these prayersticks to ask for your help in recovering the clothing of my son. He went out to hoe his field at Badger Place. The Tarantula who lives there was friendly and helped him. On the third day he suggested that they exchange clothing, that he might see how fine he looked. He gave him his white shirt and trousers and moccasins and leggins and his wristguard. The Tarantula stepped back toward his hole and said, 'This is the way you look.' At last he went into his hole, and he took with him all the clothing of my son. When he did not come home that night, I looked for him, and when I came to Owl Spring Owl Mother heard me crying and asked what was the matter. She told me where my son was, and I asked her how we should recover his clothing. She said, 'The priests shall make prayersticks for the Ahaiyute and they will help you to recover the clothing of your son.' I went and found my son, and he would not come home. My wife took food to her son, and I went to the priests. We all met in our ceremonial room and worked on the prayersticks. When they were finished, the priests told me to bring them here and ask you for your help." The Ahaiyute answered, "Of course, we are glad to help you but not today. Go home and tell your people to make paper-bread for the fourth day. Tell your wife to take food to her son, and take something for him to lie on at night."

The boy's father went home. His mother had hoped the Ahaiyute would help them immediately. She asked, "Are they going to help you?" He answered "Yes, but not for four days." The mother was very sad but the father said, "We cannot help it. They want me to tell the bow priest to make proclamation that everyone shall make paper-bread."

The boy's father went out and went to the house of the bow priest. He said, "Sit down." His wife brought out food. The boy's father said, "No, I am not hungry. Thank you." The bow priest asked, "What is it that you want? Maybe you are in a hurry." The boy's father answered, "The Ahaiyute have asked that you make proclamation that all the people make paper-bread for the fourth day." The bow priest answered, "I will call it out immediately." The boy's father said, "Thank you. Be happy all night." He went home, and he said to his wife, "I shall take out food to my son and something for him to sleep on." So the boy's mother got the paper-bread and the venison, and his father took the bear skin and the blanket and took them to Badger Place for his son. Again the boy cried. He was ashamed of his nakedness. As soon as his father got there, he put the blanket around him and spread out the bear skin, and his father put out the food and he ate. He was very hungry. When he had finished he wrapped what was left up in his blanket, and his father told him that the Ahaiyute would help him to recover his clothes on the fourth day. He said, "I have been to the Ahaiyute and they will come to our aid in four days. They asked me to have the bow priest make proclamation that everyone make paper-bread in four days. In this way they are going to help to get your clothes. For four days you will remain here and we shall bring you food." His son answered, "Very well, I will wait here for you."

While his father went out to visit his son, the bow priest made proclamation from the house-tops. He said, "My people, for three days you will all work making paper-bread, and on the fourth day the Ahaiyute will come down and use the paper-bread to make their deer." The people said, "What do you suppose he wants? How will they use it to make deer?"

When the fourth day came, early in the morning before sunrise the Ahaiyute came to Matsaḳa. Ahaiyute called out, "The hiders are hiding."[1] As soon as he heard the Ahaiyute coming, the father of the boy went to the bow priest to ask him to call out that the women should bring their paper-bread to the house of the bow priest. The bow priest went up on the top of the house. The Ahaiyute were still a mile from the village. He called, "My people, bring the paper-bread to my house. The Ahaiyute are coming in." The women sifted the paper-bread in willow baskets and made meal and every house took a small basket of this paper-bread meal and carried it to the bow priest. When everybody had brought their baskets, the bow priest spread out a buckskin and they emptied their meal upon it. They went home. No one was left in the house but the bow priest, Pekwin and the chief priests of the four directions.

The Ahaiyute came. They went into the house of the priest. He had set warm water in the fireplace. The Ahaiyute said, "How have you lived these days, my fathers, my mothers, my children?" They answered, "Happily, thank you." The priest said, "Sit down." They sat down. When they had sat down, they asked for warm water, and when it was brought, they poured it into the paper-bread meal and stirred it with their dirty hands. They made coyotes and deer, rabbits and field-mice. They used all the meal. When they had made these, the Ahaiyute took the figures and went out to Badger Place. They set them down near the hole of the Tarantula. Then they cried out again, "The hiders are hiding." They called out just as if they had killed Navaho. The Tarantula heard them, and came up to the entrance of his hole dressed in his fine clothes. He thought, "I wonder what is going on around here. Perhaps the girls will like me as well as they like that nice handsome boy." All the people were out chasing game. They kept crying, "Anybody who is around here, help us to kill deer." The Tarantula cried too, "Which way, which way?" He ran out of his hole, and all the people ran after him and grabbed him. They said, "Take off your clothes." He was confused and he pulled them off one by one. The deer ran off and scattered, but the people got the clothing of the boy.

The Ahaiyute came and spoke to the Tarantula. They said, "We are going to give you a new name. You did wrong. After this everybody who comes across you will step upon you. You will be called Ohatcika. Everybody will hate you."

The Ahaiyute took the clothes to the boy. They said, "Here are your clothes, but do not wear them right away. Wait for four days. Take them with you and in four days you may put them on." The

---

[1] Or in Cushing's translation, "The skulkers are skulking"; a cry of the scalp dance.

father of the boy came up to where they stood. He said, "Thank you, Ahaiyute. I will remember you, and I will see that you receive your prayersticks every year." They said to him, "Thank you. We are glad to have helped you." The Ahaiyute went back to their home.

The father and his son also went back to their house, but the boy went back wearing the old blanket. Before, everybody had wanted to marry him, but he looked poor now. After four days he put on his good clothes, but nobody cared for him any more. He married a girl who was not pretty. That is why today the handsomest boy marries a homely girl; his mother thought he was too valuable to marry any of the girls who asked him. And that is why we always hate the Tarantula and step upon him when we see him.

LAZY BONES (6)[1]

Notes, 309

They were living in Matsaka. A poor girl lived with her grandmother on the outskirts of the village to the southwest. The priest had a handsome son and four daughters. His sisters and their mother thought everything of this boy. One day he went out to his field to work. Everybody in the village liked to see him. All the girls wished that they might marry him, but they were ashamed to talk to him. He went to his field and as he was coming home at evening the poor girl went out to get water. She was big and tall and bald-headed. She had had sores on her head and had had to cut her hair. She didn't know how to make a fire or to cook. They called her Lazy Bones. While she filled the jar the boy was washing his hands on his way home. The girl was ashamed because she was big and shingle-haired, but the boy asked her if he could have a drink from her gourd. "All right." She didn't think of marrying that boy, because she was big and shingle-haired and could not do anything. She gave him a drink and the boy said, "Thank you." The priest's son liked the girl and thought that she would have been pretty if she had had good hair and could have made fires and cooked. The boy said, "Could you come again tomorrow?" "Yes, I will be here."

The next evening the girl washed her face and put on better clothes. She said to her grandmother, "Fix the fire, and have supper ready, for the priest's son spoke to me." Her grandmother was happy. She put out paper-bread for their evening meal. The girl took her jar and went to the river. She had a ragged black woman's-

---

[1] The story is called "Genitals Shown".

dress over her hair. The boy liked her. She got to the river and filled the jar. She pretended that she didn't see the boy, but he said, "You have come, haven't you?" "Yes." "Give me a drink?" "Yes." She dipped up the water and gave it to the boy. He asked, "May I go with you to your house?" "Yes, if you wish, if you think that your mother and father and sisters would like it. But if you don't think that they would like it, it will be all right if you don't come." "Oh that's all right. I don't mind what they say." So they went home to the girl's house. It was just about dark and no one saw them. Her grandmother was excited. She had not expected such fortune. She thought to herself, "My poor granddaughter, now we are having the priest's son." There was the priest's son following her granddaughter down the ladder. He had on a blue shirt and white trousers, and his best turquoise necklaces and shell beads. The grandmother said, "Sit down, sit down, have a seat, have a seat!" She was kind and flustered. The girl set her jar down. They had nothing but some paper-bread for the evening meal. The grandmother remembered that she had some matcepi[1] and she went into the store room and got a package of it. They ate pinches of matcepi with the paper-bread.

After they were through the poor grandmother went into the other room, so as to let her granddaughter and the priest's son sleep in the good room. The boy got up early and went to his field before breakfast. Over there his sisters and mother were waiting for him and thinking how he was married to the nicest girl in the village. About noon he came home and they were very kind to him. The boy was sleepy and lay down and the sisters asked him to eat. He said, "All right."

Again when evening came he went to the girl's house. Again for the evening meal the grandmother set out paper-bread and matcepi. After they had finished the grandmother went into the other room and left the best room for them to sleep in. The boy left early in the morning for his field. While he was working in the field the grandmother said to the girl, "Now you are going to show that you are married; go and get a basket of corn to grind for them today." So she put on her grandmother's old moccasins[2] and she put the ragged woman's-dress over her head. The people thought that she was going to work "for her fathers."[3]

They heard someone coming up the ladder and stepping in. Right away the boy's sisters did not like it. They looked angrily at her.

---

[1] Guts of rabbits roasted in ashes and wrapped in corn husks for future use.

[2] Because she had none of her own.

[3] I. e. for the priests' families. For this custom see II: 60; 78; 170.

They didn't even ask her to sit down. The youngest sister said, "Sit down," and pushed a stump over towards her with her feet. The sisters went back into the other room and paid no attention to her. They told their mother, "That girl is married to our brother." The mother was just as rude. She went into the room where the girl was and she said to her, "You are coming?" She brought out just paper-bread and put it before the girl. She did not give her anything else. Poor girl, she ate just a little and said, "Thank you." Then she said, "I have come to grind." His mother went into the other room and picked out the hardest corn.[1] She filled a great big basket. The girl shelled the corn all alone; the mother and sisters did not help her at all.[2] After it was all shelled she put it in the basket and picked up all the kernels that had scattered and put them in the basket. Poor girl, she said, "I am going," and she went out.[3]

She went to her house. She said nothing to her grandmother of the way they had treated her at the priest's house, but the grandmother saw that the kernels were hard as glass, and she said, "Oh, my granddaughter, this shows that they did not like you."[4] The girl was ashamed. Tears ran down her cheeks.

Old Woman Spider in the ceiling saw her. She said, "You have to grind, don't you? I will help you. I am coming down the ladder." The girl looked up to see who was talking. "I am Spider Woman. I live in the rafters. I am grateful that you are kind and do not break my house. You have let me live here, and I will help you. Your husband is coming soon, and as soon as he has gone to his field I will help you." The girl felt a little better, but she was not sure yet. Her husband came. She stopped grinding while he was in the room. She gave him his noon meal, and was very kind to him.[5] When he had eaten his noon meal he went back to the fields.

As soon as he was gone Old Woman Spider came down and sat beside the girl. Poor girl, she had not finished her first grinding in her first metate, and still she had a whole basket full. Spider went up and sat in the nape of her neck (under the hair braid) and she ground and ground, and she was not tired. Poor girl, she looked so funny; she did not have hair enough to cover the spider. Her grandmother said, "Why, my child, you do it so fast." She was happy. She saw how well the girl was doing. It seemed as if it were easy.

---

[1] The so-called popcorn.

[2] Very impolite.

[3] If they had not been so rude she would have stayed there to grind.

[4] The narrator bowed his head over his clasped hands in imitation of the old woman's grief.

[5] "The way brides always are."

10*

At the priest's house the boy's sisters were wondering if she would be able to grind that popcorn. "I wonder if she is doing it," they would say. "She is as lazy as can be. Maybe she is not doing it fine." So they sent the youngest sister to find out what she was doing. They said to her, "Ask if your brother is there, and say that our father wants him." The little girl went to Lazy Bones' house. She heard someone coming up the ladder. There was the little girl coming down. The grandmother said, "Sit down, sit down." The girl was grinding as easily as could be. The little girl stood by her and said, "Where is my brother?" "He went to the field." "Our father wants him." "You will find him in the field." All the time while she was talking the girl was grinding. The little girl ran home just as fast as she could and slid right down the ladder, calling out, "She is grinding and grinding. I never saw anything like it. The basket is almost full and she does it as easily as can be." The sisters laughed. They did not believe her. "I'm not joking," she said. "One of you go over too." They said, "Nobody can grind popcorn." The little girl told the mother. The mother did not believe it either. The little sister said, "You had better cook a feast for her." She did not believe her, but she got out the raw green corn and scraped it with a stone knife and put it into the stew. She had it ready for the girl.

Pretty soon Lazy Bones finished her grinding and piled it in the basket. It made a great pile straight up, for there was lots of corn.[1] She put her old dress over her head, and Old Woman Spider said, "I'm going up to my house, and whenever you clean up, you must be careful not to kill me." She went back to her web. The girl took the basket on her head, and went up the ladder. Her grandmother was smiling to think how well she had done. She walked to the priest's house, and the women in the village said, "Oh my, look at that meal! Lazy Bones must be married to the priest's son." The girls all ran out to see and they were jealous. There was the great, high-piled basket of cornmeal on her head. She was proud of that, even if she was wearing ragged clothes. But the girls in the priest's house disliked her, no matter if she did grind as nobody else could. She came in with her great basket of cornmeal. They said, "You are coming, aren't you?" They were amazed when they saw the big basket of flour. She set it down, and the mother picked it up and took it into the grinding room. They had the feast ready for her, and brought out the stew and paper-bread. She ate, and the mother said to herself, "I shall give you my nice moccasins, because you

[1] This grinding should be paid for by clothes given the bride by the groom's mother.

have done so well with the hard work." She felt that she liked her now. She brought out moccasins and buckskin (for puttees) and she made up the bundle. She went into the other room again, and took a large bowl for her to carry home the rest of the stew in. She took her woman's-dress and in it she put paper-bread. The girl put the dress on her back and tied it over her chest and she carried the bowl of stew on her head. There was no way for her to take the bundle so the little sister went along to carry it.

She went to her grandmother's house. Her grandmother thought, "Poor grandchild, I wonder what you will bring, maybe a little stew, but maybe they won't give you anything but paper-bread." Then the grandmother saw the girl with the bundle on her back and the bowl in her hand and she said, "That is nice, that is nice!" The little girl on the roof was listening to what she said. Finally she came in and the old woman was ashamed. She said, "Sit down, sit down, have a seat, have a seat." Then she saw the bundle of the moccasins and buckskin and she was happier than ever. The little girl gave her the bundle and went home. She told her mother how happy the old grandmother was.

Again, there was to be a rabbit hunt, and on the third day the girl went to the boy's house to get the corn to grind that night. She wore her nice white buckskin puttees and moccasins, and she was much better-looking. But the sisters were not nice to her. The older ones hated her and called, "There she comes, shingle-haired!" Again the girl came in and the sisters told her to sit down. She sat down and they brought paper-bread. After she had eaten, the mother asked, "What have you come to ask?" "Tomorrow there is to be a rabbit hunt, so I came to get corn to grind tonight for your sweet corncake (hepaloka)." "All right." She went into the other room and picked out the hard corn again. She brought a bowlful. The girl sat down and shelled the ears, then she picked up all the scattered kernels and put them into the basket. She said to the eldest, "I am going." "All right."

She went home and put it into the grinding stone, and again Old Spider Woman came down from the rafters. She sat in the nape of her neck and her hair was so thin that it scarcely covered her. She ground the corn as easily as could be. Just at evening she got it all done, and she put the water on the fire. Spider went up into her web. The grandmother went over and chewed the corn meal.[1] The girl put half the boiling water into the bowl and took the stirring sticks and stirred it a long time until it was smooth. Then she took the little bowl of chewed meal and poured that into

---

[1] The action of the saliva furnishes the sweetening.

the rest. It made it thinner. When she had stirred this smooth, she put in more meal to make it thick so that it couldn't boil over the pot. In the other room she made the oven. She set the flat stones upright at right angles in the fireplace, and inside of them she made a deep bed of coals. Over this she put another flat stone and she got clay and plastered it into the chinks. She covered the cakes with corn husks and put them on the oven stones and put another flat stone on top and plastered it again.

While she was making the oven the grandmother went out to Corn Mountain to find the bees. She went hobbling along, and she came to where the bees were. She said, "I am going to ask you to come tonight to sweeten my granddaughter's corncakes so that her mother- and father-in-law and sisters will like it." They said, "We will come. Tell your granddaughter to make holes for us with her finger in the plaster of the oven and we will come." The grandmother came home and told her granddaughter, and she made the holes for the bees. She put the corncakes in just as her grandmother said.

The priest's son came home, and she went into the other room and brought out paper-bread for the evening meal. They went to sleep. Everybody was cooking meat so that they would be ready for the hunt. Poor girl and her grandmother! they did not have any meat to boil. The grandmother was sleeping in the room where the corn cake was baking and the boy and girl were sleeping in the first inner room. The old woman could hardly sleep for thinking about the coming of the bees. They came down the chimney, and she heard them buzzing. They went into the holes of the oven and left their honey, and they went out up the chimney again. The grandmother keep thinking, "I wonder how the corncake will be." She was wishing that daylight would come so that she might know how the corncake would be.

The next morning they waked early. The husband didn't go to the field because he wanted to taste the corncake. The girl went into the grandmother's room and took it out of the oven. She took it into the first room and set it down and looked at it and right away she liked that corncake. Her husband said, "May I have a piece?" "No, it is your mother's. If she gives me some you may have some." She took the fibre ring (support for hot pots) and put it on her head. Her husband lifted up the pot and put it on her head. She took it to his house. While the grandmother cleaned the house, the girl went over to the priest's house. Her mother-in-law was waiting for her. They heard her come in, and they said, "There she is coming down." The mother said, "Coming, aren't you?" "Yes, here is the sweet corncake." She put it down, and they told her to sit down. They got out paper-bread and they all ate together. The mother took the bowl of corncake and tasted it, and right away she said, "Oh my daughters, come and taste how good your sister's corncake is." They came and put their fingers in and they exclaimed, "My, what a good pudding!" The oldest one took a taste and said, "My sister, how did you make this?" "I made it just as you do." The father and all the rest liked the corncake. They were all happy. They treated her just as if they had always liked her. She ate just a little, for she knew that her husband and grandmother were waiting for her. She said, "I am going." Her mother went into the other room and she got a big bowl of venison stew and brought it out. Then she brought a roll of paper-bread. She went into the back room again and the girl could see a row of dresses hanging there. The mother took a woman's dress and a belt and she tied them with the paper-bread and brought the bundle out and gave it to the girl. The girl was very happy to have the dress and the belt. The mother said, "Did you make corncake for yourself?" "I made it just for you." "Perhaps brother (i. e. her son) would like to have some." The mother got out a small bowl and gave it to her full of pudding. The little sister helped her take the things home. The girls in the village saw her with the big bowl of stew and the corncake and the big bundle on her back, and they said, "There she comes, Lazy Bones! She is not fit to have that boy. She is no good. How shall we get her husband away from her? We shall find some way." The girl went home. The grandmother was happy when she saw the big bowl of stew and the corncake and the big bundle on her back. She heard how kindly her father- and mother-in-law had treated her. She untied the bundle and there was the dress and belt, and she hung them over the deer antlers.

The next day they were dancing kokokci, and the girl was anxious to go, because now she had this new dress and new belt and new moccasins. When she heard the dancers coming in before daylight she kept waking every few minutes because she was thinking about the dress. She waked up. She built a fire. She had plenty of flour now, because every day when she began to grind Grandmother Spider came down. She helped her grandmother make paper-bread every morning. "I had better wash my hair," she thought. "I am going to the dance." None of it was longer than her bangs. She washed her hair, and her husband's hair, so that they might go to see the dancers. She put on her dress, and her belt, and her moccasins. Just as the dancers were coming out, she was there in the plaza. She had her white buckskin puttees and moccasins on, and her nice woman's dress. Again the girls in the village said, "There is that Shingle-hair. How shall we get her husband away from her so that we can marry him?" They were jealous because they thought that she wasn't fit to marry that nice boy. They were surprised that when nobody cared for her she should have nicer clothes than theirs, and they were jealous.

That evening after the dancers went in she went home. Her husband had liked to see his wife dressed so nicely in the plaza and he was in a hurry to embrace her. They played together. The next morning the girls were talking, and they said, "What shall we do to take that Lazy Bones' husband? She is shingle-haired. We will have the bow priest make a proclamation that the girls will have a contest in the plaza, and whoever has the longest hair will marry the priest's son."

The girls sent their youngest sister to the bow priest. He and his wife heard someone coming. They said, "Someone is coming." They looked up and the little girl was coming in. They were eating the evening meal. They asked her to sit down, so she sat down and ate with them. She ate a little and said, "Thank you." Then the priest said, "What is it that you have come to say?" "My older sisters are sending me over here to ask that you make proclamation tonight that whoever wishes to marry the priest's son shall come to the plaza. Whoever has the longest hair shall have him. We want you to call this out." "When did you want this?" "For the fourth day." "I will do this." "Thank you." She went home. Her sisters were waiting for her. She came in and they asked her, "What did the bow priest say?" "He will call it out after he has finished his evening meal. It will be done on the fourth day." They were pleased because they knew that they had long hair, and that the girl's was shingled. They began grinding corn to be pretty when the day came.[1] When they finished grinding, every night they washed their hair so that it would be nice and glossy.

The bow priest called it out: "In four days the girls who wish to marry the priest's son will come to the plaza and whoever has the longest hair shall have him." The boy and his wife went to the top of their roof and they heard what the bow priest said. She was very sad. The husband felt sad too because he knew that the girls had longer hair than his wife and he hated to leave her. He liked her very much. His wife said, "He called that out because they don't like me. If you really want to stay with me we will find some way to do something. If we don't they will get you." The boy felt sorry for his wife and wondered how to make her hair grow. "Is there

[1] "The fine meal sticking to their arms makes the skin whiter."

any way to make your hair grow before the fourth day?" he asked. "Yes, sweetheart. I have a grandmother who lives up here. I can call her if you want me to." "Yes, I shall be glad if anybody can help you because I love you and I want to stay with you."

When the girl's husband was asleep Grandmother Spider came down and sat on the stone bench. The girl was sitting on the floor. Old Spider Woman spit on her fingers and wet the ends of the girl's hair. She took the girl's stirring sticks and rolled the ends of her hair around the sticks and pulled it till it was down below her shoulders. She folded it up and wrapped it into a queue. The girl was happy, and when the boy waked up she had a queue. He was as glad as could be. She was glad too. She was not ashamed to be seen now, and she went out without a blanket over her head.[1] Before the contest the girls saw her coming out with her queue and they said, "I guess it is her grandmother's."[2]

The next day when her husband was in the fields, Old Spider Woman called her again, and came and sat behind her. She spat on her fingers and wet the ends of her hair. She took the girls' stirring stick and wound her hair around it and pulled and pulled until her hair came down to her waist. Then she said, "Now my daughter, feel your hair. It is down to your waist." She felt it and it was long. She was as pleased as could be, for it was long thick hair, and she had a big queue. Old Spider Woman tied it up and went back to the rafters. She went up to her web. The girl's husband came in again, and he was happy because his wife looked just as he had always wanted her to look. She was not a bit ashamed any more. She went to grind for her mother-in-law and now she had a big queue. The girls were more jealous every time she came out. She didn't care now for she had nice clothes and a nice queue and her husband loved her.

Again the third day the boy was not home and Old Spider Woman called her again and the girl came and sat in front of her. She unwound the black-dyed yarn from her queue. Then she went to the metate and got the rubbing stone and wet it. She wrapped the girl's hair around it and pulled four times. It came to her buttocks. She wrapped her bangs around the stone and twisted them to make them curly. When she was through she went back to the ceiling. The girl's husband came home and he was as happy as could be. His wife was prettier than ever, and her hair was thicker.

---

[1] "She had never done this before."

[2] "The old women used to cut off their queues when they had lots of lice and fasten them on whenever they were going out."

After the noon meal he went to his father's house. He told his wife, "Tomorrow will be the fourth day and the girls will meet in the plaza. I will find out what to do." He came to his father's house and he asked, "Father, tomorrow will be the fourth day and the girls want me to marry the one who has the longest hair. The bow priest has made proclamation. What shall I do?" "Isn't there any way for you to get help from somebody so that your wife's hair will grow longer? At noon the girl will go to the plaza when the bow priest comes for her. But you should not go to the plaza from your wife's house. Come here and dress in your best clothes." "That was all I came to ask you. Thank you, father." He went home. His sisters who had hated his wife at first were sorry now that she might not be able to keep their brother. They thought that she had short hair.

When evening came Lazy Bones felt sad. She was not sure. She thought that maybe some girl had still longer hair than she had. She worried about it that night, and her husband too. The next morning in that house that had asked for this contest they washed their hair and brushed their dresses with the hair brush. Lazy Bones woke up and washed her hair and her husband's hair. After the morning meal, the bow priest called out that they were ready. The boy went to his own house, and the girl washed her hair. It fell to her buttocks. Old Spider Woman came down again. Right away she pulled off the yarn wrapping and picked up the rubbing stone. She brushed out the hair, wrapped it around the rubbing stone and pulled it four times. It fell to her knees. Old Woman Spider put the stone away, spat on the hair and rolled it up and tied it with the yarn into a great big queue. She was so pretty! Then Old Spider Woman went up to her web again. The girl brushed her bangs and took a stirring stick and rolled them on it to make it curl. She put on her white puttees and moccasins and her dress, and her belt and blanket. She sat and waited for the bow priest to come.

About noon the bow priest went first to the house of the girls who had asked for the contest. The others in the village said, "Those are the girls who wanted to marry the priest's son." They made fun of them. The bow priest went in and everybody was waiting for him to bring them out to the bench in the big plaza. He asked if they were all ready. They all had nice hair and they had done it up in the best fashion. Their mother had dressed it for them. They said, "All ready." So they got their blankets and put them over their heads and followed the bow priest up the ladder. Everybody was waiting for the girls to come. There was the eldest sister, and two next, and the little sister, and they all went down to the big plaza. Their seats were ready for them, facing north. There were six, one for each of the contestants and one for the priest's son. The bow priest took each girl to her seat and moved her to the six directions and made her sit down.

He went to the boy's house. They heard him coming. When he came in they asked him to sit down, but he said, "No, thank you. Are you ready?" "Yes." The boy was dressed in his best. He put his blanket on, and he followed the bow priest, who took him to the plaza where the girls were. When they got there, the bow priest moved him in every direction, and made him sit down on his seat next to the youngest girl. Again the bow priest went to the girl's house. He asked, "Are you ready?" "Yes." She got up and took her blanket. She looked very pretty with her nice clothes and her large queue. She looked nicer than the other girls but they thought that they had longer hair. She came in following the bow priest. The four sisters nudged each other. The bow priest put his hands on her shoulders and moved her in every direction and made her sit.

Everybody was on the tops of the houses and standing all around. The bow priest said to the priest's son, "You are the priest's son and whoever has the longest hair you shall marry. You shall go to each girl, and you shall take down her hair and marry the one who has the longest." The boy laid aside his blanket where he was sitting and the bow priest took him to the eldest sister. He took off her yarn wrapping and made her stand up, and her hair came down to her waist. Then he went to the next girl and took off the yarn wrapping. She stood up, and her hair fell to her buttocks. He passed to the next and took off the yarn wrapping from her hair. When she stood up her hair fell just below her buttocks. He came to the youngest, and took off the yarn wrapping from her hair. It came down to her thighs when she stood up. Then he came to his wife, and took off the yarn wrapping from her hair. When she stood it came to her knees. The people all laughed and the four girls cried and drew their blankets over their faces and ran home. The boy took his wife and they went home. Everybody laughed; these girls who had wanted to take the husband of Lazy Bones had been fooled.

Again there was another house which had four girls and these girls went to get water. These first girls said to them, "Somehow we must get that girl's husband away from her. She is darker than we are; perhaps that would be the best way. The girl who has the best light-colored, fat, smooth (i. e. not hairy) legs[1] shall marry

---

[1] Even a girl not otherwise beautiful will be chosen for a dance in Zuni if her arms and legs are plump and hairless.

the priest's son." They told the youngest sister to go to the bow priest and ask him to make proclamation. She went that same evening. The bow priest and his wife were at the evening meal when they heard the girl coming. The bow priest nudged his wife and said, "There is another one coming." They asked her to sit down and eat with them. She sat down and ate a little and said, "Thank you." The bow priest asked her, "What have you come to say?" "My sisters are sending me over to ask you to make proclamation that whoever has the best, light-colored, smooth legs like a baby's shall marry the priest's son." "All right, I shall call it out when I have finished my evening meal." "Thank you. I am going." She went out. The girls at their home were very anxious to hear what she had to say. As soon as she came in and had sat down, they asked her what the bow priest had said. She told them that he had said that as soon as he had finished his evening meal he would call it out. They were pleased, for they thought that they were going to have the priest's son because his wife did not have as pretty legs as they had. After a while they heard the priest call it out. They went out and pretended that they didn't know anything about it. He called, "On the fourth day in the plaza the girls will meet and the one who has the best light-colored, fat, smooth legs shall marry the priest's son." The boy and his wife went out and listened too. The girl had nice big legs, but they were dark. Her husband told her not to worry for he thought she had nice legs, but she was afraid.

The next day he went to the field again. The girl went into the inner room to get some corn and she prayed,[1] "You are my mothers, and you will always be here no matter how often I come in here for corn. My store of corn will always increase." Yellow Corn Mother said, "I know you are worried about the fourth day you have to go to the plaza. Come in here when your husband is away and I will wash your legs and they will be made as beautiful as can be." "All right, thank you, my mothers." She came out very happy. She shelled the corn, and told her grandmother to parch it for her to grind. When it had popped she took off her puttees in order to grind with bare legs so the meal would powder them.[2] She ground easily and when she had finished she piled the meal into a bowl. She told her grandmother to watch for her husband from the roof so that she could come out quickly when he came. She took a bowl of cornmeal and a bowl of water into the corn room while her grandmother watched on the roof. Corn Mother heard her coming

---

[1] As usual.

[2] "Whoever grinds gets lighter every day."

in and she turned into a person. The girl set the bowl of water down on the floor and Corn Mother told her to put in her right foot. With her hands Corn Mother washed her right leg, and it turned all light and yellow and fat and beautiful. She put her left foot in the bowl and Corn Mother washed that with her hands and it too turned light and yellow and fat and beautiful. She said, "This is all, my child." "Thank you." The girl took her bowl of water and as she was going out she looked back and there was not anybody there.[1]

When the fourth day came the girl was not troubled at all. In the morning after they had eaten the bow priest called it out. When the boy heard this he went to his own house. As soon as he had gone the girl went into the corn room again. Yellow Corn Mother was waiting for her (as a person). She dipped her hand in the yellow water (i. e. colored with yellow cornmeal) and washed her right leg first, and then her right arm and hand. Then she dipped her hand in the yellow water, and washed her left leg and arm and hand. She dipped her hand in again and washed her face. She was very pretty when Corn Mother finished. The girl said, "Thank you," and went out into the other room. She sprinkled the rest of the water over the floor.[2] She dried herself and put on footless yarn stockings and waited for the bow priest.

The bow priest came out and went to the house of the girls who had asked for this contest. He went in and asked, "Are you ready?" "Yes." They had no moccasins on, nor puttees, just yarn leggins. They followed the bow priest to the plaza. There were six seats ready and he motioned them toward the six directions and seated them. Again he went to the priest's house and as he came in he asked the boy, "Are you ready?" "Yes." He pulled his blanket about him and followed the bow priest to the plaza. The priest moved him in the six directions and seated him next to the youngest sister. Again he went to the girl's house. He called to her, "Are you ready?" "Yes." She was very beautiful, the most beautiful woman they had ever seen. Right away he knew that she was the best girl. She was very kind to him. As soon as the people saw them coming they said, "How pretty she is." He moved her in the six directions and seated her. Then he turned to the boy and said, "You are the priest's son. You shall get up and begin with the eldest sister and take off her stockings. Whoever has the fattest, smoothest and most beautiful legs you shall marry." The priest's son went to the

---

[1] "This is why people's right feet and hands are bigger than the left ones, for Corn Mother washed the right foot first."

[2] To keep the luck in the house. For instance one never throws outside the water in which a turquoise bracelet has been washed.

eldest sister. She held up her legs and he pulled off her stockings. They were rather pretty legs. He went to the next sister. He pulled off her stockings and she stretched out her legs. They were nice and yellow-skinned, but they were not fat. He went to the next sister, and he pulled off her stockings. She held out her legs. They were nice and yellow-skinned and fat but they were a little hairy. He went to the youngest sister and pulled off her stockings. She held up her legs. They were very pretty legs, yellow-skinned, smooth, and fat. He went to his wife and pulled off her stockings. She held up her legs. They were the most beautiful legs ever seen, the yellow-est-skinned and the smoothest and the fattest. Right away these girls pulled their blankets over their faces and ran to their homes. Everybody laughed at them. The priest's son took his wife home.

That evening in a third house the girls said, "That girl isn't fit to marry the priest's son. What can we do to get her away? She has no dimples. We have looked at her closely and she didn't have any." One of them said, "Did you look at her closely? I would not like to fail after these two contests." "I did. She hasn't any." "Let us call a contest and have it proclaimed that whoever has the prettiest dimples shall marry the priest's son." They sent the young-est sister to the home of the bow priest. He and his wife were eating their evening meal when they heard the girl coming. She came and they asked her to sit down and eat with them. She sat down and ate a little. Then the bow priest asked, "What is it that you have come to say?" "My sisters have sent me to ask you to make proc-lamation that whoever has the prettiest dimples shall marry the priest's son." "All right. I shall call it out when I have finished my evening meal." "Thank you, I am going." She went out. When she got home, her sisters could hardly wait to hear what the bow priest had said. When she had sat down they said, "What did he say?" "He said that he will make the proclamation after he has finished his evening meal." "We are happy." They were pleased because nobody had dimples like theirs. They were sure that they were going to marry the priest's son. The boy and his wife went out and listened. The wife was afraid this time. Her husband said, "Maybe you will get some."

When the fourth day came the boy went to his house in the morning. The girl was worried; she was afraid that she was going to lose her husband. Just then Spider Woman came down. She dipped her baton stick in corn pollen. She stood before the girl and said, "My child, close your lips." The girl closed her lips. Spider Woman took the baton and poked her in the cheeks. "Now smile," she said. The girl smiled and she was *so* pretty; she had the nicest dimples. She wasn't afraid any more.

The bow priest went to the house of the girls who had asked for the contest. He called to them, "Are you ready ?" "Yes." He took them to the plaza where there were six seats waiting for them. He moved them to the six directions and seated them, the eldest one first. Then he went to the house of the priest's son. The boy was all ready. The bow priest came in and asked, "Are you ready ?" and he answered, "Yes," and followed him to the plaza. He moved him in the six directions and seated him next to the youngest sister. Then he went to the girl's house. She had put on her best clothes and looked very pretty. He said, "Are you ready ?" and she answered, "Yes." She followed him to the plaza. He moved her in the six directions and seated her. Then he said to the boy, "You are the priest's son. You shall stand in front of each one, and each one shall smile. Whoever has the biggest and prettiest dimples, you shall marry." The boy stood in front of the eldest sister. She smiled. Her dimples were rather pretty. He stood in front of the next sister. She smiled. Her dimples were nice but they were too big. He stood in front of the next sister. She had very pretty dimples, but they were not deep enough. He stood in front of the youngest sister. Her dimples were very pretty when she smiled. Then he stood in front of his wife. When she smiled her dimples were so beautiful, that the other girls hid their faces in their blankets and ran home. Everybody laughed at them. This was the third time that the girls had not won in the contest they had asked for. The priest's son embraced his wife and they went home very happy.

There was another house which had four girls and these girls said to them, "We must get that girl's husband away from her. He is too good for her." They planned what they could do. They wanted to be very careful for she had won in the other contests. One of the girls said, "Let us go and ask the bow priest to make proclamation that whoever has the biggest genitals is to marry the priest's son." They agreed to this and sent the youngest sister. She went to the house of the bow priest, and he was eating the evening meal with his wife. They heard her coming, and he said, "There is another one coming." When she came in they asked her to sit down and eat with them. She ate a little, and then the bow priest asked her, "What is it that you have come to ask ?" "My sisters have sent me to ask you to make proclamation that whoever has the biggest genitals shall marry the priest's son." "All right. I shall proclaim it when I have finished my evening meal." "That is all that I have come to say. I am going." She went out.

When she got home her sisters could hardly wait until she had seated herself, to ask what the bow priest had said. She told them that he would call it out that whoever had the biggest genitals was to marry the priest's son. They were very happy for they were sure that they were going to win this time. The boy and his wife heard the proclamation. They hoped that something would happen this time too.

On the fourth day when the husband had gone to the fields, Spider Woman came down from the ceiling. She laid the girl on the floor and took a big gourd and cut it in half. She took the seeds from the gourd and put water in it. She washed the girl's genitals with the water and they grew big like the gourd. The girl was very happy for she was sure that she would be able to keep her husband.

The bow priest came out of his house and went first to the house of the girls who had called for the contest. He asked, "Are you ready ?" "Yes." They followed him to the plaza where the seats were already waiting. He took each one and moved her in the six directions and made her sit down. Then he went to the priest's house where the son was waiting. He said, "Are you ready ?" The boy was dressed in his best. He answered, "Yes," and followed the bow priest to the plaza. The bow priest moved him in the six directions and seated him next to the girls. Then he went to the girl's house and brought her. When she had been moved in all directions and made to sit down, the bow priest put a blanket on the ground and said, "You are the priest's son. You shall go up to each girl and make her lie down on this embroidered ceremonial blanket and pull back her skirt and whoever has the biggest genitals you are to marry." The priest's son went to each one in turn and made her lie down on the embroidered ceremonial blanket. He pulled back her skirt. These girls all had big genitals, but those of his wife were the biggest. The other girls were ashamed. They covered their faces and ran home just as fast as they could. Everybody laughed at them. The boy embraced his wife, and they went home. They were very happy. That is why despised persons marry the nicest people in the pueblo, and then they get to be nice (kokci) people too.

THE GAMBLER WHO MARRIES MOUNTAIN LION'S SISTER (7)[1]

Notes, 311

A long time ago the people lived at Matsaḳa, and the village chief's son, about twenty-two years old, gambled all day with the iankolowe. He gambled all the time and lost all he had. He lost his necklaces and blankets and fields and he lost his sister. Pekwin

---

[1] Recorded by Ruth Bunzel.

won everything he had. Then his father scolded him. The people gambled all the time in the winter. He told the boy to go away and not stay home because he lost everything he had. The boy went away. He had nothing and he slept in the fields and on the hills. He got to a place called Press and Corner (Ehatane). There lived a Mountain Lion and his sister. Mountain Lion's sister was not married, and the Mountain Lion went down from Cipapolima and told his sister, "If any young man comes here and he looks in at your door, keep on weaving and after you pull out the stick if he is still there just go back to your work. If after four times he has not gone away this man is your husband and you must marry him no matter how poor he may be." That is what her brother told her and he went out to Cipapolima.

One day a man came from Kachina Village called Hupomotce. He walked right in and called out the girl's name, Kuyapelitsa. He called her by name and she answered. The man went in and the girl took the man as her husband. He stayed one night and in the morning he went away to the northeast to hunt deer. The girl stayed there.

One afternoon a Coyote came. He looked in the door and the girl looked up and saw someone's shadow. She turned around. Coyote had hidden. She started weaving again, and Coyote looked in again and the girl saw his shadow and turned and looked, and Coyote was looking in the door. The girl said to Coyote, "Why don't you hide, Coyote? If you hide you will be my husband." Coyote had seen the poor man before (the man who lost at gambling). He was hungry and went down to Zuni Lake, near Black Rock, and he went into the lake and washed himself. And after he had washed himself he rolled in the sand to dry and after that he was a nice looking Coyote. He went back to where the girl was, and soon she moved and looked up and the Coyote was standing hiding. Then the girl started work again and pulled the stick out and looked up and there was Coyote again. She thought, "Coyote is fooling me because I told him." Then Coyote was looking; Coyote had gone again. The fourth time the girl looked up, there was Coyote standing in the door, and she said, "Coyote, you are fooling me. You have been here before." She scolded Coyote and Coyote went a little way off and said, "I think I will look for that young man and if I find him I will tell him what the girl wants. Maybe the girl will marry the young man and the young man will be my friend and give me something to eat." He went along looking for the young man.

He found him lying in the shade of a tree. He told him, "Well, friend, let us go and let the girl see us. And if you look in the door

11

and the girl looks up and sees you, you just hide and if she starts
to work look in again. When she looks up, hide again a second time.
And then she will put in some thread and start to work again and
then she will look up again and you hide again. Then when she starts
to work and puts the stick in the loom she will look around again.
Stand right there in the door and she will see you and she will
marry you. I will stay there and be your friend and all you have
to do is to give me something to eat." The young man went with
Coyote because he was very poor and hungry and naked. He went
to the house and looked in the door and the girl turned and looked
and he hid. After a while the girl worked again and he looked in
again and when he did not move she turned around and he hid
again a second time. Then the girl worked again and he looked in
the door and after a while she looked up again and he hid again the
third time. After a while she worked again and then he moved and
she looked up and there he was standing in the door. "Now you
will be my husband," said the girl, and the boy went into the house.
She gave him plenty to eat, bread and venison and corn, and later
she gave him clothes to wear. In the night the girl said, "You are
lucky you have married me. You did what my brother told you.
Now you have married me. But Coyote told you that." He said,
"Yes, Coyote told me that." She said, "Well, you had better call in
poor Coyote and gave him something to eat." He went out after
Coyote and brought him into the house and the girl gave him
venison. The young man and Coyote stayed in the house. Next
morning Mountain Lion Girl told him, "You had better make
yourself some clothes. You know how to make clothes." She went
into the back room and brought out some buckskin and the young
man made a buckskin shirt and buckskin trousers and buckskin
moccasins. And after he had finished his clothes the girl went into
the back room and brought out a necklace of turquoise and gave
it to the young man and put turquoise in his ears. Now he was well
fixed and a nice looking young man.

He stayed with the girl ten or twelve days. One night the girl
asked him, "Don't you want to go down to Matsaḳa and see what
the people are doing?" The young man said no. He and Coyote
went out to hunt deer. He killed deer on Big Mesa and skinned
them. It was near sunset and the people were gambling at Matsaḳa,
and one side was losing. He heard what the people were talking about
because he was quite near. He heard them saying they would
gamble again in four days. He went back to the girl's house and
took her venison. The girl put supper before him and they sat
down and ate. Coyote spoke to the girl. "Matsaḳa people had lots

of fun this afternoon. They were gambling and one side lost and
called another gambling game in four days." The girl said, "Is
that so?" Coyote said, "Yes." Then the girl told her husband,
"Can't you go?" "No. I don't care to go. If I go I will lose everything
you gave me, your necklace and turquoise, and my shirt and my
trousers and moccasins. I cannot go because my shirt and trousers
and moccasins and turquoise belong to you." Then the girl said,
"These things you are wearing belong to you. They don't belong
to me any more because I gave them to you." Then she said, "If
you go I am willing to help you. I have things in the back rooms
(for you to wager) and maybe you can get even. Maybe you can
win your sister back. Your father and mother worry all the time.
I will help you gamble." "No, I don't think I want to go," he said.
Three days passed and they were to gamble the next day at five
o'clock. The girl warmed some water and washed the young man's
head and washed Coyote's body, and told him, "You go tonight and
stay all night where the people are gambling. Take prayer meal
and corn pollen and native tobacco and before sunrise go up to
Corn Mountain. Go up to god[1] and he will help you. And I will help
you gamble too." Then the young man changed his mind and said,
"All right, I will go." And the girl went into the back room and
brought out some fetishes and wrapped them in deerskin and put
them on Coyote's back, and tied the bundle on with deerskin
straps. She brought out deerskins and a few dozen buckskins and
a couple dozen women's-dresses and ceremonial blankets and coral
and turquoise and shell beads and a bowl and prayer meal. The
woman gave the young man native tobacco and he went to Matsaka.
Soon he reached Matsaka. To the east of the village was one old
man all by himself. The people did not like him because he was
poor. He was all alone. The young man said, "I won't go to my
own house because my father does not like me and my mother will
scold me. I think I will go into this old man's house." He did not
go to the house where people were meeting. The old man looked at
the young man and knew he was the village chief's son and the
old man said, "Sit down." Coyote came too, and he asked him to
sit down. They both sat down and the old man gave them corn mush
and they ate some supper. After supper some of the people had gone
to sleep, and the young man spoke to the old man. "Why don't you
go to one of the houses where they are meeting?" The old man went
to the bow priest's house. Many people were there and when he
came in he sat down in the corner by the fireplace and took prayer
meal and shell and offered them to the dead and the Ahaiyute. Then

---

[1] I. e. the Ahaiyute.

the old man went home and told the young man the sixth man had won. The young man took some bread and shells and cornmeal and turquoise and corn pollen and native tobacco and went down to the edge of Corn Mountain to the Ahaiyute shrine. When he got there he sat down and prayed and somebody listened to him. He told him, "My boy, you are too late." He did not know who was speaking. Then the young man said, "I don't care for omens. I just want to give this to the Ahaiyute and the night people." And he put his offerings on the ground and went to the old man's house. The old man and Coyote were waiting for him.

Meanwhile his wife set up an altar in her house. She did not go to sleep at all. She waited for two nights and one day. As soon as the young man came into the old man's house he gave him a cigarette and the young man told him, "Someone spoke to me, 'My boy, you are too late,' and I said, 'What do I care for omens?' I said that." The old man said, "I guess it will be all right. We can go to sleep now." Next morning, after the morning meal, about three o'clock in the afternoon they called a meeting in the plaza. After the people got there the betting started and the young man and Coyote went out. He sat on top of the ladder and people looked and Pekwin told him, "My son, you had better come down, so that you can get even." The young man said, "All right, I will come down." Then he said to Coyote, "You had better go to the old man's house and get my things." Coyote brought out buckskins and women's dresses and belts and necklaces and earrings and other things. Pekwin brought his valuable things and he bet with the whole town, lots of beads and necklaces and dresses and everything that they had. Many people bet against him and the young man still had some things left. He gave four buckskins to the old man and the old man bet the four buckskins. The young man told Pekwin, "Bring my sister and I will bet whatever I have left. And bring your two eldest daughters. Bring the three girls." Pekwin went and got his two girls and the daughter of the village chief. After a while he took the stone and threw it up and said, "Which side do you want?" And the young man said, "Which side do you want?" The young man said, "White," and Pekwin chose black. He threw it and it came down black side up. They covered sticks with blankets and the young man guessed and in the first sticks there was no ball, and in the second there was no ball, but the third stick had the ball.[1] Then it was his turn to throw. He covered the sticks. He called spider and spider came and wove his web around the ball and every time anyone took a stick he pulled the ball away. He won all

[1] The winning play.

the time. Then the young man went back to his father's house and took his sister with him. He greeted his father, and told them to give him everything in the house, "I brought my sister and Pekwin's daughters." He won many things and everyone in the town was poor. Now everything was in his house, and his sister and Pekwin's two daughters. He went back to his wife's house and he took her jars and bowls and everything she had asked for, and when he got there his wife was waiting for him in the house.

Now all the people were poor and they were angry and did not know what to do. The men held a council and they sent one man to the Hopi and asked them to come and kill the girl and the young man on the fourth day.

Mountain Lion came back from Cipapolima. He got home about sunset. He came in and talked to his sister and brother-in-law and said, "Well, tomorrow the Hopi people will come and kill you and my sister. We have to go to Cipapolima at daybreak tomorrow. The girl heated water and washed the young man's head and she washed Coyote and her brother and herself. Mountain Lion told his brother-in-law, "Listen to me and I will do something." Then he sat down facing the east and he said, "Oo-hoo-hoo." "Now do it too," he said, and his sister cried in the same way, "Oo-hoo-hoo." Then his brother-in-law cried in the same way. Coyote did not know how. Next morning just before daylight they all went away and went to Cipapolima. The Hopi people came and the house was empty. The Hopi went in and they thought the people had been gone a long time. The Hopi were mad and said, "Now we will destroy the Matsaḳa people. Why did they send for us?" And they went down to Matsaḳa and killed the people. Then they went home and had a war dance. Then the Matsaḳa people went to Hopi and fought with them and killed many Hopi and brought home the scalps and had a war dance. This is the reason why the Zuni fought against the Hopi people and the Hopi fought the Zuni a long time ago.

THE GIRL WHO MARRIES A KACHINA (7)[1]

Notes, 165

A long time ago they were dancing the winter dance series. Many different dancers came in the Mixed Dance. One had a little red mouth and a green face and blue eyes and feathers on the top of his head and they called him Ayu Tsawaki. A certain young girl, not an important girl, but just an ordinary girl, went into the kiva to

[1] Recorded by Ruth Bunzel.

see the dance. The kachinas came in and with them was Ayu Tsawaki. He said all the time, "Ayu... Ayu...," and the girl liked it, and thought it was a nice dance. The kachinas left and went into another kiva and the girl followed them. At the last kiva the girl waited outside. After a while the kachinas finished and wanted to go home. They came to where the girl was waiting, and the girl said, "I would like to go with you." Ayu Tsawaki said, "No, you cannot go." She said, "Yes, I want to go." They said, "No, you cannot go." She asked them four times. They took her with them to Kachina Village. She went into the sacred lake and stayed there with Ayu Tsawaki. She saw many kachinas there and she thought they were better than Ayu Tsawaki.

One day they were going to have a dance at Zuni and the Mixed Dance wanted to come and dance. The girl wanted to come with them. She came with the kachinas and when they went into the kiva the girl ran away. She hid in the fourth room of someone's house. The kachinas went into every kiva and did not see the girl. They asked the people where she had gone, but no one knew where she was. The kachinas went back home.

After four or five days the winter dance came, and many different dancers came, Muluktaka, Tcakwena, Kokokci and Ayu Tsawaki and the Ḳana·kwe. Ayu Tsawaki did not come to dance, but he came to look for his wife. He came after the other kachinas, looking for his wife. He was crying and the people asked him what was the matter and he sang his song and cried. Then Koyemci said, "Has anyone seen our grandson's wife?" No one had seen her. After a while they went into the fourth kiva, and still he did not find her. They went into the fifth kiva and he was crying, but he did not see her there. About midnight the girl turned around and saw him, and knew it was her husband, and she pulled her blanket over her head. After a while the Koyemci asked the people again, "Has anyone seen our grandson's wife?" Then the people said, "You had better look for yourself," because the people knew she was there. Soon the thin one, Muyapone, looked around and found the girl, and he took her to Kachina Village. After she had been there four days she could not come back any more. That is the reason that a Zuni girl, when she sees a nice looking kachina, does not want him for her husband. They are afraid of that. That is all.

THE GIRL WHO MARRIES A BIRD (6)

Notes, 312

The people were living at Ḳakima. Down to the south lived Onoliḳa (the long tailed chat). He always came to get a drink just as the four daughters of the village priest were coming to get water from the spring. The girls said to each other, "Who is that pretty little bird who comes every evening to drink? Let us catch that little bird." Next evening they waited until he came to the spring. They waited and waited and a fine young man came there and said, "What are you waiting for?" They said, "We are waiting to catch Onołika." "He won't come this evening. He drank lots last night and tonight he won't come." "Yes, he comes every evening." The boy said, "No, he drank lots yesterday, he is not going to come." They talked and they gave that boy a drink. The boy went home and told his grandmother what the girls had said. He said, "Tomorrow those girls are going to catch me. What shall I do?" His grandmother said, "The girls want to catch you to marry you. You must marry those four girls." "All right."

The next evening he came as a bird. The four girls were waiting in the sunflower patch and they chased Onołika. He ran along the ground as if his wing were broken. He led them on until they were close to his house. Then he ran ahead of them into the middle of some sunflowers and stood up a fine boy. The girls peered into the sunflower patch and they saw this handsome boy. They said, "Where is the Onołika that flew into this patch?" "I did not see any." "Yes, he just came in here." At last he said, "I am Onołika. Why do you want to catch me?" They said, "Because he is so pretty." He said, "This is my dress." The three younger sisters asked the elder sister if she liked that dress and she said, "Yes." So Onołika married the eldest sister and the other girls went home.[1]

The eldest sister lived with Onołika and after four nights he went to the girl's house. That is why when boys and girls marry they always live in the girl's mother's house.

THE GIRL WHO MARRIES THE HORNED SERPENT
Notes, 312
Published only in abstract
A (3); B (3)

THE HUNTER IS PURSUED BY WOMEN
Notes, 313

A. HE IS PURSUED BY THE WOMAN WITH THE TOOTHED VAGINA (8)

The people were living in Hawiku. A young man was a great hunter; he always killed many deer. One day he came to a tree,

---

[1] A concession to Zuni custom. See Introduction, p. xv.

and in the branches of it Crazy Woman[1] was sitting. She said to him, "Where are you going, my dear?" "I'm going hunting." "Wait a minute, and I'll go with you." The young man was frightened, and he ran. She jumped down from the tree and followed in pursuit.

The youth came to the hole of Gopher Man. He said, "Where are you going, boy?" "Somebody's coming after me." "Come in here. If you put your foot in my hole, it will grow large for you." He put his foot in the hole, and immediately it was large enough for him to enter. He went in, and Gopher said to him, "Get into my right cheek and hide." "But your mouth is too small to hold me." "It will get big enough." He went in. Gopher looked as if he had a toothache.

Crazy Woman came running up, and she stopped by Gopher's hole. "I think that boy went in here." Gopher was lying holding his cheek, and he spoke as if he were in great pain. He said, "What is it you have come to ask?" "Send out that boy who went into your hole." "I didn't see anybody come into this hole. You disturb me. I have a toothache, and your voice is loud." She said, louder than ever, "Send out that boy. I know he's in there." The Gopher only groaned. She lifted her hand and slapped Gopher on the cheek, and the youth ran out. Gopher Man grabbed for her, and tried to pull her down, but she escaped. She wanted to follow the youth.

He ran till he came to the hole of Badger Man. He was lying in the sunshine and he heard the boy coming running. "Grandfather, will you save me? Somebody is running after me." "Yes, I will help you. Come right in here, and climb into my mouth." The boy went in, and went down into his stomach. The Badger Man lay there looking just as if he would be in child-birth in two or three days. But his face showed that he was a man.

Crazy Woman came up and stopped at the hole of Badger Man. "Where is that boy who went into your hole?" "Went in here? I don't know what you're talking about. I am suffering in child-birth and you bother me! I didn't see any boy." Again Crazy Woman said, "That boy's tracks stop here. I know he's in here." Badger Man said, "Come on in, then, and look for him. There's nobody in here but me, and I am suffering in child-birth." Crazy Woman answered, "I shall not go in there. Send him out." Again he said, "Come on in and look." Finally she went in. She didn't see anyone, and she was angry, and she hit him hard, and the boy jumped out and ran out of the hole. Badger Man jumped at her

---

[1] *Halic'ona* the crazy one. Any oversexed woman may be called *halic'ona*.

and pulled her down. She had a hard time to get away, but she struggled hard. She escaped him and ran after the youth again.

The boy ran down toward Hawiku. The ceremonies of the medicine societies were in progress. He saw the light from the Big Fire Society room, and he ran down the ladder as fast as he could. He called, "Somebody is coming after me!" They said, "Sit down among the drummers over in their corner. She will not get you there."

They heard someone climbing the ladder. She stood at the hatchway and called in (in a ridiculous voice), "Where is my husband ?" Nobody answered her. She called again, "Where is my husband ? I know he went in here." At last they said, "Nobody came in here. We are having our meeting of the medicine society. No boys are in this room with us." "Yes, I know he went in here." Finally she went down. The people ran to hiding as soon as they saw her wild looks and her gray hair. She searched for the young man. When she got close, he ran out and escaped to the west side of Hawiku. He came to the cave where Goat Man lived. (Goat Man has the body of a goat, a human head, and an enormous penis.) He said, "Can you save me ?" "Yes, sit down right where you are and I will save you." He sat down. He thought to himself, "How can I be saved ? I have nothing to cover me from her." Just then the woman came. Her gray hair was standing out from her head, and her appearance was wild. She looked into the cave and saw the young man sitting beside Goat Man. She called to him, "Come out, come out. Come here to me." The boy thought to himself, "She will get me this time." Goat Man said, "Come on in yourself and get him if you want him." She called again, "Come out. Come here to me." Goat Man said again, "Come in and get him." The fourth time she went as he said. As she stepped into the cave Goat Man seized her and threw her on the ground and had intercourse with her. The boy ran out and escaped. Goat Man would not let her go. He said, "This is what you wanted. You could not get the boy, and I will give you what you want most." She was exhausted. He would not stop. At last he killed her. That is why there are no women any more who have toothed vaginas.

B. HE IS PURSUED BY CORPSE GIRLS (3)

They were living at Itiwana. A boy went out to hunt in the winter. He took his lunch, and his rabbit-stick in his belt, and his stone axe.[1] He put on his fur boots. He hunted all day, and toward

---

[1] To split open the dead logs in which the rabbits took refuge.

night the snow began to fall, and it grew dark so that he lost his way and could not get to Itiwana. He tramped around in the falling snow, and at last he came to Ḳakima. He entered the first house, and in it were four beautiful girls. They greeted him and they said, "How have you lived these many days ?" "Happily." "Sit down," they said to him. He sat down. He was surprised to see such beautiful girls in this old ruin. They brought out the evening meal, and they said, "Eat. Eat lots." He took the paper-bread and dipped it into the stew. He saw the stew was only flies boiled to a mush. They said to him, "Eat. Eat lots." But he only took pinches of the paper-bread.

They made up the bed. They asked him to sleep with them. They made the bed with the boy in the middle and two girls on each side. They went to bed. He talked to them and played with them, but he was afraid and did not have intercourse with them. He went to sleep. Just at midnight he waked up and sat up straight in bed. On both sides of him were sleeping two skeletons covered with dried flesh. There were great holes where their eyes had been, and their arms and legs were shrunk to the bone. He jumped and ran as fast as he could from that house. At last he saw a light and went toward it. It was another house in Ḳakima. He went in. There were four girls and they greeted him. He went in. They asked him to go to bed with them. Pretty soon the four girls with whom he had first taken refuge came in through the hatchway. They looked as they had when he woke up at midnight. They said to the girls in this house, "Shall we come in and dance for you ?" They said, "Yes," and they came in. There were a great number of dead people and the whole house was full of them. They began to dance jigging up and down, and rattling their bones. The boy was frightened. At last he said that he must go out to ease himself. The girls said, "Come right back." He went out. Immediately he ran as fast as he could, and he came to the hole of Gopher. He said to him, "Can you save me ?" He said, "Get into my right cheek, and I will hide you." He went in, and Gopher held his cheek as if he had the toothache. The eldest skeleton girl came to Gopher's hole. She called in, "Send out my husband. He is in your hole." Gopher said to her, "Nobody came in here. You disturb my toothache." She said, "Send out my husband." When she said this the fourth time, she slapped Gopher on the cheek, and the hunter ran out.

He came to the cave of Goat Man. He said to him, "Can you save me ?" He said, "Sit right where you are and I will save you." He sat down. The skeleton girl came to the cave. She looked in and saw the hunter. She called, "Send out my husband." Goat Man said,

"Come in and get him." The fourth time he said this, she came in.
Goat Man seized her and threw her on the ground and had intercourse with her. The hunter ran out and went home. Goat Man
would not let the skeleton girl go. She was exhausted, but he would
not stop. At last he killed her. A goat was born of her, and that is
why we do not eat the flesh of goats.[1]

C. HE IS PURSUED BY ROLLING SKULL (7)

The people were living at Matsaḳa. A young man was a great
hunter. He went every day after deer. One day he was far from
home at sunset, and it was dark and raining. He saw smoke from
a house in Halona, and thought to himself, "I will go and get
shelter there." He climbed to the top of the roof and looked down
the hatchway. Inside a fine-looking woman was sitting by the
fireplace tying her daughter's hair. He went into the house, and the
woman said, "Sit down." He sat down, and the girl brought out
food and the man ate. When he had finished he said, "Thank you."
The woman said to him, "Where were you going?" He answered,
"My home is in Matsaḳa, and I was hunting deer." She said, "It
is too dark for you to find your way now. Stay here tonight." "All
right." The old woman said, "Will you have my daughter tonight?"
"I think so." The girl was beautiful. When the bed was made in the
inner room, the girl and the hunter went in to sleep.

Next morning at daybreak the hunter woke. The house was an
old ruin, and all the good blankets he had gone to sleep on were bits
of rag. The girl was a skeleton. Her arm lay over the hunter's
shoulder, and when he jumped the bones rattled as he threw it off.
He was terrified. He ran to the ladder and started off as fast as he
could. He could hear the old woman's skull rolling after him.

At Hawiku they were dancing the yaya dance. The hunter ran
among them, and cried, "Somebody is chasing me. Save me." They
said, "Go into the circle and dance with the girls." He danced the
yaya. The skull came rolling into the plaza. It called out, "Where
is my daughter's husband? She is crying for her husband." The skull
rolled right into the dance. The girls screamed and the men ran
in every direction. The hunter ran off as fast as he could.

He came to a Navaho camp. They were dancing the war dance.
He called out, "Save me! Save me! Someone is chasing me." They
said, "We will." They took off his clothing, and put on Navaho
costume and did his hair Navaho fashion and hung a quiver over
his shoulder. The skull came. It called out, "Where is my daughter's

[1] Because they are the children of a dead person.

husband? Have you seen my daughter's husband?" It rolled right up to the hunter, and he ran off as fast as he could.

He came to Laguna. They were dancing the harvest dance. He cried out, "Save me. Save me. Someone is chasing me." They said, "Dance with us. Take this bow in your hand." He went into the dance. The skull came. It cried, "Where is my daughter's husband? Have you seen my daughter's husband? She is crying for him." It rolled right among the dancers. They scattered, and the hunter ran as fast as he could.

He came to bluebirds in a piñon tree. Bluebird Chief said to the hunter, "Why are you running?" He answered, "Someone is chasing me. Save me!" "Come up here and climb under my wing." He climbed up the piñon, and hid under the bird's wing. The skull came. It called out, "Where is my daughter's husband? Have you seen my daughter's husband?" The bluebirds tittered, "Ha, ha, ha, ha! We haven't seen your daughter's husband." The skull called again, "Where is my daughter's husband? Have you seen my daughter's husband?" The bluebirds tittered, "Ha, ha, ha, ha. We haven't seen your daughter's husband." The skull came right up the tree, and up to Bluebird Chief. The hunter jumped out from under his wing and ran off as fast as he could.

He came to a large lake with sunflowers growing around it. The biggest sunflower said to him, "Why are you running?" He said, "Someone is chasing me. Save me." "Come up on my ear." The hunter climbed up and sat on the big leaf of the sunflower. The skull came. It called, "Where is my daughter's husband? Have you seen my daughter's husband?" The sunflowers said, "No, we didn't see your daughter's husband." The skull called, "Sunflowers, you have seen my daughter's husband." "No, we didn't see your daughter's husband." The skull shook the biggest sunflower, and the hunter fell down and ran as fast as he could to the east.

He came to Porcupine. He cried, "Save me. Someone is chasing me." Porcupine said, "Come into my house. Get piñon gum and put it a hand deep inside the door." When he had done this, he sat down by Porcupine. The skull came. "Where is my husband? *(sic)* Have you seen my husband?" Porcupine said, "No, I have not seen your husband." "Yes, his tracks went in here. Send out my husband." "Come in and get him." "Send him out to me." "No, if you want him come in and get him." The fourth time Skull came into Porcupine's house. It stuck fast in the piñon gum, and Porcupine set fire to the gum and burned Skull and destroyed it. The hunter stayed with Porcupine and married Porcupine Girl.

In Matsaḳa his mother and father were worried about their son.

At the end of one year the father went to the priests of the council. They sent men out to follow his tracks, but they could not find any trace of him.

The hunter lived with Porcupine Girl and he trapped woodrats for his father-in-law. After four years he was setting his traps down by Caliente, and he lay down in the shade. He heard a noise in the sky. He heard it again. Presently he looked up, and he saw an eagle just above him. The eagle came down and lit in the tree. It took off its eagle dress, and it was a pretty girl. She said, "What are you doing around here?" The boy did not answer. She came down the tree, and they talked together. She said, "Let me fix your hair." She fixed his hair, and they had a good time together. At sunset the girl said, "I must go home." The hunter said, "I will go too." She answered, "If you are sure you want to go, I will carry you. Shut your eyes, for if you look once, you will fall to the ground." She put on her eagle dress, and he sat on her shoulders. He took tight hold and shut his eyes. Eagle Girl flew to the west. She went up through the sky. At last she came to the eagle rock and lit upon it. She said, "Open your eyes now." He looked. He did not recognize the country, the hills were all strange. He looked straight down: there he could see the earth below just as big as this (circle made by thumbs and middle fingers of two hands). Just below him he saw Ashes Spring (at Caliente) and he heard drumming there (of the Ne'we·kwe living in that spring).

They started for the Eagle country. They came first to the country of the blackbirds; after that to the country of the bluebirds, the nighthawks, the red woodpeckers, the chickenhawks, the crows, the buzzard (cutsina), the cedar-wood chickenhawk, and the red-tailed chickenhawk. At last they came to the country of the eagles.

The Eagles return, remove their coats and are human beings. He marries Eagle Girl. Eagle Chief drops from a height and kindles fire in order that his son-in-law may have cooked meat and the eagles' coats are spotted in the smoke. His Eagle wife gives him an eagle coat and teaches him to fly and hunt. One day he meets Chicken Hawk Girl. He likes her and marries her. He has to eat lizards and insects with the Chicken Hawks. He wants venison again and at his direction his Chicken Hawk wife gets his eagle coat from the house of the Eagles and returns it after each use. One day while he is hunting in his eagle costume he meets his Eagle wife. She is mourning for him. He comforts her and they are reconciled. However, at his father-in-law's direction he goes to get good food from an old man and woman in a white house and there falls in with girls from the pueblo of the dead. They follow

him to the eagle house and his wife tells him he will be safe if he
does not laugh when they dance. He breaks the taboo and is
snatched off by the corpse girls. By the help of the old man and
woman he destroys the pueblo of the dead but decides to escape
from the sky in his frayed eagle suit. His wife pursues him and
snatches it from him because of his unfaithfulness. He falls to earth
and returns in death to his first wife, the skeleton girl whose mother
pursued him as a rolling skull. See same incidents, I: 133—135.

D. HE IS PURSUED BY ATOCLE (8)

The people were living at Ḳakima. The priest had four daughters
and one son. He was the only son. His sisters loved him. Every
day he went out to hunt rabbits down to the south near Nose
Point.

One day it was cold and it was snowing hard. He killed six
rabbits and he found a cave. He thought he would sleep there over
night. He gathered wood and built a fire and roasted his rabbits.
He was just beginning to eat when he heard a call "okla, okla."
It was Atocle. He trembled. He thought to himself, "If she comes
to eat me I will give her the rabbits." Atocle came to the door
of the cave and she said, "Give me some food." The boy said, "Here
they are." "How many did you kill?" "I will give them all to you.
Eat them all up." He threw her the six rabbits and Atocle ate them
all down whole. When she had finished she said, "Now I shall come
in and spend the night with you." The boy was frightened to death.
He thought, "If she stays all night she will eat me. I will make
an excuse and go outside and run home." He sat as far as he
could from Atocle and he said, "I have to go outside to defecate.
I will come right back." He went out and he took some cornmeal
from the cornhusk in his belt. He scattered it over the excrement
and said, "When Atocle calls, answer 'Wait a minute'." He sprinkled
the cornmeal and he ran towards home. Pretty soon Atocle called,
"Are you ready to come in?" "Wait a minute." She called again,
"You ready to come in?" "Wait a minute." She called again,
"You ready to come in?" "Wait a minute." The fourth time
Atocle called the excrement wasn't steaming any more. It could
hardly answer, but it said, "Wait a minute."

The boy was running as hard as he could. He had only sheepskin
shoes on. His feet were frost bitten and swollen. He could hardly
run. When he got within sight of the pueblo he called out. His
sister heard him and said, "Somebody is out there." They ran
out and about two miles from their home they found their brother.
He was swollen with the cold and his feet were black with frostbite.

They pulled his sheepskin shoes off and wrapped him in a woman's dress. The eldest carried him a little way and when she was tired the next carried him and after that the next one. They all four (in turn) carried him until they got almost to his house.

Seven times Atocle called. The fifth time the excrement did not answer at all. At last Atocle went out to look for the boy. She said, "Why, you ran away, didn't you ? I was going to sleep with you just like a friend, but as soon as I looked at you, you were frightened to death. You shall be punished because you were afraid of me. In four days you shall die and become Atocle."

They brought the boy into his mother's house. He was sick from exposure and in four days he died and became Atocle. That is why we know when people die they become kachinas.

KIOTAKE MARRIES THE ŁAMANA (6)

Notes, 316

The people were living at Itiwana. A little boy and his grandmother were living at Hecokta. He had sores at the corners of his mouth, and he was very ugly. His name was Kiotake.

The girls of Itiwana used to go every evening to the old well with their jars, and the little boy heard that while they were going for water the boys spoke to them and asked for water to drink.[1] One day he thought to himself that he would go to Itiwana and wait by the path to the well and speak to the girls when they came with their jars. He said to his grandmother, "I am going to Itiwana to wait for the girls when they come to get water at the well. I shall have a drink over there," he said. His grandmother told him to act nicely and behave like a grown-up boy so that the girls would like him. He put on his wildcat skin and started toward Itiwana. He got there, and stood close by the path where the girls come by to the well. At last the girls began to come out of their houses. They were nice-looking girls, and they were dressed up in white moccasins with deerskin puttees and black woven women's-dresses, and red-and-black-bordered white blankets. Their arms were bare. They carried their jars on their heads and supported them with their right arms. They walked down to the well to get water, and they filled their jars and came back. Kiotake stood close to the well, and when they came up he said to them, "Let me drink." The girls looked at him as if they did not see him at all. They walked right on without answering.

---

[1] That is, he heard that this was the time for courtship.

He went home to his grandmother. He said, "All the girls gave me drinks." His grandmother was happy at what he told her. She said, "I will treat your sores so they will be healed and the girls will like you." She went out to get spruce gum, and soap-weed roots to wash her grandchild's head. She brought them in. Next morning after they had eaten their morning meal, she washed his head, and she took wooden nippers[1] and picked off his lice. When she had finished, she cleaned a stick and burned out his sores. He did not complain because he wanted to get married. Afterwards his grandmother covered each sore with spruce gum. They thought it would cure them all right away that very evening.

Kiotake was impatient for evening to come. Right away he began to dress. He looked all over his grandmother's house and he found some selenite (once used for windows) to use as a mirror. He found his grandfather's bow-guard and put it on his right wrist, and he thought, "Now I am a rich boy like the other boys. I think the girls will speak to me this evening." He looked at himself in the mirror and admired himself. He moved the bow-guard up and down his arm. "Now I am a handsome man," he said to himself.

When evening came he took his wildcat skin from the deer-antler on the wall, and he took his mirror again and admired himself. He went to Itiwana and stationed himself close by the well where he was the night before. At last the girls began to come from their houses with their water-jars upon their heads. They were nice-looking girls, and they were dressed in their white moccasins and puttees and black blanket dresses and white blankets. They walked down toward the well. The boys of Itiwana had heard that the night before a strange boy had been waiting at the well and had asked for water. That night they went down to the well to watch. They saw him standing close by the well. Two of the girls went down to fill their jars, and when they came out, Kiotake walked over close to them and said, "Let me have a drink." The girls looked around at him, and said, "No," and they laughed at him. They went home. Presently other girls came to the well, and he walked out close to them and asked for a drink, but they said, "No," and they laughed. Presently other girls came to the well, and he walked out close to them and asked for a drink, but they said, "No," and they laughed. All the time the boys were jeering at him. Presently another girl came to the well, and he was ashamed to ask her for water. When she came out ot the well she looked around at him and smiled because he looked so funny. He thought that she

---

[1] These are two sticks between which the lice are taken. They are no longer in use.

smiled because she liked him. He said to himself, "Ah, tomorrow I shall be married."

He walked back to Hecokta, and he was happy because the girl had smiled at him. He said to his grandmother, "A girl smiled at me. I shall be married tomorrow!" His grandmother was delighted, and she set to work on a rabbit-skin blanket for their bed when they should be married. She worked all night and all day. Next day they had only mush for their dinner. The boy spent all day looking at himself in the mirror. He did no work, and he did not help his grandmother. He only thought how handsome he was.

When evening came he put on his wildcat skin again and went to Itiwana. He stood just where he had before. The boys came out to make fun of him again, and they said, "There he comes. He's come again." They made a plan that next night one of the boys should dress in a girl's costume and wait for him and marry him. They said, "Tomorrow night we will do this." They went into an empty kiva to make their plans. They borrowed the dress of one of the boys' sisters, and they said, "She shall be a priest's daughter."

The boy stood by the well and the girls came from their houses to get the water. They filled their jars and they came up out of the well. He asked if he could have a drink, and the girls said, "No. You have sores." At last one of the girls said, "Yes." Everybody laughed when she let him drink. When he had had his drink, she poured out the water from her jar onto the ground and went back to the well and rinsed the gourd and the jar. Then she filled her jar afresh. The boy was terribly ashamed, but he had got his drink this time. He walked home and told his grandmother that he could marry the next night.

All the next day his grandmother worked on a rabbit-skin blanket to give to the girl when she came to grind for her.[1] She got snow-birds ready to cook for her when she came.[2] Her grandson took up his mirror and all day he admired himself in it. He thought, "Now I am a handsome man."

When evening came he said to his grandmother, "If I do not come home till late in the night, don't wait for me. I'll be married tonight."

That night when he came toward Itiwana everybody was watching for him. They knew why he came, and they knew that night he was going to marry this łamana[3] in Itiwana. He came in and

---

[1] "They had no black blanket" to make the customary present of a woman's dress.

[2] This is said to be unbecoming, as it was too precipitous. She should not have been so sure.

[3] That is, a berdache, a man who has assumed woman's dress.

12

stood where he had stood before, and the boys told everyone
that the girls were not to go for water till this łamana had gone
down with his jar. He was all dressed up in white moccasins and
white deer-skin puttees and the woman's blanket dress and a red-
and-black-bordered white blanket. He walked along just like a
woman.[1] He went into the well, and everybody was watching from
the tops of the houses. He came out and the boy asked him, "Let
me drink." He said, "Yes," and he stooped down so the boy could
drink.[2] When he had finished he put the water that was left in the
gourd back in his jar.[3] The łamana said to him, "Where do you
live ?" He answered, "I live in Hecokta." "Have you a mother and
father ?" "No, I live with my grandmother." "Will you come home
to my house ?" The boy said, "Oh yes." The łamana said, "Follow
me." They went into the village, and they stood by the corner of
a kiva that was next the łamana's house. He said to the little boy,
"I don't want to take you into my house. We will go into the kiva,[4]
and I will ask my parents if I can marry you."

They went into the kiva. The łamana set down his jar, and he
said, "Sit down and wait a minute, and I will go and ask my mother
and my father." He went into an inner room, and pretended to
talk to someone. In a minute he came back. He said, "It's all right.
We can be married tonight." He brought out all the food they
had put ready there, and set it before him. The little boy wanted
his companion to make up the bed right away, but he said, "Wait
a little." At last he made the bed, but he said, "We will not sleep
together till the morning." So Kiotake spent all night there.

His grandmother was delighted when he did not come; she
thought he was surely married. Early before sunrise she got up and
she came way down to Itiwana. She wanted to tell everyone that
her grandson was married in some house. She went into the first
house and she said, "May I have a fire ?[5] My fire went out. My
grandson was married last night, and I was so worried waiting for
him I let my fire go out." So she told them her grandson was
married. When she had got outside with the coal she dropped it,
and she went into another house and she said, "May I have a fire ?
My fire went out. My grandson was married last night and I was
thinking about him and I let my fire go out." They gave her a coal

---

[1] That is, slowly and heavily. It is a great joke for a woman to walk like a
man, or a man like a woman.
[2] This is another joke, that the "girl" should be tall and the boy short.
[3] This is very polite.
[4] In present-day Zuni a kiva is used as any empty room would be.
[5] A live coal in a loop of cedar bark.

and she went out and dropped it and went into a third house and she said, "Will you give me a coal for my fire? My grandson was married last night and thinking about him I let the fire go out." They gave her a coal, and she went outside and dropped it and went into a fourth house and said, "Will you give me a coal for my fire? My grandson was married last night, and I thought about him and let my fire go out."

While she was going around for her fire, telling everybody her grandson was married, in the kiva her grandson went in to sleep with his "bride." When he discovered that it was a man, he gave a great cry so that everybody heard him. He cried,

> Kiotake, muwe, muwe.
> Kiotake, muwe, muwe.

When they heard him, everybody laughed and laughed till they couldn't laugh any more. The "bride" laughed too, and he took back the dresses to the girls from whom they were borrowed.

Kiotake went home crying all the way,

> Kiotake, muwe, muwe.
> Kiotake, muwe, muwe.

He got home before his grandmother, and there was the fire going brightly and his grandmother was over in Itiwana borrowing coals so she could spread the news. At last somebody told her that her grandson had gone home crying because his "girl" was a man. She dropped her coal, and she ran toward home crying,

> It was not really a girl. It was a man. Muwe, muwe.
> It was not really a girl. It was a man. Muwe, muwe.

All the way home she cried. When she got home, they both cried. That is why nobody makes anything beforehand to give to their daughter-in-law, but they wait till their son has been married for four days.

THE PRIEST'S SON BECOMES AN EAGLE (8)

Notes, 316

They were living in Hawiku. The village priest had one son and four daughters. All the girls in the village wished to marry this son of the priest. Every night a girl came with a basket of flour on her head and climbed up the ladder. The boy and his father were eating their supper. The father said, "You ought to be a married man, the girls are all anxious to marry you. Choose one to be your wife." The girl came down the ladder. She was dressed in white moccasins, and she had a fine red-and-black-bordered white blanket over her shoulders. His mother said, "You're coming, aren't you?" The girl said, "Yes." The boy's mother asked her to eat with them. She ate, and after eating she said, "Thank you." They said to her, "What is it that you have come to ask?" She said, "I was thinking of your son." The father and mother said to her, "Go with him into the inner room."

In this room the boy stayed every day weaving a white blanket. It was in the loom. He said to the girl, "We must not sleep together tonight. In the morning come to this room and weave this blanket, and if you are able to do this, you shall be my wife. If you are not, we shall not marry." That night they slept apart.

Next morning she got up to grind before the father and mother of the boy had waked. When the mother had made ready the morning meal and they had eaten, the girl went back into the inner room, and tried to weave the blanket, but she could not. When she found that she could not, she went back to her home weeping. She was ashamed. (Repeat for two more off our sisters.) Everybody was watching the house of the priest's son. Every morning they saw a girl go home weeping.

That night the youngest sister went to the well to get water.She was wishing that someone would teach her to weave. She heard someone speak to her. She looked all about but she could not find where the voice came from. At last the voice said, "Here I am in the top of this flower-stalk." She looked, and saw that it was Spider Woman. Spider Woman said to her, "On the morning of the day you are to go to the house of the youth, come back to the spring, and I shall climb into your ear. I will go with you to his house, and teach you how to weave."

The next morning she went back to the spring, and Spider Woman climbed into her ear. She put on her white moccasins and white puttees and her white blanket, and they went to the house of the youth. His mother said, "You're coming, aren't you?" She put out a seat for her, and brought food. The girl ate, and when she finished, she said, "Thank you." The mother took away the food, and they said, "What is it that you have come to ask?" She answered, "I was thinking of your son." They said, "Go with him into the inner room."

When they had gone into the other room, he said to her, "We shall not sleep together tonight. In the morning if you are able to weave this blanket, you shall be my wife." They slept apart.

In the morning they ate their morning meal. When they had

finished, she went into the inner room, and went directly to the loom and sat down. Spider Woman said to her, "First pull out that short stick. Pull the lower bar out toward you. Now put the ball of cotton thread in between the warp." Everything that she had to do Spider Woman told her. The youth sat close beside her and he saw that she understood how to weave the blanket on his loom. He said, "My dear, now we shall be married and we shall have a long life."

That morning everyone was watching for the girl to come weeping out of the youth's house. But no one came, and they knew that she had married the youth. Her sisters were very angry. After that she always stayed in the house and did the weaving, and her husband helped his father hoeing the fields.[1]

Whenever he came home, his wife asked him, "My dear, do you love me?" Every time he came in she asked him again, "My dear, do you love me?" The youth did not like this.[2] He thought, "I must find out whether you really love me."

The next day when he and his father were hoeing in the fields he said to him, "My father, is there any way I can find out if my wife loves me?" His father answered, "My son, you can call the Apaches."

There were crows flying about the cornfield, and he told the crow, "Go to the Apaches and tell them the priest's son has called them to come against the people of Hawiku." The crow flew off to the Apaches. He sought out the Apache priest and said, "The priest's son at Hawiku has sent for you to come and fight him and his wife." The Apache said, "Very well. Tomorrow we will come." They made ready to go to Hawiku on the following day.

In the morning the priest's son told his wife to dress in her white moccasins and puttees, and to put on her blanket dress and a red-and-black bordered white blanket and over that an embroidered white blanket. He said, "I and my father are going out to our field to hoe. Bring us a lunch of parched-corn meal." She went out to the field and took the parched-corn meal. They built a shelter for her to sit in while they were working. At noon they soaked the meal and had lunch. The youth told his father to go home, and the old man went back to the village. He could see the dust in the distance where the Apaches were coming.

The Apaches crept up in ambush. They hid from cedar to cedar. At last they were near. The youth took out his arrows. He had twenty arrows and he shot them all and killed many of the enemy. When the arrows were gone the Apaches killed him and he fell. His wife ran away.

---

[1] The present division of labor. In earlier times the men were weavers.
[2] In Zuni the adage "Still waters run deep" is unquestioned.

The boy's father went to the bow priests and told them to make proclamation that in eight days they would dance the yaya dance.[1] When the eighth day came everyone was ready for the dance. All the women had dyed red wool to embroider their blanket dresses fresh, and they wore their white deer-skin moccasins and puttees. The priest's son's wife dressed also and went with her sisters to the dance. She did not give a thought to her dead husband. In the middle of the morning the dance began. The yaya leader went up to the wife and her sisters and said, "Shall I tie your blanket?" He took out his deer-bone needle and sewed together their blankets and put them into the dance circle.

The priest's son came in from the west and climbed up to the tops of the houses around the plaza. He saw his wife and her sisters going into the dance, and he saw that his wife never gave a thought to him. Soon the yaya leaders came up to the priest's son and put him also into the dance. They pushed him into the circle next to his wife. She looked up at him and recognized him. Tears ran down her cheeks. Immediately he turned into an eagle and flew up to the houses where he had been standing. Then he flew away giving his eagle cries. That is why we value eagle feathers so much, because the eagle is the priest's son.

ŁA·WA (7)

Notes, 317

They were living at Ḳakima. There was a young man who was a great hunter. Every day he killed a deer, and all the girls wanted to marry him. In Pinawa a girl said, "I will go to marry him." She took a large basket of flour on her head and came to the house of the young man. It was late in the afternoon. His mother was downstairs, and the young man was in his room on the second floor. His mother said to the girl, "What have you come to ask?" "Thinking of your son, I have come." She said to her young daughter, "Call your brother." The girl went up into the upper room and sang:

Aneła·wa[2], ła·wa[3], ła·wa.

She said, "Somebody has come." They went into the room where the girl was waiting. He said to her, "What have you come to ask?" "I have come to marry you." "Throw your flour against my white

---

[1] "Because he was a Cumaikoli." This is part of the plan he and his son laid to measure the wife's affection.

[2] Chickenhawk.

[3] An edible green plant "like a wild cabbage". Also the name of the hunter.

shell. If it sticks you shall be my wife." He took her to the upper
room. She took a handful of meal and threw it against the shell.
It fell to the ground. He said to her, "You must go. You cannot
be my wife."

In Hampasa a girl said to herself, "I will go to marry this man."
(Repeat for Hampasa, Kwakina, and Hawiku.)

At Hecokta, Atocle was living. She said, "I will got to Ḵakima.
That young man has refused all the girls who have been to marry
him." She took *la·wa* and put it in her basket. She took a handful
of corn pollen and folded it in a cloth. She put it in her basket. She
walked heavily and came to Ḵakima. All the people saw her and
ran away. All the people said, "Atocle is coming to marry Ła·wa."
She went into the house. The hunter's little sister saw her and
tried to hide. Her mother asked, "What have you come to say?"
"I have come to marry your son," (in dumb show[1].) The mother
said to her daughter, "Call your brother." She went out and sang:
Aneła·wa, ła·wa, la·wa.

Her brother came out of his room. He said, "What is it you have
come to ask?" Atocle answered, "I have come to marry you."
"Throw your flour against my shell. If it sticks I will marry you."
"All right." They went up to the other room. She took corn pollen
from her basket and threw it against the shell. Not a particle of
it fell to the floor. The young man was frightened. He looked at
her big eyes and big mouth and gray hair. Atocle said to him
(dumb-show), "Now you are my husband."

They came down. The young man's mother was frightened. She
went into the house and made a bed for them. It was late when she
called them. She said, "It is time to go to bed." The young man was
afraid. Atocle said, "Yes, it is time to go to bed." She went in with
him. She took off her dress and her moccasins. The boy made no
move. Atocle said to him, "Come. Get into bed." She pulled him
close to her. After a while he went to sleep. When she saw that he
was sleeping she took off her mask. In the morning he was sleeping
with a beautiful girl.

Atocle stayed with him. Whenever she went out she put on her
mask and the people were afraid of her. When she was with her
husband, she was a beautiful girl and ground meal all the time.
In four years she said to that young man's father, "Make a mask
like mine." He looked at it and made a mask just like hers. She
said, "Tell the bow priest that all the people shall make prayersticks
for me in four days." Everyone made prayersticks for Atocle. It

---

[1] Kachinas never speak except to give their calls.

was a great bundle. They formed in two lines and she went between carrying the bundle of prayersticks. She went back to Kachina Village.

A. PARROT GIRL (6)

Notes, 318

The people were living in Hopi. The kachina chief had a beautiful daughter, and everyone came to court her. The men made plans in the kiva and they said, "You go tonight, you go tomorrow." A·lucpa heard. He was an ugly boy and lived with his grandmother. They were very poor. He was fat and had big eyes and frizzly hair. He said, "I shall go to court the daughter of the kachina chief. Perhaps she will marry me." "Poor child, why should she marry you? She has refused all the handsomest men in Hopi." "You can't tell. Perhaps I may marry her." He went just as he was. In the priest's house they were eating their evening meal. Her mother and father said, "There is another boy coming." He came in. His skin was dark and his eyes were big and his hair was uncombed. He said, "How have you lived these days, my fathers, my mothers, my children?" "Happily, thank you. Sit down." They gave him food to eat and he said, "Thank you." "Eat lots." At last the girl's father said, "What have you to say that you have come into a strange house?" "I came thinking of your daughter. Others have asked her to marry them and she has refused. Perhaps she will marry me." The father said to his daughter, "My daughter, this boy has asked in your presence. You have heard. Let me ask you why you will not marry the men who come to court you." "Yes, my father. I do not need clothes because you have always given me all that I needed. They have brought me bundles of clothing. I need parrot feathers because you are kachina priest, and there can be no dances without parrot feathers. If any of these men bring me parrot feathers I shall marry them." A·lucpa said, "Yes, I shall try to get parrot feathers. I am glad to know what you want." He went home to his own house. He said to his grandmother, "Grandmother, the priest's daughter does not want clothing for herself. She wants parrot feathers ("clothing" for her father's children, the kachinas). How shall I get parrot feathers?" "Parrot feathers come from the south. There is only one way to get them and that is to go to the country where the parrots live." "Yes, I shall start early in the morning." Next morning he got up early. His grandmother put lumps of mush to warm in the coals and she made prayer meal and pollen for him to carry. He ate fast. His grandmother said, "Go south by the east road. You will find someone there who will help you." "All right, grandmother. Stay happily. Maybe I shall return happily and maybe I shall be killed in another country. But I am a man, not a girl, so do not worry."

He went toward the east. At Sunflower Stalk Place, Hawk was living. He always sat on a little stone near his door. The boy came. He said, "Oh, I am thirsty. Here is a spring." He knelt down to drink and he saw his reflection in the water. He was fat. He had big ears and big round eyes and his hair was frizzly. "Oh dear, how I look! Even if I get parrot feathers I'm afraid the priest's daughter will not marry me." Just then he saw Hawk. Hawk said to him, "Where are you going?" "I am going south. The priest's daughter will not marry any of the men who have asked her. She wants parrots' feathers and I am going to get them in the country of the parrots." Hawk said, "I shall go with you. I can help you." "I am glad. Thank you for going." Hawk said, "First I will give you clean clothes." "How can you? I haven't any." "Wait and see. I shall fly up in the air and drop down upon you. Face to the east. Do not be frightened." The boy faced east. Who-o-o! Hawk dropped down and seized the boy by his scalp. He shook him and his skin pulled up above his ankles. He flew up again. Who-o-o! He dropped down. He shook the boy by his hair and his skin pulled up to his thighs. He flew up again .Who-o-o! He dropped down. He shook the boy by his hair and his skin pulled up to his stomach. The fourth time he flew up. Who-o-o! He dropped down. He shook the boy by his hair and his old skin came off completely. He looked cooked[1] and as beautiful as anybody. Hawk dropped his skin on the ground. The boy said, "Where shall I hide it till we come back?" "You won't ever need it again." "I'll hide it here." Hawk said to the boy, "Get on my back so we can travel faster. You were too heavy to carry with your skin on."

They went far to the south. It was almost sunset when they arrived. Father and Mother Parrot were in their house and all the parrots were coming home for the evening meal. All around the house were rows and rows of shiny perches for them to sit on. The boy said, "How have you lived these days, my parrot priests?" "Happily, thank you. Sit down." He sat down on the seat by the north wall. The women parrots sat on one side and the men parrots on the other. Father Parrot said, "All the parrot people have returned now. What is it that you have come to say?" The

---

[1] Humans are "cooked" in distinction to the raw people, or supernaturals, and the boy's redness after his skin has been taken off is evidence of his looking like other people.

boy answered, "In Hopi all the men wished to marry the daughter of kachina priest but she would not. I heard them talking about this. I went also and her father asked her why she had refused all her suitors. She said that she did not want clothing. She wanted parrot feathers for her father's children. I came here to get parrot feathers for the priest's daughter." Parrot Father said to him, "Did you bring prayer meal?" "Yes." "We shall give you parrot feathers if you will pay us with prayer meal." The boy took his buckskin bag of prayer meal and laid it in the basket. The parrots said, "Thank you." They brought out a basket and set it in the center of the room. Father Parrot flew down and laid off his dress of feathers and left it in the basket. Others came and laid their feathers also in the basket. Father Parrot said, "Here are our feathers. Take them in the morning but sleep here with us tonight." The boy and Hawk slept that night with the parrots. When they were all asleep the two younger sisters took off their dresses. They were persons and they came down and played with them. They whispered together. "Where do you live? Will you take us when you go back to your home?" "You're joking." "No, we want to go." "Your people would not like it." "We won't tell them. Take the basket of feathers and we will start now." "How shall we get out?" "You go and we will follow." The boy got on Hawk's back. They took the feathers and went out quietly. The girls put on their parrot dresses and flew off and overtook them. They flew fast. They came to Red Rocks.

In the parrot house the girl who slept next to the younger sister woke up. She saw that the boys and the two younger sisters and the basket of feathers were gone. She said to the parrot girl who slept next to her, "Sister, sister, where are those Hopi boys? They have taken our sisters." Father Parrot woke. "We must go after them. They should have asked us whether they could take our daughters. Wear your best clothes and we will start at once." They flew fast. At Sunflower Stalk Place they overtook the others. The girls heard the noise of the parrots' wings. "Our uncles and brothers are coming." They waited for them. The parrot uncle said, "Why did you come without telling your fathers and mothers? Did the boys urge you to come?" The boys answered, "No, we told them not to come but they wanted to. They told us to start before you waked up." The uncle said, "We have nothing to say. You (girls) should have told your father and mother. If you want, you can come back now. These boys came for feathers not for wives." The girls said, "No, we shall go with our husbands." The uncle said to the elder girl, "This boy came to get parrot feathers in order to marry the priest's daughter. For your younger sister it is all right for Hawk is not married. When the boy has taken you to his house, then he shall carry the parrot feathers to the priest's daughter. After he has married her and brings you to her house you must live peaceably together. If you are jealous it will make a great deal of trouble." He said to the boy, "When you carry the parrot feathers to the priest's daughter, let your parrot wife sit at the top of the ladder so that everyone can see her. Go happily. Do as we tell you." He said to the girls, "Love your husbands. Love each other." The parrot men went back to their home.

The boy said to Hawk, "Now I shall go and get my skin." "No, you look handsome. Now the priest's daughter will marry you." Hawk took his wife into his own house. The boy said, "Stay happily. You helped me. You travel fast and easily. Come to see me sometimes." Parrot Girl took her husband on her back and they went to Hopi. It was the time of the evening meal. She flew to the house of kachina chief. In the house they heard the sound of a parrot flying. The boy came in. His arms were full of parrot feathers. They were very beautiful and shone in the light. He said, "How have you lived these days, my fathers, my mothers, my children?" "Happily, thank you." Kachina chief rose and took the feathers from the boy's arms. The girl brought a basket to hold them, and they laid them down in the center of the room. They ate together. When they had finished, they heard the Parrot talking at the top of the ladder. "What's that?" The father went to the foot of the ladder. He looked up. The boy said, "It's a parrot." She stayed there all night. The boy married the daughter of kachina chief. Next morning the people rose. Parrot Girl was still sitting on the top of the ladder. They said, "The kachina chief's daughter wanted parrot feathers. Who brought her a live parrot?" The boys who had tried to marry her were angry.

In the morning in the house of kachina chief they ate their morning meal. His wife washed the boy's head. He said, "I must go to my grandmother's. This is a parrot girl. I will take her to my grandmother's, and bring back her feathers." The father answered, "All right. Go happily. Come back soon." He took Parrot Girl and went to his grandmother's. Everybody was watching to see who had brought feathers to the priest's daughter. The boy's grandmother was sitting in the sun with her head bowed. She thought her grandson had been killed. They came to the foot of the ladder and Parrot Girl turned into a person. The boy's grandmother heard the ladder creak as they came up. There was a handsome man. She did not recognize her grandson. She drew back. He said, "How have you lived these days, grandmother?" "Yes, I am your grand-mother. I am *everybody's* grandmother." "No, I am your own grandson. I went to the south for parrot feathers." "Oh, oh, but you are so handsome[1]." She thought the girl was the priest's daughter. They went into the house and she put lumps of mush on the coals and heated them. She brought out venison and they ate their evening meal. The boy said to his grandmother, "My wife cannot eat this food. She can eat prayer meal or pollen. She is a raw person, a parrot." His grandmother brought out pollen and put it in a basket. The girl faced west and ate pollen.[2] They slept that night. The next morning his wife ate prayer meal, and the boy went back to the house of the priest's daughter. For two days Parrot Girl stayed with his grandmother. On the fourth day the boy came back. He said, "I have come for my parrot wife. I shall take her to my priest's daughter wife." He said to Parrot Girl, "Re-member and be peaceable. Love my wife and do not worry me." He said to his grandmother, "How can I make her into a cooked person?" His grandmother said, "She will have to learn to eat like cooked persons. I will bring a medicine society to cure her." His grandmother ran to a big ant-hill and told the Horned Toads. She called down the hatchway. "What is it that you have come to say?" "Please come with me. I need you. Tell the others to follow you." She ran home and set a pot on the fire. She put venison and hulled corn in it. She made a big pile of corn cakes. She got corn-husks and made lots of little packages of prayer meal. She laid them in a basket. The boy and girl were sitting waiting. The grand-mother tore fringes off her belt to give to the medicine men. Present-ly they heard the Horned Toads coming. The first Horned Toad brought a medicine bowl to set up for the spring on the altar. The second brought an ear of corn.[3] The third and fourth brought the eagle wing-feathers. They said, "How have you lived these days, my fathers, my mothers, my children?" They sat down facing the east. The grandmother rose. She took a package of prayer meal to the headman. He moved her hands to the six directions. She said, "I have needed your help to cure my daughter. She is a raw person and cannot eat as cooked persons do. You are powerful and can cure her." She gave him the prayer meal. The headman made a cross of meal upon the altar and set down the bowl. He spread a blanket and laid the girl upon it facing the east. He went four times to the altar and prayed. He growled like a bear and approached

---

[1] It is a joke that she was so surprised that she said this in front of the girl.

[2] That is, she turned so that she did not eat in front of them.

[3] As a substitute for the mili, the basis of which is a perfect ear of corn.

the girl. He sucked out insects and bugs and spit them into the circle of meal. At last there was nothing more to suck. She was cured. He said, "Now you can eat like cooked persons. Get up." She sat up. Four times he gave her water to drink. He took water in his own mouth and spat it out on his hands. He rubbed the girl's body. He took water from the altar to the boy and his grandmother and they drank. He took the cornhusk full of insects and prayer meal and went out to the east and left it there. The girl was cured. The grandmother dipped stew into bowls and put them in the center of the room. She set out corn cakes. They sat and ate and said, "Thank you." The grandmother said, "Fill your bowls and take them home with you." They were glad. They thanked her. "Stay happily." The girl ate what cooked persons do. Corn cake stuck in her throat but she dipped it in soup till it was soft. At last she could eat it. In two days she could eat like other people.

A·lucpa took her to the house of the priest's daughter. In the house they heard two persons coming. They welcomed the girl and his wife set the evening meal for her. They all ate together, the father, the mother, A·lucpa and and his two wives. The father said, "Now, my daughters, since you both want the same husband, treat each other like sisters and live happily." They both said, "Yes." They lived happily.

Next day Brother Hawk came to that house. The priest's daughter was washing A·lucpa's head and Parrot Girl was rinsing it. They saw Hawk's shadow through the hatchway. They said, "Brother is coming." The boy looked out. Hawk flew around the room four times and sat on the deer antlers. He shrugged his shoulders and dropped his coat. He was a person. "How have you lived these days?" "Happily, thank you." Parrot Girl said, "How is my sister?" "Happy, thank you." They talked together. A·lucpa said, "Be careful when you come to see me. When children are about it is not safe. I am afraid somebody might shoot you." "All right, I shall be careful." He turned into a hawk and went home.

In four days he came again. They were eating and Hawk sat on the ladder. The children saw and ran and got their arrows. They shot at him. He fell wounded. A·lucpa jumped up. "Oh dear, oh dear. This is what I was afraid of." He mourned for his hawk brother. He said, "I must take him to his home," and he carried him on his arm.[1] He came in to Hawk's house. Hawk's wife was there. "Oh my sister, my brother has been killed. I told him to come when the little children were not around but a boy saw him and killed him. Now we must bury him. What will you do now?

[1] In the crook of the arm, as a mask is carried.

Will you go back to the parrots ?" "No, take me to your house and I will be with my sister." "All right. Let us bury my brother and we will go." They buried him like a person. A·lucpa went back to his house. He said, "In four days I shall come and get you." He returned in four days and Parrot Girl went with him to his house. That is why Zunis sometimes have more than one wife.

B (7)

A poor boy lived with his grandmother at A'mosa. All the men wanted to marry the daughter of the village priest. Every night they went to ask for her, but she always asked them for parrot feathers. No one could get them. The poor boy said, "I shall go to the house of the village priest and ask for his daughter." He went to the house of the daughter of the village priest. They set food out, and greeted him, "What is it that you have come to ask ?" "Thinking of your daughter I have come." "I have nothing to say. It shall be as she wishes." At bedtime the girl made the bed and the man went into the inner room with her. She told him, "We cannot sleep together tonight. I must have parrot feathers." "Very well." They slept apart. The next morning the poor boy said, "I shall go to see if I can get parrot feathers, and I shall come back in four days." "All right."

He went to his grandmother's house and said, "Grandmother, I am going for parrot feathers. Give me a lunch to take." He took prayersticks and started for Old Mexico. When he had gone a little way, he came to Chicken Hawk. Chicken Hawk said, "I will go with you." Chicken Hawk went with him. He took medicine, chewed it, and rubbed it over his body so that he could run very fast. They came to a wide river. Horned Lizard[1] carried them across. The second night they got to Old Mexico. They came to a great cliff and he could not get up. Chicken Hawk said, "I will carry you up." The poor boy sat on his back and he flew up. On the top there was a great house. He went in. There were lots of men and girls and he asked them for feathers. They said, "What have you brought us ?" He gave them the prayersticks which he had brought, and they gave him all the parrot feathers he could carry, long tail feathers, and short tail feathers. He slept there. Late in the night when all the others were asleep, two parrot girls came down. They were young and unmarried. "Are you asleep ?" they said. He said, "No." He slept with them. Blue Parrot Girl would not

---

[1] The description resembled the Gila monster.

let him go. When he was ready to start, she said, "Go out and I will follow you."

They came to his grandmother's and Parrot Girl stayed with her, but the boy went on to the house of the village priest. He had lots of parrot feathers. He got there in the early evening. The girl set out food for him. After he had eaten, the girl asked, "Did you get feathers?" "Yes." "I shall marry you." They were married. In eight days the village priest called a Muwaiya dance, and they had many parrot feathers.

One day his wife was grinding and Blue Parrot Girl came to his house. She lit on top of the ladder poles. People saw her, and someone shot at her. She fell down dead. The boy cried. They put the body in the inner room. Chicken Hawk came and lit on the ladder. He asked, "Why are you crying?" "Blue Parrot Girl is killed." "I will cure her." The man took him into the house. He drew off her shirt and she was a young girl. She was alive. She stayed as his sister.[1]

In the witches' kiva men met every night and laid plans to marry his sister. One of them said to him, "I want to marry your sister. Will you give her to me?" "No." She knew that they were scheming to marry her. One day she asked her brother,[2] "What is it that these witch people say?" "They want to marry you." "No, I am not going to marry any witch people." The next night when he went to the kiva, the people asked, "What did your sister say?" "She is not willing to marry you." "All right." The girl's brother went home and they laid more plans. "We will make his sister marry us; we will force her," they said. They made a nice new woman's belt and put medicine on it. One of the witch men took it to the spring where she went to get water. He dropped it a little way from the spring. He lay down above, and waited for her to come. He waited all the afternoon. When she came, she saw the belt and wanted to pick it up. "No," she said to herself, "I think the witch people put it there," and she went on and drew water and filled her jar. Then the witch man came out and said to her, "Some woman has lost her belt. Why don't you pick it up?" "You pick it up for me." "No, you pick it up." "If you pick it up for me, I will marry you." "No." Four times she asked him to pick it up, and three times he refused. The last time he picked it up. As soon as he touched it, he went crazy. The girl laughed, put the water jar on her head and started for home. "That is what you would

---

[1] The conflict between Zuni monogamy and the folk tale pattern of several wives is evident here.

[2] That is, her husband whom she now called brother.

have done to me," she said. She told the witches, "Some man is crazy at the spring." The witch men went out to catch him. One man caught him and as soon as he touched him, he became crazy. Everybody who touched him became crazy.

Next night the head witch girl called the witches together again. She went out to White Rocks and gave the coyote call, and the witches came to their kiva. She said, "What shall we do to kill this man's sister? We have failed in our first attempt." They made a plan to transform her into a rattlesnake by playing a game of pitch and toss. They made a ring and put medicine upon it. Next day one of the men took this and went again to the girl. He said, "I have brought my ring. Let us play at catching. I will throw and you may catch, and you may throw and I will catch." She said, "I am busy grinding corn." He asked her four times. She said, "Give it to me and I will throw it to you. If you catch it I will marry you." He reached out to catch it, and he turned into a female rattlesnake, and went off crawling. She laughed. "So you would have done to me!" The men came and killed that rattlesnake, so another witch was dead.

The next night the witch girl gave the coyote call again and the men came to the kiva. The head witch girl said, "What shall we do to kill this woman? We have failed this second time." They said, "We must kill this man and his wife and sister." "How can we do this?" "We must make some way." "It will not be possible." The witch girl said, "There is a way. I will kill them." "All right."

She went out to the northeast (two or three miles) to a place where a Navaho had been killed. She took a long prayerstick (fore-arm length) in her waist and she put it on the ground. She waited. She heard the dead man coming. When he got there, the dead man said, "What is it that you have come to ask?" "I want you to help me kill two women and a man. I want you to come like a dead man and make them die of fright." "All right. When you get home, do not eat. Tomorrow, also, do not eat nor drink. The third day do not eat nor drink, and the fourth day do not eat nor drink. The fourth night come here again and I will come and turn you into a dead man." She went home and four days and four nights she did not eat nor drink. The fourth night she went back and the dead man came. He said, "Go first to the east and the south to Isleta, Santo Domingo, Old Mexico. Kill them everywhere, kill the Navahos in their country. Whatever you see a Navaho cooking in jars, go up and eat it, and make them die of fright." The dead man rolled around, crying like a dead man, "Me-me-me[1]."

---

[1] The rattling of the bones.

He knocked against the witch girl. Immediately she was transformed into a dead man. Her brains were running out, her eye sockets were hollow, her bones rattled. She started off to the Navaho country. They heard her coming, talking like a dead man, "Me-me-me." They said, "A dangerous person is coming." She rolled right into the camp. All the Navahos were alive. She went into the cooking house and took meat out of the pot and ate it. They all died of fright. She went on to Isleta, Santo Domingo, Old Mexico. Everywhere everybody died of fright.

She went back to her own village. The Ahaiyute knew that she was coming. They said, "We will stand together. There is a dead man coming." Younger Brother wet a stick in his mouth and laid it across the trail. The dead man could not get by. She came, and she said, "What is the matter with you two boys that you are not dead of fright?" "Nothing to be afraid of! You're nothing but a girl!" "I have killed lots of Navahos, Santo Domingos, San Filipes and Mexicans." "How can you kill people? You aren't anything!" "Take up that stick, I can't get across." "Why not? It's nothing but a little stick." "I can't get across." They took it away, and said, "How can you kill us? We aren't afraid." Younger Brother took a yellow stone and said, "Now I will kill you." He cut off the dead man's head. The head bounded up ("about two hundred feet"). He cut it off a second time, and a third time. Each time, as soon as the head hit the ground it joined with the body. It did this six times. Elder Brother said, "I have more power than you have." He took an arrow and shot it into the brush. There was a big fire. "That is how we kill people," he said. She said, "Let me try." "How?" "I am going to kill you now." She pulled out a long prayerstick and said, "Now die!" The Ahaiyute said, "Let me see it." "I won't give it to you." "It looks like mine, show it to me. I will show you mine." She did not want to, but at last she gave it to him. Ahaiyute took it and threw it into the fire. The girl cried, "I can't do anything against you. Give me my prayerstick and I can overcome you." Ahaiyute said, "I will give it back." He cut a cedar twig and drew it through his mouth. It looked just like the prayerstick. She said, "Now I can kill you!" "How?" "I will show you. Stand together." She threw the prayerstick, but it did not hurt them. Four times she threw it, but the Ahaiyute were still alive. "This prayerstick is not mine," she said. "Yes, it is," said Ahaiyute. "Now we will do something. See that cedar bush?" "Yes." They shot into it. Lightning came out. It covered her. She was gone. The Ahaiyute went back home. There were no more witches.

13

THE SON OF RAIN (7)[1]
Notes, 320

A long time ago the people were living at Kakima. One girl was living there who had never married; she had no husband. One night while she was asleep it rained and the rain dropped on her bed. She was asleep and did not know it, but next day when she woke her bed was wet with rain. After a month she knew that she was pregnant, and she thought it very strange because she had no husband and no young man had ever come to her, and she did not know by whom she had this baby. In time the baby was born and it was a boy, and she lived with her parents with her little boy.

When the boy was about eight years old he began to kill birds, and soon he killed cottontails with a stick. He asked his mother to make him a bow and arrows. His mother said, "Go and get some willow and a piece of good wood and I will make them for you." He went out to the southwest towards a cave called Picukta, where the white bears lived. As he came near he was running and the Rain Makers (Uwanami) saw him and said, "Here is our son trying to get up to that cave. Maybe the bears will kill him. We had better send him away." Then they took their lightning and threw it at him and threw him down. He got up and went on anyway. Then the Rain Makers tried again to stop him and hit him with their lightning and threw him about five hundred yards away. Heavy rain came and he could not get up to the cave. The Rain Makers were afraid the bears would kill their child.

Then the boy was angry and did not want to go on, so he went home. Next day he went out and went about in the fields looking for cottontails. A big bee came buzzing and spoke to him and said, "Well, my grandson, what are you doing here?" "I am looking for cottontails." "Let us go to the girl who has these fields." "All right." They went down to where two girls were working in the fields. They had many watermelons and sweet melons and corn. They came to one of the girls and she gave them some watermelons and he ate them and threw away the skin and the seeds and the bee carried them to the other side of the house. Then the girl asked him, "What is this? Your bee is carrying the fruit away. How can he do it?" The boy said, "Why yes, he can carry anything." The girl did not believe him. He took the string out of his moccasins and gave it to the bee and the bee carried it away. Then he took off his moccasin and threw it away and the bee carried it off. He took off his stocking and the bee carried it away. The girl took off her *pitone* and the bee carried it away. Then the girl became bold

---

[1] Recorded by Ruth Bunzel.

and took off her belt and the bee carried it away. Then she took off her dress and the bee carried that away. Then the other girl did the same and the two girls were naked. They had nothing with which to cover themselves. Then the boy said, "Well, my grandfather, you had better bring back these girls' clothes. We don't want to leave the two girls like this." Then the two girls put on their clothes and left.

The boy went back to the cave at Opaḳakwi to get oak wood for his bow and willow for the arrows. He gathered an armful of willow twigs and he found a stick of oak wood. Soon a black bear came along very angry and wanted to kill the boy. The bear said, "Why did you spoil my house?" The boy said, "I want that stick." "Why?" "My mother is going to make me a bow and arrows." The bear asked him, "Have you a sister?" He said, "No. There are only I and my mother. We live alone." "Have you no father?" "No, I have no father." The bear said, "Can you give me your mother?" He said, "I will give you my mother. My mother is young. She is only about twenty-five years old, and she is a fine looking woman. I think you will like her." The bear went into the cave and brought out a bow and arrows and a quiver of mountain-lion skin and gave them to the boy and he said, "I will come to your house tonight."

The boy went home and told his mother. She said, "You are crazy. Why did you do that? I don't want a husband." The boy said, "I did it because I wanted a bow and arrows. I didn't think you knew how to make them and he gave me this fine bow and arrows."

That night the bear did not come and next day the boy made arrows. He took flint and broke it and made good arrow heads. Then he went out and was finishing his arrow. In the afternoon he heard the bear coming. The bear came up to the top of the house where the boy was working. He was putting the stone point on his arrow. The bear came up and asked the boy, "Why are you putting charcoal on your arrow? That won't kill anything." The boy said, "You are foolish. That is not charcoal; it is stone." The bear said, "No, that is charcoal." The bear said, "I shall go and stand fifty yards away and you can shoot me and you will see that it won't hurt me." The boy said, "No, I don't want to kill you," and the bear said, "You can't kill me with that. I shall go over there and you shoot." Then the boy changed his mind and said, "All right, stand over there about a hundred yards off, and I will shoot you. But I will surely kill you." Then the bear said again, "You can't kill me with that." He went off and sat down and the boy let go

13*

his arrow and shot him and the arrow went through his heart and stuck out three inches behind. The bear groaned and fell over. The boy went over to him and said, "Why did you fall down?" He pulled out the arrow and it was covered with blood, and the bear rolled over and died. The boy went back to the house and said to his mother, "I have just killed my father. He was coming to see you and I killed him." His mother said, "Why did you kill him? You should not have done that." Then the boy sent his mother out to skin the bear.

That night the girls'[1] brothers and uncles, and the people who lived in the other house, were talking it over. They wanted to kill the boy because he had seen the two girls naked. Next day the boy went to hunt rabbits and found the bee. The bee told him, "Tomorrow night you are going to die. Someone is going to kill you. Tell your mother to make you some bread, three loaves with holes right through, and one without a hole. Take them into the mountains to the south, and hunt deer there. Stay there over night. At sunset you will see lots of dead wood and you will build a big fire under a big tree, and when the fire is burning take your four little breads out into the dark and put the one without a hole nearest the fire." He said, "All right," and he went home and told his mother to make the bread.

Next day he took the bread and he went to the top of the mesa and hunted deer all day. Near sunset he came to a place where there was plenty of wood and he brought lots of wood and made a fire. He made a big fire and about ten yards away he put down one loaf of bread, the one without a hole, and twenty feet further out he put the second one, and twenty feet further he put the third and then the fourth. Then he sat down under the tree. Soon he heard a coyote crying, "We we we we," and after a while he heard it again. He heard it four times, as if someone were crying. After a while a little way off he heard a girl; she was gasping like a dying man. The boy heard her but he was not afraid. He put more wood on his fire and sat under his tree. A little later the girl came nearer the fire, and blood was streaming from her head. The boy looked at her. Then the girl came nearer and ate the first bread. Then she came to the next one and ate that, and after a while she finished and went on to the next one and ate that. Then she finished and she came to the last bread, the one without a hole and she ate that, and right away she dropped dead. Then the boy went to the girl and took his knife and cut her body and cut her coyote shirt off and he saw that it was a girl. Then the other girl came and he took off her shirt and her mask. They were the two girls whose dresses he had taken

[1] The girls whose clothes the bee had taken away.

and whom he had seen naked. Now he wanted to kill the two girls. The girls said, "No, we cannot die," but he shot them anyway and the two girls died. Then he cut their heads off and made night-hawks out of the two girls' heads, and took their hearts and made owls and he took their livers and guts and made bats. Then he said to them, "Now you can go wherever you please." One bat went to the spring on the south and the other to the north. Then the boy went home.

That is the reason why the Zunis always go to these two springs to pray, because the two girls live in the two springs.

THE BUTTERFLY PURSUIT

A. TOMSTINAPA AND NE'WE·KWE (7)

Notes, 321

The people were living in Ketcipawa. Tomstinapa was living in the spring Maitcikawa. He used to go down towards the east about five miles and north about two miles and west about three miles. Down there eight sisters had a garden and they heard Tomstinapa going by giving his kachina call.[1] The eldest girl said to herself, "I will wait for that man and when he comes I will tell him to stop." He stopped and played with the girl. He said to her, "Let us play hide and seek. I will shut my eyes and you hide. If I find you I will cut off your head; if you find me you will cut my head off." "All right." Tomstinapa shut his eyes and the girl went into the squash blossom. He looked and looked but could not find her. He got tired and he said, "I give up. Come out." She said, "I was in the squash blossom, couldn't you find me? Now it is your turn to hide." Tomstinapa jumped into a big sunflower. The girl squeezed milk from her breast. She looked in it and saw the man in the sunflower. She called, "Come down, I see you in the sunflower." He dropped down. "I have lost my life, kill me." She seized him by his hair and cut off his head. She twisted his hair together and she cut open his chest and took out his heart. She dug a hole in the field and put his body in it and covered it with earth. She carried the heart and took up the head by the twist of hair and carried it home. The blood dripped all the way and from every drop the tenatsali grew. She got home to Ketcipawa and went into her own house. She dug a hole under the ladder and buried the head, and the heart she put in a jar and set it in the corner of the room and covered it with a woman's dress.

[1] Tomstinapa's call is a high, far-carrying note, and not to be mistaken.

That night Tomstinapa did not come home. His sisters and his mother and his father were worried about him. They wondered if some harm had come to him. His mother called Eagle and asked him to look for her son. She said, "Bring me word whether he is dead or alive." He flew up to the heavens. He went so near the sun that it burned the feathers from the top of his head, but he could not see him. He came back and said, "I cannot find him." His mother said, "Therefore you shall always be bald and eat dead animals." His father said, "I shall call the carrion fly, perhaps he can find our son." He came and said, "What is it that you have to ask?" The father said, "I want you to look for my son. If any animal dies you always find it. If my son has died I want you to bring us word." The fly said, "Which way did he go?" "He went out of this house and went down the ladder and five miles towards the east. Then he went north two miles and west about three miles and came home towards the south again." "All right." The carrion fly flew off so fast you could not watch him and he went smelling and smelling all over the country. He went five miles to the east and then north two miles and three miles again to the west and he got to the girl's field. There were eight girls working in the field and the fly buzzed about and sucked the juices of the flowers. He found the tenatsali and it was the blood of Tomstinapa. He followed the trail of the tenatsali and all along the way where the girl had carried the head, wherever the blood had dropped, these flowers were blossoming. He came to her house and under the ladder he found the flowers growing from his head (it was buried under the ladder), and flowers in the jar. He went back and Tomstinapa's father asked, "What have you found?" He said to him, "He is dead. The girl killed him. I found tenatsali growing in her field. Everywhere his blood dropped it was blossoming and from his head that is buried under the ladder." His father said, "All right, go." The carrion fly went back to his home.

The father took his flute and blew a note and a yellow butterfly came out of it.[1] He did not like it and he put it back into the flute. He blew a second note and a blue butterfly came out and he put it back in the flute. He blew a third note and a red butterfly came out and he put it back in the flute. He blew a fourth note and a white butterfly came out and he put it back in the flute. He blew a fifth note and an all-colored butterfly came out. This was beautiful and the father said, "Go to the house of the eight girls. Go five miles to the east, two miles to the north and three miles to the west and

---

[1] This magic of Tomstinapa's father is that belonging to the Paiyatamu cult, see discussion.

come to their field." The beautiful butterfly flew until he came to the tenatsali flowers. He lit in them and sucked their juice. The eight girls saw the butterfly in the flower. They were making baskets and they wanted the pattern of the butterfly's wings to use for their baskets. They said, "Let us catch the butterfly," and they ran after it. They took off their scarves and tried to catch the butterfly with them. Then they took off their belts and tried to catch the butterfly with them. Then they took off their moccasins and tried to catch the butterfly in them and last they took off their dresses and tried to catch the butterfly with them. It flew and flew until they were way up by Corn Mountain. The sisters were tired and naked and they had not caught the butterfly. They lay down in the shade of a tree and went to sleep. The butterfly was sitting on a branch of the tree and he took off his butterfly shirt and stood up a man with his hair tied up with corn husks in two horns. He was Ne'we·kwe.[1] He came down to those eight girls while they were asleep and had intercourse with them. He went up into the tree again. When he had gone Coyote came and he had intercourse with each of the eight girls also. Then he pulled out the hairs of his moustache and "planted corn" between their legs.[2] Later in the afternoon the girls woke up. They scratched and scratched between their legs. They smelled bad and were ashamed. They all got up and tried to cover their genitals with their hands. They did not know what had happened. At last they looked up and saw Ne'we·kwe in the tree. They said, "It is you that did this bad business." "No." "Yes, you must give us something to wear. We are naked." He cut off a piece of the corn husk that wrapped his hair and threw it down. When it touched the earth it became an embroidered white blanket. At last there were eight blankets and the girls put them on. Ne'we·kwe came down and he said to them, "Where are you going?" "We do not know." "I will take you to my house." He took them to Ashes Spring.[3] He went in and the eight girls lived there with their husband. He always brought them lots of venison.

B. PAIYATAMU (7)
Published only in abstract

---

[1] The Ne'we·kwe are in many respects a phallic society. Tomstinapa is obviously a variant of Paiyatamu in this story, see notes. Ne'paiyatamu (Bunzel, 1080) is a Ne'we·kwe impersonation.

[2] This is the origin of women's pubic hair.

[3] A spring associated with Ne'we·kwe.

PAIYATAMU'S GRANDSON (7)

Notes, 323

They were living at Pinawa. A boy lived with his grandmother. They were very poor and the people threw ashes and refuse into their house. When the boy grew to be a young man, he asked his grandmother, "Who is my father?" His grandmother answered, "I do not know. Go and ask the Sun." The next day the young man made prayersticks, and went to the Sun. Sun said, "What have you come to ask that you have come so far?" He said, "I want to know who my father is." The Sun answered, "I do not know who your father is. Whenever people have intercourse in the daytime that baby is my baby. Only when they have intercourse in the night, people's children belong to them." The boy went back to his grandmother's.

Next day he went out to hunt rabbits. As he was coming in at sundown with his catch, he met the eight daughters of the priests, — the daughter of the village priest, pekwin's daughter, the daughter of the elder bow priest, the daughter of the younger bow priest, and all the other priests. They said, "You're (plural) coming, aren't you? Let us have some." He gave them lumps of mush his grandmother had toasted in the ashes.[1] The girls said, "We do not eat poor stuff like this. We shall get our food at home." They threw his mush balls after him. The boy cried and went home to his grandmother.

Next day he made prayersticks. His grandmother made food for him, and he took his prayersticks and went far to the north to Paiyatamu's house. When he had gone fifteen miles he made fire and ate the mush balls. Somebody was coming. He looked and saw Mountain Lion. Mountain Lion said to him, "Are you camping here? Have you got a ceremonial hair-feather?" "Yes." He took a cactus pod, took out the fluff and tied it on the left shoulder of Mountain Lion. He took yellow clay and painted his face. Over that he made a black line and painted black vertical stripes on his body. Now he was a handsome young man. Mountain Lion stayed with the boy. Toward morning Mountain Lion went out. At a little distance he saw a deer and killed it. He took for himself only a little bit of the blood and went on and left the deer for the young man. In the morning the boy followed his tracks. He found the deer, skinned it, and packed it on his back. He went on to the north.

---

[1] Girls met young hunters and were given a piece of meat. As so often in these tales, this was a prelude to marriage. The boy in this story was not well brought up and divided his lunch with them, not his day's catch They were insulted but he did not know why.

At night he built a fire and ate. Somebody was coming. It was Bear. Bear said to him, "You are camping here tonight? Have you got a ceremonial hair-feather?" "Yes." He gave him a hair-feather made of a cactus fluff and tied it on the left shoulder of Bear. Bear stayed with him. Toward morning Bear went out and killed a deer. He took only a little piece for himself and left the rest for the boy. In the morning the boy followed Bear's tracks. He found the deer, skinned it, and packed it on his back. He went on to the north.

Next night he made a fire and ate. Somebody was coming. It was Badger. Badger said to him, "Have you a ceremonial hair-feather?" He gave him one, and that night Badger killed cotton-tail rabbits for the young man and left them for him. He went on to the north. Next day he made camp. Wolf came. He gave him a ceremonial feather and Wolf went out and killed antelope for him. He skinned the antelope and packed it on his back. He went on to the north.

He came to Spider Woman's house. She said to him, "Where are you going?" "I am going to Paiyatamu's house." Spider said to him, "I will go with you. Put me in your ear, and I will help you." He put Spider Woman in his ear and went on.

That evening they saw Paiyatamu's house. Paiyatamu was sitting outside of his door. He was an old, old man with gray hair. Spider Woman said to the young man, "Say to him, 'Hello, my grandfather'." The young man said to him, "Hello, my grandfather." Paiyatamu said to him, "I have no grandson." The young man said to him, "Yes, you are my grandfather." The old man went back into the house and brought corn. He said, "My son has no child." Paiyatamu's eight daughters were grinding flour at the grinding stone. The young man spoke to them and said, "Hello, my aunts." They did not answer him. Spider said to him, "Ask your aunts, 'Where is my father?'" They did not answer him. Paiyatamu said, "I will send to the kiva and bring my son." He sent a messenger and his son came. Paiyatamu said to him, "You have come." "Yes." The boy said to Paiyatamu's son, "How have you lived these days, my father." His father answered, "Do not call yourself my son. We shall see whether you are a son of mine." He went into the next room, took a square (sacred) stone and made a spring of water. He said to the young man, "Come, your aunts will wash your hair." They pushed him into the spring. Spider Woman let her thread down through the water. The young man laid hold on it and climbed up.

He said to Paiyatamu's eight daughters, "Tell my father to come." They called his father, and his father said to him, "If you can do as I do you are a son of mine." He took him into the other room. There was a great mountain of glass, smooth as ice. His father climbed to the top and stood there. He said to his son, "If you can climb this you may say 'My father' and I will answer you." Spider lay her thread against the mountain of glass and the young man climbed to the top. "Hello, my father." "Hello, my son."

They came down. His father brought out a sash and a flute.[1] The flute he threw into the thick brush. "If you can find the flute, you are my son." Spider directed him and he went to the place where his father had thrown the flute and picked it up. "My son, you are my child." His son said to him, "You are my father. When the people went for water to the spring at Pinawa, you urinated on a yellow flower, *hatsoliko*[2]." "Yes." "I am that child."

He called his eight sisters and told them to get water. They went into the other room and heated the water. They got a crystal and made it red hot. His father touched his son's hand with it and the skin cracked. He touched his other hand and the skin of that hand cracked. He touched his foot and the skin cracked. He touched his other foot and the skin cracked. He took a crook and pulled the skin off. He stood up a beautiful young man. His father said to him, "Throw your skin in the river, it is dirty. You are a different man." He went to throw his skin in the water.

As soon as he came back his father's eight sisters made suds and washed his hair. They dressed it and combed it. They put the best yellow parrot feathers on his head and dressed him in a white shirt. They tied a sash and a belt around his waist and fastened a fox skin at his back. They gave him socks and tied yarn below his knees. They put on blue moccasins on his feet. They hung a bandolier of black and white beads over one shoulder and fastened the wrist guard on his wrist. They painted his face with shiny black paint in straight lines under his eyes and a vertical line on his chin, and they made a spot on each cheek.[3] When they had dressed him, his father said, "My son, you must return to your home. The eight daughters of the priests, the daughter of the village priest, pekwin's daughter, the daughters of the two bow priests, will come to marry you. Do not sleep with them, they are enemies. They have insulted you. When the priest's daughter is ready to sleep, tell her to look up. Take your stone knife and cut off her head. Knot her hair together and tie the head to a stick. Cut her body open and take out her heart. When you have killed them all, put their heads and

---

[1] The special property of Paiyatamu.
[2] A thistle.
[3] This is the costume of Paiyatamu.

their hearts in your flute. Each night go out and sleep by the fire with your grandmother. Next night another priest's daughter will come to marry you. Do the same to her. The next night another priest's daughter will come. Do the same to her. The fourth night another will come. Do the same to her. When you have killed them all, come back here. Tell your grandmother, 'Eight days from now I will come back and bring with me eight priests' daughters.'"

Paiyatamu said to him, "My son, go back to your home now." Paiyatamu called the Rainbow and said to him, "Take my son back to his home in Pinawa." The young man sat down on the rainbow as on a chair. "Close your eyes." The rainbow shot through the air and came to the earth a little distance from Pinawa. The Rainbow said to him, "In eight days, if you want me, call me and I will come." "All right." Rainbow went back. The young man went to his home. It was filled with ashes. Before night the house was clean and he went out into the village. The people had never seen him before. He was very handsome, and beautifully dressed. The daughter of the village priest saw him and she said to her mother, "Somebody has come to that old woman's house. He is a handsome man. I want to go to marry him." "All right." She put a great basket of corn on her head and went to the young man's house. His grandmother said, "Somebody is coming." The girl stood at the hatchway and called to the grandmother, "Ca. Lift me down." The grandmother took the basket of corn into the house and emptied it into the grinding stones. She sat down and they gave her food to eat. When she had eaten the grandmother said, "What is it you have come to ask?" She answered, "Thinking of that young man I have come." His grandmother said to her, "I cannot answer for my son. My son, what is your wish?" "I will marry this girl." "All right." His grandmother went out to make the bed. She came back and told her grandson, "I have made the bed." The young man said to the daughter of the village priest, "Let us go in." The girl went in with him. He took off his moccasins and the girl went to bed. He said, "Look up." While she was looking he took his stone knife and cut off her head. He tied her hair together (to carry it by). He cut her body and took out the heart. He put the head and the heart on a shelf. He dug a hole in the floor and threw in her body. He went out to the room where his grandmother was. "Why have you come out, my grandson?" He lay down by the fireplace and slept.

Next night Pekwin's daughter came to the hatchway (Repeat as above for the eight daughters of the priests.)

After eight days, when he had finished his morning meal, he took the heads and hearts of the rain priests' daughters and put them into his flute. He said to his grandmother, "I must go to my father. If the fathers or sisters of any of these girls come to ask for me, tell them I am hunting, and that I will come back in eight days, and bring back all the girls." "All right." He went a little distance from Pinawa and called the Rainbow. Rainbow came and he sat down on his neck. Rainbow shot into the air and came to the house of Paiyatamu. Paiyatamu and his eight sisters were sitting along one side of a white embroidered blanket. His father said to him, "My son, put your flute in your mouth and blow hard. Face the east." He faced east and blew upon his flute. The daughter of the village priest jumped out of his flute and sat down naked on the ceremonial blanket. She was in a perspiration. "I am tired." Paiyatamu's sisters said, "She is ugly. She is frowsy and hot." One of them went and brought an embroidered white blanket and put it around her. The young man blew again upon his flute. He faced north and Pekwin's daughter jumped out of the flute. She sat down naked on the ceremonial blanket. Paiyatamu's sisters said, "Ha, she is ugly." One of them brought up a ceremonial blanket and put it around her. (Repeat for the eight girls.)

Paiyatamu went into the next room and brought corn. His sisters shelled it and he told the eight girls to grind. His sisters took medicine in their mouths and spit it over the corn to make it hard as stone. The eight girls ground and ground, but they could not make meal of it. They hurt their hands and cried, but they could not make flour, for the corn was like stone. Paiyatamu's sisters said, "Ha, they are no good, they cannot grind." They went to the grinding stones and immediately it became fine meal.

That night Paiyatamu taught his son the songs of the priests. Every night for eight nights he taught him the songs of the retreats of the priesthoods.

In Pinawa, after seven days, the village priest told his wife to make paper-bread. She ground and she needed her daughter's help. She went to the grandmother to get her daughter. She went in. There were eight baskets standing by the grinding stone. Grandmother looked up and saw her. "Sit down." "I must not sit down. I came to find my daughter. I want her to help me to make paper-bread." "My grandson went up to his father's house. He will return tomorrow evening and bring back all the girls." The wife of the village priest returned to her home. People knew that something was wrong. Pekwin's wife went to get her daughter's basket. The wife of the bow priest went to get her daughter's basket. The wife of the younger bow priest went to get her daughter's basket. The mothers of all the eight girls went to get their daughters' baskets. They all wept and said, "Our daughters are dead." The people in the village got ready and said, "Let us kill the old woman. Her grandson has killed our daughters."

At Paiyatamu's house Paiyatamu taught the eight girls the songs of the priests. He said to them, "Your fathers are priests. They do not know how to pray and I have taught you. When you get home each of you shall teach your own father. Tell him that you have brought back his prayers for the retreats. When you go back to your home, always be faithful to my son." "All right." The next day he called the Rainbow. He came and the eight girls and the young man sat on his neck. He shot through the air and carried them close to Pinawa.

It was the eighth day. The people of Pinawa came out ready to kill the grandmother. They brought stones and knives and ropes. The old woman said, "Let me look for my son. He promised to bring home the eight girls by sunset. If he does not come by that time, kill me. I shall not live long anyway. It is best that you should take my life. I am not afraid to die, but I want to wait for my son's promise." One of the leaders said, "Poor woman, she is right. We should wait. If he comes we shall be sorry. If he does not come, we can kill her." The grandmother went out and searched the horizon. She saw her grandson coming with the eight girls. She called to the people. "Somebody is coming. I think it is my grandson." People looked. Those who were coming were all dressed in white embroidered blankets. People said, "She is right. It is good that we did not kill her." Each of the girls went to her own house. The village priest's daughter went to her father's house; Pekwin's daughter to her father's house; the daughters of the bow priests chiefs' to their fathers' houses. That night each of the girls taught her father the prayers of the retreat. For four nights they taught their fathers. They called the rain. The eight girls and Paiyatamu made prayersticks, and planted them for rain. They went into their house and prayed. For eight days and eight nights it rained. There was much water. They ended their retreat. The village priest went into his room for his retreat. It rained. For eight days and eight nights the rain fell. He ended his retreat. Pekwin went into his room for his retreat. For eight days and eight nights it rained. He ended his retreat. The bow priests went in for their retreat. For eight days and eight nights it rained. They ended their retreats. The water already came up to the tops of the houses. All the seven villages went up to the top of Corn Mountain to escape the flood. For forty days and forty nights it rained all the time. All the animals were killed, the deer, the antelope, the birds, rabbits, bears, wolves and coyotes. The water came up to the top of the mesa and still it was rising. The priests and Paiyatamu met together. They said, "How can we stop the flood ?" At last one of them said, "The village priest has a daughter who has never been married, and whose body is perfect. He has a son also. Let us ask for these two. If they are willing to save us the flood will be stopped." The village priest was very sorrowful, but he had to save his people. His son and his daughter said also, "We must save our people. In four days you will take us to the edge of the cliff and throw us down into the water." Everyone made prayersticks and ground prayer meal and gave to the son and daughter of the village priest. After three days they made the prayersticks. The women and girls ground white cornmeal and took turquoise and shells and coral, and gave to the son and daughter of the village priest. Next morning the girl and boy dressed themselves in their best clothes. They put on embroidered white blankets and beads and took the great bundle of prayersticks which the people had made for them. They made the boy stand to the west and the girl to the east. The village priest took his basket of meal and "made the road" for them. He brought them to the edge of the cliff and threw them down into the water with their bundle of prayersticks. They sank to the bottom of the flood. When they were half way down they became pinnacles of rock, the boy to the right, the girl to the left.

The flood retreated. In two months the water was gone but the ground was too soft to walk on. In six months the ground was dry, and the people came came down from the mesa. They had been there four years.

This is why, if any girl, when she is married, wants a girl or boy baby, after six months she will take a little stone from the Boy or the Girl at Corn Mountain. She will grind it and put it in water and drink it. After six months she will have a child, a girl if she took stone from the Girl; a boy if she took stone from the Boy.

THE CORN MAIDENS MARRY (7)

Notes, 325

They were living at Hecokta. All the people of the seven towns went there to gamble. They had no women[1] and they gambled all the time. One man made a deer-mask. He put it on and went south. An A'mosa boy dressed all in his nice clothes and wearing lots of

---

[1] That is, there were not enough women to go around.

beads went south to hunt. He saw the deer, and it went south about half a mile. Then it turned and went northwest close to Hecokta. Along about sunset the deer went into a cedar bush, and a man came out. The A'mosa boy went up to the man, and he said, "Where are you going?" The A'mosa boy said, "A deer went in there." The other said, "Let the deer alone. Come to my house." He went to his house. They brought out the evening meal. After they had eaten, lots of men came into the house. Everybody gambled. That boy lost everything. He lost all his nice clothes, and his beads and everything. Next morning he went off poor.

That day a man of Hecokta went hunting deer to the southwest. He came to Hanłipiŋka. He had seen no deer. About sunset he got there. Now there were seven sisters that lived there; nobody knew they were living there. They were Yellow Corn, and Red Corn, and Blue Corn, and White Corn, and Black Corn, and Speckled Corn, and Sweet Corn. That night Red Corn and Blue Corn went to get water. They put water in their jars, and they saw this man. He had never seen girls before. He didn't know anything about them. He saw these girls, and he saw they were good-looking girls, and he was afraid. He went back. Then he wanted to go into their house. He said, "May I come in with you into your house?" Red Corn Girl said to him, "I don't think my sister Yellow Corn will let a man come into our house." She went in to ask Yellow Corn if the young man could come into their house. Yellow Corn said, "No." Red Corn went back to tell the young man that her sister would not let him come.

Next evening at the same time White Corn and Speckled Corn went out to get water at the well. The young man came again, and asked if he might go into their house. He went with them to the house they lived. He wanted very much to go in now. White Corn went in to ask Yellow Corn if the young man could come in. Again she said, "No." He went home. Next day he came back at the same time. Black Corn and Sweet Corn came out to get water in their jars. He went with them to their house, and Black Corn went in to ask her sister if the young man could come into their house. Yellow Corn was angry, so she said, "Yes." He came in. He wanted to take one of those girls to his home with him. Their sister said, "If you want to take one of these girls home with you, Red Corn shall go with you." So he took her to Hecokta. He didn't gamble any more. He spent all his time with his wife; he was always thinking about her.

The men who were gambling noticed that he never came any more, and late one night the headman said to one of the gamblers,

"Go tell that man to come here and gamble. He never comes here any more." One of the men went out. He climbed up the ladder of the boy's house without making any noise, and he heard the girl talking and playing. The man went in. He saw the girl, and he asked, "Where did you get that girl?" "If you won't tell, I'll tell you where I got this girl." "I won't tell. I need a girl." "All right, I'll get you a girl." So the boy stayed there that night, and next morning the (first) boy went back to Hanłipiŋka. He got Blue Corn Girl and brought her to Hecokta.

Next night when they were gambling they sent another young man to get these two to come to gamble. He went softly up the ladder of the boy's house, and he heard two girls inside. He went in. He saw two nice girls. He asked, "Where did you get those girls?" "If you won't tell, I'll tell you where we got these girls." "I won't tell. I need a girl." "All right, I'll get you a girl." So the boy stayed there that night with the two boys. Now there were three boys. Next morning the boy went to Hanłipiŋka, and got another girl. He got White Corn Girl. He brought her back to Hecokta. Now there were three girls.

Next night those who were gambling sent another young man to bring the three who did not come to gamble. He went softly up the ladder of the boy's house, and he heard three girls talking. He went in, and he saw three nice girls. He said, "Where did you get those girls?" "If you won't tell, I'll tell you where we got these girls." He said, "I won't tell. I need a girl." "All right, I'll get you a girl." So the boy stayed there that night with the three boys. Now there were four boys. Next morning the boy went to Hanłipiŋka, and got another girl. He got Speckled Corn Girl. He brought her to Hecokta. Now there were four girls.

Next night those who were gambling sent another boy to bring the boys who did not come to gamble. He went out, and went softly up the ladder to the boy's house, and he heard four girls. He went in and he saw four nice girls. He said, "Where did you get these girls?" "If you won't tell I'll tell where I got these girls." "I won't tell. I need a girl." "All right, I'll get you a girl." So the boy stayed that night. Next morning the first boy went down to Hanłipiŋka, and got another girl. He got Black Corn Girl. He brought her back to Hecokta.

Next night five boys did not come to the gambling. They sent another boy to tell them to come to gamble. He went up to the boy's house quietly and he heard five girls. He went in, and he saw five nice-looking girls. He said, "Where did you get these girls?" "If you won't tell, I'll tell you where we got these girls." "I won't tell." "All right, I'll get you a girl." So the last boy stayed all night with the five boys. Now there were six. The next morning the boy went to Hanłipiŋka and brought back another girl. He brought back Yellow Corn Girl. He brought her to Hecokta.

Sweet Corn Girl was left all by herself. She was lonely, and she grew very thin and weak. One night Ne'we·kwe[1] came. He came by the Milky Way. He went right into the house at Hanłipiŋka, and Sweet Corn Girl was all alone. She was sick, and she had nothing to eat. She had just a very little corn-pollen left. Ne'we·kwe greeted her. She said, "I don't know where my sisters went." He said, "I know. Don't you want to go there?" She said, "I don't know. I am so weak." He said, "I'll make you strong." There were only three grains of corn left in her hair. He went up to the Milky Way.[2] He made a cigarette and lit it. He blew out the smoke, and made a cloud.[3] Pretty soon it began to rain. It rained hard. Next morning Ne'we·kwe went to Hanłipiŋka, and he found Sweet Corn Girl standing up, and in her hair were the three grains of corn. He planted them. Next day it rained. The next day it rained. For four days it rained, and the corn came up, lots of sweet corn, and in four days it was eared.

These six men were living in Hecokta. One day they went to hunt deer, and these six girls were left all alone. Yellow Corn sister said to her sisters, "We are very foolish. We ought to go higher up." They went down into the floor. That evening the men came home. The girls were gone.

Sweet Corn grew and the corn tassels shone white. Ne'we·kwe came. He gathered the corn ears and put the pollen in his basket. He took it to his house. In the morning Sweet Corn Girl was alive. He said to her, "Your sisters have disappeared. Find them and bring them and bring them back." "How can I go where my sisters are?" "Wait." He got corn stalks and cut four lengths, each with a joint. He cut each length down the middle and removed the pith. He marked his coliwe sticks.[4] He gave her arrowheads to carry with her. She put on beautiful clothes, a new embroidered ceremonial blanket, and strings of beads. She was beautiful. Ne'we·kwe took his flute and drew her in. He blew a note and she came out a yellow butterfly. He blew her to Hecokta. She lit on the pole of the ladder where they gambled. Presently one of the gamblers went out and the butterfly flew away. She turned into a beautiful girl with fine

---

[1] Ne'we·kwe brings the Corn Maidens on the last day of Ca'lako. Bunzel 917.
[2] Always associated with the Ne'we·kwe.
[3] The usual sympathetic magic.
[4] Stevenson 328—33.

14

clothes and beads. He saw her coming. He went down the ladder and told the gamblers, "A beautiful girl is coming. Perhaps she is one of our wives." "It can't be." "Perhaps. She is very beautiful." Presently she came down the ladder. She said, "I am looking for my sisters." "Yes, we married your sisters. Six of them were our wives. One day we went hunting deer. When we came home they had gone and the house was all closed except the fireplace." They gambled. She bet her hand on the throw and the gambler bet his hands against hers. She picked up her gambling sticks and threw them. They turned into tektcitci (brown birds with yellow and black markings on the breast).[1] She won. She threw again and they wagered their feet on the throw. Her gambling sticks turned into bluebirds. The third time she threw they wagered their hearts and her sticks became blackbirds. The fourth time they wagered their necks and her sticks became snowbirds. The gamblers said, "We lose our lives." Then the six Corn Sisters came down the ladder.[2] They got their sister and went up to their own home. At the top qf the ladder she took her arrowheads from her dress and threw them down the hatchway.[3] The house caved in and all the gamblers were killed. The seven sisters went home.

THE BOY WHO HAD TO LEARN TO MARRY (8)
Notes, 326

They were living in Hopi on the first mesa. A little boy lived with his grandmother. He was ugly and he never grew big. He was thin and poor. Every day he went out hunting snow birds. They thought he was a good hunter because he always brought in snow birds.[4]

All the people despised him and threw rubbish at him. He saw the other boys talk to the girls when they went to get water from

---

[1] It is a common Zuni idea that a game that depends on throwing to a great distance may be supernaturally won when the missile is transformed into a bird. In coliwe, however, the count depends upon the sides of the counters which fall face upwards and the incident seems misplaced. Perhaps some connecting link is taken for granted in the account.

[2] Games are efficacious in calling the rain, the Corn Maidens, etc. Most games may be played for these ends.

[3] The Corn Sisters are traditionally offended by being the object of sex desire and they punish men who have been guilty of such behavior. Ne'we·k-we is the means for recovering the Corn Maidens in this story as in the more usual Corn Maidens stories, I: 20 sq.

[4] "In those times the only game were snow birds and rabbits."

the spring in the evening, and his grandmother said, "Take your canteen and act like a grown man. Be polite and do as the girls tell you." He took his canteen and went down to the spring. After they had filled their jars he said to them, "Please give me water to drink." The girls laughed at him. At last one of them was sorry and she gave him water. They came back from the spring. He was ahead walking like a lord and the girls laughed at him as they came behind.

The father of the girl who had given him water, thought to himself, "That little boy is a good hunter. It will be well if he marries my daughter."

The next evening the girls went again to get water and the little boy waited for them. The girls came and filled their jars and the little boy said, "Please fill my canteen." The girl said, "I will fill it for you." She filled it and the water that was left in her gourd she threw over him (to show that she liked him). The rest of the girls said, "Come, we must go home. You walk first," they said to the little boy. So he went ahead again walking as proud as the night before. The girl who had given him water whispered to him, "Wait for me and come to my house." He said, right out loud, "Why should I wait for you? Why should I come to your house?" He did not know anything about marrying. His grandmother had not expected that he would want to marry that night and she had not told him anything. He said, "Wait until I run home with my canteen of water." He went to his grandmother and he said, "The girl who gave me water wants me to come to her house. Why should I go to her house? Perhaps she wants me to work for her father." His grandmother said, "So a girl asked you to come to her house. That is good. Go and keep your mouth shut. Eat just a pinch when they set food before you. Sit quiet and keep your eyes on your bow guard." He ran back and caught up with the girl and she said, "Walk behind me," so he fell in behind her and walked just as she did.[1] They got to her ladder and the girl went up first. As she was above him he looked up under her dress and he wondered what that was. They went up and came down again into her house. Her mother and father and sisters were all kind and welcomed him. They said, "You are coming, aren't you." The girl answered, "Yes, we are coming." The boy remembered that his grandmother had told him to keep his mouth shut and he did not say a word. Her mother said to the girl, "Set out the evening meal."

---

[1] This is a joke; men walk easily and with grace but women heavily and flatfootedly. It is a great joke for a woman to walk like a man or a man like a woman.

She got out meat and paper bread and they sat down. The boy remembered that his grandmother had told him to eat just a pinch. He did not eat of the meat nor take paper bread. He picked up a crumb from the floor and ate it. When they were through the men sat back and the girls took the things away. The boy remembered that his grandmother had told him to look at (through) his bow guard, so he took it off and held it up in front of his face and stared through his bow guard. After a while the girl's mother went in and fixed the bed and she said to her daughter, "Go to bed in the inner room, my child." The boy thought to himself, "Why have I got to sleep in this house? I live with my grandmother." He wondered what he would do when he got into the inner room. They went in and the girl took off her dress and sat down on the edge of the bed and the boy stood up stiff beside her. The girl said, "Sit down beside me." "All right." "Lie down on the bed." She pulled him towards her. Then she took his hand and drew it over her breasts. She touched his thighs with her fingers. It tickled him and he squealed and ran out of that house and home to his grandmother. His grandmother said, "What are you coming home for now?" He said, "That girl wanted me to stay all night in her house. She made a bed for me and she drew my hand down over her shoulders. I touched two hillocks on her chest." The grandmother sat down and said, "My poor child, come here." She opened her dress and showed him her breasts and drew his hand over them. She said, "This is what you touched. You shouldn't run away. It is hard enough to get married and now this nice girl wants to marry you. You must go back and be her husband." "I like her in the daytime but at night I think I shall run away from her."

His grandmother said, "Poor grandson, you do not know what's good for you." She dropped off her dress. She took his hand and made him feel her genitals. "This is the way women are." She showed him everything. He stayed that night in his grandmother's home.

Next morning while they were still eating their morning meal the girl came to his house. She was dressed up with white buckskin puttees and moccasins and a good, new woman's dress and blanket. On her head she carried a big basket of meal. She got to the top of the ladder and the grandmother said, "You're coming, aren't you?" "Yes, I'm coming." The little boy and his grandmother were eating their morning meal of snow birds and paper bread. The grandmother made the girl sit down by the boy and eat with them. She took the basket of meal into the inner room and emptied it and filled it with dried peaches and snow birds broiled on long spits. When the girl had finished eating she said to the grandmother, "Let me stay and grind for you." So they put the basket of peaches and snow birds in the corner of the room and the grandmother brought out ears of corn and the girl shelled them. The grandmother parched the corn and the girl ground it in the grinding stones. The grandmother put the cooking pot on the fire and went into the inner room to get dried meat. She cut it into small pieces and put them in the pot. She went back into the inner room again and got corn and shelled it and soaked it and split off the skins in the grinding stone. She winnowed it and put the kernels into the pot with the meat. She let it boil all day so that the girl could take it home that night.[1] The little boy went out to hunt rabbits. He worked hard for he was going to take the rabbits to the girl's mother and father. Just as soon as he had got enough he came back home to his grandmother for he knew the girl was working there. The boy brought his rabbits into the house, walking like a grown man. He laid the rabbits in a row on the floor with their heads to the east. It was not yet twilight and the girl had already finished her grinding.[2] His grandmother was getting a lunch ready for the girl. As soon as she had finished setting it out she went into the inner room and got four perfect ears of corn to put between the legs of the dead rabbits. She prayed, "We are glad you have reached our house, return again other days." She sprinkled prayer meal over them. When she had finished she sat down and ate with the girl. The boy sat beside her and ate too. When the girl had finished eating she got up and said, "Thank you." The grandmother had the big bowl of stew ready and she set it down for the girl. She took four rolls of paper bread. She laid her own white blanket down on the ground. She put the rolls of paper bread inside and the girl tied the blanket over her chest. She took the bowl of stew on her left hand and went to her mother's house. She emptied the stew into her mother's bowl and the paper bread into her mother's basket. She folded up the boy's grandmother's white blanket to take back with the grandmother's bowl and went to get her dried peaches and broiled snow birds. When she got there the little boy picked up his four rabbits and his grandmother showed him how to take them to the girl's mother and father. The girl took her basket of dried peaches and snow birds and walked ahead and he walked behind like a grown up man. Just as the girl stepped off the ladder onto the roof the grandmother got hold of the little boy on the ladder and said in his ear, "Don't be scared tonight. Stay with the girl." They

---

[1] "The way my grandmother made it."
[2] This shows that she was quick in the work.

went to the girl's house and her mother was very happy when the girl brought in dried peaches and snow birds and the boy his four rabbits. They thought they would have enough to eat for a long time. The girl made up the bed again and they went into the inner room. This time he remembered what his grandmother had taught him and he was not afraid. He stayed all night and married that girl.

Next morning the little boy waked his wife and told her to make lunch for him so that he could go out to hunt. His wife got paper bread and folded it in a blanket. He tied it around his waist. He went toward the west looking for deer but he could not find any. There was snow on the ground and lots of tracks but he wandered around and could not find any deer. Spider Woman heard him crying. She said, "Look up here. What are you crying for?" He looked and looked but he couldn't find anybody. "Here I am where the bark is cracked. Tell me, what is the matter?" He looked and saw Spider Woman and he said, "I am crying because I am tired. I came out to hunt deer for my wife. I am just married and I can't find anything to take her. I can't give her the bridal costume[1] but if I could kill a big deer it would be just the same." Spider Woman said, "I will help you. We shall have to climb this high mountain." The boy looked up and saw the cliff and he said, "How can we get up there?" "I shall go up first and shall let my ball of thread down to you. Hold on to it. When I draw you up do not open your eyes. If you do you will fall." "Thank you." Spider Woman climbed the cliff and let down her ball. The boy held on to it and Spider Woman drew up the web. The boy closed his eyes and she pulled him to the top of the cliff. They started out. Spider Woman climbed into the boy's ear. She said, "I am going to take you to White Bear. He will help you to hunt the animals." "How far is it?" "His cave is close by. He has all the great stone hunting knives and he will show you four. The first is the largest but do not take that. The second is large too but do not take that. The third is wrapped in sinew but do not take that. The fourth is the smallest and is wrapped in sinew. Take that one. Whenever it is thrown it kills deer." They came to the big cave where White Bear lived and the boy went inside. He was lying down and White Bear said to him, "My grandchild, what are you coming here for? I am the kind of animal that children are afraid of. I shall not hurt you for I am good to children like you who are not afraid of me. What is it you want to ask? There is deep snow on the ground and no one comes to ask help when the snow is deep on the ground (because

---

[1] The story is laid in Hopi where the bridal costume is always given the bride by the groom and his relatives.

hunting is easy then)." "Yes, I do not like to ask help when deep snow is on the ground but I have just married a wife. She chose me because I am a good hunter and I cannot find any snow birds or rabbits or deer. I have to find someone to help me. Will you ?" "Yes, I will help you to hunt the deer. I shall not chase them but I shall stay here and cause you to kill them. I will give you a knife." He went into an inner cave and brought out the stone knives. Spider Woman said in his ear, "Do not choose the good knives." White Bear brought them out and said, "Choose whichever you want. Take the biggest one." "The big one is a good knife but I shall not take it. I shall take the smallest one." "You had better take the biggest one." "No, I shall take the smallest one." He chose the smallest knife.

White Bear said, "Stand ready. I shall go to the west and growl and the deer will run toward you." White Bear went to the west and growled and presently the deer came running toward the little boy. There was a big buck in the lead. The boy stood straight behind a tree and when the buck ran past him, he threw his knife. It struck the head of the buck and he fell to the ground. The boy ran to him and breathed the last breath from the deer's nostrils. It died. White Bear came up again and said, "Now you have a deer to take to your home." "Yes, thank you. I shall give you the pluck." The boy cut open the deer and took out the pluck and cleaned it and gave it to White Bear. He returned the stone knife to White Bear and Spider Woman said, "I will get a sunflower stalk to put in with the meat. It (the pack) will be light to carry." She found a sunflower and cut a stalk and brought it to the boy. He stuck it in his pack of venison and pulled it up on his shoulders. He said, "I am going now." He and Spider Woman started toward their home. When they came to the cliff Spider Woman told the boy to catch hold of the web and she would let him down. She said, "Keep your eyes closed." When he got to the bottom he called, "I am on the ground," and Spider Woman came down also. When they got almost to the Hopi country (home) Spider Woman said, "This is my home, I shall stay here." "All right, grandmother, good-by. You will help me again some day."

He went on to his own house. It was late in the evening and his wife was waiting for him. He climbed up the ladder to the roof, carrying his big pack. He called out to his wife, "Ca. Come and lift me down." The father and mother said, "Go out, he is bringing something in." The girl went up and helped him hand down the deer. The father and mother came to the bottom of the ladder and helped. They laid out the deer like a person with his head to the east. They put strings of beads around his neck and the mother went into the inner room and got a perfect ear of corn to lay between his legs. They covered him with a red and black bordered white blanket and then with an embroidered white blanket. So they clothed the deer. The mother went again into the inner room and brought out prayer meal and everyone prayed saying, "We are happy that you have reached here. You will be alive again and return here some day." They sprinkled the cornmeal. They were happy that they had the great buck.

The girl gave the boy something to eat. They always lived happily because the boy married before he knew anything about girls. That is why parents always want their girls to marry the best men and the boy's parents always want their sons to marry pretty, industrious girls.

REED[1] BOYS AND THEIR GRANDMOTHER (7)

Notes, 327

They were living in Kwakina, in Pinawa, and in Halona. Pinawa and Halona ran against each other in a kick-stick race. Pinawa always won and the people in Halona complained, saying, "What shall we do?" They called a council and they said, "We must go to the two Reed Boys who live down by Zuni river." They sent one of the priests to ask the help of the Reed Boys. They were living with their grandmother. The Reed Boys said to the priest, "Go to Kwakina. An old woman lives there with her grandson. Ask him to come to Pinawa and race in four days." "All right."

They went to Kwakina. All the people of Halona were praying for help. In Kwakina the little boy lived with his grandmother. They were poor and people threw ashes and refuse into their house. The priest said to them, "We have come to ask you to race for us. Come down and race at Pinawa." "Why do you want me to race for you?" "We always race with Pinawa and they always win from us." The young boy said, "How can I do this? I am poor, I have nothing to wager on the race." "Never mind. Our grandfather will come in three days. He will bring everything that you need to wager." "All right. I will come."

At sunset they started back. They came to Halona. The priest said to the boy, "We will go to the house of the village priest. All the priests of the council will gather there." The priest and the boy came to the hatchway. They went in. The village priest said to them, "Sit down." They sat down. He said, "What is it that you

---

[1] Lakaia, the reed which is used in ceremonial cigarettes.

have come to ask?" "I have come to ask you to call a stick-race
in four days. We will race with Pinawa." "Very well. I will call
the race." "Thank you."

The boy went out from the house of the village priest. He came
down to the edge of the creek and he ran as fast as he could to the
house of the Reed Boys. He came in. They set supper before him
and they said, "Come here tomorrow. In the afternoon we will
race with you. We will kick the stick around the race course (fifteen
miles)." "All right. I will come." He went home. Next day, early
in the afternoon he went to the house of the Reed Boys. Their
grandmother set food before them. Elder Brother Ahaiyute came
also. They gave him food. He said, "Are you going to race?"
"Yes." He said to the Reed Boys, "You two race on one side and
we two will race on the other." "All right." They made the kick
sticks and painted them. It was the middle of the afternoon.
"Which way shall we run?" "We shall go to Caliente and then
through Pescado. We shall go the other side of Hecokta, and home
again. In three hours we will be back. We will come in before sunset."
They set off. The Reed Boys ran on one side and Elder Brother
Ahaiyute ran with the young boy. They came past Hawiku. Pekwin's son was hoeing corn in his field. He saw how fast they were
running and how the young boy ran as fast as the others. He was
going to race in four days. He went home and made yarn for a
stocking.[1]

The runners got home before sunset. Their grandmother brought
food and they ate. When they had eaten they appointed the next
day to practice. For four days they practiced running.

On the third day Tciktcałaci[2] came to Reed's house. He carried a
great basket. It was filled with venison and buckskin and blankets
and women's dresses and belts and necklaces of all kinds. He gave
them all to the young boy to stake on the race. The boy went into
retreat at Reed's house. He made himself ready for the race. Next
morning he started for Pinawa with the Reed Boys. They came to
the house of the village priest. All the people had brought out all
their possessions to stake on the race. The Reed Boys made a bundle
of prayersticks for the boy and they said, "Go outside the village
and dig a hole and plant it." He took it outside and buried it to a
depth of his forearm.[3]

The son of the village priest of Halona had married the daughter
of the village priest of Pinawa. Pekwin's son (who had seen the

---

[1] He was going to bet the stocking on the race.
[2] Sweet Man. "He eats only sweet food." Bunzel 1070, for Tcałaci.
[3] Only especially potent offerings are buried at such a depth.

racer) told him what he had seen; that the boy had supernatural power and would win the race against Pinawa. The son of the village priest went to his father-in-law. He had it in his mind to say, "Do not bet against them. Get them to race for us." Reed Boy knew that he was going to make trouble. He went to the window of the house of the village priest. Just as the boy sat down to speak to his father, he spat at him and he became a summer bird. He flew off to the east. He got to Halona. Everyone was at Pinawa to see the race. One old man and one old woman had stayed at home. They took him into their house and fed him, and gave him food and a blanket and a buckskin shirt.

That night the Reed Boys went to Kwakina with the young boy. He went into retreat in his own house (for the race with Pinawa). At the home of Reed Boys, the two grandmothers[1] sang all night, and made themselves young and beautiful. In the morning they were old again. They set out to go to the race. They came to Halona. The son[2] of the village priest had been clothed by the old man and old woman. He saw these two beautiful young women and said to them, "Come to my house." They went with him. It was time for the race. The women said, "We were on our way to see the foot-race." The young man said, "No, don't let's go now." "We can go and come back very soon." They started.

The Ahaiyute[3] were coming to the race. They called to the son of the village priest, "Where are you going?" "We are going to the footrace." The Ahaiyute said, "Come with us. You shall have these two young girls for your wives." "How shall we go?" "We shall make a scalp dance," (i. e., go in ceremonial scalp dance style.) They formed in line. Elder Brother Ahaiyute walked first and behind him Reed Boy's grandmother. Behind her walked the son of the village priest, behind him the grandmother of the young runner at Kwakina. Behind her walked Younger Brother Ahaiyute. They came to Halona[4] and they bet all they possessed on the stick race. The son of the village priest took those two young girls as his wives. Pekwin's son[5] came. The village priest's son said to him, "I will let you have one of my wives." "All right." He took the young boy's grandmother and the village priest's son took the grandmother of the Reed Boys.

---

[1] Of the despised boy of Kwakina, and of the Reed Boys.
[2] He had been turned into the summer bird.
[3] Elder Brother Ahaiyute did not run of course in the final race. He had only practiced with the despised boy and given him power.
[4] *Sic.* A slip for Pinawa.
[5] Who had told him how the race would come out.

They raced at Pinawa. The runners went through Caliente and through Pescado and back around Hecokta. They came back to Caliente, and home again to Pinawa. The young boy won everything. So Halona won over Pinawa. The young boy who had won the race and the Reed Boys took all that they had won on the race and went to their homes.

The son of the village priest and Pekwin's son went to their homes at Pinawa and took their new wives. That night they slept with them. In the morning when the son of the village priest woke he was lying with an old, old woman. Her eyes were almost shut. She was skin and bones. She was too weak to sit up and she scratched herself all the time. He jumped up. He ran to the house of Pekwin's son. His wife was just as old. She had gray hair and was bent double. The two young men were angry. They would not talk to their wives. They drove them away. The two old women went off leaning on their canes. They were too weak to travel.

There was no rain. The people were hungry. Every day the wind blew and they could not bring the rain. They called a council. The son of the village priest went out to hunt. He went toward the west along the Zuni creek.[1] He saw a young girl cleaning buckskin in the water. He said to himself, "That is a pretty girl." They talked together. The village priest's son said, "I see you have had something to eat. I am all skin and bones. Feed me, I am starving." The girl brought venison and paper-bread. He ate and he said, "I will go to your house with you." "No." "Why not?" "You have a wife." "No." "Yes. You had a beautiful wife, but in the morning you did not care for her. You threw her out." The priest's son was ashamed. He said, "Yes. I had a beautiful girl for my wife and in the morning she was old and wrinkled. She was doubled over and could not walk." "Maybe I would be the same. You would turn me out." "No." "I don't think I want you." "I want to live with you and have something to eat." The young girl said, "When I am old and too weak to sit up, and scratch myself all the time, will you turn me out?" "No. I don't care how old you are. You shall always stay with me." He took Reed Boys' grandmother back to his house.

They slept together. Next morning when he awoke, he was lying with an old woman. Her eyes were almost shut. She was skin and bones. She was too weak to sit up and she scratched herself all the time. She yawned. He felt bad. He drew away from her. She said, "Bring me water." He got some water for her. "Thank —— —— you." (She could hardly talk.) The young man went out hunting. He left her alone.

[1] Near the home of Reed Boys.

Next day he went to the same place. He saw the beautiful girl washing buckskin again at the creek. He said to her, "Give me food." She said, "No. You threw me out and I will not live with you again." She went back to her home and the young man went to Halona.

In four days another young man was out hunting. He was a poor boy and lived with his grandmother. People threw their refuse and ashes into their house. He saw that pretty girl, Reed Boys' grandmother, washing buckskin at the creek. He was bashful, but she called to him, "Why don't you talk to me? Don't you like me?" "I am ashamed." "Come with me." She got soap-weed root and made suds. She washed his hair. The young man thanked her. She brought out venison and paper bread. At sunset the girl said, "I must go." "I will go with you." "No, don't come. Maybe in the morning you will not like me. You will turn me out. It has happened twice." "No. Whatever happens you will always stay with me." She took him to her home. She set before him all the food that he could eat. He slept with that girl. In the morning she was old and wrinkled. She could hardly talk. She scratched herself all the time. The boy did not care. He was happy. She tried to raise herself on the blankets but she was too weak. He put his arm behind her shoulders and raised her. He put her clothes on her and dressed her. She said, "Give me a drink." He warmed water and put it to her lips. "Thank — — — you." He did not care. He went out to get wood to make the fire for breakfast. When he came in with it he saw his wife again. She was pretty and plump. She said to him, "My dear husband, let me make the fire." She went to the other room and brought out venison and paper bread and melons. She set breakfast before him. The young man was very happy. She said to him, "Go into the other room. Get buckskin and make moccasins and shirts and trousers." He went into the other room and brought out all kinds of clothing. He was very handsome. She said, "Bring beads and put them on." He brought coral and turquoise and white shell and put it around his neck. He stayed with that girl and they were very happy. That night they slept together. In the morning she was old and wrinkled again. She was not strong enough to lift herself up on the blankets. He put his arm behind her shoulders and lifted her. He brought her water and went out again to bring in wood. When he came in she was a young girl again. For four nights they lived together and every morning she was an old woman. On the fifth morning, when he woke, she was a plump young girl. He was very happy. She got up and ground flour. She ground the yellow corn and the blue corn, the white corn, the red corn, the black corn, the all-colors corn. She had just a little flour. She said to her husband, "Get me a great sack." He said, "I think you do not need such a big sack." "Yes, I want a large one." She put the little bit of flour into the great sack and tied the mouth.[1] They started to his home. He said, "I am bringing my wife." They welcomed her. Next morning she was an old woman again. The young man said to his father and mother, "Never mind, she is a beautiful young girl." For four mornings she was an old woman. The fifth morning she woke up a plump young girl. She worked for them and brought much rain. The people had food again and her husband was rich and powerful.

THE MANNIKIN WIFE (8)[2]

Notes, 328

The people were living on First Mesa.[3] The son of the priest was called Cikantiwa. He was handsome, and he had three sisters and one brother. In the summer he worked for his father in the field, and tended the corn and squash and beans and melons and watermelons. He was bashful, and every night he slept in the field in the shelter there.

One day he wanted to marry. He went out to the field where he had been hoeing and took a pile of weeds to his shelter, and laid them in a corner. He told his family that next day he was to marry a girl from some other village. He said she had come to his field while he was hoeing. His family were glad, and they began to get the clothes ready for his wife.[4] He was not satisfied. He wanted to have the buckskin given on that first night; he did not want to wait to have it with the rest of the clothes. His family gave him the buckskin, and he took it back to the shelter. He sewed it into a human form and stuffed it. He made hair for it from the ravellings of his blanket, and laid the mannikin on the bed of weeds. All that night he talked to her and played with her.

Next morning he went to his family and they had the marriage clothes ready for him. He told them that his wife was exceedingly bashful and that it would not be wise for them to come to see her. They gave him everything, — the black blanket dress and the

---

[1] It multiplied magically of course and filled the sack.

[2] A Hopi story, told in Zuni by the late Tutsena (Hopi name) or Kopekwin. He died about 1910. He was Badger clan.

[3] That is, Hopi.

[4] This is the characteristic activity of the groom's family in Hopi, not in Zuni. The gift of the buckskin is, however, characteristically Zunian.

red-and-black bordered blanket, and the woman's belt and the white moccasins, and the footless black stockings. They gave him also a second set.[1] When he reached the shelter again, he dressed her in the new clothes, and put her in a sitting position.

His mother thought to herself, "Shall I go to the field? I should like to see the girl who is living with my son." His mother went out, and came to the field. She listened and she heard a conversation. A woman's voice said, "I think she is coming to roast some corn. Build the fire, maybe she wants to come in." Her son's voice answered, "No, she won't come in. I told her you were ashamed." His mother thought, "Maybe the girl is afraid that his mother is an ugly person." She thought after all she would go home. As soon as she had returned, she told her daughters, "I heard your brother's wife talking. She told brother to build the fire to roast the corn, but he said, 'No, she won't come in', so I came home. I think he doesn't want us to visit his wife." His sisters too were very anxious to see his wife, but they said, "Anyway on the fourth day we shall see her."

The boy talked all that night to his mannikin and to himself, and he played with her. He didn't know any better. He was ashamed with all the nice-looking girls who wanted to marry him, so he had to make this mannikin for a wife. That noon he went home and told his people to be ready. He said, "We shall come this evening. But my wife will not come into this room. Get ready a room on the upper floor for her. When evening comes, leave that room empty for I will bring her at any time."

He went back to the field, and his sisters made ready the room. When evening came, he dressed the mannikin with all the new clothes. He put on the white moccasins and the woman's blanket-dress and tied the belt and the blanket and put over her the white marriage blanket.[2] Then he tied her with buckskin thongs to his shoulder. He started after it was very dark so that no one would see him.

When he came to the ladder of his house, he set the mannikin by the ladder and went up, and all his people said, "He has come." He ran quickly around the outer wall so that his family would not hear his steps, and came again to the foot of the ladder. This time he took the mannikin on his back and climbed the ladder, stepping like a woman[3]; and his family said, "There comes his wife."

---

[1] This is the characteristic Hopi gift of two sets of the women's wedding outfit from the groom's family.

[2] This is the Hopi wedding costume, not Zuni.

[3] A man and woman traditionally walk in very different fashion. It is a great joke to say of anyone that he walks like a person of the opposite sex.

All that night he talked to her just as he had in the shelter, and he answered himself in a woman's voice. He went into the family room to get food for her. His sisters had everything ready. His father said to him, "No matter if she is ashamed, tomorrow before sunrise we must wash her head.[1] We will tell our relatives to come tomorrow." The boy was troubled. He went back to his own room and ate and talked to the mannikin. He didn't know what to do the following morning. When he went to bed, he couldn't sleep. He tossed all night.

Just before morning he heard a voice from the next room, the sound of a girl grinding. The girl said to him, "Are you asleep? I am coming out, because I am sorry for you. You are in trouble. I am Corn Woman, and I will help you."

The next morning the family of the boy were ready to wash the head of his wife. Corn Woman went with him down the ladder, and they washed her head. She was very beautiful. After her head was washed, she ground with his three sisters.[2]

On the fourth day, she asked his mother for the stone on which to make paper-bread. His mother had a stone ready, and she brought out everything to make paper-bread. The girl started laying out the paper-bread on the hot stone, and they saw she was very skillful. She was almost through, and there was just enough batter to make two more sheets of the bread, when they heard something like the noise of the Great Shell[3] blowing. It was the sound of a whirlwind coming from the west. It came toward the house with a terrible noise. It entered the hatchway and went directly to the Corn Woman. She had her belt tied tightly about her, but the wind lifted her skirt and stripped all her clothing from her. The people cried out, and she tried to cover herself with her hands. She was naked. Then she told them what the boy had done, and that it was the mannikin who had come to get her clothes.

All the male relatives came to make a new set of clothes for this wife.[4] When they had the clothes ready on the fourth day, she put them on, and she thought to herself, "Now I have my own clothes."

On the eighth day after the whirlwind, she told her husband, "I shall go into the corn-room where I lived before. I shall become corn

---

[1] A principal wedding observance in Hopi. In Zuni the bride and groom wash each other's heads.

[2] This is Hopi custom again. In Zuni the girl goes alone to the groom's house and sometimes grinds, but the groom does not accompany her on this visit.

[3] Great Shell is a medicine bundle.

[4] Hopi, not Zuni, custom.

again. I shall be Corn Mother[1], and your corn room will never be empty. The boy said, "I love you; I wish to go in with you that I may be with you always." They went in together, and she became the Corn Mother, and he became yapotone.[2]

On the next day the people did not hear any sound in their room; they looked for them, but the room was empty. Then they went into the corn-room, and there lay two ears of corn, one branched ear and one full, perfect, straight ear. They said, "It is our son's wife and his child[3], and it is our son." They were sorry that they had lost their son and his wife, but they were glad that their corn would always increase. That is why in a store-room they always lay down first the corn mother and on top of her the yapotone, and around them they place their children. And that is why when a baby boy is born they always put the yapotone beside him; and by the mother they put a mother ear.[4]

THE PRIEST'S SON WHO LOST EVERYTHING AT GAMBLING (8)

Notes, 329

They were living at Itiwana. The priest had an only son. He was a valuable boy and never got into fights. One day in the big plaza they played tacoliwe, and the priest's son went to his mother to get something to wager on his play. She gave him gladly a black woman's dress and a woman's belt. They set up the circle of stones and he threw the lots down on the center stone. He won. He was happy. He took all the things the others had wagered and they went home sad. He took his winnings home and his mother was pleased. The boys who lost said, "Tomorrow we shall play and beat him. We shall take paper bread and prayer meal and put it down for the Ahaiyute. We are playing their games. If we do this they will be on our side, and we shall win all he has in his house." They went to their mothers and asked for corn meal and paper bread and valuable stones to grind with the corn meal. Their mothers took the corn meal and ground valuable stones in it and put it in the corn

---

[1] The Mother Corn in the storeroom is thought to bear children daily and prevent the corn stores from running low.

[2] The fully kernelled, straight ear of corn that represents the male. It is the basis to which the macaw feathers and wicker standard are added in making the mili, the personal fetish of the members of the curing orders of the medicine societies. In every storeroom a Mother Corn and a yapotone lie together by their "children", the store of corn.

[3] The branched ear represents the pregnant woman, i. e. the woman and her child.

[4] By the side of a baby girl a common ear of corn is placed.

husk and folded it.[1] They took paper bread and put it in the corn husk and rolled it up. One of the boys was older than the others and they went to his house. All together they went toward the east to Eastern Road,[2] and they said, "They are powerful and they will come down and get it." So they scratched the earth and poured in the prayer meal from their corn husks and they prayed, "You will be on our side, and not on that of the priest's son. He doesn't think to give you anything. We have brought you this because it is your game, and now you will be on our side." They prayed and put it in the ground. They went home. They had gone just a little way when they heard the Ahaiyute calling and they did not turn around. They said to each other, "I guess they're happy. I guess they came out to get it. Don't any of you turn around." They walked on, and as they went they talked. "I wonder if he will be on our side." "I guess he said that (called out) because he is pleased."

Next morning they were ready to start another game. They called the boy to play with them. He had a father who was a priest, but he never thought to take the prayer meal and paper bread to the Ahaiyute. The boy brought out a woman's belt to wager. They said to him, "Go in and get more. You won last time."[3] He went in and got two black women's-dresses and a woman's belt and a buckskin. They made the bets. They sat in a circle. They said, "You start," because they had taken offerings to the Ahaiyute and they knew that they were going to win. He threw the lots on the center stone and two of them fell red side up (or "flat") and the other fell white side up (or "on back"). (This counted two). He threw again, and again two fell red side up (counted two). Again he threw: this time all three fell white side up (counted five). He threw for the last time, and one fell red side up and two white (counted three). He was sad. The others threw. Two were red side up and one white (counted two). They threw again. Three fell red side up (counted ten). They threw again and both times three white sides fell upward (each throw counted five.) They were happy. They played again, but the priest's boy could not win. He was way behind. At last they won. Then they said, "We have won; you have lost your things." The boy was sad. He went home. His mother felt sorry, but she did not scold him.

He said, "I am going to try again and get my clothes back. I am going to make the lapotciwe."[4] So he cut the corn cob and put in

---

[1] For prayer meal.

[2] Shrine of Ahaiyute near Zuni.

[3] One wagers on successive games what one has won before.

[4] Contrast Stevenson, 342.

15

the sharpened deer antler in one end, and in the other end he put feathers. He said, "I shall tell these boys to be ready to play tomorrow." He went to the house of the oldest boy and they said, "Sit down." They asked him right away, "What have you come to say ?" "I am coming over here to let you know that you will work on your lapotciwe. I am going to try tomorrow to get my clothes back. We shall play tomorrow." "All right, we shall be ready. After I have had my meal I shall go to tell the others." "All right." The boy went home. The older boy went and told the others to come to his house to work on the lapotciwe. They came in as soon as they were called. They asked, "What have you to say ?" "The priest's son came to tell us that he is going to try to get back his clothes tomorrow and he wants us to have the lapotciwe ready." They told the woman in that house that they needed the feathers and she brought out the box. They took the tip of a deer's antler and they sharpened it fine as a needle and stuck it in one end (of a corn cob). They put feathers at the other end. They finished.

They got ready to take the prayer meal and paper bread out to Wool Mountain. When they arrived there they scratched the ground and emptied the corn husk and prayed to the Ahaiyute, "You will be on our side and not on that of the priest's son. He doesn't think to give you anything. We have brought you this because it is your game, and you will be on our side." They came home and they said, "I wonder if we shall win tomorrow. Last time we won we heard the Ahaiyute." They were scared. The oldest said, "I hope it will be the same for we always try to do right."

The boy's mother and father never thought about telling him to take out offerings to the Ahaiyute. As soon as he had finished his lapotciwe he went to sleep. Next morning again, those boys went out before sunrise, and waited for the sun to rise and sprinkled prayer meal and prayed, "Father Sun, all this day be on our side and help us." The priest's son was still asleep at sunrise and his father and mother did not wake him to go out to pray. He woke up after the sun had risen, and they ate their morning meal. Afterwards he cut a little piece of buckskin with his tool of deer antler and laid it on the ground. He took black paint (akwena) and put it on his tool and made a little black spot on the buckskin for the bull's eye. He folded it small and said to his mother, "I am ready, mother. What shall I bet today ?" His mother thought he would win this time. She brought out a big buckskin, a white blanket, a woman's dress, and a woman's belt. She piled them up. The boy laid the belt down on the floor and piled the rest on top and carried it on his back by the belt. He went to the big plaza again. The other boys were coming at the same time. They said, "We are coming at the same time, aren't we?" "Yes." He laid his piece of buckskin (target) down. He told the boys to be first. The oldest boy threw the first throw. It just grazed the mark. The second time he threw it just grazed, and the third and the fourth time. Then the priest's boy threw. It grazed each time. The second boy's first throw grazed, but his second hit the bull's eye. All his other throws just grazed, and those of the third boy also. The last boy made one hit in the bull's eye. The priest's boy tried again, but all his throws were wide of the mark. The boys took up the buckskin pack, and the priest's son lost everything that he had wagered. All the people called out that the boy had lost, and his mother went in and cried because he had lost all her valuable things. She did not speak to her son when he came in. He said, "Mother, please give me food. I am hungry." She stopped crying and gave him paper bread and dried meat. She felt very sad, and his father felt sad also. But they still had many valuable things. The boy said, "Don't worry, mother. I am going to try again tomorrow. I shall try Hidden Ball."[1]

Again he went to the boys and asked them to be ready to play this game. They said, "All right, we shall be ready to play this game tomorrow." Again they went to their houses as before and got the prayer meal and put it in the corn husks. They went to Corn Mountain and put it down under Corn Mountain. They prayed, "You will be on our side and not on the side of the priest's son. He does not think to bring you anything. We have brought you this because it is your game and you will be on our side." As they turned their backs they heard "Who-oo." They asked, "Do you hear the owl?" "What is that for?" "That is good luck." So they walked home and didn't turn around.

The priest's son was asleep. He went to bed as soon as he came from the boys' house.

Next morning the boys got up early and went up and waited for the sun. As it rose they prayed, "Father Sun, when daylight comes, be on our side." After the sun was up the priest's son woke up and had his morning meal. The oldest boy went to the Ahaiyute house where the game was. He asked the mother of that house if they could borrow it, and she said, "Yes." They brought it out—the hollowed sticks and the ball. They went to get the things they were to bet. Again the priest's boy asked his mother what he was to bet. She brought out two buckskins and two women's dresses. He did these up in a pack and put it on his shoulders and went out to the

---

[1] The game is always kept in the Ahaiyute house (81) where it is renewed every December.

big plaza. He laid it down. The boys asked, "Which side are you going to choose ?" "The left" (east). They put red paint on one side of a stone disk. The eldest asked the youngest which he would choose. He answered, "The one which is not painted." So the oldest threw it up and the white side was up. It was good luck, and he played first. Poor boy, he (priest's son) sang as loud as he could every funny song he could sing. He had not even chosen a Rat man (to hold the one hundred and six tally straws) and he stepped on them (bad omen). When he had hidden the ball two of the other side came to guess the ball.[1] They had decided with each other which to take first, so they chose two and they were empty. They skipped the next cup and picked up the end one. There was the ball! So right away they picked up the bundle of counters and put them on their side, and the poor boy sat and cried. The other side sang funny songs as loud as they could, and they were happy because they had guessed the ball right. So they pulled their blankets up over their heads, to hide the ball. The Rat man came and held their tally straws and he gnawed at them. After they had hidden, they sat up straight, and the priest's son was wondering which to choose. He thought it was in the far end cup, and he touched the one at the near end first, and there was the ball! They all laughed and threw sand at him, and he went over to the Rat man and got ten tally sticks and brought them over to the other side and the Rat man gnawed at them. Again they hid the ball, and he came again and chose. He thought it was in the second cup and he picked up the end cup first. There was the ball. It counted another ten against him. Every time he lost.

About night he felt that he was starving. He thought that he would go home and get some lunch.[2] His mother asked, "Is it on your side ?" "No. It is on their side. I was coming to get something to eat." "No wonder it is on their side! They don't go home to get something to eat and lose valuable things." His mother was very cross to him. She brought out paper bread and he took just a little and went out. He ate as he watched them hiding the ball. When they had finished he went to guess. He thought it was in the first cup and he touched the third and there was the ball again! Again this counted ten against him. About midnight he had exhausted all the counters and the other side had won. The boys took all the things home. Poor boy, he was afraid to go home to his mother, so he lay down where he was and slept until sunrise.

---

[1] To win, the ball must be discovered in the third hiding place uncovered.
[2] This is sure to bring failure.

When day came he walked into his house, and his mother and father were looking out to see if they were still playing. Everybody said that he had lost all his bundle, and his mother and father were crying. When he came in they scolded him and said, "We gave you all the valuable things we have. You are our only child, but we don't want you any more." The tears ran down his cheeks and he didn't ask for anything to eat. He had with him the valuable stones that he carried in his belt, and he walked out. He went to Corn Mountain. He said, "I hate to go back to my house after they have scolded me. All the people know I have lost all these things. I will go where nobody knows me. I had better pray this time. Maybe I lost because I didn't pray. Perhaps the other boys prayed. I will pray. Maybe my forefathers will take care of me while I am around here, turned out by my mother and father." He went toward Corn Mountain, and at Red Mountain he sat down and rested.

He thought he would go to the people of the east. He was hungry and miserable. He wept. Spider Grandmother lived in the rocks, and she heard the boy crying and asked, "What is the trouble?" He looked up and down and in every direction and stared, but could see nothing. He wiped his tears and answered, "I am right here." "I thought you were crying?" "I wasn't crying." "I thought I heard you crying." The boy thought to himself that it always helps to tell the truth, so he said, "I was miserable. I was playing games and I lost. My mother and father didn't like me any more. I am going to the people of the East. Besides I am hungry. I came without anything to eat." Spider said to him, "Come in and eat." "Where are you?" "I am right here in this hole. My house is small, but you can come in." The boy heard the voice and he tried to see where to go. It said again, "I am a little spider. You cannot see me." The boy stood there and said, "It is so small, I can't get in." "Yes, just step, and you will be able to get in." So he stepped and he walked right in. It was just like a cave inside. The boy went in and passed her, and she was behind him. She turned into a person. She brought out a little greencorn cake (ground and baked between stones) from an inner room (cave) and put it in a little basket. Every time he ate it another took its place in the basket. He was full, and felt strong. He said, "Thank you." "That is all right. I am always glad to help people who are in trouble." She gave him two cakes to take with him. She knew that he was a valuable boy because of his buckskin leggins (unfringed) tied with the narrow woven belt, and his blue wool shirt and trousers. He stuck the cakes into his wide belt and said, "I shall come to see you again." He was very happy.

He started on. When he was tired, he said, "My grandmother

always put a broom straw (of redtop) in any bundle that was heavy. I shall put one in my belt and make myself go lightly." So he looked about and found one and put it in his belt. He prayed, "Straw, make me walk easily and travel fast." He went on fast. He went past Nutria and that night he came near Laguna. "I had better sleep here," he said to himself. He sat down to eat his cakes. He saw a light to the north side, and he said, "That is Laguna, and I better go over there now. I will not eat my cakes. I will go before I sleep." He went towards the light. He said, "I had better eat my cakes before I get into that house. Maybe they have bad things in that house." He got to the house. It had a little low opening with a heavy door that was pulled aside or closed by a thong.[1] He called, "I am coming." The door made a noise and they said, "Come in, whoever you are." He came in. He was a nice boy, dressed nicely. There was a man and his wife in the room. They asked him to sit down. He sat down. The woman saw that he had come a long way. She brought out cornbread and warmed it in the coals, and she brought out venison. He ate, and while he did so he heard a noise in the other room. He kept looking toward it. A pretty girl was in there. She was shy. Right away she liked that boy.

In Itiwana his mother and father worried about him. Every evening they went up and sat on their roof and they prayed, "Come back again, if only for a few days." They were sorry they had scolded him. There was nobody coming or going and they were lonely. They thought, "He was not worse than other boys, and now perhaps he is killed." They cried.

He finished his supper and said, "Thank you." What was left of the corn bread he put back. He took out his bag of native tobacco, and the man asked, "Where did you come from ?" "Itiwana. I am a priest's son. I played games and lost. My mother and father didn't care for me any more so I have come here." "Do you know every game ? Do you know keconiwe ? ("buckskin deer, a Laguna game.") Could you and I play a game tonight ?" "If you want to." He went out to ease himself before they started. The girl went out one door when the boy went out of the other. She said to him, "Is my father going to play the game with you ?" "Yes." "You don't know how to play our games. I am going to help you because I love you. I will give you this so that you will beat my father." She tore out a finger nail and stuck it in the boy's palm. "By and by, when my father doesn't like you, I am going to run away with you," she said. The boy went in and the girl pretended to go to bed in the middle

[1] "As they always have at Laguna."

room. Her mother went to bed too, way back in the same room. The man said, "Which will you choose?" The boy said, "I choose blue." The man said, "I choose red." The man asked, "What do you bet?" He took out the bag with the four valuable stones in it and said, "I bet these." The man got up and picked out four big buckskins; he said, "I bet these." The man dealt, and blue came first and red last, so the man lost. Then he dealt again and the blue came up. The boy won the buckskins. They played and played, and every time the boy won. He won all the things in that house. The man was angry. He said, "You must stay here a few days. I shall try to take back my buckskins and valuable things. Let us sleep." He showed him the inner room (on the other side of the main room) and gave him blankets. He slept hard for he was tired.

The next morning he walked around to see the village. The girl got up; she wasn't shy now. The woman called them to the morning meal. He came in. They had cornmeal cakes again, warmed in the coals. After they had finished the man went to work in his fields. The boy thought he would walk again. He went to the east to Laguna, and some of the men were nice to him and questioned him. He told them, "I am a priest's son from Itiwana and I came out here to visit." "What house do you stay in?" "In the house on the west side, by itself." "Those people are witches." But some said, "Those are nice people." In the evening he said, "Goodby. I may come again." He went back to the house. They were just ready for the evening meal. The man didn't like the boy, but pretended that he did. After the meal they smoked the native tobacco. About ten o'clock the man said, "I want you to do something." The yard was full of tall trees, and he said to the boy, "You must clear this ground before morning or you shall die." "I can't do this. I shall die." The man went in and he and his wife went to sleep. They slept hard. The girl called them, "Mother! Father!" When they did not answer, and she knew that they were fast asleep, she went out. She pulled out a long hair, ran to the boy, and said, "You take one end of this hair, and I will hold the other while you run with it." He ran, and all the trees were cut down by the hair. Then the girl said, "In the morning my mother will look to see if all the ground is cleared. She will come out and urinate and all the trees will grow up as before. You must watch so that she will not come out." The girl went in to sleep again. At earliest dawn the boy was watching the house door. The woman peeped out, and as she went to pull the door open, the boy ran up and pulled it shut. She went back to her husband and said, "The boy has cut all the trees, and he won't let me go out to urinate." The man got up and looked out. "He must have supernatural power," he said.

The boy went into his room and slept all day. At the evening meal the woman called the boy. He came in and ate with them. The girl pretended to be on her father's side. Afterward the two men smoked native tobacco, and talked. The man asked about the people in Itiwana. "We do not have much rain,"[1] he said. When it was late, the man said to the boy, "Let's go over and see what you shall do to-night." They went out. The man pointed to a river way off. He said, "If you don't make that river run through my ground, you shall die." The man went in and the boy went to the river and stood there. "I cannot do this," he said. "I cannot make such a ditch. I shall die." When the girl thought that her father and mother were asleep, she called, "Father, mother!" They did not answer. She went out to the boy. She pulled out a long hair and said, "You take one end, and I will take the other. Run with it, and this will make the river run through my father's yard. But in the morning when my mother tries to come out to urinate, you must not let her get out, or she will close it up again." Very early in the morning, the mother got up and tried to go out to urinate, for she saw that the boy had made the river flow through their land. The boy ran to the door and would not let her out. She went back to her husband and told him what he had done. The man hated him, and he said, "Yes indeed, you have supernatural power!" The boy smiled and went in and slept all day.

At the time of the evening meal the woman called him, and he came and ate with them. After the meal they smoked and talked. When it was late the man asked the boy to go out with him. He told him, "If you do not lift that round mountain (a mile away) I will kill you." The boy was sure that he could not do this. The girl thought that her hair was not long enough. So she dressed herself up with nice bracelets and necklaces and went out to meet the boy. "We shall run away," she told him. He asked, "Where shall we go?" "East to the farming villages of Laguna. If they don't find us we shall made a circle and go around to Zuni."

They did this. They were never tired. They passed Laguna and went towards the east. When daylight came the mother and father could not hear their daughter getting the morning meal. The mother waited, then she looked into the other room but there was no meal. The girl was gone, and the mountain was still there. She ran back to her husband and said, "We have no daughter now!" "She will come again! We will get her back. Get the morning meal ready so that I can go after my daughter." The mother hurried and warmed the corn bread. She set out nothing else. After they had

---

[1] That is, he did not boast.

finished eating, the father said, "Where shall I go?" He went out
and turned into a big whirlwind.

The girl kept turning around to look. She thought, "Father will
be coming about this time." She saw the whirlwind and said, "That
is my father." She nudged the boy, and he turned into a bony
donkey and she turned into a female donkey. The whirlwind saw
no one. It went on past them and came back and met them again.
It went back home, and they changed themselves into persons
again. When he got home his wife said, "What did you see?" "I
saw a bony male donkey and a female donkey." "They must have
been the ones." The woman was angry. The man said, "The boy
has more power than we have. We think we know something, but
he escapes us." His wife said, "I thought you were going to bring
our daughter back, but now I am going." She turned into a little
whirlwind. The girl turned and saw the little whirlwind coming.
They got to a spring and she nudged her husband and he turned
into a fish, and she turned into a little fish. The whirlwind saw the
little fish, but did not recognize them. She came home and the man
said, "Did you bring your daughter back?" "I saw two little fish
in the water. I guess these are the ones." The man said, "I am going
this time." He went in a big whirlwind. The girl looked around and
saw the big whirlwind coming. She nudged her husband and he
turned into an apple tree, and she was a little apple tree. The
whirlwind saw them, but he did not know who they were. When he
came home, his wife asked him, "Did you find your daughter?"
"No, I only saw a big apple tree and a little apple tree." "They
must have been the ones. I shall go this time." She transformed
herself into a little whirlwind and went in search of them. The girl
saw the whirlwind coming. She nudged her husband, and he became
a dove, and she turned into a female dove. They were sitting on a
post when the whirlwind passed. It did not recognize them, and
returned home. The girl said, "This is the last time they will come."
When the mother got home, her husband asked her if she had
brought his daughter back. She said, "No, I only saw two doves
sitting on a post." "They must have been the ones. We can't help it.
He must have more power than we have."

The girl and her husband turned around to go towards Zuni. They
made a big circle. After one day and one night they came to Red
Mountain. They were hungry. At night they came to where Spider
Woman lived. The boy said, "Let us stop here. I can't help it, I am
hungry." The girl was tired. They went there, and Spider Woman
was waiting. She was sitting outside. She said, "That is my friend
coming. He is bringing a girl." Then she said, "You are coming,

aren't you?" "Yes." She asked them to come in and they said, "Yes." They stepped in, and it was a big hole. A year had passed since he had been there. Spider Woman asked them to sit down, then she went into the other room and brought out green-corn cakes again. They sat down and ate. The boy ate lots. but the girl was shy. They said, "Thank you." Spider asked how he had liked his journey. He answered, "I liked it. This girl is from Laguna, and she is coming with me." "That is nice." "We are going now. We may come again someday."

They came by way of Owl Spring (south of Corn Mountain). They got a drink and rested there. He could see Zuni, and it made him very happy. About noon they rested.[1] They came to Badger Place. He asked the girl to wait there while he came in to his people to ask their permission (for marriage). He came in, and the girl waited at the spring. The people on the roofs saw him coming in. He was dressed differently (like the people of Laguna), he had his hair in bangs, and a white shirt, and a belt without any black in it (red and green), and they said, "Someone is coming in. It must be somebody from the east." Everybody came out to look. The boys knew him. One of them went to tell his mother, "Your son whom you scolded is coming back." She said, "I do not believe it. Maybe he died long ago." Lots of people came in and said, "It is your boy." The boy came into the village, and they made the mother go up on the top of the roof and go down to meet him. She felt sick she was so excited. They came in. They called out to a boy, "Go tell his father to come in from his fields." He went and said to the priest, "Your wife wants you to come home. Your boy came home this morning." He ran as fast as he could. He was so glad to see him back, he skipped steps on the ladder. He embraced his son and said, "We should not have sent you to another place! We will not find fault any more." They set out food for him, and his mother brought out a great slab of jerked venison and spread it over the coals. She brought out paper bread, and the boy ate. When he had finished he said, "Thank you." Then he said, "Mother and father, over there is a girl at the spring in Badger Place. She is a good looking girl. I want to bring her home. When I left here and went to their house, her father played his game with me. She helped me, and I always won. He was angry with me, and tried to get the better of me. He wanted me to clear the ground in his yard, and cut all the trees down in one night. I could not do this by myself, so this girl helped me. She took one of her hairs, and I held one end and she held the other. We ran, and all the trees were cut down.

---

[1] "They were not married yet."

The next night he wanted me to make the river flow through his land. Again she helped me, and her father could not kill me. The third night, he asked me to move a round mountain. The girl thought that she could not do this, so she ran away with me. Her father and mother tried to get her back again, but they were not able to do this. I want to marry her here. She is at the spring. She wanted me to ask you before we came over here." Lots of people came into the house to greet the boy and they heard what he said. The mother and father said, "Yes, child, we want you to do as you wish. We are glad, for we have no girl in this house. We shall be glad to have her come to this house." The people who heard told the others that the priest's son had a nice girl at the spring.

A one-eyed witch heard this, and she went to the spring and climbed up the trees hanging over the water. The witch called to the girl. She was sitting close by the water and the witch could see the girl's reflection, and she thought that it was hers. "How pretty I am," she thought. She found out that it was the girl who was coming to marry the priest's son. She told her to come up into the tree, and said, "I can comb your hair before you go to the priest's house." She asked her four times, and the girl thought, "I had better go." The witch took a little stick and tangled it in her hair, and she turned into a blue dove and the old witch was the girl. She waited for the boy. He was slow.[1] He told his mother to be ready. Everybody watched while he went out to get the girl to marry her. He got to the spring and there was the girl. He didn't see the difference. The dove was trying to talk to her husband, but she was afraid to do it before the witch. He said, "It is all right. My mother wants us to come to be married." The poor dove followed. When they got there, there were lots of people in his father's house to greet his wife. She looked pretty outside, but she had one eye inside. They all breathed from their hands, and made her sit down. They brought out paper bread. Everybody was happy. That evening the boy was anxious for it to get dark. The dove was sitting on the pole of the tall house ladder. The old people were saying, "The priest's boy is married now." His father went out. The dove said, "Dear father, will you see if there is any way to change me again into a person ? The old witch woman came to the spring and touched me, and I turned into a dove. She took my shape, and she is down there with my husband. Please help me turn into a person again." The father went down to the boy. He was with his wife, and he told him, "This is not your wife. This one is a witch. Your wife is a little blue dove. This witch changed shapes with her at the spring." So

---

[1] "He should have hurried."

the boy hated his "wife" and he did not lie with her. He just sat and pretended to play with her. His father went out and got a medicine society man and they came back. He went to the witch and touched her with his crook. Then he touched the blue dove and they changed shapes again. They threw out the old witch. They said, "What makes you do witch things? Go away from here!" So she went out, and there was the beautiful wife again, and they were married happily. That is why we hate witch people.

THE MAN WHO MARRIED THE DONKEY (8)
Notes, 331

The people were living in Matsaḵa. The son of the village priest was handsome and worked hard in the fields, but he was bashful with girls. Nevertheless they wished to marry him.

One day he was working with his father in the field, and his father said, "It is time to go home." His son answered, "I am not ready yet." "Very well. I am going now. Come later." His father started home.

When he was alone, he went over to Badger Place where the horses were pasturing. He found a female. Presently she passed urine, and afterwards the muscles contracted. When this happened he put his fingers in. He thought, "It is a great deal of trouble to take a human wife. If I go with the animals it will be no trouble." He tried to have intercourse with the mare, but she was too wild. She kicked him. He was not discouraged. He thought, "Tomorrow I will come again and try."

He went home. He was very happy; he thought about what he had just done. When he reached his house, they were eating the evening meal. His sisters said, "Brother is just coming in." His father answered, "Yes, he stayed in the fields to give the horses a drink at Badger Spring." He came in. His mother and sisters said, "Eat." He ate, and when he had finished, he said, "Tomorrow I am going out to the fields before the sun gets hot. I shall start before breakfast." He thought he would get to the field before anyone was up. His father answered, "That is a good plan. You will work in the cool of the day." "When the sun is hot in the middle of the day, I shall come home, and go out to work again in the evening."

In the morning he went out to the fields before anyone was up. He went directly to Badger Place where the horses and donkeys were pastured. As he came up, the horses ran off; only the donkeys were left. He thought to himself, "I don't like these Gray-bodies,[1] but it is hard to manage the mares. I will try these." He had no

---
[1] A common vituperative word, and a name for donkeys.

trouble with the donkeys, and he had intercourse first with one and then with another. Then he went back to hoeing. After awhile he came back and tried another. He used all of them, but the first one was the best. He thought how much better this was than taking a human wife. He could always go over to the donkeys after he'd worked a little while. He felt that he had a home in Badger Place; he only went to Matsaka for his meals.

The corn was about knee-high.[1] One day he went to his home for the evening meal. His mother was roasting venison for him. She said, "Why is it that you are so late? You never used to be late." He answered, "It is because I have hoed so much corn." His father said, "I shall come out with you to see how much you have done." "That is good. I shall follow soon." His father went. He was pleased that his son had hoed such a great patch of corn. The youth ate his meal and rested, and he said, "I had better go to my field. Father will be waiting for me there." He went out to the corn-field. His father was hoeing there. The son said, "Father, go back home now. I shall finish this hoeing by myself." His father answered, "Thank you, my child, I am glad to hear you speak in this way. I shall go home and do other work." His father went home, and took out a buckskin and cut out moccasins for his son. He wanted to make him a gift for the work he had done in the corn-field.

The youth watched his father out of sight, and went back to where the donkeys were. He always went to his own special female now. He had intercourse with her, and took her over where there was good grass for her.

Every day he repeated this. Sometimes his father brought his meal to him in the field. He was always happy; he thought all the time how sensible he had been not to take a human wife and have all that trouble. He thought that this way he would never have any trouble. He did not know that his donkey was pregnant;[2] he had never thought of this.

The corn was beginning to leaf. In Matsaka four women came to the house of the priest's son, carrying baskets of meal on their heads. The eldest had a basket of yellow corn meal; the next a basket of blue corn meal; the next, a basket of red corn meal, and the youngest a basket of white corn meal. The youth was sitting by the fire-place. His father and mother were happy when they saw the women enter; they thought that now their son would marry.

---

[1] It was explained that the season of animal heat is in June and runs into July.

[2] Impregnation is never so certain as when there is sexual intercourse between human beings and animals, it is said.

The girls said to them, "My fathers, my mothers, how have you lived these many days?" "Happily. You're coming, aren't you? Sit down." The mother took the basket of yellow corn meal from the eldest sister, the father took the basket of blue corn meal from the next eldest, and the two sisters of the youth took the baskets of red and white corn meal from the two younger sisters. They took them into the inner room and emptied them; they brought out paper bread and dried peaches and set them before the women. They said, "Eat." The girls ate a little, and they said, "Thank you." The father of the youth said to them, "What is it that you wish to ask that you come to my house bringing cornmeal?" They answered, "We desire to marry your son." The father answered, "It is for him to decide." He spoke to his son, and said, "My son, will you marry these girls?" The youth sat with his head bowed, and he made no answer.

His mother made the bed for them. She said, "Your bed is ready." The girls went into the inner room. They lay two on either side of the pallet. The youth came, and he lay in the middle. He took no notice of them at all. He did not speak to them nor play with them. Before sunrise the women said, "We had better go home. He does not take any notice of us." They rose and dressed and went out into the other room. The youth's mother was there. She said, "Why are you going out so soon? It is not yet time." They answered, "Yes, but he does not take any notice of us. We are going now." His mother said, "He should be ashamed." She brought out their baskets. She filled the first with large beans, and the second with dried peaches, the third with dried venison, and the fourth with tiny speckled beans. On the top of the basket of the eldest sister she placed a woman's blanket dress; on the second, a piece of buckskin; on the third a woman's blanket and on the basket of the youngest a woman's belt.[1] The women were happy over their presents. They said, "We are going." The mother answered, "Go then."

The mother went into the room where her son was. She was angry. She said, "Why would you not marry? They were good girls, and good-looking." He did not answer a word. He would not give any reason. Presently he got up and went again to Badger Place.

He went straight to his donkey. Four times he had intercourse, and the fifth time she would not allow it. She kicked. He tied her hind legs, and tried again. Again she succeeded in throwing him off. He was angry and said, "Well, I will try another one." He went

---

[1] These are presents very much out of the ordinary, and are given as an indication of her shame at her son's behavior.

to donkey after donkey, but not one of them would let him approach her.[1] The youth said to himself, "I thought the animals would go with me, but now not one of them will do this any more. I should have married those girls."

The people all through the village found out that he had refused to marry the four girls. Everybody was talking about it. Nobody valued him any more because he had not married the girls. He stayed in the house all the time. All winter he stayed there making moccasins.

When spring came he went out to plant his field. He thought that now he must take a wife. On his way to plant he came to the river where the girls go down to get water. He asked them for a drink out of their jars. Not one of them would give it to him, because they all knew how he had treated the girls who came to marry him. He had to kneel down and drink out of the river. He went on to Badger Place. He had got over expecting the animals to let him approach them and he did not give them a thought. He planted his corn field. He thought, "Perhaps some girl will come this way with lunch for her father, and I can talk with her." But no one came.

After his day's work he walked home. He did not come into the house, for he wanted to stay in the yard and watch the girls. His mother called, "The meal is ready." He said, "I'm going out a little while." He went down where the girls go to get water at sunset. He stood by the path, and stuck out his foot in front of the girls as they came along. He said, "Stop. Where are you going?" The girls did not like him. They said, "Don't do that!" They kicked his foot aside and went on. When the next girls came, he held out his foot again, and said, "Stop. Where are you going?" They said, "Don't. Go away." They kicked his foot aside and went on. When the next girls came, he stuck out his foot again, and said, "Stop." They said, "Don't," and they kicked aside his foot. Presently other girls came and he stuck out his foot and said, "Stop." They said, "Don't do that," and they kicked aside his foot and went on. Finally all the girls had gone down to the spring. They filled their jars and came back. He stuck out his foot and said, "Give me a drink out of your jar." They said, "No, we haven't time." They went on. Another pair of girls came from the spring, and he said, "Give me a drink." They said, "No, we haven't time." A third pair of girls came from the spring and he said to them, "Give me a drink." They answered, "We haven't time." A fourth pair of girls came from the spring, and he said, "Give me a drink." They

---

[1] The season of heat was past.

answered, "We haven't time." Finally all the girls had come from the spring and gone to their homes.

Every evening he did this. At last some of the girls said, "Perhaps we might speak to the priest's son. He is handsome." Next evening they saw him again on their way to fetch water. They said, "There is the priest's son. If he talks to us, what shall we do tonight ?" One of the girls answered, "Let's talk to him. They say he never talks to girls." They came on. They were playing at Corn-Leaves-Marked.[1] They had a supply of the leaves inside their dresses. The youth said, "Let me see your Corn-Leaves-Marked." They said, "What do you mean ?" "I saw you put them in your dresses. Let me show you what I can do; I can make them better than you. Come over by the spring and we can sit down and make them. They went over by the spring, and sat down together. The girls gave one of their leaves to the youth and he folded it and made a pattern. He unfolded it, and held it to the light. It was a good pattern. Another of the girls said, "Make me one too." So he took another leaf and made a pattern on it, and gave it back to her. He said to the elder of the girls, "Come again tomorrow and we shall play this game again." She said, "All right. I shall come again to-morrow at this same time." The girls went on to the spring and filled their jars. He said, "Give me a drink." They gave him water. When the eldest gave him a drink, what was left in her gourd she threw over him.[2] He cried out, "Oh, you made me shiver! Don't throw water on me. We (i. e., I and a wife) are pregnant. You will have to make me a new bowl."

He went home, and went into the house. His mother said, "We have waited a long time for you. The dinner is cold. You had better eat right away." The son sat down and ate. He was happy; he was proud of himself that the girls had played with him. He ate as fast as he could, and when he had finished, he said, "I am going out now." He put on his blanket, and went over to the yard in front of the

---

[1] Corn leaves are folded through a number of times, and marked in patterns by the teeth. When unfolded they display "belt" patterns.

[2] This is the conventional way of showing preference for a sweetheart in these courtships on the way to get water in the evenings. The conversation that follows refers to the fact that if water is thus thrown over a man while his wife is pregnant — or if his father's sister baptizes him after he has participated in a ceremony — the child when it is born will have diarrhea. To prevent this, the woman who threw the water, or who washed his head, must make a new bowl and give the child a drink. The same taboo attaches to the mother, so that if a woman discovers she was pregnant when she underwent the rite of head-washing, she will receive a new bowl from the aunt who baptized her, and be given a drink immediately to remove the consequences.

house of the girls. He hoped someone would come out. He went up
toward the ladder, and he coughed loud. He waited till midnight but
she did not come out. He thought to himself, "Tomorrow night you
will come out and we shall talk together."

He went back to his home. He came in. His mother said, "You
stayed out late, I thought you weren't coming in. I made your bed
right back of the ladder." He went to sleep. All night he thought of
the girls he had talked to at the spring. In the morning when he
woke, he took up the fawn-skin bag of seed corn.[1] He went out to
the fields. He thought to himself, "This is the way I shall be working
for my wife by this time next year." He fell to work with the planting stick; he pushed it into the ground, and dropped in the seed
corn. He worked hard. At noon he stopped to rest, but he did not
take time to go home for lunch. He sat in the shade, and he noticed
the donkeys. He thought to himself, "I don't care for them any more.
They wouldn't let me go with them anyway. I will chase them off."
He took up sticks and ran at the donkeys and chased them off. His
donkey was almost come to her time, but he had not thought of
that. He went back to his planting. He was happy. When the afternoon was well over, he stood on his mark and his shadow reached
to the bush.[2] It was time to go home, so he walked in to Matsaḳa.
He was tired. He came in to his house. His mother said, "Supper is
all ready for you. I knew you would be tired, and I got everything
ready." "Yes, I have to go out again, and I'm glad to have supper
first." He sat down and ate. He hurried as fast as he could; he was
afraid someone else would talk to those girls.

When he had finished his meal, he went to his room, and put
on his head-band. He walked out to the spring. He stood by the
path, and the girls came to fetch the water. He stuck out his foot,
and they said, "Don't. Let us by." "I'll let you by, if you will give
me a drink when you come from the spring." They promised, and
he let them past. Every girl that came along he stopped in the
same fashion, and at last the girls he was looking for came along the
path. They said, "Have you got corn leaves?" The youth answered,
"I have brought you women's belts." They thought that was a fine
present. He took out corn leaves and made "belts". He gave them
to them. They said, "How nice!" He thought that he was making
them a great present, and that they would be of great use to them.

---

[1] This would be lying near the ladder ready for the first person up in the
morning to take it to the fields.

[2] Time is not told by the position of the sun in the sky, but by the shadow
cast between two well-known points by a man's length; or by the moment
when the shadow of a wall reaches a certain place, etc.

16

He said, "Shall we go to the spring and play ?" The elder answered, "I don't think we have time tonight. Our mother told us not to be so long tonight." "But I have brought more corn leaves." "To-morrow night we can do this." The girls went on to the spring, and he waited for them to fill their jars. They all walked back together toward the village. He walked with the elder. He said, "After supper I'll come over to your house and wait in the yard. I came last night. I coughed but you did not come out. Finally I had to go back home again. If you tell me you will come out, I'll come again tonight after supper." The girl answered, "If my father goes to his kiva, I will come out. He doesn't want me to go out after dark." "All right."

The youth went again to his home. He couldn't wait. He went up and down the ladder; he sat a little on top of the roof, and came in again. He saw the girl come out of her house with the floor sweepings. He hid over by the dirt pile. She went over with her bundle and emptied it. He came out. He said, "What did you throw away then ?" "Dirt." "My, you threw away all your luck!" "Don't worry. I don't like to have the sweepings around. I gave corn meal to the sun so he wouldn't take my luck."[1] The youth said, "I hope he won't take your luck. Where is your father ? Is he eating his supper ? Does he know you're talking to me ?" "No, I don't think so. I told my sisters not to tell our father till I am sure you want to marry me." "I'm sure I want to marry you. It's better to tell your mother first." The girl said, "I must go back now. They didn't expect me to go out. I didn't tell where I was going." "Shall I come around again soon ?" "If my father goes out. I heard him say he was going to his kiva. You can watch him, and see what he does. If he goes out, come close to the house where my mother's ovens are."

The youth waited out by the corrals, watching till her father should go to his kiva. He did not come out of the house. At last the youth thought to himself, "I think he came out while I was looking another way." He went up toward the ovens. Just as he got there, her father came out. The boy rushed back toward the corrals. The father did not notice him at all. The boy was pleased at his luck. He thought to himself, "I'll be with that girl tonight."

He went back to the ovens and immediately the girl came out of the house and joined him. In her house her mother was grinding with her two sisters. The youngest said, "Do you know where our eldest sister is going ?" The mother said, "I think she wants to talk

---

[1] If one throws out refuse between sunset and sunrise, one throws away one's luck. The corn meal that may be given in the sun to remove the taboo is thrown into the bundle of dirt.

to somebody." "I know who he is." "Who is he, then ?" "He's the son of the village priest." Immediately the mother said, "I don't want her to talk to that boy. He wouldn't marry the girls who went courting. He is bad. He is not like his father. I shall go and call her in."

She came across[1] and put her head out of the hatchway. She could see her daughter over by the ovens, and she called, "Come in, and finish your grinding. If not, I shall call your father." The girl answered, "I'll be in pretty soon." "Right now. I shall call your father." The girl said to the youth, "I shall have to go." He answered, "Tell your mother and father who it is. Tell her it is the son of the village priest." He thought he was valuable. The girl said, "Yes." She thought she would not be scolded if she told.

She went into the house. Her mother said, "Didn't you have any better sense than to talk to that son of the village priest ? If I see you with him again, I'll tell your father and I will whip you." The girl had nothing to say. She came in, and went across and took her mother's place at the mealing stones. She was angry. She nudged her sisters and said in an undertone, "Did you tell our mother who it was ?" They said, "No." "How did she find it out ?" She said to her sisters, "If they make trouble about my marrying him, I will go to his house to live." She ground hard all the evening.

Her mother and sisters went to bed. The girls slept together, but the elder kept on grinding. The youth was still waiting out-doors. He thought the girl would come out again when she had told her mother that it was the son of the village priest. He could hear the girl grinding in the house still, so he still waited. Her mother said, "It is time to go to bed." Her daughter paid no attention; she went on grinding with all her might, striking the stones together hard. Over and over her mother said, "Go to bed now," but she paid no attention. The fire went out, but still she kept on grinding. Her mother said, "You'll break the stone. Come to bed. If you don't get over your temper, I'll tell your father." Finally her mother dropped off to sleep, and the girl came across and got into her bed with her dress on. When the boy did not hear any more grinding he went home. He thought, "Maybe her mother is telling her which day we shall be married." He went home and went to bed. All his family knew now that he had a sweetheart.

When the girl's father came in, her mother did not tell him what had happened. Next morning the girl did not come to eat the

---

[1] The phrase for coming out from behind the mealing stones is the same as for passing a threshold.

16*

morning meal with them.[1] Then her mother told her father about the son of the village priest. Her father did not speak to her angrily. He said, "My daughter, perhaps you thought that the son of the village priest was a good boy. But we know what he has done. Everyone talks of it. We do not want you to marry him." The girl said nothing. Still she did not eat. After he had talked with her, her father took his fawnskin bag of seeds and went out to plant. The girl kept thinking to herself, "I will marry you anyway because I like you. I will go to your mother's to live."

The brother of the girl's mother had a feast that day for those who were helping with his planting. The girl's mother went to help. When the three sisters were left alone, the eldest put on her moccasins. She thought, "I shall have to go without meal. My mother would not let me take meal. I shall grind for his mother at her house."[2] Her sisters said, "Where are you going?" She answered, "Not anywhere. I'm never going to enter this house again." She went out.

Her sisters climbed the ladder to watch which way she went. She walked right to the house of the village priest's son. They said, "She should be ashamed! To go right to the house of a boy when she is not married to him!"

The boy's mother was spinning, and his two sisters were grinding. His mother was surprised to see the girl coming down the ladder. She said, "You're coming?" "Yes." The mother went to the inner room and brought out paper-bread. The girl ate, and when she had finished, she said, "Thank you." They said, "Eat lots." The mother took away the basket, and she said, "Now talk."[3] The girl said, "I have come to grind for you." The mother said, "There is no more corn ready."[4] She went into the corn-room and brought out ears of corn and placed them beside her. The girl shelled them, and when she had finished she picked up from the floor every kernel that had been scattered. When she had finished she thought that the mother would parch it for her, but instead she said, "When you have ground it coarse, I will parch it." The girl was unhappy. She took her corn and went across to the grinding stone and set to work to break up the kernels. It was hard work, but at last she finished.

---

[1] This is the conventional way to show anger; to work hard and angrily, and not to eat or talk.

[2] This is still the conventional Hopi practice, but in Zuni it has become customary to take the meal as a gift from the girl's family rather than to consider her grinding of it the proof of her ability as a housewife.

[3] This is not the usual polite phrase.

[4] If she had been glad to accept her, she would have said, "Go across and grind with my daughters."

The mother put a bowl on the fire, and parched the corn. When she had finished she gave the corn to the girl, and she took the place of one of the sisters at the fine-grinding stones. The mother said to the daughter, "Make the meal ready. Set out the paper bread and the chili paper bread. I think brother will be coming soon."

When the meal was ready, the mother told the girls, "Come across." They sat down. The youth came in. He was surprised to see the girl there. His mother said, "You're coming, aren't you?" "I was tired this morning, and I came home for the mid-day meal." His mother got up and set a stool for him next to the girl. He sat down and they ate. When they had finished, the girl went over to the bench[1] and the boy came and sat beside her. The two girls and their mother took what was left of the paper bread and went into the inner room. The boy said, "What did you come for? Did you come to stay here?" "Yes, I came to marry you." "What did your mother say last night?" "She didn't say anything." "Did she tell you to come here?" "No. I didn't tell her I was coming. I thought I better come here and stay tonight." "That is good if your mother and father want to have it that way." "I don't think they will find fault." When the mother and sisters came back into the room, they stopped talking together, for the girl was ashamed.

The sisters put the girl's meal into the second mealing-stone and the boy went back to his field again. The girl ground. The mother said, "I will get peaches ready for you to take home tonight." She went into the inner room, and brought out dried peaches. She washed the pot and put in water. She washed the peaches and put them over the fire. The girl went on grinding. She ground better that the boy's sisters ever ground.

In the afternoon the girl's mother thought she had better go home to see how her daughters were getting on. She was worried because her eldest daughter had been in such a temper. She came in. Her two daughters were grinding. She said, "Where is your sister?" They answered, "You scolded her, and she would not eat. She has gone to the house of the village priest's son." "Is this the truth?" "Yes." The mother wept. The sisters said, "You should not have scolded her so." She kept on crying bitterly. The girl's father came in. He said, "What it the trouble?" The girl's mother said, "The girl has gone to the boy's house. She is grinding over there." Her father looked sad. He said, "She will come back if we pay no attention. Maybe that boy will get more sense (and be a good husband). He is the son of the village priest. Maybe if we say nothing

---

[1] "She does not say 'Thank you' this time, because it is her second meal there."

to anyone, they will come back here and live." The girl's mother said, "Yes, that is best." The mother went back to her work at her brother's, and she said nothing to anyone. She was always thinking about her daughter, but she did not speak of it.

The girl finished her grinding. She put the meal into a basket. It was full, and very fine. The boy's mother was pleased. She said to her daughters, "Come and set out the evening meal. We shall eat together." They set out the meal, and about sunset the girl finished sweeping up her mealing stone and came across. The boy came in. His mother said, "You're coming, aren't you? Sit down and rest a little while your sisters set out the meal." The girls set out paper bread and dried peaches. The father came in. He was surprised to see the girl there. He lowered his voice when he saw her. He said, "Put the stumps[1] around and we will eat." They sat down and ate. When the girl had finished, she rose and went back and sat on the bench. The mother said, "I have your peaches ready for you. I will get you paper bread also." The girl said, "No. I am not going home tonight. I am going to stay here." His mother said, "Oh! Well, that will be all right." She was glad. They all sat and talked together, and when bed-time came, the mother made up the bed for them in the inner room, and they went in to sleep together. So the village priest's son had a wife now.

They lived together at his house for eight days. In Badger Place the donkey gave birth to the child of the village priest's son. It had a body and neck like a donkey, and its ears were big like a donkey's, but it had a human face. When he was four days old he could walk and talk like a man. About four days after this, his mother said to him, "You cannot live on weeds alone. You are half-human. You must have corn to eat. You have a human father. He does not come often to Badger Place, but when he comes you will know him for he always wears white-sacking shirt and trousers. Some wear blue woven shirts, but he always wears white."

The youth came out to his field. The little donkey ran in front of him and jumped and walked on his hind legs. He tried to make him see that he was human. The youth only said, "What is the matter with that little donkey? That is his mother over there." He tried to drive off the little donkey. At last the little donkey went back to his mother. She said to him, "What did your father say to you?" "He didn't say anything to me." "If you told him that you were his child, he might kill you. He is married now, and he will not want you around. When his father comes, then you shall tell him that you are the child of his son."

---

[1] Sawed-off tree stumps are often used as seats, though the tales usually assume that people are sitting on the floor, which is also common practice.

They waited for the youth's father to come to his field. At last
they saw him coming. The donkey said to her child, "There is your
grandfather. Run and jump around him. He will try to chase you
off, and at last a stick will hit you. Then tell him that you are of his
blood. He will treat you honorably. If he does not believe what you
have told him, show your face and he will recognize you." The little
donkey ran over to the field and jumped and ran about. He broke
the stalks of the young corn. The man took up a stick and threw it
at him. He dodged and it did not hit him. Again he came running
up to him through the young corn plants, and again he threw a
stick at him. When he threw the fourth stick, it hit him, and he
cried out, "Ouch, grandfather! Don't hit me. I have your son's
blood." The man said, "What is that foolish thing saying?" The
little donkey turned his face to him, and said, "My grandfather, let
us talk together. Last spring your son was working in this field,
and he thought it was a great deal of trouble to have a human
wife. He saw the horses and the donkeys and he thought he would
take a wife from them. He went to the mares, but they would not
let him have intercourse with them. They kicked him. Finally he
went to the donkeys. He picked out my mother, and when he had
intercourse with her four times, I was conceived. That is why I am
the child of your son. I am half human and I cannot eat weeds
alone; I need corn also to eat. Go back and bring me human food
to eat. I belong to your human people." The man was troubled.
He said, "My child, I am not sure. Wait till I ask my son. Then I
will bring you food." "Yes, that is best. I am sure he will tell you
the truth."

The priest was troubled. He did not know what could be done. He
prayed and he said, "My forefathers, my people, grant that this
little donkey shall keep this secret away from all the people, and
let me think of some way to be rid of this creature."

He went home. He was sad. He could hardly eat. He said to his
son, "My child, did you water the horses?" His son answered,
"No, I thought you had watered them. That is why I did not."
"After supper we will go together." They finished their evening
meal, and they went out. His son knew that he had something to
say to him, but still he did not think about the little donkey.

He waited for his father to speak. His father began, "My son, I
have something to say to you. Speak the truth to me. If you tell
this, I will consider and decide what it is best to do without further
talk." His son's heart beat; he thought that someone had seen him
when he had intercourse with the donkey. His father continued,
"This morning I was working in my field, and a little donkey ran

all around me. He trampled down the young corn plants. I chased him out and threw sticks at him. At last one of the sticks hit him, and he called out, 'Grandfather, do not hit me; I am your own blood.' He told me that you are his father. Last year you had intercourse with his mother; at the fourth time he was conceived. He showed me his face, and he has a nose that is just like yours. I fear that this is true. I want to be rid of this little donkey, and I will never tell anyone about this, not even your mother nor sisters. If you do not tell the truth, perhaps someone will discover this." His son said, "Yes, my father. It is terrible to tell you that I have done these things. I thought it was a great deal of trouble to take a human wife, and I thought that if I took a wife among the animals I could live with you always."

His father answered, "My son, this is not the custom of the Zunis. I think our forefathers have sent you this to teach you to think right. My child, I hope no one will find this out. I am trying to think what to do. If people go to Badger Place, the little donkey may tell them that he is your child. I will decide what can be done, but first I wished to learn from you the truth. Now I will go to talk again to my grandchild." The youth went home troubled. He thought to himself, "Why did I do this? I must have been crazy." When he reached home, he did not know what to say. That night he could not sleep. He wept.

His father went to Badger Place. The little donkey came jumping toward him. It crossed his mind that he could kill it then and there. But he could not. He could not forget that he was of his blood. He spoke kindly. He said, "I have brought nothing to feed you. We did not have anything left to-night. I have something to say to you. I want to ask you to stay away from people. Do not let them find out about you. If you will do this, I will value you. If people saw you, they might find out what my son has done. That would cause trouble for your father. I shall always bring you human food." The little donkey said, "Very well. I shall tell my mother, and we shall stay away from others." "I am glad you are willing to do this. I shall see you again tomorrow."

He went back to his home. He kept always asking his forefathers to make him think what he should do. When he got home, he sat with bowed head. His wife said to him, "Why are you sad?" He answered, "I am tired." His wife went to bed. He went into the inner room and brought out the sticks of tenatsali.[1] He bit a little from the sticks. He prayed, "Now my children, when I sleep, come and tell me what I am to do. Tell me the truth in my dream; tell

---

[1] Medicine sticks. See I: 34.

me what it is right to do. You know what my son has done; he did not know any better. Please show me what to do so that people may never discover this thing he has done." He chewed the tenatsali, and lay down alone to sleep. His wife wondered what it was that he had eaten. She was used to his eating tenatsali at the times of his retreats, but now she could not understand.

He fell asleep. The little Tenatsali Youths came down the ladder. They said, "Our father, I think you never told your son what it meant to have intercourse and to take a wife. You never instructed him how to do right. That is why he did this thing. We have punished you both. The priests should know better than the outside people,[1] but you have neglected this. You shall always tell your sons how to win girls for their wives, and how to have intercourse with them, and how to take care of them. Your girls you shall tell how to conceive children. You are a priest but you have not done these things. The poor[2] people know them, but not the priest." The village priest answered, "My children, you are right. I did not think to talk this over with them. I thought my son would know better than I. Now shame has come upon us both. My son has a child that is half-donkey, half-human." The Tenatsali Youths answered, "We know this is true. You are both to blame. Now you shall take your most valuable turquoise, and you shall make two crooks and two prayersticks for the Ahaiyute. Go with them straight to Corn Mountain, and ask them to help you to be rid of this little donkey. They know what to do. They have supernatural power."

At daylight the village priest waked. He was surprised to find himself still in bed. He thought, "You Tenatsali Youths are right. You have told me what I needed to know." He rose immediately and built a fire. His wife was surprised. She said to him, "What makes you wake so early?" "I did not sleep well. I am tired of staying in bed."

He got out his box of valuable feathers, and selected the feathers for the Ahaiyute. He took out two feathers from the body of the turkey, two jay's feathers, two chaparral cock feathers, and two of the onoḷiḳa, one of each for each of the Ahaiyute. He laid them out, each kind together. He cut two prayersticks and two crooks, and he made the one for Elder Brother the longer, and the one for Younger Brother the shorter. His wife wondered to see him working with the feathers, for he was not a member of a medicine society, and it was not the time of his retreats. She said, "Why are you

---

[1] That is, lay persons.

[2] As always, in the sense of being without ceremonial possessions.

working with your feathers?" He answered, "Never mind. I am a priest, and I have this knowledge to work on prayersticks and crooks."

He took the sticks he had cut for the crooks, and he bent one end over in position, and tied it with soap-weed fibre. He laid them in the basket, and he worked on the straight stick for the Elder Brother Ahaiyute. He took up the feather from the body of the turkey and he put it against the stick and wound it with wrappings of cotton string. He took up the feather of the jay, and he placed it against the stick and wound it with cotton; he took up the feather of the chaparral cock and placed it against the stick and wound it with cotton; last he took up the feather of the little brown bird and finished the wrapping of the prayerstick. He placed it in the basket, and he made the stick also for Younger Brother.

He took up the larger of the crooks, and he took eagle-tail feathers and the feathers of the chaparral cock and of the jay. and he bound them to the crook. When he had finished he laid this also in the basket and made the crook for Younger Brother. When he had finished, he set the basket in the corner and covered it with a skirt. He went to get the black from-the-beginning paint;[1] he painted the sticks with the sacred black paint of the priesthoods.

When the morning meal was ready, they sat down and ate. He was sorrowful, and his son also. They could not eat. The father thought again of his dream and it comforted him a little. He waited till it was time to start (about nine o'clock). Then he bundled the crook and the prayerstick for Elder Brother Ahaiyute in a wrapping of corn-husk, and the crook and the prayerstick for Younger Brother he wrapped also in corn-husk. He put them again in the basket, and he went in and selected his most valuable turquoise and his buckskin bag.[2] He brought them out into the outer room. He took a piece of petrified wood, and spread a skin over his knee. He put the turquoise on the skin, and with his piece of petrified wood he crushed the turquoise. When he had a handful of the dust, he put it into his buckskin bag. He asked his wife for freshly ground corn-meal of the white corn. When it was ready, he mixed it with the turquoise dust in his bag. He took the bag of prayer meal, and the prayersticks and the crooks in their corn-husk wrapping and he wrapped them again with corn-husk into a single bundle. He started for Corn Mountain.

---

[1] The sacred and distinctive possession of the priesthoods.
[2] A small bag carried at the belt, holding prayermeal.

No matter how ashamed he was to be seen setting out with feathers to plant at that time of the year,[1] he went out toward the east. The people saw him going with his bundle of feathers, and they said, "I saw the village priest go out today with prayersticks." Some said, "He is going out to pray for rains." Others said, "Perhaps he has prayed for an earthquake."[2]

Some men who had donkeys pastured at Badger Place went out to look after their animals. The mother donkey saw them coming. She was jealous of the human wife of the village priest's son, and she said to her child, "My child, those men are coming to get their donkeys. Walk like a man and go up to them and tell them who your father is." The little donkey walked like a man and went over where the men were coming. The men called out to each other, "Look at that donkey walking!" They laughed and laughed. They ran to chase it. When they made it run, it got down on all-fours like a donkey again. They came up close to it. It said to them, "Do you know why I walk like this?" They stood still when they heard it talk. They said, "Is it for good that you are talking?" (i. e. "does this mean that something dreadful is going to happen?") He answered, "It is for good that I am talking. I am half human." They said, "How can this be?" He answered, "I am the child of the village priest's son. Last spring he was working here in his field and he took a wife from the animals. The horses did not like this, so he had intercourse with the donkeys. That is how it happened that I am a person." They said, "Can this be true? The village priest's son?" "Yes, I have already told my grandfather about this a few days ago. I should like to know my father." They said, "He is married now." The little donkey said, "That is why he never comes here any more." They asked him, "Do you want to send any message to your father?" He answered, "Ask him to bring me human food to eat. I cannot eat weeds all the time." "We will tell him to come and bring you food. We are going now." They went home. They talked together of what the donkey had told them. They felt that it was a terrible thing. They said, "We must not tell of this. If we tell, our village priest will be angry at us. We will keep this secret till others find it out." They went home. They kept thinking of this thing. They did not tell even their wives.

---

[1] It was not the season of his priesthood's retreat. Even members of medicine societies plant regularly only at full moon. If they go out at other times to plant for a sick person, of course everyone knows who is being cured. Plantings after a death, and after a ceremonial impersonation are also recognized by everyone. Secret plantings are always suspect. See also I: 86; 90.

[2] That is, perhaps he is doing evil for his own ends. See references above.

The village priest went on up Corn Mountain. He climbed to the top, and came where the Ahaiyute lived. They heard him coming and they said, "Grandmother, somebody's coming." He came in, and said, "My fathers, my mothers, my children, how have you lived these days?" "Happily, thank you. Sit down." They saw that he was in a hurry, and they did not offer him food. They said, "What is it that you have to ask of us that you come up Corn Mountain so fast?" He sat with his head hanging. He said, "My children, my youths, I have come to ask you to help me. I am ashamed to tell you of this matter. It is a terrible thing. Last year my son took a donkey to wife; she became pregnant. One day I went out to my field and a little donkey came playing and jumping around me. I threw sticks at him, and at last I hit him. He talked to me. He said, 'Your son made my mother pregnant. I am his child.' I was sorrowful. I have eaten nothing since. I can do nothing. Last night I ate tenatsali. They told me to come to you and ask for your help. That is why I have made prayersticks and crooks for you. I finished them and I came here. Help me." They answered, "Yes, we are always glad to help our people." They picked up the prayersticks and crooks that he had brought and put them in an inner room. They came back and they said, "Our father, we will help you to be rid of this creature. We will take care that you never see it again." He answered, "I am very happy. I will go back and wait for you to perform this." "We will surely do this. If we do not do it today, in four days we will perform this." "I am going. Be happy all days."

He went home. He was still sorrowful that the Ahaiyute should be about to kill the little donkey, because his blood (flesh) was in it. He walked home. He came in. His wife was wondering all the time what he had done that day, but she did not dare to ask. She said, "We have finished our midday meal. Will you eat now?" He said, "No, I will eat the evening meal. I am going out to my field."[1]

As soon as he had left their house, the Ahaiyute said to their grandmother, "What shall we do, grandmother?" She answered, "My dear children, you will have to kill it. Bury it like a human being." "Then must we take prayermeal?" (to sprinkle on the body) "No. Kill the creature and put it in a deep crevice washed out by the rains. Put its head to the east. But if you sprinkle meal upon it, it will go to Kachina Village and trouble our forefathers. Bury it without meal. Take a hair from the left side of my head. When you have buried the little donkey, each of you shall take one

---
[1] Because he was sorrowful, he avoided his family.

end of my hair, and you shall carry it around the bunch of donkeys there, and make them all ugly so that hereafter no one will ever care to take one for a wife." They pulled out a hair from the left side of her head; it was very short. They took up their bows and arrows so that if anyone saw them they would think they were out hunting.

They went to the west side of Corn Mountain to see if everyone had gone home from Badger Place. They had to wait till almost sunset. At last there was no one in sight, and they climbed down the west side of Corn Mountain. It was a hard climb, and it was almost dark. They come to Badger Place, and they played with the little donkey. He reared up like a man, and one of them cut his throat, and the other sent his arrow through his heart. He fell dead. His mother came up, and cried out, and grieved over her child. The Ahaiyute took up the body of the little donkey and carried it to a deep crevice washed out by the rains, and put him in it. They put his head to the east. When they had buried him, they said, "Now we must transform the donkeys." They each took one end of the hair from their grandmother's head. They said, "Now we are making you as ugly as you can possibly be so that no one will ever care for you again. No young man will ever look at you, and only old men will ride on you." They pulled the hair, and it stretched out to an immense length (about 100 feet). They were surprised, for their grandmother's hair was short. They carried it completely around the bunch of donkeys. That is why no young men ride on donkeys.

BAT YOUTH (3)
Notes, 334

The people were living at Pinawa; there were four sisters who lived together. At a little distance lived Bat Youth with his grandmother. Every evening he went to beat the drum for these girls while they were grinding corn.

One night after the girls were through grinding, Bat Youth started for home and the girls went to bed. They slept together on one blanket. The boy, however, only made a pretense of going home; he came back and opened the hatchway carefully and came down the ladder. He stood still to see if they were really asleep. "Are you asleep? all asleep?" he asked. They did not answer, so he knew they were asleep, and he went to the youngest one and lay with her. When he had finished, he went to the next older sister, and lay with her. Then he went to the next older sister, and lay with her. Then he lay with the next older, and finally with the eldest. Not one of them woke. He went out.

When he was gone, the youngest woke, and she said, "I'm wet." The next sister woke, and she said, "I'm wet;" and when the next sister woke, she said the same thing; and the eldest also. They said, "It is that Bat Youth who has done this. Let us run after him and pay him back." They ran all the way to his home, and just as he reached his ladder, they caught him. He was so frightened he could not climb it. They tore off his rabbit-skin blanket. He was naked. They left him, and he went home in shame.

Next morning the four sisters said, "Let's fly off. We are shamed. Who will want us here? We will go away." They went. Next day the youth and his grandmother also flew off, for because of what he had done they were ashamed. That is why nobody thinks bats are pretty. Nobody says when he sees a bat, "Oh, see that pretty bird flying!" And because of Bat Youth's shame bats still carry bedbugs.[1]

---

[1] Bats are supposed to be carriers of bedbugs.

DISCUSSION AND ABSTRACTS

The abstracts in this volume are discussed in relation to all Zuni tales recorded over the past fifty years, and all these previously recorded tales which differ from tales in this volume have been abstracted at the end of each section. The themes of the tales have also been discussed in relation to the beliefs and practices of Zuni culture, and the footnote to each tale gives the captions of incidents, which are alphabetically listed, with all Zuni occurrences, in the Index of Incidents, Vol. II.

The following abbreviations have been used in the references:

Cushing, F. H. Zuni Folk Tales, New York 1929. Listed 'Cushing'.

Stevenson, Mathilda Cox. The Zuni Indians. 23rd Annual Report of the Bureau of American Ethnology. Washington 1904. Listed 'Stevenson'.

Bunzel, Ruth. Introduction to Zuni Ceremonialism; Zuni Ritual Poetry; Zuni Kachinas; Zuni Texts. 47th Annual Report of the Bureau of American Ethnology. Washington 1932. Listed 'Bunzel'.

Journal of American Folk Lore. Listed JAFL.

Publications of the Museum of the American Indian, Heye Foundation. Listed Heye Museum.

Publications of the American Ethnological Society. Listed AES.

Memoirs of the American Anthropological Association. Listed MAAA.

THE EMERGENCE A (6), I: 1; B (7), I: 6

Cushing RBAE 13 : 379—447; Heye Museum 8: 20
Parsons JAFL 36 : 135—162
Stevenson 24—53; RBAE 5 : 539—541   Bunzel 549—602
Also: The Ahaiyute cut vents in the underworld people and enable them to eat, Cushing 398. The same tale was printed earlier, Cushing JAFL V (1892): 49—56.

The Sun sent his two children to the fourth world below to lead the people out into the upper world. After their emergence witches followed, bringing corn and the afterlife (death) as their gifts. The people had webbed hands and feet and Sun's children cut them into human form. They sought the middle of the earth to establish their homes, and a priest's son and daughter committed incest, and their children were the koyemci, a clowning society. In crossing a river the children in their mother's arms turned into water animals and were lost, revealing themselves later as kachinas. A waterskate finally determined the middle of the earth and the people settled there.

Zuni origin tales are extreme examples of the extent to which mere plot is dwarfed in Zuni in comparison with ceremonial interest. The familiar incidents of the Zuni origin tale occur in all the available versions and are used in supernatural validation of ceremonies. Which ceremonies are thus validated depends in large measure upon the knowledge and ceremonial affiliations of the narrator.

The first three published versions, the two of Cushing's and Stevenson's introduction to her great work on Zuni, cannot be used in detailed discussion, for Cushing's, RBAE 13, is a poeticized version that draws heavily upon his interpretive powers, and his Ahaiyute story is fragmentary. Mrs. Stevenson's story is an abstract rearranged to serve as an introduction to Zuni ceremonial. Nevertheless the main outlines and peculiarities are clear. The philosophizings and schematic analogies of the Cushing tale, RBAE 13, are characteristic of Zuni esoteric lore and the version is the most elaborate of Zuni speculative attempts at a synthesis of ceremonies, clans, societies, directions of the compass, colors and patron animals. In this version and in Stevenson's, the only ceremony the origin of which is given in detail is the Corn Dance, see above, 20—43, and notes 269.

Parsons' version is a validation of the initiation ceremony into the kachina society. It details first the origin of the kachinas and the fetishes of the initiation party and then the conduct of the ceremony. Kachinas not involved in the initiation are not mentioned.[1] The fetishes that are used in the initiation[2] are named along with the kachinas. The listings follow through the list of initiating kachinas and fetishes of the Kaklo chant as can be seen by comparison with the abbreviated mnemonic version recorded by Stevenson, 73—89. Following the initiation-ceremony origin, there is a condensed origin of the scalp ceremony and a still more condensed origin of medicine societies and of the institution of Łewekwe. As Dr. Parsons says, the account is not esoteric.

Version A (6) is another non-esoteric variant of the Emergence. The Ahaiyute are born of the Sun's rays falling on mist and go to the lowest world to lead the emergence of the people. The usual incidents of the story are followed by a long detailed account

---

[1] Parsons JAFL 36 : 149, "four younger brothers" are the two Nawico and the two Anahoho. Tsitsiḳa, "great grandfather of the Koyemci", RBAE V: 547, names the children at initiation. Culawitsi, of the initiation party, is not mentioned.

[2] "Wotsana" is sutiḳa, the bird fetish which accompanies Kolowisi at the ceremony. See Stevenson, 100.

of the actual events of the ceremony of the initiation of boys and of the łewekwe ceremony, both of which are reserved for another volume, Zuni Ceremonial Tales.

Version B (7) is quite different in spite of the fact that most of the same incidents are repeated. I took it down without text in 1925 from the same informant from whom, in 1927, Bunzel obtained the text account, 547—603. The text version ends, however, with the settlement of Itiwana while B continues with accounts of the institution of the ceremony of the initiation of boys; the Łewekwe (both of which are reserved for the volume of Ceremonial Tales); the departure of the Corn Maidens and the institution of molawia, above, 24—43. All the ceremonies of which origin accounts are introduced into the other versions are thus introduced in B, and comparison between the ceremonial accounts is reserved for the volume of Ceremonial Tales.

B is an esoteric priestly version which is a validation of the four priestly medicine bundles, ka'eto·we, tcu'eto·we, mu'eto·we and łe'eto·we, which figure so much more prominently in the traditional Zuni ritual prayers than in Zuni ceremonial of the present day. The alignment of priestly bundles has apparently changed in present practice and the native priests can give no more satisfactory account of the old groupings than an ethnologist's guess. The esoteric origin version of the priesthoods, Bunzel and B, above, preserves this old grouping instead of mentioning the now existing major priesthoods, teciwani, pałtowa, onawa and hekapawa. The fixed and word-perfect form of this esoteric origin myth is well attested by the two recordings mentioned above. The version taken without text is not printed except for the incidents not included in Bunzel, for all deviations between the two versions are those due to lack of text control. The smallest details, the order of the incidents, even the stylistic peculiarities, are identical.

On the other hand, the tale, Cushing 398, of the Ahaiyute who descend to the lower world on their inverted magic shield because they hear cries of distress, overcome sham enemies for the under-world people and cut vents in their bodies to enable them to eat, is an example of the Zuni fondness for recasting incidents of their emergence myth to serve as humorous tales for evening entertainment. The incidents selected conform closely to those in Version A, but no emergence is mentioned. It is a popular story of an "opposite" world where people throw away good food, making use of it only to sniff at, where they are overcome by bunch grass waved in their faces but have bodies too soft to be hurt by the blow of a war club, where their dangerous enemies are bluejays and pots of

17

boiling mush with earrings of onions. This "opposite" world
figures also in a European tale recorded in Zuni, JAFL 35 : 64.
The Ahaiyute in this Cushing tale are quarrelsome little boys who
pick a fight, not dignified supernatural guides as in emergence
tales of the other type.

A (6), I: 1—6.[1] Sun took pity on the crowded condition of the
underworld and created his sons, the Ahaiyute, by projecting his
rays upon the mist overhanging the upper world. The twins
immediately chose their Ahaiyute shrines and in four days were
old enough to go to the fourth underground world to lead the people
into the upper world. They consulted in turn the priests of the
six directions. They planted four trees which grew magically and
from which the Ahaiyute made prayersticks by which the people
ascended. When they first reached the light of the upper world
tears of pain ran from their eyes, and sunflowers and buttercups
grew from their tears.

Witches came as stragglers[2] out of the emergence hole and when
they overtook the people were admitted to their company because
they brought the gifts of corn and of life after death. The latter
they demonstrated by killing a child and showing it happy in its
afterlife.

The Ahaiyute cut exits in the people, who up to this time had
lived by smelling food. They also slit their webbed hands into
fingers and cut off their horns and tails.[3] The people were too
numerous and had to separate. The two parties were given choices
between the dull colored egg of the parrot and the beautiful egg
of the crow.[4] The ones who chose the beautiful egg came to Zuni
and therefore crows are nuisances in Zuni cornfields, but the
people to the south have valuable parrots.

The leader of the people sent the priest's son and daughter
ahead to look over the country. They committed incest, and with

---

[1] Indexed: Magical impregnation: sun's rays falling on mist. Emergence
from fourth world below. Witches come forth at emergence. Origin of
corn due to witches. Origin of death and afterlife due to witches. Cutting
of first people. Choice of eggs. Incest of brother and sister with birth of
Koyemci. Origin of kachinas from lost children. Middle of earth, waterskate
determines the.

[2] The stragglers were monsters. Cushing RBAE 13 : 384.

[3] Those who refused remained monkeys. Cushing RBAE 13 : 417.

[4] These eggs were produced by the first Pekwin when he struck the solid
rock with his ceremonial staff. Cushing RBAE 13 : 385. Parsons JAFL
36 : 141 gives this tale as an incident of the separation of the people into
two bands on migration; Cushing 385, as the origin of the ceremonial
division into summer (macaw) and winter (crow) people; Stevenson 40,
as the origin of the two subdivisions of the Dogwood clan. Version B
relates the incident, without making it a test theme, as the reason why
there are crows in Zuni and corn is not kernelled to the tip of the ear.

their children became the Koyemci.[1] Father Koyemci created a river by marking the ground with his foot,[2] and when the people crossed it, their children became water animals, descending into the lower world as the first kachinas. When the leaders of the people were shown Kachina Village, where the Koyemci and the kachinas now lived, they were reconciled to the loss of their children, and their priests received instructions from them in prayerstick making.

The waterspider was called to locate the exact center of the world and the people settled at Zuni.

(Followed by the account of the first initiation of boys and institution of the Łewekwe ceremony, reserved for volume of Zuni Ceremonial Tales.)

B (7), I: 6.[3] The Sun desired someone to give him prayersticks. Therefore he sent his two children, Ka'eto·we's Two Mouths, to the fourth womb of the earth to bring the people to the upper world. They descended on their lightning arrow. The people in the lower world had no light and were tailed and horned and had webbed hands. The two leaders sent by Sun conferred with the priests of the six directions in succession and they agreed to the ascent. The leaders summoned in succession Eagle, cokapiso, Chicken Hawk, Hummingbird, Locust (who penetrates solids) and Reed (from which prayersticks are made) to search out their road. The first four failed, the fifth got almost to the surface of the earth and the last penetrated the crust. From the Sulphur Smelling Underworld the leaders set up a pine tree as a ladder to the next world above, the Soot Underworld, a spruce as a ladder to the next world, the Fog Underworld, a piñon as a ladder to the

---

[1] The mother of the Koyemci is impersonated as Komokätsik. She lives in Kachina Village but the Koyemci live in Koyemci Mountain. It is she who gives birth to the kachina dolls which the kachinas bring to children at the winter dance series. Bunzel 1014.

[2] A reference to this tale, Bunzel 1015, adds that the sister was menstruating at the time of the incestuous cohabitation and for this reason springs were formed which gave rise to the sacred lake of Kachina Village.

[3] *Only in abstract. Published with text, Bunzel 549—602.* Indexed: Emergence from fourth world below. Arrow, travel on lightning. Bird search: road to upper world. Locust and Reed penetrate crust of earth. Witches come forth at the emergence. Origin of corn due to witches. Origin of death and afterlife due to witches. Cutting of first people, horns and tails of first people cut by leaders. Food is made edible by birds' regurgitation. Choice of eggs. Incest of brother and sister with birth of koyemci. Origin of kachinas. Girls washing garments or skins betray their people. Kana·kwe, war with. Magical impregnation: foam on waterfall. Visit to Sun. Separable soul: Kana·kwe leader's heart is in her rattle. Kana·kwe survivors bring medicine bundle to Zuni. Animals contest for daylight. Middle of earth, waterskate determines the.

next world, the Wing Underworld, a cottonwood as a ladder to the upper world. In each underworld the priests of the societies sang their song sequences and those who sat in the first row are those who know the songs and in the fourth row those who do not. The sunlight of the upper world was too strong for their eyes and caused tears to roll down their faces.[1] Spider sitting in the ear of a Dogwood clan priest taught him to identify the four chief medicine bundles, ka′eto·we, tcu′eto·we, mu′eto·we, le′eto·we, and to name the months of the calender. This priest was then made Pekwin and the sun put in his charge but he was given no medicine bundle.[2]

After four years (days) the earth shook and Mexicans and witches came out of the hole of emergence. The latter brought corn as their gift to the people, and also instituted death and after-life. They asked for a child whom they made sick and after she had died they showed her to the people playing happily in the under-world.

The people started toward the Middle, stopping at named springs. At the first spring the leaders cut the tails and horns from the people. At another spring they planted corn and it was un-palatable till Raven had chewed it for them, and hard until Owl had chewed it for them. The people separated into two bands both seeking the Middle; those journeying to the south took a macaw egg and the tip of a corn ear, the others a crow egg and the butt of a corn ear.[3]

They got to the site of Kachina Village and a brother and sister climbed the hill to lay out the route for the people to take. They committed incest and became father and mother of the Koyemci.[4] Father Koyemci made the Little Colorado by drawing his foot across the sand and when the women of the first band[5] crossed with their children the latter turned into watersnakes and frogs, and were later found to have become the kachinas and to have founded Kachina Village. The remainder of the mothers kept tight hold of their children and did not lose them.[6]

---

[1] When the morning star rose they thought it was the Sun. Stevenson RBAE 5 : 540.

[2] Pekwin has no eto·ne.

[3] This is said to be the reason why Zuni (i. e. north) has crows instead of valuable macaws, and badly filled ears of corn instead of fully filled. See p. 258, n. 4.

[4] Their first born, was Kołamana (supernatural maiden), the transvestite ap-pearing in the Kana·kwe dance, Cushing; Stevenson. The latter adds that this impersonation was made a transvestite by the Kana·kwe giantess leader after his capture, to subdue him (she mistakenly calls him Kokokci before his change of sex).

[5] These were the Bear and Crane, Cushing RBAE 13 : 404; the Bear, Corn and Sandhill Crane clan, Stevenson RBAE 5 : 541; Lewekwe, Stevenson 33.

[6] Their hands nevertheless became webbed, and the Ahaiyute cut them into fingers. RBAE 5: 541.

Two Neᐧweᐧkwe went to spy out their route and saw two girls washing garments in the stream at Hanłipinḳa. They killed[1] and scalped them, and returned to their (ḳaᐧetoᐧwe) people to await the attack they had provoked. To lead in this coming conflict (i. e. with the Ḳanaᐧkwe) the two Ahaiyute were born from the foam of the waterfall, and they instituted the comatowe song cycle (i. e. war songs).

Meanwhile the prey animals contested with the birds of prey in a hidden-ball game for the privilege of hunting in the daytime. Spider and Squirrel were on the side of the birds and Owl on the side of the animals. Squirrel was sluggish and lay by the fire but Spider directed him so that he won for his side by finding the ball in Owl's hand while Owl was dancing. When the bird's side guessed, Spider moved the ball under the winning cup by means of his web. Therefore Owl and the prey animals hunt at night. See above, 10; notes, 264.

Those who possessed Łeᐧetowe separated from the others and with their snow-bringing powers went to the north.

The conflict with the Ḳanaᐧkwe blocked their progress. The Ḳanaᐧkwe had an invulnerable giant woman as their leader. Younger Brother Ahaiyute went to his father the Sun for help and was told that she kept her heart in her rattle. Sun gave him turquoise rabbit sticks for himself and his brother, with which the giantess was slain. Her people fled and an old woman and two children were adopted into the Zuni tribe because they brought their medicine bundle, the Black Corn etoᐧne, to Zuni. See notes, "The Ḳanaᐧkwe", below.

The people came toward Itiwana. They asked the waterskate to determine the exact center of the earth. He tried Halona first and then Itiwana. They built Zuni where his heart had rested.

(Followed by institution of the boys' initiation rites, of the Łewekwe ceremony, reserved for volume of Zuni Ceremonial Tales, and of the Corn Maidens and molawia rites, I: 24—43.)

THE ḲANAᐧKWE, I: 6—10

THE KANAᐧKWE CONCEAL THE GAME[2]

Stevenson 36—46   Cushing RBAE 2 : 22—24; RBAE 13:424
Parsons JAFL 36 : 142   Bunzel 597, 599
Benedict "The Emergence" B, preceding tale.

The Ḳanaᐧkwe story is one of the best known in Zuni and is often given as part of the emergence story. The form given here in version A is said to be that used in the Ḳanaᐧkwe priesthood.

---

[1] Ne'weᐧkwe behavior goes by contraries, i. e. is of the order of "backward" speech.

[2] Indexed: Ḳanaᐧkwe, war with. Sinew bowstrings slack in rain. Separable soul: Ḳanaᐧkwe's leader's heart is in her rattle, B.

It agrees with RBAE 2 : 22 and differs from all others in the absence of reference to the Ḵanaꞏkwe giant woman leader who kept her heart in her rattle. It also gives the final victory to the Ḵanaꞏkwe and makes this the reason why kachina gifts at dances do not include venison, whereas it is regularly among the Ḵanaꞏkwe gifts. The informant who told this version, in giving the tale by allusion as part of the origin tale, Bunzel 599, tells the usual Ḵanaꞏkwe story as in all the above versions except RBAE 2 : 22: In order to overcome the Ḵanaꞏkwe the Ahaiyute are created (or ascend to their Sun father for weapons), find the heart of the giant woman leader in her rattle and destroy her. All Ḵanaꞏkwe but two children are killed and these bring the black corn etoꞏne to Zuni. In all versions but Bunzel (and, as above, RBAE 2:22), the Ḵanaꞏkwe string their bows with yucca in a rainstorm while the usual sinew bowstrings of the people become slack from rain, and the three kachinas who appear in all Ḵanaꞏkwe dances are captured at this time by the victors. The story should be compared with that of Citsuḵa, I: 18.

Cushing RBAE 2 : 22—24 gives the story in the form of the widespread *Liberation of Game.* Familiar incidents such as the role of the Ahaiyute, the giantess leader with her heart in her rattle, the bowstrings too slack from the rain, are not present in this version. He translates Ḵanaꞏkwe "Snail People" and Ḵamaḵa, their traditional home, "Place of Snails". The story is as follows: the Ḵanaꞏkwe shut all game in their canyon as in a corral and the people of Kachina Village starved for lack of food. The Calako (see Crow's discovery of game, B, below; Calako is a giant bird impersonation, RBAE 2 : 22, n. 3) followed a stray elk and found where the game was imprisoned. With the help of Beast Gods the people of Kachina Village liberated the game and the habits of these animals were fixed according to incidents at the time of their liberation.

A (7), I: 6. The hunting surrounds of the kachinas and the Ḵanaꞏkwe overlapped and they quarreled. Therefore the Ḵanaꞏkwe hid all the game on earth in their corrals. The Kachinas came to do battle bringing the rain with them. The rain, however, slacked their sinew bowstrings and the Ḵanaꞏkwe strung theirs with yucca. They thus won the battle, capturing three of the enemy (named below.)

B (3), I: 8[1]. This version differs from the preceding in including the incident of Crow's discovery of the hidden game animals; in

---

[1] *Published only in abstract.*

stating that the Ḵana·kwe did not know how to string bows with sinew; that the leader's heart was in her rattle; that the great Ḵana·kwe outcry "Huita, Huita" (the Ḵana·kwe call in all dances) was responsible for their winning the battle; that Blue Ḵana·kwe captured Sayałia, hitting his horn with his arrow (which leaves a hole in his mask at the present time), Black Ḵana·kwe captured Itsipoca, a Koyemci (whose mouth is still drawn with crying), and Yellow Ḵana·kwe, Kołamana; and that the Ahaiyute overcame Ḵana·kwe's giant leader by shooting her heart which she carried in her rattle.

THE ḴANA·KWE CHILDREN BRING THEIR MEDICINE BUNDLE (7), I:8[1]

> Cushing RBAE 13 : 424   Stevenson (a) 43; (b) 44
> Parsons JAFL 36 : 145   Bunzel 600; ms, abstracted below

The medicine bundle of the Ḵana·kwe, associated with the black corn clan, is the single instance of folkloristic elaboration of Zuni eto·we. The usual story, sometimes alluded to rather than related in the origin stories, is that in order to destroy the Ḵana·kwe the people were given the war rites of the comatowe song cycle (Bunzel 597, Parsons 144, Cushing 419ff.) and the use of the sulphuric fumes of Big Shell (Cushing 424, 425, Parsons 145, Stevenson 45; Bunzel 600, gives the sulphuric smell as that of their own, Ḵana·kwe, bodies.) A Ḵana·kwe boy and girl, or a boy and girl and their grandmother, saved themselves from these poison fumes by inhaling medicine and were discovered and adopted by their conquerors because they possessed a medicine bundle. Stevenson gives also a version like the one printed here: that the girl and boy were sole survivors after the destruction of the Ḵana·kwe and to save themselves from starvation joined the enemy with their medicine bundle, were given a husband and a wife and adopted into the Corn clan. The present version substitutes abandonment in famine, a favorite Zuni introduction, for the usual defeat of the Ḵana·kwe.

The Bunzel ms version is the form in which the Ḵana·kwe story is told as origin of the Ḵana·kwe dance:

The Ḵana·kwe rounded up all the game and locked it up. The Kachina Village people made war on the Ḵana·kwe, who captured three of the kachinas. The Ḵana·kwe escaped underground to a spring near Acoma. They left behind two children who set out to follow their people. They went first to Hawiku, then to Itiwana, and were adopted by Black Corn Clan because of their medicine

---

[1] Indexed: Children deserted in famine.

bundle. They set out to find their people, promising to return. They returned with the Ḳanaˑkwe dance, but this proved dangerous and people died. Therefore, the Ḳanaˑkwe instructed the Zuni people to copy their masks, and impersonate the dancers.

During a famine at Ḳamaḳa, the home of the Ḳanaˑkwe, after the latter's defeat by the Zunis, the Ḳanaˑkwe went to Acoma deserting a boy and his younger sister. The children lived on woodrats the boy snared. In order to save themselves from starvation they sought out a pueblo of their enemies. They had (Ḳanaˑkwe) snout mouths and appeared strange to the people; when they showed their black corn medicine bundle, they were adopted and given spouses.

THE ANIMALS PLAY HIDDEN BALL (7), I: 10[1]
Parsons JAFL 43 : 44   Bunzel 598
Vide Stevenson 339, note c

The widespread story of the animals' council which determined daylight or the seasons retains in the Parsons version alone the widespread incident associated with it: the origin of the chipmunk's stripes. In that version "Squirrel" is sitting too close to the fire and his back is scorched. The tale is never told in Zuni as an origin of daylight or the seasons but as the reason why prey animals and owls hunt by night. They lost the game to the birds because their player, Squirrel, guessed that Owl had cheated and concealed the ball in his own hand. This incident is referred to in the Stevenson note above.

At Hanłipinḳa the prey animals played hidden ball with the birds of prey to determine which group should hunt in the day time. The Ahaiyute brought the implements of the game and were to give the decision according to which side was ahead at daybreak. Squirrel, however, was on the birds' side and Owl on the animals'. Before dawn Squirrel was choosing and he uncovered the ball which Owl had hidden in his hand. When his side hid the ball in turn, Spider covered it with his web and put it under the losing cup so that the prey animals lost the game. For this reason Squirrel is a day animal and Owl a night bird while prey animals hunt by night.

---

[1] Indexed: Animals contest for daylight. Helpful animals: Spider goes underground to move ball in game.

THE FLOOD, A (8), I:10; B (3), I:12

Cushing RBAE 13 : 429	Parsons JAFL 36 : 161
Stevenson 61; RBAE 5 : 539	Benedict I:200

The people take refuge upon Corn Mountain from a great flood.

The story of the great flood, when the people were forced to take refuge on top of Corn Mesa, is found in all the older versions of the Emergence. It is loosely and variously integrated with the other incidents, and is not included in more recently recorded origin tales. Both the stories of the flood given here are set in Zuni in non-mythological times and are stories of punishment for sex offenses. It may be, considering how often the theme occurs in accounts of drought and famine, that sex offenses are implied in older accounts but the Stevenson version does not refer to any cause of the flood; the Cushing version lays it to the inaccuracy of Waterskate in indicating the navel of the earth at Halona across the river from the correct Itiwana, adding that "the first priest did evil"; the Parsons version says "for some reason Ocean was angry."

Nor do either of the present versions relate, as all the older versions do, the sacrifice of the village priest's son and daughter to the supernaturals that caused the flood. This tale is known to everyone in Zuni as the origin of the Girl and Boy cliffs to the west of Corn Mountain where are located important fertility shrines sought by pregnant women, or women desiring pregnancy. In the present collection this story of human sacrifice is told as the consequence of the acquisition of the rain songs of the priests' retreats by Paiyatamu's grandson, a consequence of supernatural blessing and not of human sin, 1: 200.

Cushing, in addition to the tale just discussed, gives a different Flood story, RBAE 13 : 421 ff., which is likewise a consequence of supernatural blessing. When the people were given the enormously powerful war songs of the *comatowe* cycle, which are likewise weather control, wind and flood ripped open the earth. The Ahaiyute dried the foam in their hair so that it became the warhoods of the bow priesthood, and established the landmarks (mountains).

The introduction to version A is the incident: *Apparition impersonated to punish evildoers*, which is incorporated also in other tales, see Index, Vol. II. The sex offense punished by the flood is specifically intercourse between members of the same clan.

A (8), I: 10.[1] After the people had settled in Itiwana the corn clan sinned and the young people lived together promiscuously.

---

[1] Indexed: Apparition impersonated to punish evildoers. Flood and earthquake, people take refuge on mesa from great.

One member of the clan, son of a priest, obtained power from his dead uncle and came as an apparition of the dead to the pueblo. When the people saw him they ran to the mesa to escape the earthquake and flood that follow the appearance of the dead. The priest's son's own grandmother was overtaken in the flood which he let loose in his character as Kolowisi. This was the origin of the taboo on sexual relations between members of the same clan.

B (3), I: 12[1]. The bow priest and Pekwin led the people on a picnic so that they could slide on a certain frozen pond. The young people committed sex offenses and there was an earthquake. The people took refuge on Corn Mountain, and when they returned they had no corn stores. They were starving. Fathers and mothers ate their children in secret. One boy tried to save his little brother and Spider Woman fed them inexhaustible food which they took back to their people. However the sex taboos were still not observed and after three more earthquakes the flood filled the valley and turned all the people it overtook into frogs and watersnakes. People took refuge on Corn Mountain. After the flood receded it was found that those who had sinned had been turned to stone (in the form of frogs, etc.) Since that time sex taboos have been observed.

The Origin of the Uwanami (7), I: 15[2]

The kachina trap six men who have lost to them in a game of hidden ball in Kachina Village, and these become the Uwanami (rain makers).

This story like the two preceding are not placed in mythical times. It is my impression that this tale is made up of common elements on the analogy of the origin of the kachinas and the origin of the world of the dead, that is, in all three cases people are lost for some reason and rediscovered, and the searchers are told that they have become sources of blessing to the people on earth. The story does not occur in any of the older collections.

A despised young man living with his grandmother gets Spider Woman's help in gambling by giving her a cigarette. When he hides the ball she drags it in her web under the wrong cup, and when he guesses his opponent's ball she spies out for him which cup it is under. The people of the village are summoned by Pautiwa

---

[1] Indexed: Flood and earthquake, people take refuge on mesa from great. Inexhaustible food. Helpful animals: Spider Woman, inexhaustible food.
[2] Indexed: Despised youth wins gambling game. Helpful animals: Spider goes underground to move ball in game.

to Kachina Village to gamble with the kachinas, and all the people provide themselves with goods to stake on the game. The kachinas stake deer and antelope. In the first four games the kachinas win, and the six men who lose to them are trapped under the floor. The people choose the despised young man to choose for them, and Spider helps him as before so that the kachinas lose all their deer. The kachinas show the people the six men sitting three and three in an inner room from which mist issues; they have become the Uwanami and they tell the people to pray to them. For this reason the priests make a pilgrimage to the Sacred Lake every fourth year at the beginning of the summer rain dances, and for this reason people go to Kachina Village when they die.

THE THEFT OF THE SUN AND MOON (7), I : 16[1]

In order to get light for their hunting Coyote and Eagle steal from the kachinas the boxes in which they keep the sun and moon. Coyote disobeys instructions, opens the box and lets them escape to the sky.

The tale of the bird, usually Raven, who wanted the sun so that he could see to hunt, found the owners who kept Sun in a box and flew off with it, is one of the most important origin stories of the Northwest Coast. Boas' discussion, RBAE 31 : 641—648, includes versions from all the Northwest Coast and Puget Sound. In Zuni it is an isolated tale not integrated with the usual origin cycle and such elements as a wooden box receptacle and Coyote's shame at having his "chief" carry the bundle are out of place in Zuni custom. It would seem probable that this tale is current among the Southwest Athabascans but the informant had heard it from a Zuni priest and did not know an Athabascan analogue. None has so far been recorded.

Coyote and Eagle were hunting companions. Coyote never caught anything and he complained to Eagle that it was so dark he could not see. Therefore they set out to find the sun and moon. On the journey Coyote was almost drowned trying to swim a wide river. At last they came to Kachina Village. The kachinas kept the sun and moon in boxes which they opened when they wanted light. Eagle borrowed them, flying with them toward his home. Coyote ran along on the ground begging to carry the boxes. He was ashamed to have his chief carry them. At the fourth request Eagle consented and as soon as Coyote was left behind he opened the boxes. The sun and moon rose to the sky, taking with them all their warmth. That is why there is winter.

---

[1] Indexed: Theft of Light. Pandora.

CITSUᴋ̣A (8), I : 18[1]

The kachina force the great hunter Citsuka to come to their lake by hiding the deer over the whole country. When he comes to Kachina Village in search of food, Pautiwa takes him as his son-in-law.

The tale of the supernaturals who hid the deer and how they were released by Citsuka's marriage among the game owners is variously told. In all versions the plot uses a familiar incident which is often a part of the Kana·kwe story: the discovery of women washing a buckskin, which betrays the fact that their people alone have food. It is obvious that more and more Kana·kwe material has been incorporated in later versions.

In the Stevenson version, the owners of deer are the Black Ravens, "kwalaci kwina", and no reason for their monopoly of game is given. As soon as Citsuka has established an entrée among them by marrying one of their daughters he betrays them to Pautiwa. For this betrayal and for his liberation of the deer he is rewarded by marriage with Pautiwa's daughter. There is no reference to conflict between the kachinas and the game owners. The incident of the origin of the habits of prey animals is introduced when Citsuka calls the beast gods of Cipapolima to feast at the liberation of deer, and their behavior on this occasion Citsuka makes characteristic of their species for all time.

The version Bunzel 925 makes the owners of deer not Black Ravens but Black Crows, koko a·kwin·e, i. e. by the familiar Zuni pun, "Black Gods". These "Black Gods", like the Kana·kwe,[2] get into a fight with the kachinas of Kachina Village when their game-surrounds overlap and they impound all the game. Citsuka while he is hunting vainly in a famine comes upon two of their women washing buckskin. He marries one and is given charge of the corral in which all game has been secreted. Pautiwa, swiming around as a duck, sees him eating venison and promises him his daughter in marriage if he betrays the Owners of Game. To release the game, Citsuka confines a wild animal in each corral and pops salt in his fire that night, which frightens the deer so that they run off and scatter over the earth. He marries Pautiwa's daughter.

In Bunzel 929 and the present version, the story is told without reference to black gods or the Raven people. The kachinas plot to get Citsuka as their son-in-law because he is a good hunter and they hide the deer to force him to travel the long distance to their

---

[1] Indexed: Girls washing skins or garments betray their people.
[2] Cushing gives "Black People" for the Kana·kwe, RBAE 13: 424—6.

country. As soon as he comes into Pautiwa's presence the latter offers him his daughter and plenty of deer: the marriage is not arranged in payment for any betrayal of the Owners of Deer or for providing the kachinas again with game. The distribution of game over the earth is hardly even implied.

The Stevenson incident of Citsuḳa's eating his ears, little hairy deer tails from his mask, occurs again in the present version, as also Citsuḳa's association with Kwelele. The reflection of the myth in ceremony is explicitly stated in the last paragraph of the present version: "that is why he is doing this now" i. e. in the calendric ceremonies.

Citsuḳa and Kwelele lived with their grandmother at Cipapolima far in the east. Citsuḳa was such a famous hunter that the kachinas hid the game to force him to come to their country in search of food. He and his family were forced to eat the tiny deer tails that form the ears of Citsuḳa's mask. In order to obtain game he followed the heat lightning to the southwest and at the lake of Kachina Village he saw two kachina girls washing buckskin. By this he knew their people could find deer. They took him to Pautiwa, who betrothed his daughter to him. He spent the spring at Kachina Village with his wife and the autumn in Cipapolima with his grandmother, returning at winter solstice from the east to Zuni, where he met his father-in-law and returned with him to Kachina Village. This is the basis for Citsuḳa's yearly travels (in ritual.)

THE CORN MAIDENS, A (7), I : 20; B (8), I : 24

Cushing, RBAE 13 : 431—445   Parsons, JAFL 29 : 392—399
    Heye Museum 8 : 38—54   Bunzel, 914; 918
Stevenson, 48—49, 51—54

The Corn Maidens are insulted by the people and hide themselves away, causing a long famine. They are ceremonially recovered and institute the corn ceremonials.

The abstracts of this story published by Parsons and Stevenson and the long embellished account by Cushing obscure the narrative form of this incident. All the versions, including the present one, are deeply colored by the observances of the Corn Dance and the molawia, but the incident is nevertheless a narrative told in the usual Zuni style, as was indicated also in the Cushing version in Heye Museum 8.

The principal divergences in the account have to do with the amount and detail of ceremonial incorporations. Version A was told as the concluding incident of the version of the Emergence B,

I : 6. It is the ceremonial account of the Corn Maidens and the institution of the ceremony of molawia. Bunzel 918 is the same narrator's short abstract of the same material and was given as a myth of the Corn Maidens. Version B on the other hand is the exoteric version of the famine caused by the departure of corn, and Bunzel 914 is a condensation of this same tale by a member of the same family. Version B is a "four nights" form of the tale and is full of cultural detail which well illustrates the value set in Zuni narrative style upon the elaboration of the events of pueblo life. The recall of the people who had taken refuge from famine in Acoma and Hopi and the processes of divination with tenatsali and jimson weed are fully expanded. In these versions the escape of the Corn Maidens is simply an animistic phrasing of famine caused when the corn in the storerooms acts upon its resentment of the carelessness of the people, and hides itself. (The story of this resentment and the ensuing famine is told also in the tale, II: 26.) Duck (Pautiwa in duck form, Bunzel 915) hides them. The priests try divining and seek aid in vain from tenatsali, jimson weed, and the Ahaiyute. They ask Ne'we·kwe Youth. He requires the priests to keep a strict retreat to assist him and succeeds.

A variety of ceremonial aspects are stressed in the different versions. In the Parsons account, recorded from a Ne'we·kwe man, Ne'we·kwe Youth's ceremonial father who prepares him for the search and receives him back afterwards is a Sand Hill Crane man, which office formerly had to be held by a member of that clan. The rabbit gives, not the Ne'we·kwe whistle as in the present versions, but its tongue which is placed in Ne'we·kwe Youth's mouth during the ceremonial taboo on speaking. In the Stevenson version the two elder Corn Maidens accompany the two bow priests to distant springs for water to pour in he·patina, an important rite of molawia not mentioned in the present versions. In the Cushing version the tale begins with an account of the institution of the cokowe (water) party of the Corn Dance and of Paiyatamu's bringing his Dew Maidens to participate in the dance opposite the Corn Maidens. Ne'we·kwe Youth, when he is asked to seek the Corn Maidens, clowns in characteristic fashion, using backward speech, and has to be ceremonially discharmed. He institutes the offering of water at He·patina and has four youths perfect in body chosen to carry the gourds of sacred water.

A certain confusion occurs between Ne'we·kwe and Paiyatamu. In the Stevenson version, Paiyatamu (Keresan: *youth*), the patron of the Flute cult associated with the Corn Dance, is confused with the masked impersonation Ne'paiyatamu (Ne'we·kwe Youth), who recovers the Corn Maidens and is impersonated at molawia as Bitsitsi. This is the more understandable as there is a lack of clear distinction in Zuni between the masked impersonation Ne'paiyatamu, the unmasked Bitsitsi, and the Paiyatamu of the Flute cult, an order of the Little Fire and Bedbug medicine societies. In the Stevenson version, Paiyatamu is also the would-be violator of the Corn Maidens, but this, if not an error, is certainly an idiosyncracy of the narrator; Version A makes the bow priest the violator, the Parsons version the Ahaiyute, their supernatural equivalent; Cushing credits the flute dancers with desire for the Corn Maidens, and the non-esoteric versions explain the departure of the Corn Maidens as due to the carelessness of the people in the use of corn.

The most inexplicable discrepancy in the versions is Cushing's substitution of Citsuka for Pautiwa in his account of the molawia ceremony. In all descriptions of this ceremony, Pautiwa represents the duck and always appears, Citsuka never. Cushing identifies Citsuka as a black god whereas he is always ritually referred to as a white god. It is impossible to understand at the present time what this divergence may signify and it seems most likely an error. Version A gives Duck as the hider of the Corn Maidens and assumes the hearer's knowledge that Pautiwa is his kachina equivalent who appears in the procession at molawia. Stevenson elaborates the incident: the Corn Maidens escape to their home in Keyatiwa Spring and send Black Corn to Kachina Village asking for help. Father Koyemci (a regular participant in the molawia procession) and Pautiwa accompany her back in the form of ducks and cover the Corn Maidens with their wings.

A (7), I:20[1]. During one of the nights that the six Corn Maidens spent in the shelter of boughs in the plaza during the Corn Dance, the bow priest desired the eldest sister and when she went outside attempted to lay hands on her. The Corn Maidens were offended and escaped to the ocean in the southeast, taking the corn in the pueblo with them. Duck hid them, diving under the water of the ocean with the six Corn Maidens under her wings. Famine descended on the people when the corn was gone and they endured it for seven years. The priests of the council met every night. They summoned Eagle, Cokapiso, Chicken Hawk and Crow to find the maidens. The latter, who always smells out corn, found kernels under the ocean but did not recognize it as corn. Hummingbird also failed. They then summoned Ne'we·kwe Youth, who directed

---

[1] Told as concluding incident of Emergence tale B, I: 6.

Indexed: Corn Maidens are offended at being the objects of sexual desire. Famine is caused by loss of Corn Maidens. Bird search: Corn Maidens. Corn Maidens, loss and recovery of by a Ne'we·kwe impersonation.

the council to keep the strictest retreat during his search and to make prayersticks for him. With the power given by this retreat he found the Corn Maidens and they came into Zuni as they do in the molawia ceremony the last day of Cala'ko. In the night the Corn Maidens went to all the houses and filled the storerooms.

B (8), I:24.[1] The people ignored the observance in regard to corn, using flour to fill their game bags and treating the kernels carelessly. Therefore all corn departed from Zuni, and Duck hid the six corn sisters under her wing in her nest by the ocean far to the southeast.

The people took refuge from the famine in Acoma and Hopi but the village priest sent a runner to recall them that the village might be reunited in the search for the corn maidens. The priests of the council called the Tenatsali Youths, who searched four nights, and Jimson Weed Youth who searched one and who fed the village priest's little son with his leaves that the latter might divine. The Ahaiyute were also called and also failed, creating the Milky Way as they rode over the world. For the fourth attempt the priests called Ne'we·kwe Headman to summon the supernatural, Duck, who lived in Ashes Spring. He required the strictest fast and retreat of the priests and succeeded in his search, returning in the character of Bitsitsi with the corn mothers (i. e., the institution of molawia).

Salt Woman Migrates (8), I : 43[2]

Stevenson 58   Bunzel 1032

Salt Woman and Turquoise Man once lived near Zuni. They removed to a distance in order to make themselves more valuable. When the priests followed Salt Woman to her new home they discovered the tenatsali youths and learned how to use their medicine.[1]

The story of Salt Woman and Turquoise Man's removal from Black Rock Lake to their present homes is told also in the Bunzel version but the ceremonial associations of the tale are unlike. The present version "belongs" to tenatsali, and the Bunzel version is a kachina origin tale of Salt Woman. It therefore tells how Salt Woman was adopted into the mixed dance (in which she appears in Zuni) by the kachinas of Kachina Village.

Salt Woman lived only a few miles from Zuni in Black Rock Springs. Turquoise Man lived near her. The people came often to supply themselves and it was the custom for boys and girls to

---

[1] Indexed: Famine is caused by misuse of corn in game. Famine is caused by loss of Corn Maidens. Origin of the Milky Way. Corn Maidens, loss and recovery of by a Ne'we·kwe impersonation.

[2] Indexed: Salt Woman, migrations of.

gather salt under the leadership of a bow priest. After a time they became careless and soiled her flesh and wasted it. Therefore Salt Woman went to Turquoise Man and together they set out to find themselves new homes. When they found their salt was gone, the priests of the council made prayersticks and two priests went with two runners to follow her trail. It was salty and marked by landmarks she had created on her journey. They were led on their way to the home of the tenatsali youths (the country where tenatsali is gathered) and were instructed in the uses of tenatsali in divining. When they reached Salt Lake they were punished for the people's carelessness first by having their feet badly cut by the salt when they waded into the lake to fill their bags, and second by not being able to find the road back to Zuni without long wandering. Salt Woman gave them salt, and instructions that mature men should come after her flesh from this time. She told them to put the kachina society duck feather on her prayersticks. When men returned to Zuni after gathering salt the first time they were to be washed by their father's sisters. These aunts were to bring a present and receive salt in return. On later trips the taboos might be relaxed.

TAIL BY TAIL (8), I : 49[1]

Cushing 230   Parsons JAFL 31 : 231   Bunzel 922

The coyotes lose their lives stealing from the Ḳana·kwe, and Saiyaḷia skins them for his costume.

This kachina origin story well illustrates the acculturation of a folk tale in Zuni. The Cushing version recorded fifty years ago is obviously the European incident of "Tail by Tail" where the first animal in a chain hanging teeth by tail breaks wind and they all fall to death. Cushing's version is as follows: The coyotes wanted the Ḳana·kwe's children, who lived on top of Corn Mountain, and they planned to hold each other by the tail *to climb up*. They were strictly warned not to break wind. One of them *sneezed*, however, and they all died and their skins were taken by Saiyaḷi'a for his collar. The trick is obviously misunderstood, as also in the Parsons version where the *bottom* coyote breaks wind and all fall. In the present version the folly of *ascending* a mountain by holding tails is avoided by modifying the trick so that the taboo against breaking wind is reinterpreted as a means to secure flatulency (i. e. lightness) and render the ascent possible.

The fully ritualized and acculturated form of the tale is published in Bunzel 922. Every detail has been fitted into Zuni custom. In the first place it accounts carefully for the fact that the action of

---

[1] Indexed: Tail by Tail.

the story takes place on Corn Mountain. The Ḳanaʻkwe traditionally live at Ḳamaḳa, and the story in all versions takes place on the cliffs of Corn Mountain. Therefore the Bunzel version describes that after the winter solstice ceremony the Ahaiyute started for their home on Corn Mountain. Before the Saiyaḷiʼa started for Kachina Village they went hunting to get animal skins for their costumes. They accompanied the Ahaiyute in the direction of Corn Mountain. (This is understood to be after the last day of the winter solstice ceremony, the great day on which Pautiwa and the four Sayaḷiʼa visit the kivas late at night to send out the old year. The Ahaiyute have been down to the pueblo to get the prayersticks that have been planted for them at the great winter solstice plantings.) As the Ahaiyute climbed the mountain, leaving the Saiyaḷiʼa hunting below, they were so happy that they kept giving the happy calls that the Ḳanaʻkwe give at a throw-away. Four coyotes heard these, and ran up saying, "Where is the throw-away?" The Ahaiyute wanted the Saiyaḷiʼa to have these coyote skins to wear so they said, "Down below." "How could we get down?" "Stick a corn cob in your anus and you'll float down gently." They jumped off and were killed. So the Saiyaḷiʼa got the coyotes' skins to wear around their necks. In this final version there is nothing left of the old misunderstood European incident of "Tail by Tail" but the fact is obvious that the various versions are variants of one tale.

The Coyotes plotted to attend the Ḳanaʻkwe's throw-away dance and get the corn boiled on the cob which they tossed out to the people. Since the Ḳanaʻkwe lived on the top of Corn Mountain the coyotes stoppered their anuses with corn cob in order that the accumulation of wind should make them light enough to ascend. They almost got there when one of them pulled out his corn cob and broke wind, and they all fell down dead. Saiyaḷiʼa came by and skinned the coyotes and that's why he always uses their skins for collars.

THE BOY WHO BROKE HIS VOWS (3) I : 50[1]

Stevenson RBAE 5 : 554 Bunzel 605 (text)
Bunzel 1003 Benedict ms. "Boy who broke his Vows",
 reserved for volume, Zuni Ceremonial
 Tales.

A boy newly initiated into the Kachina Society betrays to his uninitiated playmates the fact that the kachina dancers are men of the pueblo dressed up in masks. He is ceremonially killed by the most dangerous kachinas.

---

[1] *Published only in abstract.* Indexed: Boy who broke his vows.

This is one of the most often repeated stories in Zuni. According to the occasion it is told in very different ways. The form in which it is told by the Kachina Chief at the close of the initiation ceremony is given in text, Bunzel 605, and the "eight nights' story" is reserved for the volume of Ceremonial Tales, in which version the initiation and its associated ceremonies are meticulously described as a part of the tale. It is also a favorite kiva story, a form represented by the present version. The child who was punished is named as Kaiyu'ani in all versions. The Kachina Chief's version, Bunzel 605, is introduced by the origin, during the period when the people lived on Corn Mountain, of the winter solstice ceremony and the winter dance series. The present version introduces the story with a resumé of the main incidents of the origin tale, and the Bunzel version 1003, where the tale is told as the origin of the masks of scare kachinas, makes no attempt to place the story in mythical times. The kachinas who take part in the execution vary somewhat in different versions: in Bunzel 605 the only scare kachina is Temtemci, and he is accompanied by the Saiyaɫi'a and the Koyemci. In Bunzel 1003 the kachinas who carry stone knives are all named: Homatci, Hainawi, Temtemci and Ahute ("to stamp on the ground"), and the Ahaiyute accompany them. The Ahaiyute finally locate Kaiyu'ani and protect him from the fury of the scare kachinas till they bring him to the plaza where the execution takes place.

The present version is introduced by an abbreviated account of the incestuous birth of the Koyemci, the origin of the first kachinas when children became frogs crossing the river, the water-skate's location of the Middle of the Earth, and the flood. The people lived on Corn Mountain during the flood and held an initiation. Kaiyu'ani was initiated and warned not to tell that the kachinas were men in masks. During the next winter dance series, however, Kaiyu'ani with the other children was playing at the river modelling clay figures of the kachinas. He did not want his play interrupted and told the children the dancers were only their fathers and their uncles dressed up in masks. Therefore the chiefs of the Kachina society summoned the dangerous kachinas, Temtemci, Ahute, Homatci and Hainawi. They came with the Sayaɫia, broke open the boy's house where he lay hidden, and with their stone knives cut off his head. They left his body lying and kicked his head to Kachina Village.

ADDITIONAL INCIDENTS OF THE EMERGENCE
First Beings

Both Cushing and Stevenson give to A'wonawil'ona (those who hold the roads, i. e. life spans of men) an interpretation colored by monotheistic deism, and Mrs. Stevenson even likens this deity to the Greek Athena. In reality Those-who-hold-the-Roads is not the creator of the world and a figure of the Zuni pantheon, but a collective term, see Bunzel 486, by which any being is addressed in prayer. The confusion in use is due to the fact that the missionaries have used the term, as Mrs. Stevenson did, for God.

The Cushing account of creation is distinctive because it attributes the origin of life to the cohabitation of the Sun Father and Earth Mother, a myth current among the Yuman tribes but not recognized, as far as can be discovered, by Zuni priests or laymen at the present time.

A.[1] A'wonwil'ona became the Sun Father and formed the Earth Mother and Sky Father of balls of his cuticle. They cohabited and life was conceived in the fourth womb of the Earth. Earth repulsed the Sky when she was with child and they withdrew from each other to their present positions.[2] Earth Mother created the landmarks of earth, and of her warm breath touched by the cold breath of the Sky rain-giving clouds were formed. Sky created the stars, which symbolize also their terrestrial reflections, the corn kernels. *Cushing RBAE 13: 379—81.*

B.[3] A'wonawil'ona, Sun, Moon, and First Priest and First Priestess, were the primal beings. The first created clouds and earth-waters; First Priest of his spittle created stars, and First Priestess of her spittle created the earth. Of the two latter the people of Zuni were born in a rapid succession of births in the underworld. *Stevenson RBAE 23: 23—4.*

Ḳaklo[4]

The village priest had four sons: Ḳaklo, two Anahoho, and Siwelushiwa; and one daughter Siwiluhsita. He sent the eldest,

---

[1] Indexed: Creation from cuticle. Origin of life in cohabitation of earth and sky.

[2] Sky is lifted by the bow of the Primal Twins. Cushing RBAE 13 : 382; Heye Museum 8 : 25.

[3] Indexed: Origin from spittle.

[4] Indexed: Incest of brother and sister with birth of koyemci. Origin of kachinas from lost children.

  Stevenson has a reference to this story in RBAE 5 : 544. Ḳaklo weeps because he is blinded and cannot guide the people during the migration. Duck comes to his aid. — Ḳaklo is an important impersonation in the initiation ceremony. No reference to the tale has been found in recent years and it is certainly not generally known today.

and then the two next eldest, to search out the route to the Middle. They did not return. He sent the youngest boy and girl. They cohabited and the koyemci were born. The kachinas originated in crossing a river. Meanwhile Ḳaklo had become blind with weeping, his face coursed with tears (as his mask) and his voice cracked like the Duck's, who, the wisest of all creatures, answered his duck-like call. She guided him by the sound of his ceremonial shells he put around her neck, to a great body of water which he could not cross. Rainbow Worm heard the shells and promised if he received prayersticks to carry Ḳaklo across the water. As Ḳaklo gave him the sticks the rainbow printed itself on Ḳaklo's mask. Rainbow set him down on the northern shore of the Sacred Lake and from the nearby Koyemci Mountain he heard the babblings of the offspring of his transformed brother and sister and learned the misfortunes of his people. In Kachina Village (below the lake) the kachinas heard the cries of Duck near Kachina Village and Pautiwa sent a Salimopiya to summon Duck. Pautiwa told Duck that at the sound of the ceremonial shells of Ḳaklo, which he wore, the madness of the koyemci would pass away, and they would carry Ḳaklo on a litter to Kachina Village where he was to be taught his chant. His sight was restored when Culawitsi lit new fire. The koyemci waited for him on the shore of the lake and bore him back to his people, singing about the prairie dogs that watched them from their holes. In this way was instituted the coming of Ḳaklo (at initiation of children). He told the people their lost children had become kachinas and recited his chant in the six kivas. He breathed into the mouths of four hearers, who thereby became the Ḳaklo cult group. The koyemci bore him back to the west. The two Anahoho sought their brother meanwhile all through the ruined cities of their people, and led by the Salimopiya they returned now with faces blackened and marked with their own hand-prints in their despair. They were beside themselves and climbed to the housetops, looking down all the chimneys to find their brother, and, when they did not see him, throwing the chimney pots to the ground. People brought them other pots and baskets; they looked into all of them as if they were chimneys and threw them to the ground where the Salimopiya destroyed them as offerings to the dead and the kachinas. *Cushing RBAE 13:398.*

THE GREAT CONFLAGRATION[1]

The "ripening" of the earth by fire is not mentioned in recent origin tales but it is a common belief in Zuni and given as the origin of diminutive animal fetishes, etc.

A. The earth was still soft and there were many monsters. To prepare it for habitation the Primal Twins shot their lightning

[1] Indexed: Conflagration, world. Game, Ahaiyute kill their playmates in, B.

arrows and the earth heaved and was covered with fire. Lime is believed to be the burned bones of animals caught in this fire and lava, *apkunia*, their burned blood. *Cushing RBAE 13: 389; ibid 2: 14; Heye Museum 8: 32.*

B. The Ahaiyute had power to cut each other in two with their turquoise rabbit sticks. Neither suffered harm, but when human children begged to play the game the latter did not revive. Therefore the people were angry at the Ahaiyute who shot their arrows at the sun and caused fire to sweep the country. Animals were shrunken and burned to stone (fetishes) and corn was converted to the burned stores now found. *Stevenson RBAE 23: 57.*

ADDITIONAL TALES OF THE SUPERNATURALS

The kachinas are characters in Zuni tales of all kinds and are therefore included under other sections of this collection; for references see Index of Proper Names, in forthcoming volume Zuni Ceremonial Tales. Besides the role the kachinas play in the usual Zuni folklore, the ceremonial tales reserved for the volume of Ceremonial Tales are chiefly concerned with incidents of kachinas and kachina impersonators. The kachina tales recorded by other students which are abstracted here are those that for various reasons do not find place in the other groups of tales in these volumes.

POCIYANKI

Pociyanki is a supernatural patron of the medicine societies. He is not impersonated as a kachina. He is addressed in cult prayers, Bunzel 805, where he is named doubly from Keresan prototypes: Iyatiku ("mother," the corn fetish of the Keres), Pociyanki (culture hero of certain eastern pueblos). The incidents given by Parsons below are the usual Keresan tales of their supernaturals. Pociyanki is referred to Cushing RBAE 13 : 388; 426; Stevenson 49. In RBAE 2: 16 he is described as a culture hero who appeared on earth as a poor despised boy, and is the patron of the medicine societies.

A.[1] In the beginning Poshiyanki was created in the waters of the earth as counterpart to the Sun in the sky above. He journeyed to the Sun to pray him to deliver mankind from the dark inner womb of Earth, and in answer to his prayers Sun impregnated foam and the Primal Twins were born to lead the people to the upper world. *Cushing RBAE 13: 381.*

---

[1] Magical impregnation: Sun's rays on mist or foam.

B.[1] Poshiyanki and Lea (Spanish *rei*) held a contest of their magic powers. The former was short and the latter tall and the former proposed to test which one should be touched first by the rays of the rising sun. Poshiyanki won. The second contest was of ownership of animals. Lea called domestic animals and Poshiyanki game animals and game birds. Poshiyanki won for he had four times as many as Lea. Poshiyanki taught all the ceremonies of the medicine societies. When he disappeared under the earth, he did not die. Poshaiyanki is also credited with bringing the domestic animals, note 2. *Parsons JAFL 31: 262.*

C. Poshaiyanki contested with Shumaekoli as to their rain powers, and Poshaiyanki lost. They matched their animals and Shumaekoli lost, having only woodrat, deer, jackrabbit and rabbit, and Poshaiyanki all the rest. Poshaiyanki's brother forbade him to continue these contests and stoned him when he refused. *Parsons JAFL 43: 5.*

THE SANTU

The Santu is a Mexican santo toward which Zuni observes the usual rites of a medicine bundle. The two major ceremonies are the lying-in of the santu, *santu tcalia*, which falls four days after the end of the New Year taboo, and during which clay objects representing wealth are made by anyone desiring to do so and placed around her altar for magical impregnation; and the autumn santu dance during which the santu is placed in a shelter of boughs in the plaza before the church and is entertained for four days by a dance danced by the young people of both sexes from six or seven years old to nineteen or twenty. The dancers are divided into two sets which dance alternately and join forces for the final appearance. It is one of the most charming dances in Zuni and is described in tales reserved for "Zuni Ceremonial Tales." See also Parsons MAAA 4 : 171.

Until Cushing's time, RBAE 13 : 337, the santu was housed in a shrine in the old Spanish church now in ruins. She was a Virgin of Guadelupe and in 1871 was carried off by a party of vandal Americans. A St. Francis was substituted, but the Zuni continue to regard the santu as feminine and she is called our maiden, *elle*. She is housed now like any medicine bundle in the house of her "father", and anyone may visit her and leave pennies in her dish, asking for healing or fertility. This is done chiefly by Mexicans. The Zuni associate her specifically with fertility: women obtain blessing in childbirth, and men good fortune with domestic animals.

[1] Test: Sun's rays strike first.

The long ceremonial tale of the Santu which is reserved for "Zuni Ceremonial Tales" includes *Magical impregnation: sun impregnates maiden,* an adaptation of the birth in the manger, and various medieval incidents of the Virgin. The following is a version of the same tale:

A Mexican girl was impregnated by Sun and when they saw she was pregnant the soldiers guarding her attempted to kill her. She was saved by Sun and directed to go to Zuni. As she went she blessed those who pleased her and cursed those who did not. Her twins[1] (girls) were born at Kachina Village in a corral, and the pig and dogs who licked the babies were blessed with many offspring and the mule who did not was refused offspring. In Zuni the twins became santus and the younger went south to other Zuni tribes. The mother chose to go to Acoma with the he·matsi dancers.[2] *Parsons JAFL 31: 258.*

THE GAMBLER OVERCOME BY THE AHAIYUTE[3]

This story should be compared with the tales in the usual Ahaiyute cycle where the Ahaiyute are overcome and eaten as a feast, thereupon killing their victors and emerging alive from their noses. In this tale the Ahaiyute are saved before they are actually eaten, and take revenge. The Cushing version names the gambler as Mitsina, a kachina not otherwise mentioned, and describes his mask and costume. In Culin's "Chess and Playing Cards" p. 782, Smithsonian Museum, Report of National Museum 1896, Cushing refers to this tale, describing Mitsina as the Eagle Star God and attributing to this incident the eaglefeathers still used to decorate the war canes, which are the property of the Ahaiyute. The Boas version does not identify the gambler as an impersonation.

A. Mitsina was a bad kachina and therefore barred from Kachina Village by the kachinas. He lived alone and killed those who lost to him in coliwe. The Ahaiyute twins of Face Mountain lost to him and were trussed before the fire in preparation for his feast when the Ahaiyute twins of Corn Mountain, staking their Ahaiyute weapons on the game, overcame him and set them free. They distributed all the stores the gambler had accumulated and plucked out his eyes. He found a piece of pitch which he lighted to guide him to Kachina Village. Eagles and Crows, who before this were

---

[1] Variant: She had one child, who became the santu, JAFL 31: 259, note 1.

[2] Indexed: Magical impregnation: Sun impregnates maiden.

[3] Gambler overcome by the Ahaiyute. Origin of spotted or black plumage in fire, A.

white, flapped into his pitch light and the feathers took on their present coloring. Mitsina is represented in the dance with holes in his mask for eyes, a wretched loincloth and a torch of pitch pine. *Cushing 385.*

B. A gambler named Takyel'aci won the lives of the Ahaiyute twins in a game of coliwe. Their grandmother took the Ahaiyute coliwe sticks to four girls and sent them to save their "brothers." The first three lost but the youngest burned the gambler's set of sticks and won when she substituted the ones Ahaiyute grandmother had given her. When the Ahaiyute were released, they cut out the gambler's eyes and threw them to the east and west as morning stars. The gambler took a crystal ball and transformed it into a ball of fire which he rolled after the Ahaiyute. They told all the people to close their doors, however, and the ball of fire rolled past harmlessly. *Boas JAFL 43: 45.*

KACHINA ORIGINS

Origin accounts of various kachinas are included in Bunzel's discussion of "Zuni Kachinas". Very few of them make use of widespread folklore incidents; typically they describe some event at Kachina Village or on the occasion of a kachina dance in Zuni that is said to have set a custom. They were told by Informants 8 and 3. Those tales in "Zuni Kachinas" which are part of the usual Zuni origin cycle have already been discussed.

ATOCLE.[1] When the earth was soft Atocle (Su'uki) used to steal and eat the babies their mothers had put down while they worked in the fields. She was a cannibal with bare feet and long toenails. The people finally tracked her to her cave to the south of Zuni (Su'ukonakwi) and killed and buried her. One of her pursuers made a mask resembling her so that she could dance at Zuni and came in for the mixed dance. At first mothers hid their children but then they used her to frighten them and make them mind. She put two little children in her basket to frighten them but in four days they died. Since then she shakes her stick at them instead. *Bunzel 938.*

TCILILI. When the earth was soft Tcilili stepped on the babies their mothers had laid down in the fields while they worked. His big feet killed them (as an impersonation he wears bear's paws on his feet) and he ate them. The people sent him away, and he comes sometimes as a solo dancer with Towa Tcakwena. *Bunzel 1020.*

---

[1] Indexed: Origin of mask, Atocle.

AHE'A (HE·MOKÄTSIK[1]). In Kachina Village when all the kachinas were ready to come to Zuni for the initiation their old great-grand-mother protested that Kolowisi (horned serpent fetish) should not come without her. The kachinas thought she was too ugly and left her behind, but she followed them and at last they let her come to bring the blessing of her old age to Zuni and to suckle Kolowisi at the initiation. *Bunzel 986.*

O'WIWI. The grandfather of the Mahetinaca is an old, old man who followed his grandchildren and joined their dance though they were secretly ashamed of him and tried to leave him behind. He is a hunting kachina and brings his animal fetishes setting them out ceremonially and feeding them with the blood of game. He tried to take a human wife and at last one girl who was very poor accepted him. When he removed his costume he was young, and had all kinds of valuable possessions. *Bunzel 1063.*

NAWICO. Nawico is the sweet corn (which he brings in the bundle of willow sticks he carries in his hands). When the customs of the initiation were being instituted they asked Nawico to watch the shadow of the church till it reached a certain point and indicated that it was time to whip the initiates. This is why he comes at initiation of boys into the kachina society. *Bunzel 991.*

UPO'YONA. When the customs of the initiation were being instituted, they sought someone to sit in a swing in the kiva and echo the calls of the kachinas in the plaza. They asked Pautiwa for his son Upo'yona, and therefore he comes at initiation. *Bunzel 996.*

ANAHOHO. These kachinas have existed since the emergence. They wear crow-feather collars and give warning of evil as crows do, especially warning of Navaho raids. They dipped their hands in the blood of the slain Navaho and marked their masks with bloody hand marks, as they appear today. Since they foretell evil their office is equally to take away evil by exorcism. *Bunzel 994.*

KUKUCULI. All the directions were represented by kachinas except the sky. They called the sky person. He was Kukuculi and the headmen of Kachina Village made the buckskin bundle the Mixed Dance uses for a drum and assigned him as solo dancer of that dance. *Bunzel 1026.*

LAGUNA TCAKWENA. In the beginning there was only one Tcakwena dance in Zuni, the Towa Tcakwena. As an act of friend-ship the dancers from Zuni went to Laguna and danced Tcakwena for four days. They learned Laguna songs and dancing positions there, and when they returned people liked the new style of the dance and always retained it along with the old form. They brought a Laguna kachina with them, Hatacuku, who always comes paired and whose mask resembles the Koyemci masks but is not surrounded with ritual. *Bunzel 1023.*

TOMSTINAPA.[1] Pautiwa sent Tomstinapa as solo dancer with the mixed dance "to bring his sweet voice to Zuni." His call is noted for its beauty. *Bunzel 1024.*

BEAR KACHINA. In the beginning the Beast Gods of the medicine societies lived at Cipapolima and sent White Bear to guard the south and Black Bear the east, Mountain Lion the north, Wildcat the west, Knife Wing the sky and Badger the world below. Black Bear hibernated and when he woke at the first thunder of spring he was lonely and started for Kachina Village to find company. He lived there and they put him into the mixed dance. He is a medicine society member and after he has danced in the mixed dance, a medicine society entertains him and gives him a bundle of prayersticks to take back to his home in Cipapolima. *Bunzel 1028.*

YA'ANA. On days when the people of Zuni plant prayersticks the kachinas wait in Kachina Village to receive them. One day one kachina went hunting and when he got back there were no prayersticks for him. He cried and the tears are to be seen now on his mask and his call is Ya'ana (alas!). *Bunzel 1040.*

DEER KACHINA. In the beginning the people had no game but rabbits and small birds. The hunters' society had a rabbit hunt and the kachinas at Kachina Village listened to hear whether they prayed for deer. At last the society sang their deer songs and the kachinas sent Hehe'a out to get a young deer to take to Zuni. Coyote went too. He chased the deer and taught the people to kill and skin it and lay it out with prayer meal. Then the deer was alive again and returned to Kachina Village. *Bunzel 1041.*

HETSULULU.[2] In the beginning a good pekwin planned a dough-ball game to make his people happy during the days after the winter dances when the kachinas had gone away. The breadstuff they threw in the game was an offering to the kachinas and pleased them. Pautiwa misunderstood and thought the priests had called a kachina to come to Zuni, so he selected a poor little kachina who had no (human) father and mother to make prayersticks for him. The kachinas dressed him though he had no valuable beads to wear, and gave him clay balls to throw in the game. He went to Zuni

---

[1] For the full tale of how Tomstinapa came to be solo dancer of Tcakwena, see "Tomstinapa and Kukuculi," reserved for "Zuni Ceremonial Tales".

[2] Contrast this story with: Famine is caused by misuse of corn in a game.

and when the people began to play he gave his call and joined them. (The people put the clay balls in their storerooms to increase their corn.) He always comes for this game and sometimes in the mixed dance. *Bunzel 1048.*

THE GREASE BOYS.[1] Two boys lived with their grandmother on the sand hill south of Zuni. They lived on woodrats. They were so poor they had no clothing at all and they were ashamed to be seen naked. Their grandmother told them to go to Kachina Village and ask the kachinas for clothing. The kachinas clothed them, gave them dried venison and told them to dance in Zuni with the mixed dance. Because they had no moccasins, they were to take turns carrying each other on their backs. Their grandmother was very happy because they would not be lonesome any more. *Bunzel 1051.*

MAHETINACA.[2] Four Bat Girls (not yet made ugly) accosted a boy at the spring and took him to their home. On the fifth day they left him alone while they went food gathering and Butterfly Girl took him to her house. She had Spider Woman spin her web over her house to keep out the Bat Girls. When they tried to break in, the web caught in their hands and feet and made them webbed and the soot and burnt corn Butterfly Girl blew over the web made them black. They retaliated by giving the Butterflies bedbugs. While they were mourning over their mishap a Mahetinaca came. They scorned him because he was ugly and covered him with the dirt they had been covered with. Mahetinaca has always been disliked since this time. *Bunzel 1057.*

EAGLE (K'ÄK'ALI). The eagle impersonations are said to have been brought with the Hilili dance (in which snakes are worn) forty years ago from Hopi in order to ensure eagles' nesting on Corn Mountain. *Bunzel 1067.*

NAHALICO (CRAZY GRANDCHILD). Nahalico was condemned to wear a headdress of four stiff turkey wing feathers to punish him for hunting turkeys secretly and wantonly. This is why he is called crazy. *Bunzel 1078.*

YEBITCAI. Yebitcai were Navaho impersonations which the latter offered the Zuni seventy-five years ago to cure their epidemic of mumps(?). It is danced around an open fire at night. Since then Zuni men have danced this dance. *Bunzel 1083.*

---

[1] Indexed: Kachinas at Kachina Village provide clothing.
[2] Indexed: Helpful animals: Spider protects with web. Cp: Origin of black plumage in fire.

II. THE AHAIYUTE ADVENTURES

The stories included in this section make up a loosely coordinated Ahaiyute cycle of which the chief themes are ridding the earth of monsters and the twins' acquisition of rain-making powers. The Ahaiyute figure, of course, not only in this popular cycle but in tales of every sort. Their birth and leadership at the Emergence has already been described in the discussion of that story, and they are the heroes in any number of tales of courtship and witches and deserted children that are included in other sections of this collection.

The series of Ahaiyute adventures as it exists today contains some of the most widespread incidents represented in Zuni. Incidents such as *Underground to the Monster* and the *Cannibal Eagle*, with its trick of crawling into a moosehide to be carried to the eyrie, of deceiving the eagles by false evidence of death, its conversation with the eaglets about their parents' return, are told over great areas to the north of the pueblos. Incidents of the latter tale are recorded from the Mackenzie Valley[1] and the Plateau[2]. Other widespread tales in this cycle are the *Cliff Ogre*[3], the *Toothed Vagina Woman*, and the European tale of the *Changed Headbands*. With the exception of the last, these incidents are all stories of western North America, and their prominence in the pueblos[4] seems most likely due to pueblo contact with the Navaho and Apache[5]. This makes more interesting the fact that fifty years ago this cycle was not told of the Ahaiyute. The Ahaiyute in Cushing's tales are the supernaturals who gave to Zuni the great *comatowe* rites connected with war and weather control[6], the mischievous boys who tease their grandmother, kill Cliff Ogre, and obtain the rain making powers, and the quarrelsome youths who pick fights in an "opposite" world before the emergence and cut the first people into final shape, see Index. The incidents, *Underground to the Monster*, *Cannibal Eagle* and the *Ghost Pursuit*, though Cushing does not tell them of the Ahaiyute, he gives as a popular tale of a hero who is the son of Rain. Even the names of the Ahaiyute were not the same in Cushing's time. He gives always Ahaiyute for elder brother and Matsailema for younger brother[7]. At present Ahaiyute is their collective name, Matsailema the elder

---

[1] E. g. Conversation with Eaglets, Petitot 114, Hare Indians.
[2] E. G. False blood and brains, Boas, RBAE 31: 613.
[3] Bibliography, Waterman JAFL 27 : 49.
[4] For Sia, Stevenson RBAE 11 : 47, 52; for Cochiti, Dumarest MAAA 6 : 218.
[5] For Navaho, Matthews MAFL 6 —135; for Apache, Opler ms.
[6] RBAE 13 : 421.
[7] Cushing 65.

and Uyuyewi the younger, the two latter being forms of the usual Keresan names. Mrs. Stevenson reverses the terms for elder and younger brother. She refers to them always as the gods of war but it is probable that her informants called them the Ahaiyute.

The *Theft of Rainmaking Objects* is a strictly pueblo tale and is found in practically all pueblo collections. The usual pueblo introduction to this tale, the Old Woman Giantess who carries off the two boys in her basket after several escapes, is not known in Zuni. The *Death in the Nose* incident is a tale that belongs specifically to Zuni. The sequence *Death in the Nose; Theft of Rainmaking Implements; Sham Pursuit; Drowned Grandmother*, is fairly fixed in Zuni mythology, see table below. The *Sham Pursuit*[1] is a favorite pueblo tale and quite common on the Plains.

The usual pueblo incident of the Ahaiyute, the *Visit to the Sun*, their father, to obtain powers occurs in the *Kana·kwe, War with the*, see Index, and is often told of other heroes. Similar incidents, *Travels with Sun*, and the *Father quest*, are told in various tales in Zuni but never of the Ahaiyute.[2]

The *Ghost Pursuit* is a common pueblo origin tale of the scalp dance, a ceremony under the protection of the Ahaiyute.

The combination of incidents in the various tales of the Ahaiyute cycle may be seen from the following table: —

The Adventures

A, Ahaiyute overcome Monsters, A (7), I: 51.
   B, (7), I: 56.
   C, (8), I: 62.
D, Ahaiyute obtain Ceremonial Objects (8), I: 68.
   E, (3), I: 75.
   F, Parsons JAFL 43 :32—35.
   G, Handy JAFL 31 : 462.
H, Bunzel AES 15 : 282.

I, Cushing, 175—184.
J, Loc. cit. 381.
K, Loc. cit. 425.
L, Parsons JAFL 36 : 155.
M, Stevenson 49.
N, Bunzel AES 15 : 281.
O, Boas, JAFL 35 : 79.
P, "The Son of Rain" (not the Ahaiyute), Cushing 65.
Q, Handy JAFL 31: 462.

---

[1] Bibliography BBAE 59 : 97. It has been recorded also for the Lassik, JAFL 19: 137.

[2] For these incidents see Index of Incidents, vol. II.

	A	B	C	D	E	F	G	H	I	J	K	L	M	N	O	P	Q
Contest with Bear																P : 65	
Underground to the Monster	A	B				F								N^1	O^2	P : 79	
Death in the Eyes	A	B														P : 72	
Cliff Ogre	A	B									K					P : 75	
Headbands changed	A																
Toothed Vagina Woman	A																
Cannibal Eagles		B		D												P : 84	
Descent of Cliff: Bat Woman		B														P : 87	
Death in the Nose		B		D	E	F		H									Q
Theft of Rain-Making Implements		B		D^3	E^4		G		I^5								
Sham Pursuit		B		D	E	F				J							
Powers tried on Grandmother		B		D^6	E^6	F^7	G		I^6								
Ghost Pursuit	A		C									L	M				

THE AHAIYUTE DESTROY MONSTERS
A (7), **I**: 51; B (7), **I**: 62; C (8), **I** : 68

Cushing 65 (not Ahaiyute); 425, abstracted I: 293
Parsons JAFL 43: 32
Boas JAFL 35: 79 (not Ahaiyute)
Bunzel AES 15: 281

A^8

Ahaiyute adventures: Cloud Swallower is killed from the shelter of a tunnel made by Gopher. Cannibal Owls are blinded and killed by exploding salt kernels in their fire. Cliff Ogre who has a horn on his forehead and kicks people over a cliff is thrown to his children to eat. The Ahaiyute exchange headbands with their dangerous wives and their wives' father kills the latter

---

[1] Not underground.
[2] Incorporated in a European tale.
[3] From Saiyaƚia.
[4] From Atocle.
[5] From the Uwanami.
[6] Power tried: bringing flood.
[7] Power tried: whipping rite.
[8] Indexed: Underground to the monster. Death in the eyes. Cliff ogre thrown as food to his children. Headbands changed. Toothed Vagina Woman. Origin of pubic hair from Coyote. Pursuit by dangerous women: rolling skull. Ghost Pursuit. Origin of scalp dance.

in place of their lovers. The Toothed Vagina Women are rendered harmless by artificial penises of hard wood. Coyote gives the women pubic hair. The Ahaiyute are pursued by the skull of a woman they have both slept with and killed, and her ghost is made harmless by the institution of the scalp dance.

The Ahaiyute overcame a giant elk Cloud Swallower, who ate the clouds and caused drought. Gopher tunnelled to his heart and asked Cloud Swallower for the hair over his heart with which to make a nest. In the spot thus exposed the Ahaiyute shot him from the shelter of the tunnel and escaped before the monster ripped it open with his horn. Gopher examined the monster's body and declared it lifeless and the Ahaiyute threw his organs to the sky where they became stars.

The Ahaiyute blinded and overcame the cannibal Owls by exploding salt kernels in the fire in Owls' house. They allowed two young owls to live and decreed that their food should be rabbits.

The Ahaiyute threw over the cliff a giant called Forehead Horn who used to pretend he had a cramp in his knee and kick people down a cliff where his children ate them. The children realized whom they had eaten when they got to his horn. The Ahaiyute killed the children.

The Ahaiyute overcame an old woman and her granddaughter who both appeared as young girls. They married them and exchanged headbands with them after the women were asleep. Their father came in the night and cut off the girls' heads instead of their lovers'.

The Ahaiyute took seven men with them to provide a husband apiece for the eight Toothed Vagina Women and their grandmother. They each took artificial penises of oak and of hickory. They drummed and danced for the women. At night they broke the teeth from their vaginas and left them. Coyote came and gave them his hair for their pubes. The women were harmless after that.

The Ahaiyute slept one after the other with a dangerous woman and killed her. She revived four times and they repeated. The four skulls of the women they had killed rolled after them and they took refuge in the midst of dancers, in sunflowers, under wings of bluebirds, and in the ceremony of the Knife Society at Cipapolima where they were taught the observances of the scalp and finally rendered harmless the ghost of the dead. (Followed by the account of the institution of the scalp dance, reserved for volume, Zuni Ceremonial Tales.)

B (7)[1]

This version follows very closely the Cushing tale of the Son of Rain. It opens with Cliff Ogre thrown as food to his children; Underground to the monster; Death in the eyes (owls), as in version A.

[1] Recorded by Ruth Bunzel. Indexed: Cannibal Eagles. Descent of cliff: Bat Woman. Taboo on looking. Taboo on passing through tall growth.

The Ahaiyute filled a jackrabbit's guts with blood and daubed their necks red in order that an eagle should carry them to its ledge as food for its children. The latter were afraid to touch them because they talked. The Eaglets told them their father returned with the first sprinkle of rain and their mother with the fourth. When the Eagles came, the Ahaiyute killed them both and took their feathers but spared the Eaglets, decreeing that they should eat rabbits henceforth.

They could not get down. They attracted the attention of Bat Woman below who ascended, filled her basket with downy feathers for her nest, and took the twins down in her spider web basket. Against her directions, they opened their eyes during their descent, and all fell together. They told her not to pass through a sunflower patch on her way home but she disobeyed and the feathers flew away as summer-birds.

C. The Ghost Pursuit (8)[1]

Stevenson 49 Benedict I: 54 Parsons JAFL 36 : 155; MAAA 4: 28, 29

The Ahaiyute are pursued by the skull of a woman they have both slept with and killed, and her ghost is made harmless by the institution of the scalp dance.

This tale is founded on the belief that dead victims whose ghosts have not been ceremonially dealt with by the scalp dance are dangerous. The places in which the twins take refuge differ in all tales but refuges in ceremonies of the medicine societies are popular.

Younger Brother Ahaiyute carried the lunch for a day of hunting. They found a Navaho girl who was left alone in a hogan and Younger Brother lay with her and gave her the lunch in payment. Elder Brother protested and Younger Brother directed him to do likewise and afterwards they would kill her that she might not cause further trouble between them. They did as he suggested and started for home. The girl's corpse pursued them. They ran first to Cipapolima (sixty miles) for refuge but the medicine societies were at Zuni for the annual ceremonies and they retraced their steps to Zuni. Little Fire let them sit in the midst of the crowd, Uhuhukwe behind the altar, Big Fire, Hunters' Society, and Bedbug Society put them under the protection of the beast gods, White Bear, Wildcat and Mountain Lion respectively. Ciwanakwe put them among the women so that she would not find them, Ne'we·kwe with the choir, Cuma·kwe in the middle of their women's dance, Snake Society by the headmen at the altar. Knife Society, the tenth society, taught them the rites of the scalp dance and made the ghost harmless. Followed by the account of the institution of the scalp dance, reserved for volume, Zuni Ceremonial Tales.

---

[1] Indexed: Pursuit by dangerous women:corpse. Bird tracks on altar, ambiguous. Origin of scalp dance. Pursuit through series of ceremonies.

19

THE AHAIYUTE OBTAIN THE RAIN-MAKING IMPLEMENTS

A (8), I: 68; B (3), I: 75

Cushing 175, abstracted I:293   Handy JAFL 31:462

Cp. Parsons JAFL 43 : 34

Death in the Nose

Parsons JAFL 43 : 34   Handy JAFL 31 : 463

Bunzel AES 15 : 282   Benedict I: 72

Drowned Grandmother

Cushing 183   Handy JAFL 31: 462   Cp. Parsons JAFL 43: 35

The incident of the Ahaiyute's revenge after their bodies have been consumed in a feast is told as a separate incident by Handy and Bunzel. The cannibal is identified as Atocle or Suyuki and the old woman kills them as in the version below by biting their necks while she pretends to be lousing them. They place their voices in all her domestic furnishings and accuse her of eating dung. They get into her nose and she dies, whereupon they emerge unharmed. In the Handy version they pretend death to lure their enemy into roasting them.

In Parsons and I: 72 the Ahaiyute take part in an initiation of Saiyalia boys and are killed by the whipping they receive in this ceremony. They are cooked for the initiation feast and kill the Saiyalia in the same way. In the two versions in this volume they then steal the rain-making objects, stuff the dead cannibal's skin for a sham pursuit, and finally in their absorption in bringing rain with their new game drown their grandmother in the resulting flood. In the Cushing 183 version of the Drowned Grandmother pepper plants grow from her body, and in the version, I : 74, she is rescued from drowning. The idea in these three stories is that she was the person on whom the Ahaiyute first tried out their new powers of rain-making.

The Parsons version is told to a different theme: in this tale the Ahaiyute do not go to get rain-making powers from the Saiyalia. Their objective is the Saiyalia's specific knowledge, the initiation ceremony of the kachina society. The Ahaiyute themselves lose their lives in this initiation and when they have come to life again and returned they try it out on their grandmother who is killed and comes to life again. The Zuni do not now phrase the whipping rite as a ceremonial death and resurrection, though they do so phrase the initiation into the medicine societies, and this tale gives an interesting folkloristic association with the whipping ceremony. The Cushing story of the Ahaiyute's adventure in obtaining the rain-making implements differs considerably from the other versions, see abstract below 293.

A (8)[1]

This version opens with the story of the *Cannibal Eagles*. The Ahaiyute find the Saiyaɬia initiating their children, are whipped also and die of it. The Saiyaɬia cook and eat them, but the Ahaiyute call out from everything in the room and make the Saiyaɬia sneeze them from their noses. They kill the Saiyaɬia, stuff one and drag it after them to scare their grandmother. They steal the Saiyaɬia's sacred rain implements and when they use them almost drown their grandmother. The second time they hunt for eagle feathers they are successful.

The Ahaiyute wanted eagle feathers for their arrows, but they could not reach the eagle's nest. They saw Eagle carrying a dead fawn to her ledge so they killed two young fawns the next day and clothed themselves in the skins. The mother Eagle took them to her nest as food for the young birds. When she left they took off their disguise. The eaglets told them that their mother would come back with the little rain, and their father with the big rain. The Ahaiyute killed the eaglets and filled the fawn skins with the feathers. They killed the eagles and laid them out as if for human burial. They put the feathers in their bags.

They could not get down, but Squirrel came to their aid. He brought a gourdful of pumpkin seeds ground to a meal and mixed with water, and he obtained pine seeds from Kachina Village to plant at the foot of the cliff. It grew magically and next morning they climbed down the tree and started home. Squirrel warned them not to go where there were any flowers growing or their feathers would become birds and fly away. They avoided three patches of flowers but not the fourth and the feathers became summer birds and flew away.

Their grandmother told them they must not go to Hecoktakwi where the Saiyaɬia lived. They promised to mind, as usual, and next day they started for the forbidden place. They found the Saiyaɬia initiating (Saiyalia) boys in their kiva. They entered and were whipped also. They died and the Saiyaɬia cut off their arms and legs and put them in the pot and cooked them for the newly-initiated Saiyaɬia to eat. They all feasted. Their voices (of the Ahaiyute) remained alive and called out from the Saiyaɬia's whipping blades that they had eaten dung. The Saiyaɬia broke the yucca blades and everything else. The noses of the Saiyaɬia were running and they were sneezing, and soon the Ahaiyute jumped out. The Ahaiyute caught up their bows and arrows and shot the Saiyaɬia who, when they died, turned into deer (as all kachinas are believed to do). They flayed and stuffed the largest with twigs and leaves. They took the rain-

---

[1] Indexed: Cannibal Eagles. Descent of cliff: magic tree. Helpful animals: Squirrel, inexhaustible food. Inexhaustible cup. Taboo on passing through tall growth. Death in the nose. Voices placed in domestic objects. Theft of rain-making implements. Sham pursuit. Drowned grandmother. Helpful animals: Squirrel: ascent of precipice.

making things of the Saiyaɫia, the lightning frame and the arrows and thunder stones. They dragged the stuffed deer along and before they reached their home, they called to their grandmother that they were being chased. She ran to aid them and hit the stuffed deer until she was exhausted.

After they had eaten they started to play the rain-making game. This brought so much rain that their grandmother bobbed up and down in the water. She was saved. The Ahaiyute went again for eagle feathers. They found a nest on a ledge with eaglets in it. One brother handed his brother down and he killed the eaglets, but his brother on top was unable to help him up. Another squirrel came along and brought him up on his back. This time they avoided the flower patches and got the feathers safely home.

B (3)[1]

The Ahaiyute's grandmother told them not to go to Noponikwi. They immediately went and found Atocle Woman lousing herself. They shot arrows near her to attract her attention. She loused Elder Brother and bit him in the neck so that he died. She did the same to Younger Brother. She built a fire and put the two into the pot. When she had eaten, the basket in which she parched corn, the paper-bread stone, the stirring stick, the stew pot, and everything in the room cried out, "You ate dung." She broke up everything in the house, but still they repeated the words. She began to sneeze, and sneezed the two boys out of her nose. She fell dead but immediately turned into a deer. They killed the deer and stuffed the skin with cedar bark. Then they gathered up her rain-making implements and started home, dragging the stuffed deer. They called out to their grandmother that somebody was chasing them. She covered half her face with soot and half with ashes, and picked up the largest stick of firewood and beat the deer. They laughed at her. After supper, the Ahaiyute began to play their new rain-making game. It began to rain, and the water filled the house. When they went to find their grandmother, she was floating on the water drowned.

ADDITIONAL AHAIYUTE TALES

The Ahaiyute figure in tales of every sort. For the complete list of their exploits see *Ahaiyute*, in Index of Proper Names in the forthcoming volume, Zuni Ceremonial Tales.

---

[1] Printed only in abstract. Indexed: Death in nose. Voices left in domestic objects. Sham pursuit. Theft of rainmaking implements. Drowned grandmother.

THEFT OF THE RAIN-MAKING IMPLEMENTS[1]

Rain spoiled the Ahaiyute's hunting and they planned to capture the implements for rain-making. They went south where the red House of the Gods stood in great terraces like a high mountain and secured the aid of Centipede to climb the walls. He let himself down over the altar and on the first trip took the thunderstone and on the second the lightning shaft, while the gods sat wrapped in meditation in their ceremonial room. The Ahaiyute ran home with their spoil and rolled the stone and shot the lightning shaft. The storm shook Corn Mountain and completely flooded the house of the Ahaiyute. The boys took their game to the roofs, but their grandmother was drowned below. They buried her and red peppers grew from her grave. When the rain gods knew of Centipede's part in the theft they shrivelled his body as it is today, burned from handling the lightning. *Cushing 175.*

CLIFF OGRE[2]

A cannibal giant, Foretop Knot, also called Cloud Swallower because he ate the clouds and caused famines, lived on the edge of a precipice in the mountains to the north, and kicked those who came against him into the chasm below, where they were eaten by his children. The Ahaiyute determined to overcome him and end the drought. Spider Woman wove her web over his eyes so that he was blinded, and the Ahaiyute easily avoided his kick and beat him to death. Falling, his feet drove deep into the sands and he became El Capitan of the Cañon de Chelly. The Ahaiyute twisted the necks of his children, and allowed only the two eldest to live. One is Owl, whose neck still twists in every direction, and the other Falcon, who always perches on El Capitan, calling, "Father, Father." Because of this cannibal giant, people abandoned the prehistoric pueblos of this region. *Cushing 423.*

THE AHAIYUTE RESCUE MAIDENS FROM A MONSTER[3]

This tale of the Ahaiyute's rescue of distressed maidens from the power of monsters should be compared with the usual use of this incident, in *Marriage is taught by supernaturals to those who refuse it.* In this tale no courtship theme is introduced, see I: 296.

Two daughters of the village priest went to wash their clothes at a spring near Hecokta. Atahsaia, a demon as large as an elk with

---

[1] Indexed: Theft of rain-making implements. Helpful animals: Centipede scales wall. Drowned grandmother. Origin of plants from grave.

[2] Indexed: Cliff Ogre. Helpful animals: Spider blinds monster with web.

[3] Indexed: Origin of stars: the Ahaiyute become stars; monster's body. Sham pursuit. Supernaturals are sent to shrines. Origin of Milky Way. Death in lousing. Ogres, maidens delivered from.

body covered with black and white scales, large protruding eyes and teeth like crooked fangs, lived in his cave nearby. He had claws like a bear's and carried a large flint knife and a great bow. He saw the girls and howled his war cry which Echo redoubled. He led the girls to his cave, where he was accustomed to throw the bones of his victims into a chasm below, offered them babies' bodies, which they only made a pretense of eating, and ordered them to louse him. He prepared to kill them when he loused them in turn, but the Ahaiyute of Twin Buttes, who had heard his war cry, threw their water-shield, which protected the maidens, and then their arrow, which killed the demon. They instructed the maidens in the duties of priests toward the Ahaiyute and sent them back to their home, where their father assembled the priests and made prayersticks for the Ahaiyute. The latter, left alone with the dead demon, skinned and dismembered him, throwing his organs to the sky where they became stars. *Cushing 365.*

TURTLE'S WAR PARTY[1]

This pueblo tale of the despised animals, Worm and Turtle, who go on the warpath and overcome their enemies should be compared with the Plains tale of Turtle's War Party. This tale, like that of the Plains, is a social satire on the scalp dance, but in both regions it has been thoroughly adapted to the local warpath procedures. In this pueblo tale Turtle's role in the fight has become that of a shield on the backs of the Ahaiyute. This origin of the scalp dance should be compared with the more usual Zuni versions.

The Ahaiyute did not herd their turkeys carefully and they strayed near a pueblo and were killed for their feathers. One young turkey escaped, gobbling, "I-wo-lo-ka" (murder) and the Ahaiyute planned to take revenge. They took Worm and Turtle as their warriors and made arrows. They held the preparatory feast and council for the war path and their grandmother appeared as young and made woman medicine of her cuticle. The Ahaiyute loosened the bowstrings of the enemy with rain from their water shield, Turtle clinging on Younger Brother's back shielded the Ahaiyute in the pursuit, and Worm discharged the lizard leaves he had eaten and suffocated the pursuers. The Ahaiyute scalped their enemies and brought in the scalp dance, Turtle carrying the scalp pole, and frightening the old grandmother so that she ran out with her poker to fight too. The grandmother and Turtle apportioned

---

[1] Indexed: Cp: Turtle's war party. Sinew bowstrings slackened in rain. Helpful animals: Turtle provides shield; Worm disgorges stomach contents. Cp. Odors are dangerous. Women provide woman-medicine in war. Origin of scalp dance (Turtle's war party). Cp. Death in the eyes.

between them all the roles of the scalp dance. This was so hard on them that now the scalp dance requires many performers. The huge Turtle went off to the ocean leaving only his little children behind him (reason why turtles are small), and Worm has always been small since he disgorged himself in this fight. *Cushing 317.*

THE HOPI CHILDREN BECOME BIRDS[1]

The Ahaiyute went to Hopi during the Lapaleaka dance and were offered no food except by a poor old woman. They ground blue paint and called all the children to celebrate a dance with them. The twins painted the children and told them to hold to the ends of cottonwood branches. They sang and the children became chapparal jays, while the rest of the people of the pueblo, Awatowa, turned to rock. The Ahaiyute went back to their grandmother and they all separated to live in their various shrines around Zuni. *Parsons JAFL 43: 35.*

III. TALES OF COURTSHIP
THE RABBIT HUNTRESS: A (3), I: 76; B (7), I: 84[2]
Cushing 297   Parsons JAFL 43 : 42
Cp. Cushing 365, abstracted I: 293

A girl attempting to do man's work and hunt rabbits is caught in a cave by the cannibal Atocle. The Ahaiyute save her, and Elder Brother Ahaiyute marries the girl, thus teaching her a woman's proper duties. Their children are dangerous and kill their playmates in play. With their father they go to the Ahaiyute shrines to live.

The theme of all the versions of this popular story is that of the girl who, because she had no men able to hunt for her or her old parents, has attempted a man's role and is rebuked and taught her proper duties of marriage. The earliest version, Cushing's, ends with the admonishment of marriage by the supernaturals; they do not propose marriage and she marries the next man who asks her. In the other three versions, as in so many other Zuni stories of *Marriage is taught by supernaturals to those who refuse it,* the role of the supernaturals is themselves to initiate the non-conforming mortal into the joys of marriage.

---

[1] Indexed: Despised supernaturals refused food. Supernaturals are sent to shrines.

[2] Indexed: Marriage is taught by supernaturals to those who refuse it. Maidens who perform men's duties. Ogres, maidens delivered from. Game, Ahaiyute kill their playmates in. Supernaturals are sent to shrines. Kachinas become deer when killed, A. Origin of scalp dance, B. Orpheus, B. Inhalation, transportation by, A.

Versions A and B illustrate two approved narrative devices of Zuni. Version A is told in the most popular Zuni style. The outline of the tale is expanded by the incorporation of minutiae of everyday life until the story becomes an ethnological account of e. g. the making of the sand beds at birth by a woman of the father's family (for actual practice, see Stevenson RBAE 5 : 545), the feast that closes confinement, the presentation of children to the sun.

Version B illustrates another literary device of Zuni folklore. In this tale the Rabbit Huntress theme is only the introduction to a tale the body of which is represented by the story of the twin children of supernaturals who are ceremonially sent to shrines, and the conclusion of which is the popular Orpheus tale. In tales of this type, see Introduction, I : xxxiii, the elements are often loosely held together but the narrator is expected to follow through the consequences of the elements that have gone before. The pleasure of the audience in such a version is that of hearing several familiar elements told as one tale. There is a marked interest in Zuni in this sort of manipulation of incident and the more popular combinations become fairly fixed.

The tale, Cushing 365, is a story of the rescue of girls from an ogre by the Ahaiyute, but the girls have not assumed men's duties and they are not taught marriage.

A (8). A family had no man as breadwinner and the daughter attempted to hunt rabbits for them. She was very successful and spent the night in a cave without returning home. Atocle found her but could not enter the mouth of the cave. The girl threw out all her twelve rabbits and her clothing and the kachina swallowed them. She was trying to draw out the girl with her crook when the Ahaiyute's grandmother on Twin Mountain heard her cries. She told her grandchildren and they killed Atocle, who became a deer at death. They skinned the deer and took from its stomach the rabbits and clothing. They burned up the rabbits but killed twenty-four for her and returned with her to her home. Her father offered his daughter to the Ahaiyute and Elder Brother married her. The next day the girl brought her basket of flour to the Ahaiyute's grandmother. Though Younger Brother had been jealous and angry he greeted them in friendly fashion. The grandmother gave the girl a white blanket and a black woman's-dress and a dancer's kilt and dried venison, and they returned.

In a few days his wife had twin boys. The Ahaiyute summoned his grandmother to make the sand bed for the babies. She came with great excitement and pleasure and her grandson inhaled through a straw and drew his grandmother the last part of the way. She washed the babies and put ashes on their bodies and heated sand beds. The fourth day, before sunrise, the grandmothers presented the children to the sun. When they returned Ahaiyute grandmother washed the babies again and the mother left her sand bed. The grandmother gave her her bath and dressed her and took the sand from the bed out of the house. They feasted on fresh venison which the Ahaiyute had brought the day before for this purpose. The Ahaiyute grandmother returned to her home with a great pile of paper-bread and sweet corn cakes and a foreleg of venison. Younger Brother was delighted when his grandmother returned with the food.

The Ahaiyute's children in their play dismembered their playmates and mixed up their arms and ears when they put them back. Therefore the bow priest made proclamation that the twins should be killed on the fourth day. Ahaiyute dressed his children with the dancer's sash and the leather cap of the bow priests. They walked down between the double line of the people and were killed. The grandfather of the twins went to Pekwin and asked for the four games of the Ahaiyute and for bows and arrows for his grandchildren and for the Ahaiyute. The people made the games and Pekwin took them to the house of the twins' grandparents. That evening Ahaiyute's wife made the road with prayer meal and behind her walked the two Ahaiyute and the twins (revived) with their games in their arms. The Ahaiyute and his children went to their shrines and the mother returned to her home. That is why every year the people make the implements of their games for the two pairs of Ahaiyute twins.

B (7). A girl was the sole breadwinner for her grandparents. She finally persuaded her grandfather to consent to her hunting rabbits. She found only two rabbits and lost her way in a snowstorm. She took refuge in a cave. Atocle followed her and ate her rabbits and her clothing. The grandmother of the Ahaiyute heard her cries and the Ahaiyute killed Atocle. They ripped her stomach and took out the rabbits and the clothing. They cleaned her clothing and returned it but the rabbits they left for Coyote. They killed thirty or forty rabbits for her and returned her to her home. Elder Brother married her. Twin boys were born. Their father refused to give them bows and arrows because of the danger, but they visited an Ahaiyute shrine and the Ahaiyute of the shrine gave them bows and arrows, kick stick, stone knife, and rabbit stick. When they returned they cut each other in two and the pieces joined again without harm. Their father told them not to do it to the other children but the boys begged until they did. They killed all the children. The people came against them to kill them but they and their father escaped to shrines. The rabbit huntress married again as Ahaiyute had directed before he left the pueblo, and, after a Navaho raid, this husband introduced the scalp dance (which is under the patronage of Ahaiyute). One day his wife died. Followed by the *Orpheus* story (not recorded, see same incident as conclusion, II: 133.)

THE GIRL WHO REQUIRES A SCALP OF HER SUITORS (7), I: 87[1]
Published only in abstract

Bunzel AES 15 : 123
Bunzel AES 15 : 139, abstracted below, 334.
Cf. Cushing 185, abstracted below, 335.

Ahaiyute overcomes the Apache and marries the girl who has demanded that her suitors bring her scalps. His children are dangerous and they and all the family are sent ceremonially to Ahaiyute shrines.

The text versions of this tale by Bunzel are both by informant 7, who also told the tale abstracted here. In the first of the Bunzel versions the incident of Pautiwa's disapproval is introduced 127, 130, and is badly integrated with the rest of the tale. It does not appear in my version and is an incident that belongs properly with the second Bunzel version, a tale which breaks the story abruptly with the summoning of the Apaches and follows the fortunes of Pautiwa's children by a poor maiden, children who turn out to be lame and blind and have supernatural power. The first text version differs from the one abstracted here chiefly in that, in the former, Younger Brother Ahaiyute of Salt Lake is the final suitor of the girl and plans the Apache fight to obtain for himself (not for the mortal suitor) the scalps necessary to marry the girl. The consequences, in my version, of the aid he gives the girl's final suitor (the death of the rejected suitor, and the terror of the girl at the Apache war cry) therefore do not appear in the text version. These incidents should be compared with the tales of *Death Sought by summoning the Apaches*. The concluding incident, *Supernaturals are sent to Shrines*, is told in the Bunzel version exactly as in the one abstracted here except that in the former version the Ahaiyute children get their weapons from Middle Prayerstick Place instead of Corn Mountain and when they go to their shrines the elder son is placed at the shrine Snow Hanging and the Ahaiyute father goes to Middle Prayerstick Place. The other shrines are alike.

A very different tale of the girl who requires that her suitors bring her scalps is recorded by Cushing as a story of a Hopi maiden. After others have failed, an orphan boy enlists the aid of the village dogs

---

[1] Indexed: Marriage is taught by supernaturals to those who refuse it. Tests, marriage: scalps. Supernaturals sent to shrines. Game, Ahaiyute kill their playmates in. Origin of scalp dance. Cp. Death sought by summoning the Apache.

and with their help proceeds single-handed against Zuni, returning with many scalps. The story concludes with the triumph of the boy over his jealous rivals who have challenged him to a rabbit hunt to try to bring about his downfall.

The priest's daughter of Ḵakima demanded that her suitors bring her scalps. Men came bringing marriage bundles from Matsaḵa, Pinawa, Wimpiawe, Hampasa, Kwakina and Hawiku, but they failed to obtain scalps. Up by Salt Lake a boy heard of the priest's daughter and came to court her. She refused him also because he brought no scalps and he told the Ahaiyute of Salt Lake. They made arrows for him and sent Crow to call the Apaches. The last suitor and Younger Brother Ahaiyute went down to fight them and get scalps. The girl dressed early and went to her field and was surprised by the enemy. When she was surrounded by the fight she was terrified and the last suitor she had refused reprimanded her. The suitor killed many and at last was killed himself. Younger Brother Ahaiyute cut the scalps (including the hair and ears) and hung them on cedar boughs. He distributed them to all who came so that they became bow priests. For twelve nights they danced the scalp dance. Younger Brother Ahaiyute married the girl and she had twins who grew magically in four days and asked their father for bows and arrows. He refused because they were raw people and therefore dangerous but they went to the Ahaiyute shrine on Corn Mountain and got weapons there. They played at shooting at and restoring each other. The children in the village wanted to play too. Their father forbade it but at last the twins consented. They killed all the children. The people attacked the Ahaiyute children but were pacified by a despised old man. They sent the bow priest to the Ahaiyute father, who told the priest he and his sons were raw people and advised the people to make prayersticks for them and send them ceremonially to shrines. They did so. The younger twin remained in the shrine at Twin Mountain and the elder on Corn Mountain. His mother, father, sister and brother remained at Arrow Mountain and the father Ahaiyute went to the Salt Lake. That is why all these are Ahaiyute shrines.

AHAIYUTE MARRIES THE BOW PRIEST'S DAUGHTER (8), I : 87[1]

The proud priest's daughter who has ignored three ceremonies and refused the successful hunters to whom her father promised her, accepts the dirty little Ahaiyute. The jealous young men of the village challenge him to four races, which Ahaiyute wins with supernatural assistance. In the

---

[1] Indexed: Marriage is taught by supernaturals to those who refuse it: maiden. Despised boy wins maiden. Tests, marriage: killing a deer. Contests to retain wife: stick races. Supernaturals are sent to shrines.

last race the prize is the bow priest's daughter. After he succeeds in retaining his wife, she grinds for his family, and he returns as a supernatural to his shrine.

This long tale is a good example of popular Zuni narrative style. The story outline is expanded by description of everyday life, e. g. relations between parents and a daughter, courtship, marriage, and stick race contests. The elements of the tale are all familiar; the girl who secludes herself, courtship tests, the triumph of the despised boy, here the Ahaiyute, contests to retain wives, and the dangerous children of supernaturals who are sent to shrines. These elements are here woven into a story which represents the generic daydream of a Zuni male: an unprepossessing youth wins over all comers and triumphs when challenged by the losers. With this theme is interwoven as well the daydream of the Zuni woman: a girl is able to scorn the life that occupies other people and is sought above all women, finally being loved and married by the hero.

The bow priest had a daughter who never went out among the people. She wove and ground meal and made baskets continually. Her father was anxious that she should marry that her husband might help him in the fields. At the time of the winter dance series her father urged her to join the people but she would not even look at the dancers. Her father therefore made proclamation of a ceremonial rabbit hunt in order that someone would give her a rabbit and become her sweetheart. His daughter, however, ignored the preparations of food, she did not dress herself in the new clothes her father provided, and did not go out at all when the young men took the pretty girls on their horses for the hunt. Her father was not discouraged. He asked the village priest to ask Cuma·kwe for the yaya dance. Cuma·kwe made prayersticks and chose the girls to dance. They practiced at Heiwa kiva and danced the four days' yaya (shorter form). The bow priest cut a buckskin in two for new puttees for his daughter. Again she would not touch the beautiful clothing. She ignored the food preparations and did not even go to see Cumaikoli come in. After yaya her father asked the village priest for the Corn Dance but his daughter did not go out even to see the Corn Dance. Her father was in despair. He made proclamation that his daughter should marry a hunter who brought a deer. Four young men sighted a deer and the handsomest priest's son killed it with his arrow. He went to claim the bow priest's daughter. He brought the deer and they laid it on an embroidered blanket with its head to the east. The girl would have nothing to do with the suitor. He took his deer again and left. Immediately another came and another, but the bow priest's daughter refused both. For four days hunters came bringing the game they had killed.

The Ahaiyute came. Elder Brother disclaimed his rights in the deer for "it is not nice for two to marry one girl." Younger Brother took the deer to the bow priest's house. He was small and dirty and his hair was matted. The bow priest's daughter accepted him immediately. They clothed the deer with turquoise and made the prayers over it. Ahaiyute and the bow priest's daughter went to bed. The people of Matsaḳa sent a boy to visit the bow priest and return to tell them if his daughter had accepted Ahaiyute. They were angry.

In the morning, Ahaiyute came out of the bow priest's house and went to Corn Mountain to visit his grandmother. His elder brother had brought back the lights of the deer his brother had killed and teased their grandmother, telling her he had killed his brother. That morning they were waiting for Younger Brother but Elder Brother was jealous and said he would not speak to him. When his brother came in he forgot and embraced him. They ate and Younger Brother asked his grandmother for clothing to give to his wife. She gave him an embroidered woman's dress and a buckskin. Every day he went hunting and brought his game to the bow priest's house.

The young men were jealous and wanted to overcome Ahaiyute. They asked the priest's son whom the girl had refused to ask his father to ask the bow priest for a stick race. The priest went to the bow priest's house and Ahaiyute accepted. The priest told his son and the son gathered the best runners. For four days they practiced every morning. Ahaiyute never practiced. On the third day Ahaiyute went to his grandmother to ask for help. She said, "Go to the Owl and give him prayer meal." She gave him two buckskins and two black woman's-dresses to bet on the race. The runners selected a stick-race man to have charge of the ceremony and they used his ceremonial room for their retreat. On the night before the race the four who were to run went to the east carrying food for their forefathers to observe the omens. They made their offerings and returned without looking over their shoulders. They heard a crow but they did not know whether it was a good omen or a bad one. They slept in the ceremonial room. In the morning, early, Ahaiyute went to Owl Spring. He gave Owl prayer meal and Owl directed him to pull a feather from his left wing and carry it in the race so that his opponents would become sleepy. He told him also to choose the position on the right for the race. At sunrise, in their ceremonial room, the runners drank emetic and the stick-race man made the kick stick and prayed over it. The bow priest made the stick for Ahaiyute. When it was time for the race everyone came out in their best. Ahaiyute's wife was dressed in buckskin puttees and ceremonial dress. The bow priest brought out the clothing which Ahaiyute's grandmother had given and that which his family gave. Their opponents brought out what they wished to wager. All the goods were paired one against the other. The young men and women climbed up to the housetops to watch the race. The runners went out with folded arms to the starting place, a mile south of Zuni. Stick-race man tied their hair but Ahaiyute did not have any hair to tie. Ahaiyute wore the owl's feather in his G-string. He chose to have his father mark his kick-stick in the middle. Because of the owl feather Ahaiyute ran faster than his opponents and won all of the goods that had been wagered. Both sides feasted after the race. The runners planned a second race and challenged Ahaiyute. Again the runners practiced and observed the taboos in their ceremonial room. Ahaiyute did not practice. On the third day he took the garments he had to his grandmother's and she gave them back to him to wager on the next race. She told him to go to Tecamiḳa (Echo, a masked impersonation) and take him his batons to pay him for help in the race. The bow priest made batons for Tecamiḳa and tied on the feathers and painted them. He took them to the south where Tecamiḳa lived and Tecamiḳa gave him a ball of his cuticle which would make his opponents stiff and slow as Tecamiḳa is. Ahaiyute observed none of the taboos. On the night before the race the runners went out to observe the omens. They heard a coyote but they did not know what it augured. In the morning they drank the emetic. In the afternoon everyone gathered goods to gamble upon the race and they paired them in the plaza. Ahaiyute's wife dressed herself again in her best. Ahaiyute wore in his G-string the paint Tacamiḳa had given him and therefore won the race. In the bow priest's house and in the stick race house they feasted. The runners planned a third race. They challenged Ahaiyute and he accepted.

His grandmother told him to ask Hawk for help and Hawk gave him a feather from each wing to wear in the race. His opponents observed the taboos and made sacrifices, but for omen they heard a skeleton behind them. The people wagered their possessions. During the race the bow priest sat alone in his house with crossed ankles to lock the legs of Ahaiyute's opponents, and Ahaiyute won. For the fourth race his opponents challenged Ahaiyute to wager his wife. He got feathers from Hummingbird and spewed corn pollen over him to make him yellow. The opponents heard for their omen doves quarreling and the call of a crow. The bow priest's daughter dressed herself ceremonially as the prize for the contest and the stick-race man came to take her to the plaza to sit against the pile of clothing as prize for the winner of the race. Ahaiyute won and they feasted. The stick-race man refused to let them challenge Ahaiyute again.

The bow priest's daughter ground a great basket of cornmeal for Ahaiyute's grandmother and they took it to Corn Mountain. They stopped at Ololowicḳa and pushed a stone through the rock grooves with their feet to remove weariness. They remained four days on Corn Mountain, the girl helping the Ahaiyute's grandmother and teaching her to cook, and the Ahaiyute hunting. They were very happy. On the fourth morning, before sunrise, Ahaiyute and his wife returned to Matsaḳa, the girl carrying a large basket of dried venison from the grandmother. Ahaiyute, however, was a supernatural and after a while he asked his father-in-law to ask the village priest to make Ahaiyute crooks for him and his brother. He took them with him and returned to his shrine.

THE BRIDEGROOM IS REQUIRED TO KILL A DEER
A (7), I : 121, B (7), I : 126

Cushing, 104, abstracted below, 335. Bunzel, ms, abstracted below, 336.
Parsons, MAAA 4 : 302, abstracted Bunzel, AES 15 : 165, abstracted
  below, 335. below, 336.

The two versions in this volume of the marriage test of a successful deer hunt are excellent examples of the evenhandedness of Zuni sex ethics. In both cases a young person is obstructing marriage by the test imposed, but in one case it is a man and in the other a woman. In Cushing and in version A, the essential element of the tale is the trick by which the marriage test of a successful deer hunt is rendered impossible beforehand by the person who imposes the test. The supernaturals as usual teach the unwilling youth and maiden to accept marriage as their human destiny. The theme of the Cushing version is somewhat obscured by Cushing's narrative style but the motivation is clear in its main outlines. The girl is not only taught marriage but, like the youth in "Cactus Girl" by illness, she is punished for her pride by *Death in fall from sky*, a novel use of this incident.

In the rest of the stories that make use of this marriage test, the test is one possible of accomplishment. In the Bunzel AES tale the story is an origin myth of the *Liberation of game*, and the girl is the Owner of Deer, as also Cushing. Since the Ḳana·kwe impounded the game, I : 7, in the AES myth she is the bride of a Ḳana·kwe and when she returns to her human home none of her suitors are able to bring "her children", the deer. When the despised boy prays they come; he marries the girl, and deer are thereby liberated for human use. In this form the incident of this marriage test loses all ethical implications; it is not told to illustrate in any way the theme of proud girls who scorn their suitors. This appears true also of the Parsons version though it is too slight to indicate any definite theme. The "Turtle Husband", Bunzel ms, is similarly a tale of ceremonial origins, in this case of summer solstice rites.

Version B, "The Frog Husband", is an excellent illustration of a European incident reworked to a typical Zuni theme. It is the usual story of proud maidens who refuse marriage and are taught by supernaturals to accept it. The girl is punished by her humiliation at being forced to marry a frog, but he turns out to be a kachina and is successful in the *Contests to retain a Wife*. The tale concludes with *Supernaturals return to Shrines*. The same story is told with Pautiwa's son as hero and a different marriage test, II: 153.

A. YELLOW CACTUS GIRL (7)[1]

A hunter does not want to marry. He makes a successful deer hunt the marriage test, and whenever girls court him, prays to have the deer hidden so that he can send his suitors away. Cactus Girl punishes him with illness and cures him by teaching him the blessings of marriage.

A youth was courted by girls from three towns. He told them he would know if they were virtuous if he killed a deer next day and each day he prayed to have the deer hidden because he did not want a wife. Yellow Cactus Girl came to court him and when he sent her away likewise, she upbraided him for his duplicity and took out his heart. She left her basket and returned to her home. The boy sickened and his father set out to follow the girl and bring her back to cure him. Her basket directed him. He came to the house of the eight Cactus Girls. The girl who courted his son had been sleeping day and night since she returned and refused to see him. At last she agreed but refused to return with him to cure his son. She consented at the fourth request. When she reached his home she swept the room and supported the boy so that he got up and ate. That night her mother, her sister, her aunt and her cousin came in succession as beautiful women and slept with the boy, teaching him to marry. After four nights the boy was cured and married Cactus Girl. She was supernatural and had to return to her home. She enjoined him to take as wife the next girl who asked him. The boy grieved for her, however, and followed her tracks. He found only a cave full of cactus. That is why Zunis have only one wife.

B. THE FROG HUSBAND[2]

Frog kills a deer after three suitors have failed, and wins the priest's daughter. The pueblo challenges him to a race with his wife as stake and he wins by the aid of the kachinas who come as rain. Eventually he returns to his home in Kachina Village.

---

[1] Indexed: Marriage is taught by supernaturals to those who refuse it: youth. Test, marriage: killing a deer. Heart of wrongdoer removed.

[2] Indexed: Test, marriage: killing a deer. Marriage is taught by supernaturals to those who refuse it. Contests to retain wife: stick race. Race won by storm. Supernaturals are sent to shrines.

The daughter of the village priest refused three suitors demanding that they bring her a deer. Frog went courting. He removed his frog shirt for the hunt, and Mountain Lion aided him. He fastened the venison and deer's head to a stick, resumed his Frog suit and hopped into the pueblo carrying his load. The girl could not refuse him and when they had retired for the night Frog sent her for water and removed his frog shirt. Next day he got another deer and showed himself in human form to the pueblo. The people said he must run fast to be able to get deer, so they challenged him to a stick race with his wife as the stake. Frog went to his home at Kachina Village for help and the kachinas promised to come as rain when he smoked the four cigarettes they gave him. The opposite side lost its kick stick in the flood and Frog won. Finally he returned to Kachina Village and his wife married again. When she died she rejoined Frog Man. That is why the dead live with their first spouses.

EAGLE MAN (7), I : 130[1]

Cushing 34   Bunzel AES 15 : 210 (6)
Benedict I : 173

The pet eagle to which the priest's son is devoted takes the boy to the sky because his sisters are jealous. The eagle marries the priest's son and teaches him to fly and hunt deer. Corpse Girls carry him away as their husband because he does not observe the taboo against laughing with them. He gets supernatural help and destroys their pueblo. The eagles send him home with presents and the despised old man of the pueblo ceremonially effects his return.

The widespread story of the man who goes to the sky with a sky maiden and dies because he breaks a taboo by going to a skeleton dance (for central Brazil, see Cherente, Oliveria, 18th International Congress of Americanists, New York, 1928, p. 395) is recorded by Cushing, above, in a version that closely parallels the present one; not by Bunzel. In the present version the tragic ending *Borrowed Feathers:* Eagle Girl pulls the feathers from her husband's coat in mid-air so that he is killed, Cushing 53; Bunzel 234, has been obviated by including miracles wrought by supernatural assistance. One of these miracles is the magic practise by which the pueblo of the skeletons is lifted up as on a mesa and the dead marooned, and the other that of the despised old man who by means of borrowed ceremonial objects succeeds in recovering the hero and is thenceforth honored. Another informant used

---

[1] Indexed: Eagle wife. Animal coats removed. Origin of spotted plumage. Corpse Wife. Taboo on laughing at dance of corpse girls. Despised old man has power.

the magic of the house raised into mid-air also in the tale of the Big Shell Priesthood, II : 160. In other respects Cushing's story follows the present version except that slight stock subsidiary incidents are introduced into one or the other. Thus in Cushing the eagle in its flight attracts the attention of the people in the field by singing a song instead of directing the hero to tie "sleigh" bells to his feet; the people who provide the hero with cooked meat in the sky are the storks and herons (a reference to their power of "cooking" their food in their bodies before they regurgitate it in feeding their young); when the hero escapes from the pueblo of the dead the bones follow in a cloud and Badger saves him by "shooting" his scent, *Odors are dangerous*, a favorite Shoshonean incident. Cushing on the other hand, does not include the incident of Eagle Chief's kindling fire for the hero by dropping from a height nor the discoloration of the eagles' coats in the smoke (see same informant, I : 173). Cushing's version of this story is stylistically unlike a Zuni tale.

The text version, on the other hand, by informant 6, is an excellent example of the freedom with which folklore incidents may be recombined and the care with which narrators take account of the implications of such recombination. The introduction to the Bunzel tale is the incident of *Bungler's instruction in hunting*, where a supernatural shows the ignorant hunter how to kill game without mess. The character of the hero, according to this incident, is therefore that of a bungler, and this character, set in this first incident, is kept throughout the story. He ignores the directions of the supernatural as to his route and falls in with the ghost girl; he is an inept lover with his ghost wife; the Eagle Girl laughs at him for a simpleton when he offers his rabbits to the skeleton which in the daytime represents his ghost wife; when he wishes to return to his home he deceives Eagle Girl instead of asking her help and is therefore killed. The sequence of the two marriages is reversed, and the conclusion becomes that of AES 15 : 246, etc.: at death the spouse returns to the spouse he has abandoned, here a ghost girl.

The priest's son had a pet eagle and spent all his time providing it with food. His sisters were jealous and planned to kill it. Therefore the eagle refused to eat and planned to return to the sky. The priest's son asked to go too. She took him on her wings and directed the boy to fasten bells to his legs so that they would attract the attention of his sisters in the fields as the eagle flew by. They passed through the first heaven of the crows, the second of chicken hawks, the third of night hawks, and arrived at the fourth heaven where the eagles lived. Eagle Girl set up a stone knife and ripped off her eagle coat. She was a young girl. All the eagles returned from hunting and took off their coats and were human. The priest's son married Eagle Girl. She made him an eagle suit and finally he learned to hunt. He could not eat raw meat so Eagle Chief, the father of Eagle Girl, rose to a great height and dropped down on a pile of wood, kindling it. The youth broiled venison. However, the smoke colored the white eagle coats and spotted them so that they sent him to an old man and woman near by who cooked for him. They warned him not to go to the west to the pueblo of the dead. He disobeyed and saw the bodies lying everywhere about in a large pueblo. In consequence, that night two Corpse Girls followed him to the eagle country. They fell through the hatchway like dead bodies and stood up beautiful girls. His eagle wife directed him not to laugh back at them and he would be free. He disobeyed her counsel and the girls caught him by the arms and took him to their peublo. They took him to bed with them but they stank and he did not have intercourse with them. In the morning they were dead bodies. The old man and woman who lived to the east directed him to scatter prayer meal around the pueblo and shoot an arrow into the circle he had made. The pueblo would be raised up as if on a mesa and when he shot it would be carried away to the other side of the ocean. The old woman also gave him lukewarm water to purge himself from his contact with the dead. He obeyed their instructions and overcame the pueblo of corpses. The eagle people sent him back to Zuni with new clothes and presents because his people were continually looking for him. A despised old man got supernatural help and borrowed a *mili* from a medicine man and brought back Eagle Youth. The family made the old man a member of the family and fed him. Therefore old men are still honored.

THE TARANTULA STEALS THE YOUTH'S CLOTHING (8), I: 137[1]
Cushing 345

The priest's son refuses six sisters who woo him. A tarantula tricks his clothing from him and he is shamed and marries an ugly girl. The Ahaiyute recover the lost clothing by a magic deer hunt.

The Cushing tale is an animated version collected fifty years ago. It lacks entirely the motif of the humiliation of a person who refuses marriage and hence the incident of the six sisters who court the priest's son and his concluding humiliation are omitted. The hero is described merely as a priest's son in training for a race and the tarantula accosts him while he is running his daily course. The essentials of the story are those of the present version: the manner

[1] Indexed: Cp. Marriage is taught by supernaturals to those who refuse it: youth is shamed. Tests, marriage: grinding corn. Stolen finery recovered. Paste animals are magically animated.

20*

in which Tarantula tricks the clothing from the boy, and the help of the Ahaiyute by means of a magic deer hunt for which they make the game out of paste. The same scalp dance call is used to attract Tarantula's attention, "The skulkers are skulking". Cushing's version gives four preliminary futile attempts to recover the clothing before the aid of the Ahaiyute is invoked: the people attempt to dig out the hole with hoes, and Kingfisher, Eagle and Falcon are charged to seize him as he appears at the edge of his hole. Minor variations in Cushing's version are: the paste animals are made of ground white sandstone by Ahaiyute's grandmother; Tarantula is burned in punishment and his ashes form the present little stinging insects. This incident is found widely in Asia and America, see Dähnhardt, *Natursagen*, Vol. III, 151ff.

The story has much in common with the tales of Underground Dwarfs, II : 186. The incident of the lost clothes and their recovery is used also as the introduction to the tale of the faithful wife who followed her dead husband, Bunzel ms, abstracted, II: 299.

Pekwin's son was handsome and a great hunter. He went on alternate days to hunt and to hoe his fields. All the girls wanted to marry him. Six sisters came with baskets of cornmeal to court him. He was not at home but his mother gave them presents of food. The eldest came again that evening and they went to bed together. The priest's son, however, refused to sleep with her till she had ground corn next day. His mother gave her hard popcorn and she was unable to grind it. She went home very sad.

A tarantula was jealous of the priest's son's fine clothing. He helped him hoe for two days and then proposed that he put on the boy's clothing so that the priest's son could see how he looked in the boy's clothing. The tarantula ducked into the hole and the boy was left naked.

His father searched for him late that night. At Owl Spring Owl told him where his son was and that the Ahaiyute could recover the boy's clothing. The priest found his son, and the boy's mother took him food. His father went to the priests and they made prayersticks for the Ahaiyute in the chief ceremonial room of the pueblo. Next day Pekwin took them to the Ahaiyute at their shrine at Eastern Road. Their grandmother gave him food and the Ahaiyute promised to help in four days. They directed that all the women make paper bread and pulverize it and bring it to the bow priest's ceremonial room.

On the fourth day the Ahaiyute came to this ceremonial room and stirred water into the paper-bread meal and made images of deer and rabbits and small game. They took them out and placed them near where Tarantula lived. All the people joined in the pursuit of the Ahaiyute's game. Tarantula heard them and joined too. When he had gone a little distance from his hole they caught him and stripped him of his clothing. They gave him a new name and made him hateful so that everyone would step upon him and kill him. They gave his clothes to Pekwin's son but for four days he was not to wear them. The people despised him now and he married an ugly girl, because his mother had thought he was too good for the girls who asked him. That is why handsome boys marry homely girls and that is why the tarantula is killed at sight.

Lazy Bones (6), I: 145[1]

The priest's son marries a despised girl. With supernatural aid she outstrips others in grinding hard corn for his mother and making sweet Indian corncakes, and four times she wins contests with four girls to retain the priest's son in marriage: (1) longest hair, (2) plumpest, most hairless legs, (3) dimples, (4) largest genitals.

This tale is the generic day dream of the Zuni woman. The unprepossessing girl is chosen by the handsome man and surpasses all others both in occupational and in beauty tests. The masculine counterpart of the theme is the tale, I: 87—121. Characteristically enough in view of the lack of differentiation in Zuni between day dreams of men and women, the present story was recorded from a male informant.

A handsome priest's son was a great favorite. Lazy Bones, a big, ugly girl who had had her hair shingled on account of sores, lived with her grandmother. They were poor and she had not been taught to care for the house. The priest's son met her at the spring and asked for a drink. He came to her house. Her grandmother was happy and brought out roasted rabbit's guts to eat with paperbread. He slept there and came again next night. His family supposed he had married the nicest girl in the village. On the second day the girl's grandmother told her to get a basket of corn to grind for the priest's family. They were displeased when Lazy Bones appeared as the wife of their son. They gave her popcorn, which is too hard to grind, and did not help her shell it. She took it to her home to grind and Spider Woman sat under her little hair braid and gave her supernatural power. Spider Woman was good to her because she and her grandmother had not destroyed her home in the rafters. The priest's son's four sisters sent the youngest to see if Lazy Bones was able to grind and they would not believe her report. When Lazy Bones returned with her meal the basket was piled high with the finest flour. All the people saw and knew she was married to the priest's son. His mother was glad when

---

[1] Indexed: Despised maiden wins hero. Helpful animals: Spider Woman; Bees. Contests to retain husband: beauty contests.

she saw the fine grinding and after the girl had eaten she gave her buckskin for puttees and new moccasins and a big bowl of stew and filled her blanket with paper bread. The old grandmother was overjoyed.

There was a rabbit hunt. On the third day the girl went to the priest's house to get corn to grind to make sweet corncakes for them. She wore her new high moccasins and was much more presentable. However, they gave her hard popcorn again. She ground it at home with the help of Spider Woman and after her old grandmother had masticated it (the usual way in which the cakes are sweetened), she (grandmother) went to Corn Mountain to ask the bees for honey. They told her to make holes in the plaster of the oven and while the cakes were baking they came down the chimney and deposited honey. The girl took the corncakes to the priest's house. They had never tasted such sweet corncakes. They gave her a woman's blanket dress and a belt and stew and paper bread. Next day she wore her new clothes to the dance and her husband was proud and much in love with her.

The girls of Matsaḳa were jealous and four sisters laid a plan. They sent the youngest to the bow priest to ask him to make proclamation that the girl who had the longest hair should marry the priest's son. Lazy Bones and her husband heard the proclamation and were sad. He did not want to leave her. She called Spider Woman and four times during the night or when her husband was in his field, Spider Woman rolled the girl's hair on her stirring sticks and later on the rubbing stones until it fell to her buttocks. On the fourth day, when she dressed her to appear in the plaza for the dance, she pulled it to her knees and curled her bangs. The priest's son was in his mother's house dressed in his best. The bow priest made proclamation and came separately for the four sisters, the priest's son, and for Lazy Bones, and took them to the plaza. All the people were assembled. He told the priest's son to unwrap the hair of each in turn. The four sisters had long hair, but Lazy Bones had the longest. The people laughed and the four sisters ran home with their blankets over their heads.

Another family of four girls made a plan and went to the bow priest. They asked him to make proclamation that the girl who had the plumpest white hairless arms and legs should marry the priest's son. Lazy Bones went to her corn room and prayed to Mother Corn. Yellow Corn Woman told her to grind and bring water in which she had put the fine white meal. Lazy Bones told her grandmother to warn her if her husband was seen coming and she went to the corn room, where Corn Woman became a person and washed her legs and arms, making them white and smooth. On the fourth day, when she dressed for the contest, Corn Mother washed her again. Again the bow priest came for her and the other contestants. The priest's son removed their footless stockings and his wife's legs surpassed those of all the others.

The third family of four girls challenged her to show the best dimples. Lazy Bones had no dimples. Spider Woman took a weaving stick and dipped it in corn pollen and made dimples in both cheeks. In the contest, the girls each smiled at the priest's son and his wife's dimples were the most beautiful.

The fourth family of four girls challenged her to show the largest genitals. Spider Woman filled a gourd with water and washed her and her genitals became as large as the gourd. In the plaza the bow priest laid on the ground an embroidered blanket and the priest's son put each girl upon it and exposed her genitals. His wife's were the largest and she won the fourth contest.

That is why despised people marry the nicest people in the pueblo and then they become nice also.

THE GAMBLER MARRIES MOUNTAIN LION'S SISTER (7), I : 160[1]

The unsuccessful gambler marries Mountain Lion's sister, who gives him power to recover all that he has lost, and to win all the possessions of the pueblo.

This story pictures the role of Zuni supernaturals in aiding the ruined gambler, as in other tales they come to the aid of young people who refuse to marry. It makes use of the incident, *Coyote attempts to marry Mountain Lion's sister*, cp. Cushing 215 and Handy JAFL 31 : 458, abstracted below 336.

The priest's son lost everything at gambling, including his sister, and left the village. Mountain Lion's sister had previously married a kachina but her brother had told her that she must take as her husband any man who watched her from the doorway till she looked up four times from her weaving. Coyote discovered this and told the priest's son, who took advantage of the information and married her. She clothed him well and gave him power to go back to the pueblo to retrieve his losses. He won back his sister and also Pekwin's two daughters. He won all the possessions of the village and they called the Hopi to kill him and Mountain Lion Girl. By Mountain Lion's help the youth and his wife escaped to Cipapolima and the Hopi were so angry at being foiled that they destroyed the village which had sent for them. The latter retaliated and this is the cause of the old Hopi-Zuni wars.

THE GIRL WHO MARRIES A KACHINA (7) I : 165

A girl falls in love with a kachina in the dance and after she has accompanied him as his wife is tired of her bargain and is taken to wife by another kachina.

---

[1] Indexed: Ruined gambler retrieves his losses. Coyote attempts to marry Mountain Lion's sister.

This is a realistic little story. A very different tale of the girl who married Ayu Tsawaki, a kachina not described in Bunzel RBAE 47, is told, Parsons MAAA 4 : 302, and is summarized below, 335.

A Zuni girl fell in love with Ayu Tsawaki, a kachina in the Mixed Dance, and insisted on accompanying him to Kachina Village. There she found he was only a lesser figure and when the dancers came back next time to dance in Zuni the girl hid from him in one of the kivas. He cried and searched but though the people knew where she was they would not tell him. Maiyapone took her back as his wife and after that she never could come back to Zuni. For this reason girls are afraid to fall in love with kachinas.

The Girl who marries a Bird (6), I : 166

The long-tail chat, Onoļiķa, always came to drink at the spring when the four daughters of the village priest went for water. The girls tried to find the pretty bird. He appeared as a handsome man and talked with them. The next night he came again as a bird and when they followed him into the sunflower patch they saw the handsome boy again. He married the eldest sister and that is why married couples live in the house of the girl's mother.

The Girl who marries the Horned Serpent, I : 167[1]
Published only in abstract
Cushing 93   Stevenson RBAE 5 : 544

A maiden washes at the sacred spring of the Horned Serpent (Kolowisi) and finds a little image, which becomes a human baby when she takes it up. At night it becomes the Horned Serpent and her lover. She is sent back ceremonially to his shrine.

All the versions of this tale are comparatively unelaborated. The superstition given in version B is deeply felt and carefully regarded in Zuni, where no woman ever immerses herself in bathing. The tale in the other three versions (references above, and version A) follows more closely the usual Shoshonean tale of the image a girl finds in a spring, an image which becomes a serpent at night and the girl's lover. It is associated in Zuni with Kolowisi's spring at Caliente. The story concludes in all versions with the usual *Supernaturals are sent to Shrines*. Cushing adds that as she goes off with the Serpent it becomes a handsome man.

A (3). A girl washed in the Hot Spring at Caliente (Tokanaia) and she saw a little image in the spring. She put her hand in, and

---

[1] Indexed: Water baby found in a spring becomes Horned Serpent and the husband of girl who found it. Snake Husband. Supernaturals are sent to shrines.

when she took the image out, it was a little human baby. She took it home and nursed it. That night it became the Horned Serpent and wrapped her in its coils. Her father was a priest and he commanded the people to make prayersticks for the Serpent. The people formed on both sides of the path, and the Serpent came out with his bride and passed between the double line of people. They scattered prayer meal upon them as they passed through their midst to Kachina Village.

B (3) (A "true" story commonly told by parents to their daughters to teach them not to enter water to bathe.) A Hopi girl went every day to wash her clothes in the spring where the Horned Serpent lived. As she washed, she sat in the spring the better to rinse her clothes. She became pregnant. The people knew that she was never seen with the young men, and they wondered. At last she died and they buried her. After four days they went to the grave and found that it was empty. The Horned Serpent had taken her.

The Hunter is Pursued by Women

With this group of tales should be compared also the stories of the Ghost Pursuit, which are also tales of men fleeing from a woman, in the latter case a woman they have killed; and the dance of the corpse girls, I : 134. All these groups elaborate the theme of the timid male, and there are no comparable Zuni stories of rape. See Introduction, I : xxi. This group of tales has a nightmare affect, and the pursuing female is identified successively with the woman with a toothed vagina, the female scare kachina Atocle, corpse girls, and rolling skulls. Version B is incorporated as an incident in the tale, "The Hunter is transformed into a Coyote", II : 110, and version C incorporates the story of "Eagle Man", I :130.

A. HE IS PURSUED BY THE WOMAN WITH THE TOOTHED VAGINA (8), I : 167[1]

It is only from the conclusion of this tale that it appears that the woman who pursues the hunter is Toothed Vagina Woman. Goat Man finally kills her by cohabitation and saves the hunter.

Crazy (i. e. erotic) Woman made advances to a hunter, who fled from her. Gopher Man hid him in his cheek, Badger Man in his genitals, Big Fire Society among its dancers, but she discovered him each time. At last he escaped to Goat Man who threw him

---

[1] Indexed: Cp. Pursuit through series of ceremonies. Pursuit by dangerous women: Toothed Vagina Woman. Helpful animals: Gopher hides pursued in cheek, Badger hides pursued in genitals. Killed by cohabitation.

down and killed her by cohabiting as she had wanted to kill the hunter. The conclusion states: "Therefore women no longer have toothed vaginas."

B. HE IS PURSUED BY CORPSE GIRLS (3), I: 169[1]

A hunter escapes from four girls who become corpses at midnight, is hidden by Gopher in his cheek, and saved by Goat Man, who kills Skeleton Girl by intercourse.

A rabbit hunter lost in the storm took refuge in the ruins of Ḳakima, where four beautiful maidens entertained him. The stew they gave him was made of boiled flies. They invited him to sleep with them, but he was afraid and did not have intercourse. At midnight he woke. They were skeletons covered with dried flesh. He ran out and saw a light elsewhere in Ḳakima. Four more girls invited him in. Presently the four he had abandoned came as dead persons and danced, rattling their bones. He excused himself to defecate and took refuge with a Gopher who hid him in his cheek, pretending he had a toothache. Eldest Sister Skeleton Girl discovered him and he ran to Goat Man. When Skeleton Girl came, Goat Man seized her and threw her down. He killed her by intercourse. She had a goat child and the taboo on eating goats is due to the fact that they are the offspring of the dead.

C. HE IS PURSUED BY ROLLING SKULL (7), I: 171[2]

This tale combines the pursit with a dangerous woman with "Eagle Man", I: 130. In the end the hunter returns, as often in these tales, to his first wife whom he had abandoned, here a ghost wife.

A hunter overtaken by a storm, came at sunset to a house in which a fine looking woman lived with her daughter. She gave him food and offered him her daughter to sleep with. In the morning the girl was a skeleton and the house in ruins. The hunter ran away in terror and the skull of the mother pursued him. He tried to take refuge in a Hawiku yaya dance, a Navaho war dance, a Laguna harvest dance, under a bluebird's wing, and in a sunflower's "ear", but the skull found him. Porcupine directed him to bring piñon gum and bury it a hand's depth outside his door. He took refuge with Porcupine. Skull stuck in the piñon gum and Porcupine set fire to it and destroyed Skull.

---

[1] Indexed: Corpse wife. Pursuit by dangerous women; Corpse Girls. Helpful animals: Gopher hides pursued in cheek. Killed by cohabitation.

[2] Indexed: Corpse wife. Rolling skull. Pursuit by dangerous women: rolling skull. Helpful animals: Porcupine provides gum in which rolling skull sticks. Pursuit through a series of ceremonies. Animal coats removed. Eagle wife. Origin of spotted plumage. Taboo on laughing at dance of corpse girls. Borrowed feathers.

The hunter married Porcupine Girl and trapped wood rats for her father. After four years Eagle Girl lit on a tree one day while he was hunting and turned herself into a human being. They played together all day. He wanted to go with her to her home and she carried him on her back. She flew through the bluebird's heaven, through the heavens of eight other birds, and finally reached the eagles' heaven. The eagles came home. They removed their coats and were human. The hunter could not eat his venison raw. Therefore Eagle Chief had his people gather wood and he rose to a great height dropping suddenly on the pile and kindling it. The smoke spotted the eagles' white coats and they complained, but the hunter told them they were better that way. His eagle wife gives him an eagle coat and teaches him to fly. He leaves her, however, for Chicken Hawk Girl, with whose people he has to eat insects. In order to provide himself again with venison he has Chicken Hawk Girl get his eagle coat from the eagles' house. While hunting he meets Eagle Girl mourning for him, and they are reconciled. Still on the quest for food to which he is accustomed, he falls in with girls from the pueblo of the dead who follow him to eagle village. His eagle wife tells him he will be safe if he does not laugh with them but he breaks this taboo and is snatched off by the corpse girls. He is successful in destroying the pueblo of the dead, but decides to escape to his home on the earth in his eagle coat. His wife pursues him and snatches the coat from him in punishment of his unfaithfulness. He falls to earth, and in death returns to his first wife, the skeleton girl whose mother pursued him as a rolling skull.

D. HE IS PURSUED BY ATOCLE (8), I : 174[1]

The origin of the Atocle mask. When Atocle imprisons him in a cave a rabbit hunter escapes by leaving his voice in his excrements. He dies in four days and becomes Atocle.

The rabbit hunter overtaken by a storm found refuge in a cave and was followed by Atocle. He ate his rabbits whole and entered the cave. The hunter made an excuse to leave the cave and placed his voice in his excrements which he sprinkled with cornmeal. They answered four times until they were cold. He ran toward the pueblo. His four sisters heard his calls from a great distance. When he was overcome by the cold they carried him into the pueblo but he died in four days in spite of their efforts and became Atocle because he had been afraid of the ogress. That is why it is known that people become kachinas at death.

---

[1] Indexed: Pursuit by dangerous women: Atocle. Dung informant. Origin of mask, Atocle.

KIOTAKE MARRIES THE ŁAMANA (6), I : 175[1]

The boys of Zuni carry out a trick upon the despised orphan who has been scorned by the girls going for water. They dress one of themselves in women's costume and she pretends to take Kiotake to her home. The boy and his grandmother are humiliated.

No supernaturals are introduced into this story to bring blessing to the despised. In the hands of his fellow mortals he fares badly. I have heard of this same joke being played in Mexican villages of the Rio Grande.

Kiotake was a despised boy who lived outside the village with his grandmother. He wanted to marry. He accosted the girls on their way to the well for water but they ignored him. He told his grandmother they had been nice to him and she washed and cleaned his sores and loused him. He put a bow-guard on his wrist and admired himself in the mirror. That night again the girls refused, but one girl smiled at him in amusement and he thought she was being nice to him. He told his grandmother he would marry that night and she made a rabbit skin blanket for the marriage bed. The third evening a girl gave him a drink and humiliated him by emptying her jar afterwards and drawing fresh water. His grandmother made another rabbit skin blanket to give the girl when she came to grind and got snow birds ready for her to eat. The boys in the pueblo planned to play a joke on Kiotake. One of them borrowed women's clothes and impersonated a girl going for water. When Kiotake came the fourth night she gave him a drink and pretended to take him to her house. All the people watched from their housetops the despised boy being taken to marry the łamana (berdache). The pretended girl took him to a deserted room, a kiva, and said they would sleep together in the morning. Kiotake's grandmother was happy when he did not come home. Early in the morning she went to the village and asked in house after house for a coal for her fire in order to tell that her grandson was married. While she was spreading the news Kiotake discovered the trick that had been played on him. He cried out (a traditional song calling out his name) so that everyone heard. The people told his grandmother that her grandson had gone home crying because his bride was a boy. She ran home crying also. That is why people do not make presents beforehand for the girls their sons will marry.

THE PRIEST'S SON BECOMES AN EAGLE (8), I:179[2]

The priest's son is a great weaver and requires weaving as a marriage test. Three sisters fail and the fourth succeeds because of the aid of Spider

---

[1] Indexed: Despised boy is shamed by marriage to boy posing as girl.

[2] Indexed: Tests, marriage: weaving. Helpful animals: Spider Woman. Death sought by summoning the Apache.

Woman. To test his wife's affection her husband calls the Apache. He is killed but she saves herself and in eight days dances in the dance. Her husband returns and when she recognizes him flies off as an eagle.

According to old pueblo custom men were the weavers and this story reflects this division of labor. The Zuni distrust of demonstrativeness is given extreme expression in this tale. The test of his wife's affection planned by the young husband should be compared with the more usual use of the incident *Death sought by summoning the Apaches*.

The son of the village priest remained indoors all the time weaving. Every day girls came to marry him. Three sisters came and failed. Spider Woman offered to help the youngest and sat in her ear and directed her. The priest's son married her.

Whenever he came back from work she bothered him with demonstrativeness. She kept inviting him with questions, "Do you love me ?" He thought she could not love him very much and planned to test her affection. He sent Crow to call the Apache and directed her to put on full dress and bring lunch to him in the field. The Apache came and killed him but she saved herself. His father had a yaya dance called in eight days to see if the wife would dance. She did. Her husband appeared beside her in the dance and as soon as she recognized him he flew off as an eagle. Therefore the eagle is valued (because it is a priest's son transformed).

ŁA·WA (7), I : 182[1]

The origin of the Atocle mask. Atocle marries the hunter when her corn pollen sticks to the shell on the wall after four girls have thrown their meal and failed. She finally returns to Kachina Village ceremonially after "giving" her mask as a kachina impersonation.

The widespread pueblo story of the girls who are required as a marriage test to grind meal so fine it will adhere to an upright polished surface is used also in Parsons MAAA 4 : 322, abstracted below, 337.

The girls of four towns came to marry the great hunter Ła·wa (an edible green) who lived in an upper story. He required them to throw their meal against a shell on the wall. If it stuck he would marry them. They all failed. Atocle took corn pollen and filled her carrying basket with ła·wa. She asked in dumb show to marry the hunter. Her pollen all stuck to the shell and she married the hunter. He was terrified. In the morning she was young and beautiful. She lived with Ła·wa and wore her Atocle mask only

---

[1] Indexed: Tests, marriage: meal sticks to polished object. Origin of mask, Atocle. Marriage is taught by supernaturals to those who refuse it: youth. Supernaturals are sent to shrines.

when she went out. In four years she "gave" her mask to the hunter's father. She told him to copy it and have the bow priest make proclamation that everyone make prayersticks for her. She went out between double lines of the people, and took her prayersticks to Kachina Village.

PARROT GIRL

The tale of the girl who required parrot feathers of her suitors is said in Zuni to be a Hopi tale. In both the versions the story depends upon a two-fold association: the parrot feathers are a courtship test and hence imply a human wife; and they are an occasion for flirtations with parrot girls, hence they imply a parrot wife. The narrators of the two versions develop the theme differently. In Version A the secondary wife is given moral advice by her relatives and is made human by a medicine society, whereupon she enters the boy's household as his wife. After the death of Younger Sister Parrot Girl's husband, Hawk, she also is added as a third wife and the conclusion is, therefore Zunis sometimes have more than one wife. This refers not to institutional polygamy but to aberrant instances of a sort of concubinage. Version B, on the other hand, develops the theme without calling Zuni monogamy in question: Parrot Girl stays as his sister in his house with his human wife and the story continues with the story of a *Witch Contest*.

A (6), I: 184[1]

A despised boy goes to Mexico for parrot feathers for the priest's daughter who asks them of her suitors. He is carried by Hawk. Parrot Girls marry both the youth and Hawk. The youth therefore acquires two wives and Hawk's wife becomes a third when Hawk is accidentally killed.

A poor Hopi boy who lived with his grandmother went to court the priest's daughter who had refused all suitors. She asked for parrot feathers for clothing for her father's children (kachinas) and he set out for the south to get them. Hawk carried him, after shaking him out of his ugly skin and leaving him handsome. The Parrots gave him feathers in return for prayer meal his grandmother had provided and he and Hawk spent that night with the Parrots. The two younger Parrot daughters slept with the youths secretly and planned to accompany them to their homes. At the girls' advice the four escaped together before sunrise taking the feathers. The Parrots pursued them but when the girls chose to accompany

---

[1] Indexed: Despised boy wins maiden. Test, marriage: parrot feathers. Helpful animals: Hawk insures quick travelling. Transformation into human form, ceremonial.

their husbands they gave them moral advice about loving their spouses and not being jealous. Younger Sister Parrot Girl married Hawk and stayed with him. Elder Sister flew to the priest's daughter's house and spent the night on top of the ladder while the youth presented his feathers and married the girl. Next day he took Parrot Girl to his grandmother, slept with her that night and returned to the priest's daughter. In four days he came to get Parrot Girl to live with him as co-wife. His grandmother called the Horned Toads to make it possible for her to eat human food. They functioned as a medicine society and cured her of being a raw person. The two wives lived peaceably together. Hawk came to see his friend and in spite of warnings got within bow shot of a boy who killed him. His death left his Parrot wife alone and she too lived with A·lucpa. For this reason Zunis sometimes have more than one wife.

B (7), I : 190[1]

A despised boy goes to Mexico to get parrot feathers for the priest's daughter who asks them of her suitors. A Parrot Girl follows him back home and stays as his sister. The witches want to marry her and when she refuses, vainly attempt to overcome her when she goes for water. At the fourth attempt the Ahaiyute kill the witch girl who has become a corpse in order to kill the Parrot Girl.

The daughter of the village priest refused all suitors and demanded that they bring her parrot feathers. At last a despised boy who lived alone with his grandmother courted her and set out for Old Mexico to find parrots. Chicken Hawk joined him and chewed medicine which he rubbed over his body to make him travel fast. He also carried the boy up a cliff to the house of the parrots. Gila Monster carried him across a great river. He gave the parrots prayersticks he had brought and they gave him all the feathers he could carry. He slept with two of the parrot girls and Blue Parrot Girl accompanied him back to his home. She stayed with his grandmother and he went to claim the daughter of the village priest. In eight days the village priest called a muwaiya dance and supplied the parrot feathers. Blue Parrot Girl flew to his house and lit on the top of the ladder. Someone saw her sitting there and shot her. The boy cried when they put her body in his inner room. Chicken Hawk came and revived her, and she remained in the household as his sister.

The witches wished to marry the boy's sister, but she refused. They placed a new woman's belt in the path as she went to get water. She challenged the witch man to pick it up and give it to

---

[1] Indexed: Despised youth wins maiden. Test, marriage: parrot feathers. Helpful animals: Hawk insures quick travelling. Transformation by: magic belt; pitch and toss game; catching missile. Apparition impersonated to destroy enemies. Witch contest.

her, and promised to marry him, if he did. As soon as he touched it madness struck him and she reported it to the witches. Everyone who touched the crazy man became crazy also. The second time one of the witches challenged her to a game of pitch and toss. She refused to catch the ring and promised to marry him if he would do so. When he caught it he became a female rattlesnake. Men killed the rattlesnake. The next attempt was made by the witch girl who was head of the witches' kiva. She planned to transform herself into a dead person and kill the whole family by fright. She took a prayerstick the length of her forearm to a place where a Navaho had been killed. She summoned the dead man and neither ate nor drank for four days. On the fourth night she went again and the dead man made her a corpse. She went everywhere killing the people of the eastern pueblos and Mexico. She came back toward the pueblo. The Ahaiyute heard her coming. They laid a tree across her path so that she could not cross and challenged her. The Ahaiyute cut off the corpse's head with a stone knife but it rebounded from the ground and joined the body again. They shot an arrow into the brush and caused a great fire into which they threw her long prayerstick. When she asked for it again they made a duplicate by magic but when she used it against them it was powerless. They shot again into the cedar brush. Lightning came out from it and killed her. Therefore the witches were overcome.

THE SON OF RAIN (7), I: 194[1]
Cushing 65

The Cushing tale does not include the incidents of the shamed maidens and the *Apparition impersonated to destroy enemies*, and is told as the first of a series of incidents of the Sons of Rain which are told at the present time as Ahaiyute adventures, see I : 285. The Cushing tale has the same details as the present story: the attempt of the Rain father to prevent the encounter with Bear by hurling the lightning, the boys' persistence, Bear's remark that the arrow points are nothing but charcoal, and his death when he submits to the test. This tale is still regarded as the reason why bears do not now attack people gathering wood for arrows.

A secluded maiden is impregnated by rain in her sleep. The child went to get wood for arrows and his father Uwanami (rain makers) tries to prevent an encounter with the bears who live there by hurling his lightning. He has a bee helper and bets with two girls that the bee can carry anything. The girls give their clothing, bit by bit, to be carried away and are shamed because

---

[1] Indexed: Magical impregnation: rain. Mother sold to Bear for arrow wood. Apparition impersonated to destroy enemies. Helpful animals: Bee.

he saw them naked. He persists in obtaining wood for his arrows and the black bear allows him to take it on condition that the bear marry his mother. When the bear comes he criticizes the boy's arrows and the boy bets they are good enough to kill Bear. He accepts and is killed.

The family of the girls who have been shamed plan to kill him and his bee tells him they have summoned an apparition of the dead. He overcomes this by placing doughnut shaped breads by four fires. He kills both girls and transforms their organs into nighthawks and bats.

BUTTERFLY PURSUIT, A (7), I : 197; B (7), I : 199[1]
Bunzel AES 15 : 248 (6)   Bunzel ms (7) abstracted below, 337.
Handy JAFL 31 : 456

The good runner loses a hide and seek contest with a maiden and is killed. Tenatsali grows from his blood. In punishment a butterfly lures the eight sisters to pursuit. When they are naked, the butterfly shows himself as Ne'we·kwe and punishes them by having intercourse with them in their sleep and calling Coyote to do likewise, A; the butterfly shows himself as the hero and transforms the maidens into "crazy" (zigzag flying= nymphomaniac) butterflies, B.

In both versions in this volume and the AES version, two widespread pueblo incidents, the *Hide and Seek Game* and the *Butterfly Pursuit*, are integrated into one plot. The first develops again the theme of the man overcome and killed by a dangerous woman, this time a woman who challenges him to a hide and seek game with their lives as stake. The dangerous women are however eventually punished by the magic of the family of the victim, who create a butterfly, the design on whose wings the sisters wish to copy. They are betrayed into nakedness, using all their clothes in a vain attempt to throw them over the butterfly and capture it. They are then branded with their true nymphomaniac character.

On the other hand the Bunzel ms tale "The Origin of Ne'we·kwe" uses the butterfly pursuit incident in a tale to the theme of *Marriage is taught by supernaturals to those who refuse it*. It is an origin story of Ne'we·kwe Society and is a tale of blessings obtained by supernatural marriage. In the Handy version the girl is taught the designs by butterfly girls. There is no marriage.

The text version (6) is in the best Zuni tradition. Version A (7) printed here gives the characteristic stylistic differences between Informants 6 and 7 and Version B (7) is given only in abstract.

---

[1] Indexed: Hide and Seek with dangerous maiden. Bird search. Flute music magically produces butterflies. Butterfly pursuit. Origin of pubic hair, Coyote, A. Erotic maidens transformed to butterflies, B.

21

The Bunzel version carries through consistently the identification of the hero with Ne'we·kwe: Ne'we·kwe Topknot loses at hide and seek, is killed and restored, is himself the butterfly which lures the sisters, and finally takes his own shape at the spring in order to torment them in his own licentious character as Ne'we·kwe. The flute magic which is an essential element in all versions is slurred over (it does not belong to Ne'we·kwe) and the growth of tenatsali plants from his body is not mentioned (tenatsali has no association with Ne'we·kwe). Version A is also a Ne'we·kwe story, but Tomstinapa, not Ne'we·kwe is the victim of the hide and seek game. Version B is a Paiyatamu story (i. e. of Paiyatamu cult of Little Fire and Bedbug societies) and stresses the rite at the Paiyatamu altar and the power of Paiyatamu, which is associated especially with flowers, butterflies and pleasure, i. e. he transforms the girls into "crazy" i. e. oversexed, women by his flute magic. Ne'we·kwe Topknot (Bunzel version) on the other hand strikes them with a yucca ring to effect their transformation that they should always hover over the spring where he had punished them by refusing to let them drink when they were dying of thirst. Version A records a different punishment, a conclusion added also to another tale, I: 54, by the same informant: undesired and promiscuous intercourse in sleep, here with Coyote as well as Ne'we·kwe. Afterwards Ne'we·kwe marries them and provides well for them.

A. TOMSTINAPA AND NE'WE·KWE (7). Tomstinapa lived in a spring. One of eight evil sisters heard his kachina cry and challenged him to hide and seek with their lives as stake. She hid in a squash blossom but he could not find her. He hid in a large sunflower. She drew milk from her breast and discovered him. She killed him, cut off his head, and took out his heart. Where the blood dropped, tenatsali grew. She buried the head under her ladder and kept the heart in a jar.

Tomstinapa's father called Eagle and Carrion Fly. The first failed, the latter found the tenatsali and recognized the blood of Tomstinapa. His father created butterflies from the music of his flute and chose the fifth or all-colored butterfly to lure the eight dangerous sisters. They saw the butterfly hovering over the tenatsali plants and wanted the pattern on its wings for their baskets. They tried to capture it in all the articles of their clothing till they were naked. When they fell asleep from weariness after a long pursuit the butterfly appeared as Ne'we·kwe and he and Coyote had intercourse with the girls asleep. Coyote gave them his hair between their legs (origin of pubic hair). When they awoke they were ashamed. Ne'we·kwe made embroidered white blankets for all of them from scraps of the corn husk that wrapped his fore-knot and took them to his house in the Ne'we·kwe spring. He married them and always brought them venison.

B. PAIYATAMU (7).[1] Paiyatamu was a great runner and had eight sisters. Along his daily practise course he passed the home of the eight evil maidens. One of these sisters challenged him to a hiding contest. He failed to find her when she hid in a cloud but when he crouched behind the sun she drew a drop of milk from her breast and saw the tip of his headdress reflected in it. She cut off his head and removed his heart and buried his body the depth of a man (i. e. a man's height). The blood that dripped from the head and heart became tenatsali plants. His sisters sent Eagle, Chicken Hawk, Crow and Buzzard to find him but they could not. Fly found the tenatsali and followed into the fourth inner room where the maiden kept his heart and head.

When she knew who had killed Paiyatamu his elder sister took a Paiyatamu flute and at each note a butterfly came forth in the colors of the six directions. She rejected four and sent a many-colored butterfly to lure the evil sisters. The butterfly went into the room where they were making baskets and they wanted to copy the pattern from its wings. They ran after it trying to capture it in each article of their clothing till at last they were naked. When they dropped asleep from weariness, Paiyatamu took off his butterfly disguise. He returned home and his sisters set up a Paiyatamu altar with medicine water. Paiyatamu blew his flute and at each note one of the maidens came forth as a small zigzag-flying butterfly. He condemned them to craziness (flying without direction = nymphomania) and sent one to each of the four directions to call rain.

PAIYATAMU'S GRANDSON (7), I : 200[2]

A despised boy claims to be Paiyatamu's son and is tested by his father. Paiyatamu gives him power to marry eight priests' daughters to whom he teaches the songs of the priests' summer retreats. These songs cause a flood from which the people have to take refuge on Corn Mountain. The flood is stopped by the sacrifice of the son and daughter of the village priest, who are drowned in the flood.

This tale is made up of familiar elements of Zuni folklore arranged, like the two preceding tales, around the man's day dream of overcoming the women who scorn him and of eventually making

---

[1] *Published only in abstract.*

[2] Indexed: Despised boy wins maiden. Noodle. Father quest. Helpful animals: prey animals; Spider Woman. Tests, paternity: drowning, mountain of glass, flute thrown in brush. Transformation, ceremonial. Flute music magically produces maidens. Rainbow, travel by. Flood stopped by sacrifice of boy and girl.

them serve his triumph. The boy is laughed at by the eight priest's daughters for a blunder. He gets himself made irresistible and in this form kills the eight girls who come successively to marry him. He magically recreates them by flute magic to his own purposes and they are his instruments in bringing rain ritual back to Zuni. All the wishes are given grandiose expression.

A despised boy lived with his grandmother. He asked her who his father was and she told him to ask the Sun. He went to Sun but Sun did not know. He returned home. One day as he came in from the hunt with rabbits the daughters of eight priests met him and asked for gifts. Instead of dividing his rabbits as was customary he divided his lunch with them and they were insulted. They threw the food back at him. The boy cried. He made prayersticks and went north to Paiyatamu's. On the way Mountain Lion, Bear, Badger and Wolf killed game for him, and he paid them with ceremonial hair-feathers. Spider Woman offered to guide him and she rode in his ear. They came to Paiyatamu's house. The boy addressed him as grandfather and his son as father. They tested him. Paiyatamu's son took a square stone from the altar and made a deep spring. He called the boy to have his hair washed by the eight sisters and they pushed him in. Spider Woman saved him by letting down her thread so that he could climb up. Next Paiyatamu directed him to climb a mountain of glass. Spider Woman spun her thread again and he climbed up. His father brought out the sash and flute of Paiyatamu to give to him, and threw the flute in the brush. Spider Woman directed him and he found it. When he had succeeded in these tests his father acknowledged him. His son told him, "You urinated on the thistle flower in the spring and I am that child." His father removed his son's dirty skin. After he had slit it on the palms and feet with a magic crystal he pulled it off with a medicine crook. Paiyatamu directed him to throw it in the river and the eight sisters washed his hair and dressed him in Paiyatamu costume. His father sent him back to his home to marry the eight priests' daughters who had thrown his corncakes back at him. One would come each night to marry him. He was to cut off their heads and cut out their hearts and bury their bodies in a hole. Rainbow took him back. The boy followed his father's directions and in eight days he put the girl's heads in his flute and said good-by to his grandmother. He promised to return in eight days. Rainbow carried him again to Paiyatamu's house. He faced east and blew a note on his flute. At each note a priest's daughter emerged naked. Paiyatamu's eight sisters put embroidered blankets around them and gave them hard corn to grind. Afterwards Paiyatamu taught his sons and his eight wives the songs of the priest's retreats. The girls were to take the ritual back to teach their fathers.

In Pinawa the girls' mothers came looking for their daughters at the home of the boy's grandmother. When they found they were gone they planned to kill the old woman but she begged them to wait till the eighth day. That evening Paiyatamu came with his eight wives. They went to their fathers' houses and taught them the songs of the priests' summer retreats. Next day Paiyatamu and his wives went into retreat and afterwards the priesthoods in order. Each remained eight days in retreat, in succession, and it rained all the time. Water covered the pueblo and they removed to Corn Mountain. The flood came to the top of the mesa. They asked the village priest for his young son and daughter to stop the flood. They dressed them in ceremonial costume. The boy stood to the west, the girl to the east, and holding their great bundle of prayersticks they stepped off the mesa into the flood. They became the Boy and Girl peaks of Corn Mountain. Therefore they give blessing in conception and childbirth at their shrine.

The Corn Maidens Marry (7), I : 206[1]

The six Corn Maidens are taken as wives by human husbands and escape from them. Ne'we·kwe rescues their youngest sister Sweet Corn and she summons her six sisters and destroys their human husbands.

In contrast to the usual theme of blessings received from marriage with supernaturals, this tale is one of calamity. This is due to the strong association in Zuni between the Corn Maidens and repudiation of sex in any form. Therefore when these maidens are taken by human husbands the husbands are eventually destroyed.

There were not enough women in Hecokta to go around and the young men did nothing but gamble. One man put on a deer disguise, lured a young hunter from another pueblo to join their game, and won all his clothing and necklaces from him.

One day a Hecokta gambler found seven girls living at Hanłipinḳa. They were the seven Corn Maidens. Elder Sister Yellow Corn refused at first to let him enter the house but at last he secured Red Corn as his wife and took her home. After that he never went to gamble because he was always playing with his wife. Eventually he got all the other corn sisters except Sweet Corn, the youngest, as wives for five other young gamblers. Sweet Corn was left alone and she was almost dead. Ne'we·kwe rescued her by making rain ceremonially so that the three corn kernels in her hair sprouted and grew. Before this corn had eared the six corn sisters married in Hecokta disappeared, escaping from their husbands while the latter were working. Ne'we·kwe gathered the sweet corn when it

---

[1] Indexed: Corn Maidens, loss and recovery of by Ne'we·kwe. Flute music magically produces butterflies.

was ripe and Sweet Corn Girl appeared in her own shape. He commissioned her to recover her sisters and for this purpose made a coliwe game of corn stalks and gave her a handful of arrowheads. She dressed herself in her best costume and he drew her into his flute, transforming her into a butterfly when he sounded a note. He sent her to Hecokta where she resumed her own shape and gambled with the gamblers. Her gambling sticks, when she threw them, turned each time into different birds and she won the lives of her opponents. Summoned by the game, her six sisters appeared and took her with them to their home. She threw her arrowheads down the hatchway and the roof fell upon the gamblers, punishing them for having had sex relations with the Corn Maidens.

The Boy who had to learn to marry (7), I : 210[1]

A poor boy commits all the social errors out of ignorance, and his grandmother finally teaches him how to make love. He marries the girl and receives supernatural aid in hunting.

This Zuni version of the perfect marriage celebrates the innocence of the young male as Victorian stories celebrated the innocence of the young female. In this tale the boy's naiveté is carried to the point of incorporating noodle incidents to prove his lack of worldly wisdom. His grandmother makes him ready for marriage by sleeping with him herself. The conclusion is that this is a happy marriage.

The despised boy went to the spring to speak to girls as the other boys did. One of the girls pitied him and gave him a drink. He was proud. She whispered an invitation to him. He did not know what it meant and questioned her out loud before the others. His grandmother told him to accept the girl's invitation to her house, not to talk, to eat only a pinch of food, and keep his eyes on the bow guard on his wrist (i. e. be modest, not let his eyes rove), and do whatever the girl told him. He ran back and followed the girl into her house. He obeyed literally: he followed the girl (i. e. he walked as she did, with a woman's gait, a great joke); when the family served him the evening meal he ate a pinch (i. e. he refused stew and paper-bread and picked up a crumb off the floor); when the men sat back from the meal he looked at (through) his bow guard (i. e. he took it off and held it before his face). The girl took him to bed with her but he did not understand. When she touched him he squealed (it tickled him) and ran to his grandmother. The latter let down her dress and taught him how to make love. He stayed with his grandmother that night.

---

[1] Indexed: Noodle. Helpful animals: Spider Woman. Modest choice. Despised boy wins maiden.

Next day the girl brought his grandmother a great basket of meal and the latter emptied his basket and filled it with dried peaches and snowbirds. The girl ground all day for the grandmother, who cooked a stew with hulled corn. The girl returned home with a white blanket, her bowl full of dried meat and peaches and four rolls of paper-bread in her blanket. The girl took the gift to her home and the boy walked behind carrying four rabbits he had killed. They were married.

He went out to hunt deer but he found none. Spider Woman counselled him from her place in his ear and took him up a mountain with her thread. She guided him to White Bear who owned the stone hunting knives and offered him four to choose from. Spider Woman directed him to take the least and smallest. Then White Bear called the deer and the little boy killed the largest successfully. He gave White Bear the pluck and returned the knife. Spider Woman got a dry stalk (sunflower) to make his load magically light. He took the venison home. This is why marriages are happier if boys marry before they know anything about women.

Reed Boys and their Grandmother (7), I : 216[1]

(1) The despised boy wins a stick race with the help of Reed Boys. (2) The grandmothers of the despised boy and of Reed Boys become young and marry young husbands who desert them when they wake old. They cause a drought which is only ended when another despised boy marries one of these grandmothers and through his kindness makes her permanently young.

This story loosely unites two familiar Zuni plots. For the first see *Despised boy wins stick race*. The second plot, which centers around the bridegroom's nightmare that his bride will be a hag when he wakes in the morning, is well told in Parsons JAFL 43 : 19—24, abstracted as "Supernatural Grandmothers", I: 338, where the theme of *Marriage is taught by supernaturals to those who refuse it: youth is shamed by brides who appear old in morning* is carried out in full.

Halona was constantly defeated in stick races with Pinawa. They asked the two Reed Boys for help and these told them to get a despised boy to run for them. He practised with Reed Boys and Elder Brother Ahaiyute. Tciktcałaci (kachina) brought him possessions to stake on the race and Reed Boys made prayersticks which they directed him to bury to the depth of his forearm. One of the young men saw how fast the boy ran in his practise races and he told a relative who went to the village priest of Pinawa to warn him of the danger. Reed Boy followed him and spat on him as he was about to give warning, so that he became a summer bird

---

[1] Indexed: Despised boy wins stick race. Brides appear old in morning.

and was cared for by an old man and woman who were all that were left in the pueblo of Halona because everybody had gone to see the race. The despised boy held his retreat in his house with the two Reed Boys, and his grandmother and Reed Boys' grandmother sang ceremonial songs in Reed Boys' house all night and made themselves beautiful young girls. The man who had been made a summer bird was now human and invited them to stay with him as his wives. They went to the races with the two Ahaiyute and he gave one of the wives to his friend who had watched the practise races. When they woke the morning after the race (the deserted boy had won), the two wives were old women and their husbands abandoned them. Therefore the women caused a drought. When the two deserting husbands were starving, one of them saw his wife again as a beautiful girl washing buckskin near her home. He did not recognize her. He asked her to marry him because she had plenty of food. She objected that he had abandoned one wife and that when she was old he would leave her. He swore he would not. In the morning she was old and he left her alone. When he returned she would have nothing to do with him. A despised boy came and married her. He was kind to her and nursed her. Soon she became young again and did her share of the work and clothed him beautifully. She ground cornmeal to take to his home and it increased magically. For four days she woke old in the morning but he was kind to her and afterwards she remained young always. The drought ended.

THE MANNIKIN WIFE (8), I : 221[1]

A bashful youth fashions a mannikin and tells his family he is married. A supernatural Corn Woman impersonates his mannikin and teaches him the blessings of marriage. They become the male and female corn ears of the corn storeroom.

In this tale the youth who hesistates to marry makes himself a mannikin as a substitute for a human wife, and is taught by a supernatural woman the true blessing of marriage.

The son of a priest on First Mesa (Hopi) was bashful and used to sleep in the field shelter during hoeing time. He told his family he was about to marry a girl from another pueblo who had visited him there, and he asked to be given immediately the bride's marriage gift of a buckskin. His family gave it to him, and he took it to his field shelter, stuffed it, and made hair for it from the ravellings of his blanket. He laid it on a bed of weeds and made love to it all night.

On the next day he received from his family two sets of wedding clothes for his wife and warned them not to visit his bashful wife.

---

[1] "A Hopi Story." Indexed: Marriage is taught by supernaturals to those who refuse it: youth. Supernaturals are sent to shrines.

On the fourth day he had to bring his wife home for the head washing, but he asked his sisters to prepare a room on the second story. He carried the mannikin dressed in her wedding finery. He went up the ladder twice, the second time simulating a woman's step, and spent the night talking and answering himself in a woman's voice. Before sunrise he had to take her to his family to have her head washed and he did not know what to do.

When he woke in the morning, a beautiful Corn Woman had taken the place of the mannikin. She was already grinding. His family washed her head and she ground with his sisters. On the fourth day of his visit she made paper-bread, and as she was finishing Whirlwind came with a great noise from the west and stripped off all her bridal clothes. It was the mannikin taking the clothes from Corn Woman. She was ashamed. She told the boy's family the story of the mannikin and that she had come to help him. Immediately the family began to make a new set of wedding clothes for Corn Woman herself, and they were ready on the fourth day. On the eighth day she told her husband she would go back to the corn room. She would become the Corn Mother and bless the household with corn. The priest's son loved her and accompanied her. He became the full-kernelled male ear and she the female (branched ear). His parents knew that their son's wife had been pregnant because she became the mother corn. That's why a mother corn and a male corn are placed together first in filling any corn room (to give increase), and why mother corns are placed by mothers of children, and perfect male ears by baby boys.

THE PRIEST'S SON WHO LOST EVERYTHING AT GAMBLING (8), I:224[1]

The priest's son is defeated in gambling games. The magic flight. The false bride.

The full account of Zuni gambling games in this tale introduces several European incidents which finally lead to that most satifying conclusion to a Zuni audience: the reunion of members of a family.

The priest's son wagered clothing at tacoliwe and won. His opponents challenged him to play the same game next day and they offered prayer meal to the Ahaiyute at their shrine at Eastern Road. They heard the Ahaiyute's voices for good omens. The priest's son brought out only a belt to wager but they made him go back and get as much as he had won on the previous game. The priest's son lost (game counts given). He challenged his opponents

---

[1] Indexed: Ruined gambler retrieves his posses. Helpful animals: Spider Woman provides food. Witch contests: removing a forest, diverting a river, lifting a mountain. Hair, woman's, used magically. Magic Flight. False bride. Transformation into human being, ceremonial.

to play lapotciwe. His opponents offered prayer meal to the Ahaiyute in Wool Mountain but heard no omens. They made offerings also to the sun at sunrise. The priest's son made the missile and target for the game and they all brought clothing to wager. The priest's son lost. He challenged them to the game of hidden ball. His opponents offered prayer meal to the Ahaiyute at Corn Mountain and heard the owl for good omen. Again they made offerings to the sun at sunrise. They played all day (game count given), and that evening the priest's son was hungry and went home to eat (bad omen). He lost. He was ashamed to go home and slept all night in the plaza. His father and mother wept and scolded him. Without eating, and taking only the turquoise he always carried at his belt, he left Zuni. At Red Mountain, Spider Woman took him into her house and fed him with corn cake which always multiplied. He went on and travelled easily because he stuck a straw in his belt.

In Laguna he was entertained in a house that stood by itself at the west side. The father challenged him to a Laguna game. The daughter liked him and gave him power so that he won everything in the house. The family had witch power. Next night his host challenged him to cut all of the trees in his yard. The girl pulled a long hair from her head and each took an end and they cut down the trees. She told him that if he did not prevent her mother's going out into the yard in the morning to urinate, all would grow as before. He watched and shut the door in the old woman's face. Next night her father told him to make a distant river run through their yard. The girl again pulled a hair from her head and they cut a ditch for the river. Again he prevented her mother's coming out in the morning. Next night the father told him to lift a mountain a mile distant. That night the girl doubted her power to do this and proposed that they run away to Zuni. By daylight they had gone a long distance. When her father and mother discovered she was gone, the father turned himself into a big whirlwind and pursued them. When the girl saw him coming, she turned herself into a female donkey and the boy into a bony male donkey. Her father did not recognize them. When he got home he told his wife what he had seen and she identified them. The wife went next as a little whirlwind. Her daughter turned her husband into a fish and herself into a little fish in a spring. Her mother did not recognize them but when she returned home her husband identified them. He came again in a big whirlwind. The girl changed her husband into an apple-tree and herself into a little apple-tree. Her father did not recognize them but when he returned his wife identified them. She went again as a little whirlwind and the girl changed her husband into a dove and herself into a female dove. Her mother did not recognize them, and when she returned her husband identified them. They gave up the search.

The girl and her husband continued their journey to Zuni. At Red Mountain, Spider Woman fed them again. It had been a year since the boy had passed that way. At Owl Spring the priest's son left his wife and went on to Zuni to ask permission of his parents for their marriage. While she waited, a one-eyed witch found the girl at the spring and climbed into the trees overhanging the water. The witch could see the girl's reflection and she thought is was hers. She invited the girl to come into the tree so that she could comb her hair for her appearance at the priest's house. At the fourth invitation the girl climbed up. The witch tangled her hair upon a little stick. She became a blue dove and the old witch the girl.

When the priest's son came toward the village everyone watched to see the Laguna man coming. When they recognized the priest's son, his mother was overpowered with joy and embraced her son. They sent for his father from the fields and he too was overjoyed. He told them of his marriage and they were glad. He went back to Owl Spring to get his wife. The dove followed the two, crying, but the priest's son paid no attention. The priest's family welcomed their son's wife. That evening the dove sat on the pole of the tall house ladder. The priest went out and the dove spoke to him. She asked him to change her into her own form again. The priest brought a medicine society man with his medicine crook. When he touched her with this they both returned to their true shapes. They threw out the old witch and the priest's son and the girl were married and lived happily. That is why we hate witches.

The Man who Married the Donkey (8), I : 236[1]

The son of the village priest copulates with the donkeys and refuses four girls who come with marriage gifts. When the donkeys are no longer in heat the priest's son turns to seek a girl in marriage and gradually wins a wife. When his half-human donkey offspring is born, it accosts its grandfather, the village priest, and the latter seeks supernatural help. The Ahaiyute kill the donkey child of the priest's son.

This revealing tale is no doubt founded upon the European incident of the *Mare Wife* which has been found among many tribes of the Plains. Aboriginal Indian tales of marriage with animals document not bestiality but the fundamental equivalence of men and animals in Indian belief, and their ready transformation the one into the other. The *Mare Wife* story of Zuni contrasts strongly with the Plains tale and is thoroughly characteristic of Zuni attitudes, see Introduction I : xxv. The Plains tale[2] is a story of a married woman who later finds erotic satisfaction in connection

[1] Indexed: Mare Wife. Marriage is taught by supernaturals to those who refuse it: youth. Noodle. Hair, woman's, used magically.

[2] See MAFLS 11 : 53, note 1.

with a horse; the Zuni tale is of a timid man afraid of marriage who tries mares as a substitute for women, finds them too wild, and is only disillusioned with his donkey adventure when he finds that the animal's season of heat is short. He is driven by this experience to seek a woman in marriage, and his father is blamed by the supernaturals for not having instructed his son so that he would know enough to avoid the bad expedient of bestiality in overcoming his natural fears. The supernaturals, however, are ready to help, and kill the half-human offspring.

The son of the village priest was handsome and worked hard in his fields, but he was bashful with girls. He thought it was a great deal of trouble to take a wife. Therefore when his father had left him hoeing at their fields he tried to have intercourse with the mares that were pastured there. They were too wild, so next day he tried again and had intercourse with a donkey. He arranged with his family to go to the field early each day and to stay late. His father was so pleased with all the work he did there that he gave him a buckskin as a special gift. The boy was very happy. He had chosen one particular donkey that he used regularly.

When the corn began to leaf four women came to the house of the village priest to ask for his son in marriage. They brought baskets of yellow, blue, red and white corn meal. When they asked to marry him the priest's son sat with bowed head and made no answer. His mother made up the bed for them, but all night the young man paid no attention to them. They rose early and prepared to leave. His mother was ashamed, and gave them special gifts of articles of women's costume. The young man was shamed in the eyes of the whole people.

He went out to his donkey, but she was no longer in heat and threw him off. He had nothing to do all winter but stay in the house making moccasins. Next spring he tried so scrape friendship with the girls when they went to get water, but they scorned him because of his refusal to marry the four girls. At last one pair of girls let him play at marking patterns with their teeth in folded corn leaves. She gave him a drink from her gourd and threw water over him. That night he waited outside her house after dark to get a chance to speak to her but she did not come out. Next night he offered her "a woman's belt"; he thought it was a fine present but it was only cornhusks with patterns marked on them with the teeth. That night he spoke to her before dark when she carried out the sweepings, and when her father went to his kiva, she joined him again. Her sisters told their mother who it was their sister had gone out to meet, and their mother was angry when she found it was the boy who had refused to marry. She scolded her daughter. The daughter was so angry she stayed up grinding in a temper and would not eat in the morning. Her mother told her father, and her father remonstrated with his daughter. As soon as her parents had gone out to their work, however, the girl went empty handed to the house of the village priest to grind for his mother. The mother did not great her warmly, she made her shell her own corn and break it up without parching, but the girl behaved herself so well that the mother was pleased in spite of herself. The mother suggested that she give her presents of dried peaches and paper-bread at the end of the day, but the girl had made up her mind to stay with the priest's son. Therefore his mother made up the bed for them. Both families accepted the marriage.

The donkey gave birth to the child of the priest's son. His mother told him to speak to his father when he came to hoe and ask him for corn, for he was half-human and could not live on weeds. His father took no notice, however, and his mother decided to wait and speak to the priest, his father. Next day the little donkey spoke to the priest and told him what had happened. The priest was very sad. He made an excuse to speak to his son alone and told him what the donkey had told him. His son confessed. His father went back to the fields and asked the little donkey to tell no one. He went back to his house and that night he ate tenatsali, asking the tenatsali youths for guidance. They came to him and criticized him for never having given his children sex instruction. As a priest he should have been even more careful than other people to educate his children, and he had neglected this. They instructed him to ask the help of the Ahaiyute on Corn Mountain to kill the little donkey.

The priest made prayersticks and crooks for each of the Ahaiyute. He pulverized turquoise and added it to fine-ground white corn meal. He went out to Corn Mountain. Everyone wondered that he should go out with prayersticks at a time when he had no official religious duties, and he was ashamed. He took them to Corn Mountain and told the Ahaiyute his request.

Meanwhile men had gone out to water their horses pastured near the priest's fields. The little donkey talked with them, and told them who his father was. They were shocked, and because it was a terrible thing they went home and told no one, not even their wives.

The Ahaiyute waited till no human being was in sight. They killed the little donkey, and according to the instructions their grandmother had given them they buried him "like a human being" in a deep crevice with his head to the east. They did not sprinkle prayer meal upon him, for if they had he would have gone to live in Kachina Village. Then they took one of their grand-mother's hairs, which she had given them, and according to her instructions they encircled the donkeys with it, making them ugly so that no man would ever again be tempted as the priest's son had been. That's why only old men ride donkeys now.

BAT YOUTH (3), 1 : 253[1]

Bat Youth sleeps with four girls in their sleep and they avenge themselves.

Bat Youth's exploit is well-known pueblo slander, and is attributed to living men. For its relevance to Zuni sex attitudes, see Introduction, I: xxiii.

Bat Youth lived with his grandmother, and near by lived four girls for whom he used to beat the drum while they ground their corn. One night he made sure they were all asleep and lay with each of them in turn without waking them. When they woke and discovered what had happened, they suspected Bat Youth and pursued him to pay him back. They overtook him before he reached home and he was so frightened he could not climb his ladder. They tore off his blanket and left him shamed. The youth and his grandmother flew off as bats, because of their shame, and for this reason bats carry bedbugs.

ADDITIONAL TALES OF COURTSHIP

Courtship incidents occur in many other tales in this collection. All previously recorded Zuni courtship tales, either published or in manuscript, are abstracted below. The tales, 334—337, have been discussed in connection with foregoing courtship tales and are given in order of such discussion. The tales abstracted 337—342 usually make use of incidents found elsewhere in these volumes, see Index of Incidents, Vol. II, but they are not properly analogues of tales already discussed.

MARRIAGE TESTS: SCALPS REQUIRED
Discussion, I: 298

A (7).[2] The priest's daughter demanded that her suitors bring her scalps. The Ahaiyute sent Crow to summon the Apaches to destroy the girl's village. In Kachina Village Pautiwa knew and came to Ḳakima to warn the girl of her evil ways. He got away just as the Apache descended. On his way back to Kachina Village he stayed the night with a despised girl. She had twin sons, one lame and one blind, who had supernatural power. They set out to seek their father, the blind one carrying the lame one who guided him with a rattle he held in his hand. They charmed antelope and sang for a stone knife, being successful both times. Kwelele made a fire for them. Pautiwa came to meet them and told them to go

---

[1] Indexed: Bat husband.

[2] Indexed: Test, marriage: scalps. Lame and blind are cured. Despised old man has power. Famine is caused by not entertaining supernaturals. Cp. Marriage is taught by supernaturals to those who refuse it (i. e. admonition).

to Hopi, foretelling how the Hopi would reject them. For four years, therefore, they caused a drought in Hopi because the people mauled and spat on them. At last a despised old man saw them living in the chicken coops and guessed that they might be the cause of the trouble. Four priests went to make peace with them but unsuccessfully. At last they allowed the despised old man to carry them on his back to the ceremonial room and the priests dressed them in kachina costume. The drought ended in a great thunderstorm and when lightning struck it cured one of the brothers of his blindness and the other of his lameness. They were made chief priests and Pautiwa's sisters washed them. *Bunzel AES 15: 139.*

B.[1] A Hopi maiden required that her suitors bring her scalps. An orphan boy enlisted the aid of the village dogs and descended on Zuni, getting many scalps. The unsuccessful suitors challenged him to a rabbit hunt and the cave swallows gave him rabbit sticks (sympathetic magic) and he won over his rivals. Though he was hit he healed himself. Therefore ugly boys marry. *Cushing 185.*

Marriage test: killing a deer
Discussion, I: 303.

A.[2] The Owner of Deer hides her deer and demands buckskins of her suitors. After three have failed the Ahaiyute discover the trick and force the release of the game. She imposes on them the test of scraping great piles of skins and they succeed with the aid of field mice. She marries both and twins are born. They start back to Corn Mountain to visit the Ahaiyute's grandmother and Sun snatches the wife and children to the sky. The Ahaiyute shoot at her and she falls. She is killed but the twins are unharmed and are brought up by Ahaiyute grandmother. This is the origin of the practice of adopting children. *Cushing 104.*

B.[3] A girl refused a suitor who brought her a bundle of clothing as a marriage gift, and she demanded that he bring her deer. Ayu Tsawaki came from Kachina Village. He killed deer and married her. They had twin boys who were dangerous and with their parents were ceremonially sent back to Kachina Village. *Parsons MAAA 4: 302.*

---

[1] Indexed: Test, marriage: scalps required. Despised boy wins maiden. Contests to retain wife: rabbit hunt.

[2] Indexed: Marriage is taught by supernaturals to those who refuse it: maiden. Test, marriage: killing a deer. Liberation of game. Test, marriage: scraping pile of buckskins. Animal coats removed. Helpful animals: field mice scrape buckskins in marriage test. Death of pregnant maiden in fall from sky.

[3] Indexed: Marriage is taught by supernaturals to those who refuse it: maiden. Tests, marriage: killing a deer. Supernaturals are sent to shrines.

C. OWNER OF DEER.[1] A Ḳanaˑkwe met two girls out exploring, and married one of them. She remained four years and was "mother of deer". When she left she took with her their dung, urine and hair and they promised to follow. Ḳanaˑkwe brought her in (he became a deer to carry her) and instituted the Ḳanaˑkwe dance. Four boys courted her in turn but she demanded "her children". They could not see any, however. At last Little Dirt Pile offered prayer meal to the deer and hunted successfully. So deer were liberated. *Bunzel AES 15: 165.*

D. TURTLE HUSBAND.[2] A girl would marry only a man who killed deer. Turtle came as suitor. With the help of a Koyemci he killed deer and the girl had to marry him. He removed his disguise and became a man, giving his mask to her father. She had two turtle children. In order to protect his children, Turtle Man sent for kachinas. They were entertained by the wife's brother (Badger Clan) and her father (Deer Clan). Turtle joined the kachina dance and Spider helped the wife pick her husband from among the masked dancers. He was allowed to remain with her, and the turtle children were taken to Kachina Village. Therefore Deer and Badger people go every fourth year to Kachina Village for turtles (at the initial ceremony of the summer solstice rites). *Bunzel ms.*

COYOTE ATTEMPTS TO MARRY MOUNTAIN LION'S SISTER[3]
Discussion I: 311

A. The animal Gods of Prey promised their sister in marriage to anyone who would kill the spotted demon Siuiuki. Coyote promised the demon he would become magically swift footed if he broke the bones of his legs. When he had done so he killed him. Coyote claimed Mountain Lion Girl and forced her to carry him on her back up to her home. His brothers-in-law took him hunting and he ran with the chimney swallows, fell off the cliff and was killed. *Cushing 215.*

B. Coyote found Mountain Lion Girl alone cooking for her brothers and addressed her intimately. She threatened him with having to go hunting with her brothers if he married her (see Cushing, above) and he ran off as fast as he could go and fell off the mesa and was killed. *Handy JAFL 31: 458.*

---

[1] Indexed: Tests, marriage: killing a deer. Despised boy wins maiden. Liberation of game.

[2] Indexed: Test, marriage: killing a deer. Blind choice. Helpful animals: Spider aids in blind choice. Supernaturals are sent to shrines.

[3] Indexed: Mountain Lion's sister, Coyote attempts to marry. Trick: breaking monster's legs on promise of swiftness, A.

Marriage test: Meal adheres to upright Surface[1]

A youth required as a marriage test that a ball of meal stick to an abalone shell set in the wall. Two girls came with bowls of meal and failed. A Bear Girl from Cipapolima brought cactus fruit as a gift, and her meal though coarse stuck to the shell. She had supernatural power and ground eight baskets of meal in a day.

When the Saiyataca came in at Calako and she heard their bear call she became a bear once more, taking off with her the ceremonial feather her husband had made for her at Calako. She made her husband sick and came for him as a bear, taking him to Cipapolima where the Beast Gods chastised him for having refused marriage. That is why hunters give Saiyataca's call that bears may not attack them. *Parsons MAAA 4: 322.*

The Origin of Ne'we·kwe (7)[2]

A girl spent her time making baskets, and a butterfly flew into her room. She wished to copy the patterns on his wings. She pursued him and he disappeared into Ne'we·kwe spring. She followed and was taught marriage by Ne'we·kwe. She returned home and married a poor boy, but was lightheaded (the result of her contact with Ne'we·kwe) and returned to the spring. Her children became the Ne'we·kwe society. *Bunzel ms.*

Marriage test: Ridding Field of Corn Pests[3]

A girl required of her suitors that they rid her cornfield of pests. A despised boy at last won success by digging a pitfall in her field. Coyote fell in first and boasted that he had found riches. Therefore Bear and all other animals jumped in. When it was full Coyote was able to jump out but the suitor burned all the rest. That is why girls marry despised men, and why there are so many coyote corn pests. *Cushing 288.*

Marriage Test: the pest of gnats[4]

The daughter of the village priest of Matsaka required that her suitor cultivate her corn fields and she released gnats and mosquitoes so that suitors from Pinawa, Hampasa and Kakima were overcome. A suitor from Halonawa took bitter bark to rub himself with, on the advice of his grandmother, and was on the point of

---

[1] Indexed: Marriage is taught by supernaturals to those who refuse it: youth. Test, marriage: meal sticks to shell. Cf. Bear Wife.

[2] Indexed: Marriage is taught by supernaturals to those who refuse it: maiden. Butterfly pursuit.

[3] Indexed: Despised youth wins maiden. Pitfall trick.

[4] Indexed: Test, marriage: cultivating field while maiden releases mosquitoes. False bride. Orpheus.

22

winning the maiden, but her witch sister impersonated her and both came together to the field. Not knowing which was which, the suitor, in the fight between the two women that followed, helped the wrong sister and the good sister was killed, the witch revealing herself as a crow. Followed by *Orpheus. Cushing 1—17.*

SUPERNATURAL GRANDMOTHERS[1]

A proud boy secluded himself and never went out. He refused all the women who sought to marry him. To punish him the Tenatsali Youths[2] and the two Ahaiyute transformed their grandmothers into young girls and sent them into the village at the time of the Łewekwe dance to bring the muwaiye dance[3] and tempt the proud youth to his downfall. He was tempted and danced with them. At night they cohabited with him and woke in the morning in their true form as old women. He fled and they cursed him that he should never marry. They then bestowed their favors (as young women again) on a despised boy who lived with his grandmother. They sent his grandmother to the village priest to have the bow priest make proclamation that the people come to clean the house she and the boy lived in (i. e. they had food to pay for this communal work). They feasted and the Ahaiyute brought their sacred things and the Tenatsali theirs. The old women began to teach but the boy was slow to learn. The Tenatsali learned everything quickly and were given their medicine bundles and songs and went with their grandmother to live in Tenatsali Place beyond Kachina Village. *Parsons JAFL 43: 19.*

FALSE ORACLE[4]

A Hopi girl refused her suitors and demanded deer. A·lucpa was a boy who dressed all in white and lived with his grandmother at Halona. He hid himself in a hole by the spring and sang that the girl should go to A·lucpa or the lightning would strike her. She ran home without water and her family accompanied her carrying meal. The girl married him and washed his head. He twitted her with having been frightened and when she realized the trick she struck him and ran back to Hopi. So he lost his wife. *Parsons MAAA 4: 313.*

---

[1] Indexed: Marriage is taught by supernaturals to those who refuse it: youth is shamed by brides who are old in morning. Brides appear old in morning. Despised boy wins maidens.
[2] In the tales in this volume the tenatsali are both youths, but Parsons notes them as a boy and girl, 19 n. 3.
[3] A dance in which a youth dances between two maidens. For good description see Erna Fergusson, Dancing Gods, New York, 1931, p. 78.
[4] Indexed: False oracle. Tests, marriage: killing deer.

GREASE BOY (7)[1]

The village priest had two wives. He found one of them with another man and caused a four year drought. The people were poor and went to Grease Hill to pick cactus fruit. Grease Boy lived there and made the acquaintance of a poor girl and married her. He provided food and taught the priests their rain retreats. They planted the prayersticks he had taught them to make and the drought broke. Grease Boy was a supernatural and returned to his shrine, later to Kachina Village, and his wife could not. She married again but soon died and joined Grease Boy. *Bunzel ms.*

THE GIRL WHO TRIED TO TAKE A CRICKET FOR HER HUSBAND

A girl was working in her field and she heard Cricket singing his song. She took him home and at bedtime she teased him to have fun with her. But he couldn't laugh: he could only sing, and when she tickled him (love-making) his abdomen burst and he died. *Handy JAFL 31:457.*

THE GIRL WHO MARRIED THE HUMMINGBIRD (7)[2]

Hummingbird married a girl who had rejected all suitors. The rejected suitors tried to kill him. He was dropped over a cliff and saved by Parrot. He was sent to hunt bear and Bear saved him, to hunt mountain lions with fire and Gopher saved him. He ran a race with Chicken Hawk and won in a rainstorm. He was locked in the house for four days without food and lived on the nectar of sunflowers planted by the kachinas. There was a contest of bird cages which he won with a live bird from Kachina Village. *Bunzel ms.*

SKULL HUSBAND (7)[3]

A despised boy living with his grandmother was courted by two girls at the spring. Jealous suitors killed him, but Whirlwind found his skull and brought it to his wives. It was alive at night and was their husband. The girls used the skull to kill their suitors until Horned Serpent interfered. He turned the skull into a rabbit and wooed the girls. They were faithful to their skull husband, and

---

[1] Indexed: Deserted husband causes drought. Supernaturals are sent to shrines.

[2] Indexed: Contests to retain wife: dropped over cliff; bear hunt; mountain lion hunt; stick race; confinement without food. Helpful animals: Parrot saves from death by fall; Bear saves from death in bear hunt; Gopher saves from brush fire. Race won by rainstorm. Kachinas at Kachina Village provide bird.

[3] Indexed: Despised boy wins maiden. Skull husband. Water Baby found in a spring becomes Horned Serpent and husband of girl who found it. Snake Husband. Supernaturals are sent to shrines.

22*

refused him. They bathed and found a baby in the spring. They took it home, and at night it turned into a snake (horned serpent) and lay with them. Snake was ceremonially sent back to the spring and took the girls with him. After four days he sent them home. *Bunzel ms.*

WINTER MAN AS HUSBAND (7)[1]

Winter Man accosted a girl at the spring, put her in his turquoise kick-stick and took her to his home. He made her sleep on a bed of ice but turkeys gave her their feathers; he gave her stones to grind but Mockingbird brought corn in their stead; he required her to kill a white deer, and the Ahaiyute killed it for her with Gopher's help, who tunneled to the monster's heart; he made her lift a heavy weight, and again she was successful. She sent Winter Man for firewood and he brought prayersticks. She cut off his head. *Bunzel ms.*

BUTTERFLY WIFE (7)[2]

A boy gambled and lost all he had. He left home and found a Butterfly Girl, whom he married. She forbade him to enter a certain room and when he disobeyed he found himself imprisoned in a cave. The butterflies released him but the next day he went off with Bat Woman. Butterfly Girl went after him and brought him back. He went home with his wife and with Spider's help won back what he had lost. He neglected his wife again for another woman, refusing to take her home. She took out his heart and he sickened and died, returning in death to his first wife, and living with her in summer land. *Bunzel ms.*

COYOTE HUSBAND (7)[3]

Coyote killed a girl's grandmother and put on her skin. He came home and slept with the girl. She had coyote pups. Her brother discovered what had happened, killed Coyote and buried the grandmother. He made a pitfall for coyotes. One fell in and enticed the others. The kachinas came and skinned them. *Bunzel ms.*

---

[1] Indexed: Abduction. Ogres, maidens delivered from. Tests, by ogre: grinding stone, sleeping on ice, killing deer, lifting weight. Helpful animals: turkey gives feathers for bed; mockingbird brings corn. Underground to the monster.

[2] Indexed: Ruined Gambler retrieves his losses. Taboo on forbidden room. Helpful animals: Spider finds ball in game. Return in death to first wife.

[3] Indexed: Flayer disguise. False husband. Pitfall trick.

NOODLE INCIDENTS: THE BASHFUL GROOM

The predicament of the young husband during his first days in his wife's household is a common subject of Zuni jesting. It is introduced in tales and is often told by itself without further plot.

A. The young man came back to his wife's house with a load of wood and heard his mother-in-law say to his wife, "Fix soapweed water." She was referring to a baked soapweed cake pulverized and drunk as gruel but he thought she meant the usual shampoo water. He was self-conscious about his scanty hair and went home to his grandmother. *Handy JAFL 31: 451.*

B. His grandmother made him go back again and next time he came with wood, he heard his wife's mother say to his wife, "Cook animal (flesh)." He understood it: "Cook animal (skin)," i. e. his skin blanket, and he went home to his grandmother. This time he wouldn't go back even after his grandmother had explained. *Ibid, 452.*

C. Another young husband was so ashamed at having screamed when the family kitten scratched him between the legs that he made the excuse of taking the kitten to show his grandmother, killed it and never went back. *Ibid, 452.*

D. Another brought home a deer he had killed and his wife cooked him a fresh steak from it. In salting it he got his hand caught in the neck of the salt jug. He was so ashamed he returned to his grandmother, broke the jug and refused to return. *Ibid, 453.*

Four suitors came to court the proud daughter of the cacique of San Felipe. They brought bundles, and the first peeked through the hatchway to see if he knew anyone there, lost his balance and fell into their midst; the second politely ate only a little of the parched corn offered him, but, neglecting the girl, he spent the whole night eating it in secret, first stuffing his ears so that his crunching would not wake the others; the girl's father thought dogs were crunching bones, discovered him, and he ran out ignominiously. The third similarly neglected the girl for the coveted *tcukinawe*, the sweet gruel. As he tipped the bowl toward him it slipped and fell to the floor, and he ran out. The fourth thought to wait till the girl's old aunt left the house, hid himself in the outdoor oven and slept till morning when the aunt made a fire there; his hair was frizzled by the fire and most of it burnt off, but the girl married him and men of San Felipe still have hair like this suitor's. *Cushing, Heye Museum 8: 270.*

A young bridegroom when he left to hunt in the morning was told by his father-in-law to "follow the sun", i. e. to return home at sundown, and to "run from his wood", i. e. not to let the tree fall on him. He came home panting because as soon as he cut

firewood he ran all the way home. He was shamed and went back
to his mother's house for good. II : 156.

A poor boy living with his grandmother won a girl and was told
by his grandmother to "watch his wristband", i. e. sit quietly with
downcast eyes, in his wife's house. He took off his wristband, held
it up and looked through it. His sisters-in-law said, "What's the
matter with brother?" He was ashamed and ran back to his grandmother. She said, "I meant you were to treat them well (literally,
love them) in that house." He went back, grabbed his mother-in-
law and held her in his lap. She jumped up. Then he was ashamed
and went to his grandmother. He never went back any more.
That's why boys should not think about girls till they are old
enough to behave. *Benedict ms notes.*

DATE DUE
